Faction and
Parliament

FACTION AND PARLIAMENT

Essays on Early Stuart History

EDITED BY
KEVIN SHARPE
Oriel College, Oxford

Clarendon Press · Oxford
1978

Oxford University Press, Walton Street, Oxford OX2 6DP

OXFORD LONDON GLASGOW NEW YORK

TORONTO MELBOURNE WELLINGTON CAPE TOWN

IBADAN NAIROBI DAR ES SALAAM LUSAKA

KUALA LUMPUR SINGAPORE JAKARTA HONG KONG TOKYO

DELHI BOMBAY CALCUTTA MADRAS KARACHI

British Library Cataloguing in Publication Data
Faction and Parliament.
    1. Great Britain—Politics and government
    —1603–1649
    I. Sharpe, Kevin
    320.9′41′061   JN193   77–30635

ISBN 0–19–822468–0

Printed in Great Britain by
Thomson Litho Ltd., East Kilbride, Scotland.

Preface

THIS VOLUME originated from dissatisfaction with a prevailing approach to the early Stuart period. The history of early seventeenth-century parliaments has been written from the perspective of the Civil War and the later emergence of parliament as the sovereign legislative body. A study of what those parliaments did and how they worked has been sacrificed to an account of episodes seen as 'constitutionally significant' in the development of modern parliamentary government.

For several decades now, detailed political narrative has been an unfashionable form of history. And, as far as the early Stuart period is concerned, historians for a long time rested content in the belief that enough was known to 'explain' the political crisis of the mid-seventeenth century and to understand the special importance of that century for the constitutional history of England. More recent scholarship, however, brought to light information which it was hard to accommodate to the accepted picture. And over the last few years those working on the period in detail have become convinced that our portrait of the early Stuart decades is in need of more than minor repair. Yet, though important articles have questioned many accepted explanations, the traditional interpretation of the period has survived, making but minor qualifications.

It is hoped that this volume will encourage a return to the drawing-board, rather than another repair of the old canvas. Though in discussion with the contributors I have often found a surprising level of agreement, I have not, either in commissioning or editing these contributions, attempted to present one new picture of the early seventeenth-century political world. Rather, the essays presented here, some specialized others more general, demonstrate that much more research into particular problems and thought about general interpretations is needed before a new picture can be begun. I hope that these contributions provide a stimulus for further work.

Whilst engaged on this book, I have incurred many debts, too numerous to mention them all. I shall always be grateful to Keith Baker, Anne Whiteman, and Hugh Trevor-Roper who, at various stages, excited an interest in early Stuart history. The Provost and Fellows of Oriel College, by electing me to a Hayward Research Fellowship, gave me the opportunity to continue working in the period; and the friendly assistance provided by archivists and librarians in Oxford, London, and Taunton made my studies easier and more pleasurable. I would especially like to thank His Grace the Duke of Norfolk, E.M., C.B., C.B.E., M.C. for permission to read and cite letters from Arundel Castle, and the Librarian to His Grace, Dr. Francis Steer, for his kind assistance and hospitality during my visits to Arundel.

As an editor, I owe thanks to the contributors for their efforts in writing especially for this collection, and for their patience in awaiting its completion. Christopher Brooks, Roman Cizdyn, Derek Hirst, Peter Large, John Morrill, Roger Munden, and Hugh Trevor-Roper kindly read and constructively criticized earlier drafts of the Introduction. Most of all I owe much to John Cooper and to Conrad Russell who both provided constant assistance, criticism, and encouragement. If the Introduction remains an expression of my own views, it must be the poorer for that.

Oriel College, Oxford,   KEVIN SHARPE
1977

Contents

Abbreviations

Add. MS.	Additional Manuscript
Am. Hist. Rev.	*American Historical Review*
A.P.C.	*Acts of the Privy Council*
B.I.H.R.	*Bulletin of the Institute of Historical Research*
Bodl.	Bodleian Library, Oxford
Brit. Lib.	The British Library
C.H.J.	*Cambridge Historical Journal*
C.J.	*Journals of the House of Commons*
C.S.P. Dom.	*Calendar of State Papers Domestic*
C.S.P. Venet.	*Calendar of State Papers Venetian*
D.N.B.	*Dictionary of National Biography*
Ec. H.R.	*Economic History Review*
E.H.R.	*English Historical Review*
Harl. MS.	Harleian Manuscript
H.J.	*Historical Journal*
H.L.R.O.	House of Lords Record Office
H.M.C.	Historical Manuscripts Commission
Int. Rev. Soc. Hist.	*International Review of Social History*
J.B.S.	*Journal of British Studies*
J.M.H.	*Journal of Modern History*
L.J.	*Journals of the House of Lords*
P.R.O.	Public Record Office
Rawl. MS.	Rawlinson Manuscript
Rot. Parl.	*Rotuli Parliamentorum*
S.P.	State Papers
Stat. Realm	*Statutes of the Realm*
T.R.H.S.	*Transactions of the Royal Historical Society*
V.C.H.	*Victoria County History*

For all works cited, the place of publication is London unless otherwise stated.

I. Introduction: Parliamentary History 1603–1629: In or out of Perspective?

KEVIN SHARPE

I. THE HISTORIANS' PERSPECTIVE

HISTORIANS OF the seventeenth century are not famous for their concordance. It is an irony, therefore, that one of the central points of their agreement—the special importance of the Stuart century for the political and constitutional history of England—has hampered rather than advanced their studies. If, from the textbooks of English history, the fifteenth century has stood out as the age of faction and dynastic feud, or the eighteenth century has emerged as an era of place-seeking and interest, at least the half-century before the Civil War has been famous for issue and ideology, for the triumph of liberty over prerogative, of parliament over the crown. Historians have offered many reasons for this triumph, but that it took place is one of the recognized 'facts' of the century which have to be explained but not disputed.

It is strange now to recall that 'The Winning of the Initiative by the House of Commons' originated not as the chapter of a textbook, but as the title of an interpretative lecture and essay by Professor Wallace Notestein. Notestein traced the developing procedural confidence of the House of Commons and the establishment of its claim as the foremost legislative body. It was the story of the growth of an opposition group, 'steadily year by year winning support', so that ultimately under a new leadership parliament forged chains to bind fast Stuart kings. In time, a new constitution was inevitable.[1] Even in this early essay, Professor Notestein cautiously qualified his general interpretation. As he discovered and edited more diaries and speeches, he became more interested in particular

[1] W. Notestein, *The Winning of the Initiative by the House of Commons* (1924).

problems and personalities. His last posthumous contribution reflects, perhaps, Notestein's belief in the need to present all the evidence, evidence of the confusions as well as of the confidence that characterized parliamentary debate.[2]

But the Notestein who has influenced, almost dictated, the history of early Stuart parliaments is the author of *The Winning of the Initiative*, the young scholar who, under the influence of George Burton Adams, approached English history as 'the story of how human beings have learned to govern themselves... (the story of) the slow accumulation of parliamentary rights and privileges'.[3] In the light of this perspective, Notestein's American pupils have studied English history as a means of understanding the origins of their own political development because, as one pupil put it, 'British history from its beginnings to 1776 is also in a genuine sense early American history.'[4] As recently as 1971, Professor Robert Zaller acknowledged his debt to Notestein in a book subtitled, 'A Study in Constitutional Conflict'.[5] Despite the many qualifications which Notestein made, it is this perspective in which early Stuart history has been placed.

On this side of the Atlantic, Dr. Samuel Rawson Gardiner has loomed colossus-like over early Stuart studies. Gardiner's sympathies no less than Notestein's were with the 'parliamentary cause', but his legacy has been, I think, different. Though Gardiner had a case to argue, he had undertaken a full narrative of events from the evidence available. If he often read his material with a bias, he yet presented it to his reader in his account, in the footnotes to his narrative, and in the many letters and diaries which he edited. When we read Gardiner through the ten volumes which he devoted to the period 1603 to 1642, it is the evidence of the seventeenth century which emerges more than the values of the Victorian age.[6]

[2] W. Notestein, *The House of Commons 1604–1610* (New Haven, 1971).

[3] Notestein, *Winning of the Initiative*, 3.

[4] W. H. Coates 'An Analysis of Major Conflicts in Seventeenth Century England', in *Conflict in Stuart England*, ed. W. A. Aitken and B. D. Henning (1960), 15–41. For examples of Notestein's influence, see *The Parliamentary Diary of Robert Bowyer*, ed. D. H. Willson (Minneapolis, 1941), Introduction; H. Hulme, *The Life of Sir John Eliot* (1957).

[5] R. Zaller, *The Parliament of 1621: a study in constitutional conflict* (Berkeley, 1971).

[6] S. R. Gardiner, *History of England from the Accession of James I to the Outbreak of the Civil War* (10 vols., 1883–4).

Undoubtedly Gardiner is out of date: we have new questions to ask and more material to help us answer them. Despite their limitations, studies of individual parliaments, such as Moir on 1614 and Ruigh on 1624, have undermined the notion of a monolithic House of Commons.[7] Dr. Tite and Professor Foster have shown that parliamentary procedure evolved amidst an atmosphere of doubt and uneasiness, not one of confidence.[8] But it would seem at times that their work has been in vain. 'Potted' stories of the early seventeenth century cannot accommodate the detail which Gardiner presented, nor the caveats which Notestein made, nor new discoveries which compromise the plot. In a widely read essay on the causes of the Civil War, Professor Stone still follows the old high road of constitutional crisis to civil war by the 'mile-stones' of the Apology, Bates's Case, the revival of impeachment, and the Petition of Right.[9]

It has of course been clear for some time that few men of the early seventeenth century saw a crisis inevitably impending. Professors Judson and Kenyon showed that on both 'sides' men spoke the same language—the language of law, history, and religion, of order and tradition.[10] But those who are committed to the picture of conflict easily overcome this problem: 'The winning of the initiative by the House of Commons was a radical step achieved under the smoke screen of the conservative ideology of a return to the past' (Stone).[11] Whether they could or could not justify their position, the gentlemen, puritans, and lawyers of the House of Commons won the battle for the liberty of the subject. The history of the early seventeenth century is firmly in perspective.

[7] T. Moir, *The Addled Parliament of 1614* (Oxford, 1958); R. Ruigh, *The Parliament of 1624* (Cambridge, Mass., 1971). See too M. Prestwich, *Cranfield Politics and Profits under the Early Stuarts* (Oxford, 1966), chs. VII, X. Mrs. Prestwich's book provides an important corrective to the traditional approach.

[8] C. G. C. Tite, *Impeachment and Parliamentary Judicature in Early Stuart England* (1974); E. R. Foster, *The Painful Labour of Mr. Elsyng* (Philadelphia, 1972); E. R. Foster, 'Speaking in the House of Commons', *B.I.H.R.* 43 (1970), 35–56.

[9] L. Stone, *The Causes of the English Revolution* (1972). For a critique of this work, see P. Christianson, 'The Causes of the English Revolution: a Reappraisal', *J.B.S.* XV (1976), 40–75.

[10] M. A. Judson, *The Crisis of the Constitution* (New Brunswick, 1949); J. P. Kenyon, *The Stuart Constitution* (Cambridge, 1966).

[11] L. Stone, op. cit. 93.

Historians of other centuries have reacted with surprise. Looking at the early seventeenth century from the perspective of the fifteenth, Professor Roskell concluded: 'Restiveness in opposition is not power . . . a claim to power is not the same as power acquired . . .'[12] From his studies of Tudor parliaments Professor Elton argued that 'Parliament can be shown to be constantly involved in political argument, often with the crown, without producing that breakdown . . .'[13] To Roskell and Elton, the parliaments of early Stuart England seemed not so different from earlier assemblies. But, as Elton complained, 'it would be really nice to know what happened in the parliaments of James I and Charles I . . .'[14]

The parliaments of early Stuart England then await a study free from any *a priori* perspective. Such a study will involve a full examination of what acts were passed and of what bills failed to become law; it will require detailed biographies of individual members, study of their attitudes, of the influences upon their ideas and beliefs, and of their relations with patrons, neighbours, and friends. Most important, such a study must comprehend the early Stuart nobility and the House of Lords and survey the relationship of that House with crown, Council, and Commons. It is a scholarly task which requires that same mastery of detail which Gardiner accomplished in his day.

There have already been encouraging signs. In articles and essays, Conrad Russell has not only insisted upon a return to evidence and contemporary explanations of early Stuart problems; he has challengingly dubbed the period 1509–1660 that of *The Crisis of Parliaments*.[15] He is now engaged upon a new narrative of the parliaments of the 1620s based upon a study of day-by-day proceedings and of individual M.P.s. As the narrative unfolds, so many of the old assumptions must fall away. Mr. Russell has generously and rightly acknowledged

[12] J. S. Roskell, 'Perspectives in English Parliamentary History', in *Historical Studies of the English Parliament* (2 vols., Cambridge 1970), ii. 310.

[13] G. R. Elton, review of Stone, op. cit., *H.J.* 16 (1973), 206.

[14] G. R. Elton, 'Studying the History of Parliament', in G. R. Elton, *Studies in Tudor and Stuart Politics and Government* (2 vols., Cambridge, 1974), ii. 9. See too G. R. Elton, 'A high Road to Civil War', ibid. 164–82.

[15] *The Origins of the English Civil War*, ed. C. Russell, (1973), Introduction; C. Russell, 'Parliamentary History in Perspective 1602–1629', *History*, 61 (1976), 1–27; C. Russell, *The Crisis of Parliaments* (Oxford, 1971).

his debt to Norman Ball's pioneering doctoral thesis on the
career of Sir John Eliot—the best biography of an early
Stuart M.P. and fullest study of tactics and debate in parliament.[16] Only when we have many such biographies and
studies will we understand the early seventeenth century. The
contributors to this volume have written from the belief that
we should discover more about how and why men acted as they
did before we dismiss their own interpretation of their political
problems. Together we have studied aspects of the early Stuart
parliaments in relation to local and national affairs, to personal
connection, and to social, economic, and intellectual influences.
The studies of parliamentary sessions, of particular problems,
and of personalities presented here do not provide neat interpretations of the causes of the Civil War. Rather, we have
chosen to look at the history of early seventeenth-century
parliaments from a new perspective—from the perspective of
the early Stuart period itself.

II. THE SOURCES IN PERSPECTIVE

The perspective in which the history of early Stuart parliaments is studied—the perspective which traces the evolution
of a sovereign parliament—has led to an excessive reliance
upon some types of sources and a failure to use other valuable
evidence.

The most obvious sources for the history of parliament are
the official Journals of the *two* Houses. Even the historian of
the Lower House could make more use of the reports of
speeches made at joint committees which are found in the
Lords Journals. Although it is most often consulted for its brief
summaries of speeches, the official Journal of the House of
Commons is essentially a record of the business of the House
and as such it has not been exploited. But if we are to make
use of the printed Journal to study bills and proceedings upon
bills, we must always remember the nature of the original
manuscripts from which it was compiled in the eighteenth
century. In an important but little-noticed article, Sheila
Lambert has shown that the two clerks who supervised the

---

[16] J. N. Ball, 'The Parliamentary Career of Sir John Eliot 1604–1629' (Camb. Univ.
Ph.D. thesis 1953). C. Russell, *History* (1976), 8 n. 23.

entries into the Journal before 1629 left a heterogeneous collection of notes. For some sessions, we have the clerk's original notes (meant for his own guidance) and no revised journal; for other sessions, we have the revised journal and no original notes. The entry in the printed Journal for the Parliament of 1624 is a compilation of the surviving three of five original notebooks. Not only do we then make observations about similarities and differences between one session and another from evidence which differs in its form and purpose, we often forget that we are reading the notes of two very different clerks—one was a client of the Earl of Salisbury; the other was arrested after 1621 for disaffection in parliament.[17] The last entry in the printed Journal for 1629 should lead us to exercise more caution: was it the tact of clerk John Wright or the loss of his revised journal which explains his calm reporting of that famous violent end to the session? 'Mr. Speaker delivereth a message from his Majesty. Mr. Speaker, in the name of the house, adjourneth it till tomorrow seven night.'[18]

Anyone who has kept the minutes for a committee will be aware of the inadequacies of the *Commons Journal* as a source for debates, and it is fortunate that we now have many other fuller records of speeches delivered in the House and at committee. The continuing discovery and printing of important diaries[19] has naturally attracted enthusiastic attention—so much attention that we might be in danger of not remembering the limitation of these as sources. The existence of more diaries is not necessarily evidence of the increased importance of the House of Commons. We must ask why they were kept—for the use of a patron, as a personal account, or to facilitate parliamentary business.[20] And because they are often long and detailed, we should not assume that they are accurate or complete. Though John Pym delivered probably more than twenty speeches in the Parliament of 1624, the diary of Sir William Spring, in other respects one of the fullest accounts of

[17] S. Lambert, 'The clerks and records of the House of Commons 1600–1640', *B.I.H.R.* 43 (1970), 215–31.

[18] *C.J.* i. 932; P. Laundy, *The Office of Speaker* (1964).

[19] See R. C. Johnson, 'Parliamentary Diaries of the Early Stuart Period', *B.I.H.R.* 44 (1971), 293–300.

[20] A comparison of Pym's and Simonds D'Ewes's diaries for the Parliament of 1624 shows that diaries drawn up for different purposes can vary considerably.

the session, records only eight.[21] The differences between the several diaries for the Parliaments of 1621 and 1624 should make us sceptical of relying upon any one source (when that is all we have) such as Whitelocke's diary for some weeks of 1626 or the Exact Relation for 1629. We must remember that some accounts were drawn up long after a session had ended and memories were blurred. It has been shown that Sir John Eliot's account of the Parliaments of 1624 and 1625, his *Negotium Posterorum*, was written several years later from attitudes which he had not held at the time of those parliaments.[22] Though a useful complement to the diaries, the many 'separates'—copies of speeches and proceedings found in national and local archives—are often no more reliable. 'Gathered by ignorant, careless and often unscrupulous scriveners... (they were) hastily put together for immediate circulation and profit.'[23]

Above all, the diaries and separates are, in the main, records of speeches delivered, and we should remember with Francis Bacon that 'many in this house who speak not are as wise as others that do speak.'[24] Excessive concentration on the evidence of speeches may lead us to forget many silent back-benchers and to underestimate the lawyers and antiquaries who said little but who supplied precedents and resolved questions of procedure. We may also ascribe too much importance to the rhetorical embellishments with which arguments were decorated. Undoubtedly rhetorical form is evidence which the historian cannot afford to ignore, but it is not evidence which he should use uncritically, especially since contemporaries often dismiss it as part of the ritual of parliamentary debate. James I frequently told his parliaments to 'avoid rhetorick' and criticized orations in which the style ran away with the content as more fit for universities than parliaments.[25] Sir Thomas Wentworth shared his sovereign's impatience with some members, urging his colleagues in 1614, 'let us then leave the

[21] I owe this point to a paper delivered by Conrad Russell in Oxford, 'The Parliamentary Career of John Pym 1621–1629'.

[22] J. N. Ball, 'The Parliamentary Career of Sir John Eliot'.

[23] *Commons Debates for 1629*, ed. W. Notestein (Minneapolis, 1921), xl.

[24] *Parliamentary Diary of Bowyer*, 323.

[25] *The Journal of Sir Roger Wilbraham 1593–1616*, ed. H. S. Scott, *Camden Misc.* x (1912), 74; *C.J.* i. 357.

orators and become doers'.[26] Robert Bowyer dismissed 'a long discourse' of Sir William Morrice as 'to little effect'[27] and was content to summarize a half-hour speech by Sir William Seaton in a half-page, passing over 'some preamble'.[28] To men weaned on the Scriptures, educated in the classics, and acquainted with the law, elaborate parallels, reference to philosophers and the use of precedent were as much the currency of everyday speech as our own use of the language of economics or science. At times, as in the case of Sir John Savile's speech in April 1606, the image could run away from the argument. Even the normally lucid Sir Francis Bacon delivered in 1606, 'an eloquent speech which was not long, yet impossible for men or any man to take in such sorte as he delivered the same'.[29] We may sympathize with one M.P. who envied the good fortune of the Chinese in having characters which made them less dependent upon confusing metaphors.[30] We should take care then, as did so many of those who heard the speeches, to distinguish the argument from the rhetoric. Bowyer's terse reporting of arguments is an interesting comment on the speeches reported more fully in the Cottonian manuscript Titus F. IV.

In this connection we should remember that men bred on Cicero were quick to see the advantage of a rhetorical device in order to discredit an argument. A good illustration of this is the use of argument *ad extremas*, the undermining of a position by identifying it with its most absurd or extreme effect or conclusion. In 1610, John Savile argued that if supply were once attached to the redress of grievance, all redress would subsequently have to be bought.[31] James I had to remind the House of Commons that they could not bridle him on the grounds that he might exploit a prerogative, that such an argument could no less effectively be used to limit their liberties.[32] As we shall see, the argument by reference to the

---

[26] *The Wentworth Papers 1597–1628*, ed. J. P. Cooper, Camden Soc. (1973), 76; cf. *The Letters and Life of Francis Bacon*, ed. J. Spedding (7 vols., 1861–74), vii. 179.

[27] *Parliamentary Diary of Bowyer*, 62.

[28] Ibid. 296.

[29] Ibid. 118, 165.

[30] Bodl. MS. Ashmole 1149, fo. 35.

[31] *Parliamentary Debates in 1610*, ed. S. R. Gardiner (Camden Soc., 1862), 46.

[32] *Proceedings in Parliament 1610*, ed. E. R. Foster (2 vols., New Haven, 1966), ii. 103.

extreme effect was often the expression of a genuine fear for the changes which the future might bring, but it was at times a tool of argument which came to hand and which contemporaries understood as such.[33] Francis Bacon thought that when employed by the crown such arguments distanced the king from his subjects and undermined trust and communication between crown and parliament: he urged James to abandon the 'reductio ad extremas', the 'ultimities of persuasions', and to appeal more simply to the love of his subjects.[34] Rhetorical forms were of great importance to early Stuart parliament men—Bishop John Williams even imitated Coke's gestures when he reported his speech to the Lords.[35] In order to evaluate those speeches as evidence of attitudes and beliefs, we must study the conventions, and the changes in conventions, which governed public speaking. We must understand why parliament men found Sir Edward Coke amusing.[36]

Nor should we forget the displays of emotion which were a feature of early Stuart parliaments. The frequent references to tears—of joy as well as sadness—have led a historian of a more sober century to note 'the quite unprecedented states of emotional tension in late sixteenth and early seventeenth century parliaments'.[37] Such outbursts of emotion may reflect the strain of conflict and division, but the instances do not suggest this. In 1621 Sir Edward Coke thought that James I's speech condemning the corrupt patentees should be written in gold.[38] (Evidently Elizabeth I was not the only monarch given

---

[33] Below, p. 40. See *Letters and Life of Bacon*, iii. 180–1. James I asked the Commons to distinguish his reasons from his conclusions, ibid. 184.

[34] Ibid. 368–70.

[35] *C.S.P. Dom.* 1628–9, 73.

[36] Ibid. 73. We await a good study of the style, and changes in the style, of parliamentary speeches 1603–29. Professor Kenyon contrasted the long and frequent speeches of James I with the 'clipped and curt' ones of Charles (*Stuart Constitution*, 58). Dr. S. L. Bates has argued that Eliot gained influence in parliament by the style of his orations (S. L. Bates 'The Parliamentary Speeches of Sir John Eliot', Princeton Univ. Ph.D. thesis 1971). Contemporaries certainly paid great attention to style as well as content (see e.g. *Journal of Wilbraham*, 77, *C.S.P. Dom. 1623–5*, 265; *Commons Debates in 1621*, ed. W. Notestein, F. H. Relf, and H. Simpson, (7 vols., New Haven, 1935), ii. 179). The author of 'A True Presentation' thought that some members spoke just to tell stories and to amuse, that such planned orations became fashionable to the detriment of the business of parliament (Bodl. MS. Ashmole 1149, fo. 171). In general see W. S. Howell, *Logic and Rhetoric in England 1500–1700* (Princeton, 1956).

[37] J. S. Roskell, art. cit. 321; e.g. *C.S.P. Dom. 1628–9*, 153, 156.

[38] *Commons Debates 1621*, ii. 270.

to golden speech.) Three years later, the declaration of war against Spain made the ageing Sir Edward feel seven years younger.[39] Sir John Davies compared the recovery of the Palatinate to the return of Jerusalem.[40] In 1624 Sir Benjamin Rudyerd claimed, 'we may blowe up this House without gunpowder, we may do it with our own passions'.[41] These expressions of feeling and the toleration by the House of emotional outbursts should remind us that we are studying men whose temperaments were far removed from the urbanity for which the English have become famous. When Sir John Eliot could not justify his violent behaviour against the Speaker in 1629, he suffered from no new disease—an alleged 'stop in the mind' diagnosed by Dr. Hill—he experienced the cool breeze of reason after the hot flush of temper.[42] We should take care that the history of parliament does not become a catalogue of heated moments.[43]

Historians of parliament have shown reluctance to retire from the heat of the debating chamber and to look beyond the accounts of parliamentary debates. Yet the official collections in the State Papers Domestic are rich in different types of evidence for the history of parliament. Not only are copies of speeches in these collections, especially 'official' speeches, likely to be more accurate; the notes on debate made by privy councillors or by members of parliament for the Council, provide us with good evidence of the government's evaluation of parliamentary rhetoric. Thomas Wilson's reports to Robert Cecil of the proceedings on the Union with Scotland present the invaluable perspective of a member devoted to the successful promotion of a government bill.[44] Notes from Council meetings held prior to the assembly of parliament give insights into attitudes to parliament and the reasons for its summons;[45]

[39] Ruigh, op. cit. 205; cf. *C.J.* i. 682.

[40] *C.J.* i. 509.

[41] *Memoirs of Sir Benjamin Rudyerd*, ed. J. A. Manning (1841), 80.

[42] J. E. C. Hill, *The Century of Revolution* (1961), 63.

[43] Mr. Peter Large has reminded me of the famous episode when the Rt. Hon. Michael Heseltine, M.P., swung the mace in anger in the Commons. Few would trace from this fracas the collapse of parliamentary government in our time.

[44] *C.S.P. Dom. 1603–10*, 310, 358, 335, 350. Cf. the notes taken by Edward Nicholas, Secretary to the Chancellor of the Duchy of Lancaster, *C.S.P. Dom. 1619–1623*, 323; *C.S.P. Dom. 1623–5*, 261; *C.S.P. Dom. 1628–9*, 31.

[45] *C.S.P. Dom. 1611–18*, 223, 310; *C.S.P. Dom. 1627–8*, 592. See D. H. Willson, 'Summoning and Dissolving Parliament 1603–1625', *Am. Hist. Rev.* 45 (1940), 279–300.

newsletters such as those of John Locke, Benjamin Rudyerd, and Francis Nethersole contain important hints about the ambitions and attitudes of particular court figures, about the mood of the country and the progress of elections.[46] Letters of advice sent to the king from councillors, well-meaning nobles close to the court, or even from plain folk like the beer brewer at Islington, remind us of the desire of all men for harmony between king and Commons and display a wide range of suggestions for securing an acquiescent assembly.[47] Even the well-known advice on parliament given to James I by his most able councillor Francis Bacon has not been studied seriously—presumably because Bacon has been thought blind to the inevitability of constitutional conflict which historians from their perspective have seen so clearly. It is worth recalling that the type of evidence which he studied inclined the editor of Bacon's letters, Dr. Spedding—though a man of Gardiner's generation—to more sympathy with the problems of James I and his Council and to more optimism about the possibility of good relations with parliament during his reign.[48]

Examinations of recalcitrant members—such as Phelips and Coke, Southampton and Oxford after the dissolution of the 1621 Parliament—not only remind us that the Council blamed individuals for unhappy sessions, they provide interesting insights into connections and collaborations on and off the floors of the two Houses.[49] Post-mortem analyses of the premature death of parliaments illustrate contemporary attempts to explain failures and often add vital detail to the story of a particular controversy.[50] When James I summoned some members of his parliament of 1621 to a Council meeting at which he solemnly tore their Protestation from the Journal, he stated, without contradiction, that it had been passed with less

[46] *C.S.P. Dom. 1619–1623*, 200, 231, 246; *C.S.P. Dom. 1623–5*, 122, 237, 291, 560, 267, 198; *C.S.P. Dom. 1625–6*, 82, 281. There are too, of course, the famous newsletters of John Chamberlain to Sir Dudley Carleton.

[47] *C.S.P. Dom. 1603–10*, 300; *C.S.P. Dom. 1611–18*, 196; *C.S.P. Dom. 1627–8*, 592; *C.S.P. Dom. 1628–9*, 61; Robert Triplet, beer brewer at Islington to the King, 18 Jan. 1629, *C.S.P. Dom. 1628–9*, 452.

[48] *Letters and Life of Bacon*, e.g. iii. 175, 279–80; v. 18–19, 64, 207.

[49] Somerset Record Office, Phelips MS. DD/Ph. 227(1); *C.S.P. Dom. 1619–23*, 269, 275, 333.

[50] *C.S.P. Dom. 1628–9*, 489, 499, 503.

than a third of the House present.[51] In 1629 Charles I informed the country by proclamation that the three resolutions issued by the Commons had been advanced, after the session had ended, by an outlawed man with only a few present.[52] These statements, because they are made *ex parte*, must be used with caution. But since the Journal presents us with no official record of attendance and only occasional comments about the size of the House,[53] such information can be invaluable. A thorough study of the material in the State Papers would doubtless place the history of early Stuart parliaments in a very different perspective.

For most of the early seventeenth century, thanks to the peace with Spain and the ambitious diplomatic designs of James I, there were resident in England the ambassadors of France, Spain, and the Venetian republic. Since each new envoy drew up a general report upon the state of England as he found it, we have the perspective of the representatives of the two most powerful Catholic monarchies and an influential republic across more than two decades.[54] The envoys of course noted the relative power of parliament in England. In 1604, the Venetian ambassador thought that the House of Commons would take a firm stand on its privileges; the representative of Spain expected in 1606 that there would be severe laws against Catholics because James would have to enact what parliament wanted. But, despite all, the French ambassador, Monsieur de la Boderie, had little doubt about the ultimate authority of the king.[55] The Venetian ambassador to England in 1607 went further: 'The sovereign', he informed his master, 'has now reached such a pitch of formidable power that he can do what he likes, and there is no one who would dare, either

[51] *C.S.P. Dom. 1619–23*, 326. Cf. *Stuart Royal Proclamations*, I, ed. J. F. Larkin and P. L. Hughes (Oxford, 1973), 527–34.

[52] Brit. Lib. Proclamations book, 27 Mar. 1630; R. Steele, *A Bibliography of Royal Proclamations of the Tudor and Stuart Sovereigns*, vol. i (Oxford, 1910).

[53] e.g. Sir T. Holcroft in 1606 feared 'That it will be a scandal, to shew, what we have done is done with so small a number.' *C.J.* i. 291.

[54] For a guide to sources in English and French archives see C. H. Firth, *Notes on the Diplomatic Relations of England and France 1603–1688* (Oxford, 1906).

[55] *C.S.P. Venet. 1603–7*, 142; *Spain and the Jacobean Catholics*, ed. A. J. Loomie, *Cath. Rec. Soc.* 64 (1973), 152–3; *Ambassades de Monsieur de la Boderie en Angleterre 1606–11* (4 vols., 1750), i. 94–6; ii. 100–1. De la Boderie said that when James was present at debates on the Union, 'il y en a peu qui osent parler.'

in Parliament or out of it, except at the risk of ruin, I do not say to oppose him, but even to make the smallest signs of running counter to his will.'[56] Even in 1622, the Venetian ambassador dwelt upon the power of the crown and the dependence of parliament, for its very existence, upon the king's will. Members of the Lower House, though noisy in their claims 'to order everything', the ambassador dismissed as 'semi rustics', 'mostly unaccustomed to any authority'. The House of Commons 'deliberated with great slowness, as delighting in its own authority like an inexperienced republic'.[57]

For their day-to-day observations on parliament, the ambassadors were, of course, dependent upon information, even rumour, from courtiers, M.P.s, and newsmongers. Often they cannot be relied upon, though at times their reports may reflect the views of a courtier who spoke his mind but who would not commit his opinion to the dangerous permanence of paper. Certainly the ambassadors had ears open to all opinions, and, in conjunction with other evidence, their reports may tell us much about factions at court and disagreements concerning the programme to be advanced in parliament. What strikes me most when reading the ambassadors' reports is not a picture of consistency in any one parliament (let alone of parliaments in general) but one of wavering from hope of success through stalemate and set-back to new hope. Such detailed evidence can seldom be presented, but is of vital importance. The envoys' letters offer the valuable perspective of a day's proceedings in parliament seen from the day. Their very vacillations suggest a world of flux and doubt, not one of resolution and certainty, a clash of personality not principle, a quarrel about forms and methods not about fundamentals.

Finally, we should note with the author of a tract 'Of Parliaments', that 'many grave & judicious Authors have recorded in their severall Bookes the constitution & Antiquety of a Parliament . . .'[58] Members of early Stuart parliaments and interested gentlemen, lawyers, and antiquaries had much to say about the powers, privileges, and procedures of parliament.[59]

[56] *C.S.P. Venet. 1603–7*, 508–10.
[57] *C.S.P. Venet. 1621–3*, 437–8.
[58] Brit. Lib. MS. Harl. 2043, fo. 20.
[59] I have made use principally of Bodl. MS. Tanner 84; Bodl. MS. Rawl. C 358; Bodl. MS. Ashmole 1149; Brit. Lib. MS. Harl. 6283; Brit. Lib. MS. Harl. 6810;

Some described the institution in general, some dwelt upon a particular session. Many took the form of an imaginary dialogue between an M.P. and a councillor, or an M.P. and a country gentleman. At times they echo the voice of the otherwise silent back-bencher who is lost to historical record in the anonymity of an occasional parliamentary division. These tracts reveal a range of attitudes and sympathies: one depicts M.P.s as arrogant and selfish,[60] another sees members as conservatives resisting increasingly radical pressure from the country.[61] Despite their infinite variety, however, these contemporary commentaries have been ignored by historians, largely because the authors have been dismissed as men who, despite disagreements, clung to the ideal of harmony and order when it was breaking down around them. If, however, we are prepared to lay aside the perspective which gives rise to this *a priori* objection, we may overhear the men of early Stuart England discussing their own political problems. We should listen carefully before we dismiss them.

III.   CONTEMPORARY ATTITUDES TO PARLIAMENT

In 1628 the anonymous author of *The Priviledges and Practice of Parliaments in England* briefly surveyed the nature of parliaments from their Saxon origins and catalogued their memorable achievements in passing good laws and punishing the corrupt.[62] A member of the 1628 Parliament discussed this survey in his own tract, 'A True Presentation of forepast Parliaments', which was widely circulated in manuscript and probably intended for publication.[63] The two authors disagreed only in two general respects. The author of 'A True Presentation' dismissed attempts to trace parliaments back to Saxon times or to describe parliaments in terms of what they had done. Rather, he found the best definition of parliament in its

Brit. Lib. MS. Harl. 6867; Brit. Lib. MS. Add. 36856; Som. Rec. Off. Phelips MS. DD/Ph. 227/16.

[60] Bodl. MS. Ashmole 1149.

[61] Bodl. MS. Tanner 84.

[62] *The Priviledges and Practice of Parliaments in England Collected out of the Common Lawes . . . 1628.* Cf. Brit. Lib. MS. Harl. 1128; Brit. Lib. MS. Harl. 37.

[63] 'A True Presentation of Forepast Parliamts to the viewe of present tymes and Posteritie', Bodl. MS. Ashmole 1149. This long and fascinating manuscript is unfinished, but was evidently intended for publication as an answer to the above tract. Other copies are in the Brit. Lib. MS. Lansdowne 213; Washington Folger Lib. MS. V, 6, 189.

form and structure not by its function, and parliament, as it was known to the early seventeenth century, had not its recognizable form until Henry I. He disagreed with the author of *The Priviledges and Practice of Parliaments* about the honourable achievements which were to be attributed to parliament thereafter. Such honour as it enjoyed was derived from the presence of the king, 'the one king who is head and fountaine of there honour'.[64] To the king thanks were owed for the reforms of abuses and for the judicial proceedings against corrupt ministers which recent decades had seen.[65] Such disagreements may suggest differences about the prestige of parliament. But rival claims to credit for the honourable actions of a parliament which consisted of King, Lords, and Commons scarcely constitute a conflict of authority.

Both authors agreed that kings had once made laws alone, but that now statutes were made in parliament.[66] But though it was desirable to make laws by the consent of the whole realm, 'simply to binde the King to or by those Lawes were repugnant to the nature and constitution of an absolute Monarchy'.[67] Laws anyway could not cover all circumstances and the deficiencies 'by the very intent of the makers of the statute, they doe leave to be supplied by the discretion of the executioner of the law . . .'[68]—in practice by the king and his Council.

In short, royal prerogative complemented rather than combated the liberties of parliament. They were bound, the author of 'A True Presentation' believed, by the love of father and son.[69] In a similar dialogue between 'Phileleuteros or a Parliament Man' and 'Philopolites a lover of his Countrie', the M.P. admitted that, in the past, parliaments had restrained kings, but that now they existed in 'mutual ayde and use of one another faculties'.[70] In a 'Discourse by way of Dialogue betwene a counsellor of State and a Countrey gentleman who served in the last assembly [of 1621]', the gentleman would only plead for such a parliament as had 'for ytts principal obiect

[64] Bodl. MS. Ashmole 1149, fo. 60.
[65] Ibid., fos. 31–2.
[66] *Priviledges and Practice*, 42; 'A True Presentation', fo. 97.
[67] *Priviledges and Practice*, 41; 'A True Presentation', fos. 111–12.
[68] *Priviledges and Practice*, 42.
[69] 'A True Presentation', fo. 150.
[70] Bodl. MS. Tanner 84, fo. 226.

the service of his Ma[jes]tie'.[71] Echoing James I's own sentiments expressed in 1605, he believed that kings were never so
great and glorious as when they sat in parliament. It was the
fulfilment of majesty, not a threat to it. At his examination by
a committee of the Privy Council, Sir Robert Phelips maintained that he 'well knew that neither out nor in parliament
was it fitt to jostle and contend with his Majesty's undoubted
& royal prerogative'.[72] He even agreed that members of
parliament, 'ought not to draw the veyles that princes are
pleased to sett between theyr seeret ends and comon eyes'.[73]
Since such statements would not necessarily have aided his
defence, they may be genuine expressions of his beliefs.

Of the contemporary tracts on parliament which I have
examined, only the author of an essay on 'King and Parliament', written after the Civil War, saw the parliaments of the
early seventeenth century as platforms of conflict.[74] In 1610,
Thomas Egerton, Lord Ellesmere, had warned James I of a
decline in the power of the monarchy and a rise in the
pretensions of the Commons.[75] But few commentators took such
an extreme view then or a decade later. Rather, the various
authors of tracts on parliament, be they M.P.s, antiquaries, or
country gentlemen, believed that the ideal of co-operation
between king and parliament for the enactment of good laws
could be realized in practice.

How then did they explain why it had not been realized?
How did they account for the quarrels, frustrations, and premature dissolutions which were the experience of those
parliaments?

Francis Bacon, who clung to the view that parliament was
an essential part of government, insisted that to be successful
and effective it required leadership and management. The
king, he advised, should not bargain with parliaments as he
had in 1610, but 'hold himself to the person of a gracious
king and leave them to the persons of loving and kind

---

[71] Phelips MS. DD/Ph. 227/16.
[72] Phelips MS. DD/Ph 227/1. Eighteenth-century copy of questions put to Phelips
at his examination.
[73] Phelips MS. DD/Ph. 224/83, fo. 146.
[74] Bodl. MS. Rawl. C 358, esp. fo. 41.
[75] *Proceedings in Parliament 1610*, i. 275.

subjects'.[76] Harmony and co-operation were natural provided that on the one hand the members chosen were 'fit to be advised with circa ardua regni' and that, on the other, the king's own Council was united 'and not distracted' in promoting a programme.[77] Honest men, M.P.s and councillors, who knew their duties to the public weal, could not fail to co-operate for the public benefit. James I agreed. When in 1621 parliament meddled with his prerogative by their Protestation, he singled out those 'fiery spirits' who had hastened it through when more sober men were absent from the house.[78] Attorney-General Heath blamed the unfortunate dissolution of the 1629 session on 'the untoward disposition of a few ill members of the House of Commons'. Viscount Dorchester spoke of 'the distempered carriage of some members'.[79]

Many members of the House of Commons confirmed the government's diagnosis. Sir Thomas Wentworth, in a speech to his countrymen, scorned the 'distempered heads' who 'have of late very far endeavoured to divide'.[80] Sir Simonds D'Ewes blamed 'fiery spirits' for frustrating the hopes of 1629.[81] No less, members of parliament blamed evil persons at court, the king's bad counsel, for obstructing harmonious communication between themselves and their sovereign.[82] The king, privy councillors, and members of parliament agreed that a few diseased individuals could inflict the wholesome body of co-operation with distemper.

Was this a satisfactory explanation? Or was it a fiction created in order to preserve the belief in an ideal harmony? J. P. Cooper has suggested that 'when disharmony and deadlock manifestly prevailed, scapegoats had to be found'.[83] Sir

[76] *Letters and Life of Bacon*, v. 24.

[77] Ibid. vii. 115–16; ibid. vi. 232. Bacon insisted that ridding the royal household of faction was a central prerequisite of successful relations with parliament, ibid. v. 188.

[78] *C.S.P. Dom. 1619–21*, 316.

[79] *C.S.P. Dom. 1628–9*, 489, 503.

[80] *The Stuart Constitution*, 18.

[81] *The Autobiography and Correspondence of Sir Simonds D'Ewes*, ed. J. O. Halliwell (2 vols., 1845), i. 402.

[82] There are numerous examples: see, in particular, Sir John Borough's notes on the committee proceedings of 1626 concerning the examination of members of the Council of War. Brit. Lib. MS. Harl. 6445. See below, pp. 38–42.

[83] J. P. Cooper, 'The Fall of the Stuart Monarchy', in The New Cambridge Modern History, vol. IV: *The Decline of Spain and the Thirty Years War*, ed. J. P. Cooper (Cambridge, 1970), 541.

Robert Phelips spoke almost the same biblical language when, in 1628, he suggested that there was a devil in the kingdom which they must cast out by prayer.[84] Did the devil possess few or many? John Selden, an experienced parliament man, could see no reason why 'the great noise which mad wild folks make' should disrupt an entire parliament. 'Dissentions in parliament may at length come to a good end.'[85] Few would argue that in the early seventeenth century they did come to a good end. Were, then, the M.P.s who were arrested (Sir Edwin Sandys, Sir Edward Coke, Sir Robert Phelips, Sir John Eliot) and the royal ministers impeached (Francis Bacon and Lionel Cranfield) just scapegoats? Did they take the blame for the more fundamental problems from which contemporaries shrank, but which historians have been quick to reveal? We must turn to examine those problems and how contemporaries understood them.

IV. EARLY STUART PROBLEMS

A catalogue of the 'causes' of the Civil War usually begins with the problems which Queen Elizabeth bequeathed to her successor: an impoverished crown, a puritan party which presented a threat to the established church, and a House of Commons which had become more confident and powerful. In addition, social change undermined the authority of the aristocracy and brought into the Commons men who demanded more participation in government. Under James I, the court became increasingly repugnant to the country and the fire of puritan fervour was fanned with the zeal for a war against the Habsburg Antichrist. These discontents, focused in the House of Commons, produced first conflict and then war. Few would deny that there were problems. But to recognize the problems is not to agree that they produced (even less that they were bound to produce) conflict. Some problems indeed presented as many difficulties to parliament as to the king.

The financial problems of James I undoubtedly strained more than the king's own purse strings. The king's indebtedness and extravagance need no documentation. Certainly they gave rise to criticism in parliament and to debate about the whole

[84] *C.S.P. Dom. 1628–9*, 43.
[85] *The Table Talk of John Selden*, ed. S. H. Reynolds (Oxford, 1892), 124.

basis of supply. But was royal insolvency a stick with which the House of Commons beat a recalcitrant king into making constitutional concessions? Conrad Russell has argued that the Commons never successfully used, and seldom tried to use, the weapon of withholding supply in order to gain advantages.[86] Given the procedure of granting subsidies by bill to which the king assented at the same time as giving his answer to other proposed legislation, it is difficult to see how the House could have effectively wielded such a weapon. But what is striking about the early years of James's reign is the great generosity of parliament in voting subsidies in peacetime. The grant received by James in 1606 far exceeded those granted to Elizabeth in peacetime.[87] This willingness to supply the king survived even the question of impositions which aroused suspicion and debate about a whole mode of government. Certainly in 1614 after the premature dissolution of parliament in June, the country gentlemen gave generously to a voluntary contribution which brought in at least as much as a subsidy.[88] In 1624 the Commons granted 'the greatest aid which was ever granted in parliament to be levied in so short a time'.[89] As late as 1628 a parliamentary committee was preparing to revise the customs in order to compensate Charles for revenue lost by the surrender of impositions upon trade.[90] None of these grants, however, was adequate. Rising costs lessened the real value of the subsidy granted, and an increasing problem of collecting what was voted (occasioned perhaps by the frequency and generosity of the grants) lowered the actual yield to the Exchequer. Even without Jacobean extravagance, there was a fundamental problem in government finance.

Members of parliament seem not to have been entirely blind to the problem. Dr. Harriss argues below that the sixteenth century saw a greater emphasis, in fact and in theory, on taxation by royal prerogative.[91] The author of 'A True Presentation', himself an M.P., considered (generously in the light of medieval attitudes) it parliament's duty to help relieve the

[86] C. Russell, 'Parliamentary History in Perspective'.
[87] F. Dietz, *English Public Finance*, 2 vols. (1964 edn.), ii. 389–90.
[88] Ibid. ii. 158.
[89] Ruigh, *The Parliament of 1624*, 387.
[90] J. P. Cooper, 'The Fall of the Stuart Monarchy', 557.
[91] Below, pp. 80–81.

king of his debts without inquiring too far into the cause of his impecunious state.[92] The House of Commons would be foolish, he argued, if they were to base their power on the king's poverty, for then, 'as the kinge growes rich their power grows the poorer'.[93] When they subscribed to the forced loan, when they acquiesced in the royal levy of Tonnage and Poundage after 1625, M.P.s accepted that the king could raise money *de facto* without parliament. Some believed, as did the author of 'A True Presentation', that he could tax 'iustly and honestly without a parliament'.[94] A correspondent advised Sir Robert Phelips in 1626 that it was right for him to acquiesce in the loan because the king had promised that it would not create a precedent.[95]

Debate about royal finance often centred not on whether parliament was willing to grant supply, but on whether it was the best means of endowing the crown with revenue. At the Oxford Parliament of 1625, and in the following year, Sir Edward Coke and Sir John Eliot proposed the course of acts of resumption which would re-establish a royal demesne.[96] Sir Robert Phelips, who favoured their proposal, noted with approval that in France crown lands were an inalienable fief attached to the monarchy so that subjects escaped the burden of supply.[97] The fief could be alienated only in the exceptional circumstances of war and then had to be redeemed. In this volume, Dr. Harriss shows how these medieval attitudes influenced debate about taxation and supply in early Stuart England. He has argued that disputes about royal extravagance and debate about the duty of subjects to supply the king raised no new constitutional principles. Nor did they provoke any more damaging disagreements than the fourteenth and fifteenth centuries had witnessed. Such disagreements were serious enough: the author of 'A True Presentation' reminded

[92] Bodl. MS. Ashmole 1149, fos. 140–1.

[93] Ibid. fo. 198.

[94] Ibid.

[95] Phelips MS. Dd/Ph. 219, fo. 67–67ᵛ.

[96] Bodl. MS. Tanner 276, fo. 280; Phelips MS. Dd/Ph. 216, fo. 15; J. N. Ball, 'Parliamentary Career of Sir John Eliot', 134.

[97] Phelips MS. Dd/Ph. 221, fo. 84. In 1626 Richelieu put to the Assembly of Notables in France a proposal for a grant which would finance redemption of the royal demesne. A. D. Lublinskaya, *French Absolutism: the crucial Phase, 1620–29* (Cambridge, 1968), 295–300, 314. I am grateful to Dr. John Morrill for this reference.

monarchs that if they wanted the absolute love of their subjects, they should stay out of necessity.[98] But rather than trying to control the purse for greater power, early Stuart parliaments showed concern to establish a hereditary revenue which the king enjoyed, but which he recognized it as his duty to preserve.

What then of the puritans, the first ideologically committed and organized group in English history, the van of the 'opposition' in Elizabeth's parliaments? Perhaps historians have exaggerated the effectiveness of the puritans in those parliaments which boast few acts for the reformation of the church on puritan lines. James I solved many puritan discontents by his accession to the throne. As a staunch Protestant, even predestinarian, educated by the Calvinist scholar and polemicist George Buchanan, James gave the theology of the English church a more Calvinist direction and promoted as bishops distinctly Calvinist candidates. This by no means settled all puritan grievances. Bills against pluralities and non-residence and against scandalous ministers are evidence of continuing puritan agitation; a bill for 'Restraining the Execution of Ecclesiastical Canons not confirmed by Parliament' was undoubtedly another attempt to bring the church under the authority of parliament.[99] But despite the failure of such bills, the puritans never despaired of James as they had despaired of Elizabeth—not least because the king gave their moderate petitions careful consideration.[100]

James I met no serious difficulties with the puritans—in or out of parliament—until late in his reign.[101] And then, as before in the 1560s and 1580s, the threat from Catholicism abroad led patriotic Protestant back-benchers to an alliance with the religious left. Only in 1621 (for the first time since 1604) did James request by his proclamation that those about to be chosen for parliament should be 'Protestants of the type universal'.[102] Even in 1621, with the advances of Catholicism on the continent, Sir Robert Phelips urged the House of Commons not to meddle with religion because the king could

---

[98] Bodl. MS. Ashmole 1149, fo. 199.

[99] *The House of Commons 1604–10*, 283–90.

[100] e.g. ibid. 290.

[101] Except, perhaps, the Neile Case in 1614. See *C.J.* i. 496–500; *Commons Debates 1621*, vii. 646–7.

[102] *C.S.P. Dom. 1619–21*, 472.

be relied upon to protect their church.[103] Despite his desire for a Spanish marriage for his son, few doubted James I's sincere Protestantism. When in 1624 reasons of security dictated an investigation into administrative offices held by Catholics, the Commons were relieved that 'they were found fewer than were feared'.[104]

The growth of an Arminian party in the early years of Charles I's reign promoted most discussion of religious matters. In 1625 there was no reason why the Arminian question should have led to trouble. As Dr. Tyacke has shown, in 1624 Richard Montagu was referred by the Commons to Archbishop Abbot.[105] It was Buckingham's overt support of the Arminians at the conference at York House (his London residence) and the subsequent promotion of Arminian divines which made Arminianism a 'leading issue' by 1629.[106] Undeniably this development undermined the trust in the crown of some members—notably John Pym. But even the real concern about Arminianism after 1626 cannot be understood outside the mounting anxiety over the advances made by the Catholic cause on the continent, and the increased dissatisfaction with Buckingham's policies at home and abroad.[107] The author of 'A True Presentation' observed shrewdly that had the Parliament of 1628 been less fearful of the Catholic threat, it would have avoided 'a great deal of labour and dispute about Arminianisme'.[108] In a calmer situation, Sir Robert Phelips could quite dispassionately appreciate that Calvinism 'doth give license and occasion for men dayly to invent new opinions and tumults', and reflect that religion 'ought not to pass out of its proper and peculiar center'.[109] Sir Robert Cotton, like many other M.P.s, looked to religion primarily as 'the Mother

[103] Phelips MS. Dd/Ph. 224, fo. 154.
[104] *C.S.P. Dom. 1623–5*, 238.
[105] N. R. N. Tyacke, 'Arminianism in England, in Religion and Politics 1604–1640' (Oxf. Univ. D. Phil. thesis 1968), 159.
[106] Ibid., chs VI, VII. See too N. R. N. Tyacke, 'Puritanism, Arminianism and Counter-Revolution', in *The Origins of the English Civil War*, 119–43; H. Schwartz, 'Arminianism and the English Parliament 1624–29' *J.B.S.* xii (1973), 41–69.
[107] Pym argued that not accepting the authority of parliament was a tenet of Arminianism. Buckingham's support for the Arminians at York House took the Arminian question beyond a purely religious debate.
[108] Bodl. MS. Ashmole 1149, fo. 177.
[109] Phelips MS. DD/Ph. 211, fo. 66ᵛ.

of good order'.[110] If revolutionary puritanism was a cause rather than a consequence of the Civil War, it was the child of a decade beyond the 1620s.

Problems of money and religion would have remained problems for the king and Privy Council without parliament. But the House of Commons, we are told, claimed a more active role in government as it developed in confidence. This confidence, it is said, was born of a growth in procedural efficiency; of a more educated membership (especially of an increase in lawyers and antiquaries with learning to support their claims); and of the emancipation of the gentlemen members from the control and discipline of the aristocracy.

How important, then, was parliament as an organ of government? A simple answer would be that it could participate only when it met and, as Dr. Hinton demonstrated, it met less frequently in the Elizabethan and Jacobean period.[111] One commentator observed that when it was summoned it sat for less time than was required because the king's desperate need for supply dictated short sessions.[112] Besides being the organ of public consent to supply, parliament was the supreme legislator. Judged by this standard, it declined in importance during the Elizabethan and early Stuart period, during which relatively few acts were passed.[113] Contemporaries noted with frustration the proposals and bills which never became laws. The author of 'A True Presentation' thought lengthy debates wasted valuable time;[114] John Pym omitted several speeches from his parliamentary diary because they were not intended to produce action.[115] Even in his days as a leader of the Commons, Sir Thomas Wentworth had all the impatience of a future civil servant with the Lady Mora of the Lower House. He despaired of those who fussed about privileges rather than conducted business.[116] In 1614 he proposed to encourage the

---

[110] *Cottoni Posthuma*, ed. J[ames] H[owell] (1651), p. 145.

[111] R. W. K. Hinton, 'The Decline of Parliamentary Government under Elizabeth I and the Early Stuarts', *C.H.J.* 13 (1957), 116–32.

[112] Bodl. MS. Tanner 84, fo. 235.

[113] R. W. K. Hinton, art. cit.

[114] Bodl. MS. Ashmole 1149, fo. 171.

[115] I owe this point to Conrad Russell's paper, 'The Parliamentary Career of John Pym 1621–1629'.

[116] *Wentworth Papers*, 76, 163–4.

House 'not now to relate unto our neighbours what we have said for them heare, or what they may hope for, butt to be able to show what we have dun...'[117] In every session, however, as well as prolonged debate, a battery of private bills consumed time. The enactment of private legislation was in itself an important function of parliament—perhaps another which it failed to perform satisfactorily.[118] But bills for the commonwealth were supposed to take precedence. However, attempts to ensure that private bills were dealt with early in the morning seem to have been unsuccessful.[119]

Even the great reforms debated in parliament came to nought. Little was done towards reform of the law. Despite judicial proceedings against Michell, Benet, and Mompesson in 1621, parliament passed no laws against patents until 1624.[120] In 1614 it allowed fifty-eight temporary acts to lapse by accident;[121] in 1624 it inadvertently repealed the Statute of Winchester and so left the king without statutory power to raise an army.[122] We may sympathize with Attorney-General Heath who reflected, after the dissolution of 1629, 'Now is the time to put brave and noble resolutions into *acts*...'[123] We await a good study of conciliar government in early Stuart England, but it is interesting to note that, in the summer of 1621, the Privy Council established a committee to hear and redress grievances concerning patents, informers, and high fees in Chancery.[124] Other Council commissions to inquire into buildings in London, fees in courts, or the decay of the cloth industry may all have been attempts to take up matters left unfinished by parliaments.

[117] Ibid. 167.

[118] G. R. Elton, 'Tudor Government: The Points of Contact: I. Parliament', *T.R.H.S.* 5th Series, 24 (1974), 191–5.

[119] Brit. Lib. MS. Harl. 253, fo. 33ᵛ. See 'The Moderne Forme of the Parliaments of England', Brit. Lib. MS. Harl. 6810. The author mentioned several orders passed that the house should not be troubled by private bills after nine o'clock (fo. 23ᵛ), but see *C.S.P. Dom. 1623–5*, 237.

[120] See E. R. Foster, 'The Procedure of the House of Commons against Patents and Monopolies 1621–4', in *Conflict in Stuart England*, ed. W. Aiken and B. D. Henning (1960), 57–85.

[121] Hinton, art. cit. 129.

[122] Bodl. MS. Rawl. C 358, fos. 42ᵛ–43. The author argued that the later quarrel about the militia stemmed from this oversight.

[123] *C.S.P. Dom. 1628–9*, 489.

[124] *C.S.P. Dom. 1619–23*, 274.

The procrastinations of parliamentary debate rendered it less effective as part of the executive than as the legislator. The delay in collecting money and the declining yield of subsidies rendered it ineffective as a source of supply for war or other emergencies.[125] Sessions of parliament, as the king and local officials complained, took the J.P.s and deputy-lieutenants who were elected M.P.s away from their duties in the localities. James I spoke the truth when, adjourning parliament in the summer of 1621, he told them 'that numerous foreign affairs require the presence of his councellors at his side; that the county militia which usually receive their training at this time are going without owing to the presence of their lieutenants in the parliament, and that justice is not being properly administered'.[126]

Since nearly all Stuart government was local government, parliament, as a body, played little part in the governance of England.

Early Stuart parliaments could not have claimed a large part in government by any argument concerning the efficiency of their proceedings. Certainly the early seventeenth century was a period of procedural development and the formalization of practice. We need only compare a manuscript written late in the 1620s describing 'The Moderne Forme of the Parliaments of England' with the hesitations about procedural questions documented in Bowyer's diary to see these significant developments. The ordering of business, the machinery of reading and committing bills, and judicial proceedings all followed quite an elaborate form.[127] But procedural innovations, especially the use of committees, created as many problems as they solved. They could delay rather than expedite business. Members of the Commons were usually nominated to committees by the

---

[125] The Venetian ambassador thought in 1621 that a voluntary contribution would be the best way to finance a campaign in the Palatinate, 'as the meeting of parliament, its resolutions and subsequent action are bound to take a long while and proceed very slowly.' *C.S.P. Venet. 1619–21,* 176.

[126] *C.S.P. Venet. 1621–3,* 65; *Stuart Royal Proclamations,* i. 528–30.

[127] Brit. Lib. MS. Harl. 6810 is a lengthy treatise on all aspects of parliamentary procedure. See, too, Brit. Lib. MS. Harl. 6283 and E. R. Foster, 'Speaking in the House of Commons'. We should not, however, overestimate the procedural sophistication of parliament. Henry Elsyng, clerk to the Lords, once read the roll of parliament in reverse order and nobody noticed. H. Elsyng, *The Antient Method and Manner of Holding Parliaments in England* (1660), 75.

floor, and the Clerk then wrote under the title of the bill to be committed 'the name of everyone so called upon, at least wise of such whose names in that confusion hee can distinctly heare . . . '.[128] Not only would members nominate men known to them by name, the Clerk was likely to distinguish from the confusion names which had been entered before. In short, the procedural system, let alone any political situation, tended to place relatively few men on a large number of committees. This had disadvantages: Francis Tate, the antiquary, complained that 'ever to appointe one man committee in many matters maketh the best thing neglected and great delaie in all.'[129] The committees, where the House's rule that a member may speak only once to a reading was abandoned, must have witnessed much confusion. Francis Bacon, who had seen many such committees, pessimistically exhorted the Commons in 1621 to 'let your committees tend to dispatch not to dispate'.[130] Hakewill's suggestion in 1614 that, on account of the presence of 300 new members, the question of impositions should be discussed in a full committee plunged the House into confusion.[131] Such evidence confirms Spedding's belief that 'for the solution of a difficulty which required prudent considering and delicate handling, a committee of the whole house was as unfit an instrument as could have been devised'.[132] Conferences between the Houses were but the occasion of more delays and difficulties.[133] Procedures for amending in one House bills which originated in another were extremely cumbersome:[134] the bill against informers fell victim to trouble over amendments between Lords and Commons. On another occasion, the Lower House rejected an amendment to a bill by the Lords because it was sent down on parchment, not paper.[135] Bureaucracy, as we know, need not mean efficiency.

[128] Brit. Lib. MS. Harl. 6810, fo. 27–27ᵛ; cf. *C.J.* i. 529 and Harl. MSS. 6810, 6383.

[129] Brit. Lib. MS. Harl. 253, fo. 35.

[130] *Letters and Life of Bacon*, vii. 179.

[131] *Wentworth Papers*, 68.

[132] *Letters and Life of Bacon*, v. 68.

[133] Brit. Lib. MS. Harl. 253, fo. 35 '. . . there is no one thing that hathe soe shaken the true libertie of the house as oftene conference, sometime by w[i]thdrawinge the attendance of the best members among us.'

[134] Brit. Lib. MS. Harl. 6810, fos. 33–44ᵛ.

[135] Ibid., fo. 36ᵛ. See *L. J.* i. 213–14. I owe this reference to Roger Munden.

There is no reason to think that procedural changes saw the erosion of royal influence in the House of Commons. The development of committees, especially the Committee of the Whole House with a nominated chairman, had in part undermined the authority of the Speaker, that vital instrument of royal control. But the Speaker played an important part still in Commons' debates and remained a nominee of the crown. In 1621, Sir Thomas Richardson, Speaker, was accused of sycophancy to the king.[136] Sir John Eliot thought the office of Speaker was 'filled by nullities, men selected for mere court convenience'.[137] Increasing impatience with the Speaker is not evidence for the erosion of his influence. We should anyway attach more importance to the Clerk. It was the Clerk who effectively selected members for committees, kept the roll of the House, and decided divisions by hands and voices.[138] He had great responsibilities, as contemporaries carefully observed. In listing those nominated to committees, 'he ought to doe [so] without partiallitie either to those that name or to the partie named'.[139] The statement of the obligation suggests that such impartiality had not always been preserved. Certainly the Clerk was 'a political animal' and his personal political position could be decisive. The office remained in the gift of the crown and, for the most part, the Clerk could be relied upon as a loyal agent of the king in the Commons.[140] When, after the parliament of 1621, William Mallory was examined for seditious speeches and conspiratorial conferences, the councillors reminded him, with sinister understatement, that 'yf I had bene as carefull to look to the clark as I was to the Speaker manie things had not been knowen that nowe comes to light.'[141]

Our sketch of procedure does not suggest a picture of unqualified confidence. It suggests a picture of uncertainty and confusion—one which contemporary observers drew too. The Venetian ambassador thought that the longer the Lower House

<hr/>

[136] P. Laundy, *The Office of Speaker*, 191–2.

[137] Ibid. 194.

[138] S. Lambert, art. cit.; above, pp. 6, 26.

[139] Brit. Lib. MS. Harl. 6810, fo. 27.

[140] Though we recall that one clerk was questioned by the Council in 1621; above, p. 6.

[141] Phelips MS. Dd/Ph. 216, fos. 30–1. I am grateful to Conrad Russell for the identification of Mallory. See Mr. Russell's forthcoming article in *B.I.H.R.* 1977.

discussed the union, 'the less clear becomes the road to a solution'.[142] Bacon complained that many inexperienced members of the Commons were easily distracted from business in hand.[143] In the *Commons Journals* there are reports of long silences sometimes occasioned by the ignorance of the House about procedure.[144] We might well doubt the sophistication of a House which allowed a bill to drop because the flight of a jackdaw through the chamber at the time of discussion spelled a bad omen.[145] In fact, some of the so-called 'constitutional advances' of the period owed much to the king or his Council. Though members were anxious to examine and punish the corrupt patentees in 1621, they were uncertain how to proceed. Only James I's acceptance of judicial proceedings against Mompesson, Michell, and especially Bacon overcame the 'infinite doubts' of the Commons about this procedure.[146] When the king and House of Lords denied a claim made by the Commons—the right to punish a non-member of the House, Floyd, for libels against the crown—the Lower House floundered between embarrassment and dismay.

This picture of uncertainty may lead us to question whether members of early Stuart parliaments came newly armed with an education which enabled and encouraged them to assert the authority of the Commons. Thomas Hobbes's belief that the schools and universities of England had sown the seeds of revolution has become part of orthodox explanations of the Civil War. But Hobbes himself had to cast off his classical studies to become the revolutionary theorist of *Leviathan*. The political theory of late sixteenth- and early seventeenth-century England was the theory of correspondency between the ordered macrocosm and the hierarchical microcosm of the state.[147] In the commonwealth the king was the protector, the keystone of the arch, as Wentworth put it, of that order.[148] The develop-

---

[142] *C.S.P. Venet. 1603–7*, 436.

[143] *Letters and Life of Bacon*, vii. 178.

[144] e.g. *C.J.* i. 443. Silence could at other times be a form of protest. See Russell, 'Parliamentary History in Perspective', 22.

[145] *C.J.* i. 983.

[146] As the author of 'A True Presentation' observed, Bodl. MS. Ashmole 1149, fos. 206–10; *Commons Debates 1621*, iii. 127; cf. Tite, op cit. 52.

[147] E. W. Tillyard, *The Elizabethan World Picture* (1952); W. H. Greenleaf, *Order, Empiricism and Politics: Two Traditions of English Political Thought* (1964).

[148] *The Stuart Constitution*, 18.

ing association of the nation with the monarchy and the idea of the divine right of kings, both advanced by the circumstances of the break from Rome, pointed to the crown as the source of order and government. Despite his oft-quoted description of the authority of parliament, Sir Thomas Smith still desired, for the *Republica Anglorum*, 'peace, liberty, quietness, little taking of money, few parliaments'.[149] A half-century later, Edward Forsett's *A Comparative Discourse of the Bodies Natural and Politique* (1606) ranked him among those writers 'who betray embarrassment when they attempt to fit parliament into their constitutional system'.[150]

Against this background, the concept of sovereignty was introduced into English political thought when, in 1606, Richard Knolles, the historian, translated Jean Bodin's *Six livres de la République* into English.[151] It was a concept foreign to traditional English political thinking, and some read Bodin without imbibing it. But Knolles's Bodin posed a theoretical problem which had an airing with reference to a particular case in the debate upon impositions. Some then argued that there could be no effective constraint upon the king's emergency powers.[152] While, in general, contemporary commentators seldom discussed sovereignty with reference to the English political system, it is clear from speeches, letters, and minor tracts that several antiquaries thought that the King of England met most of Bodin's criteria for a sovereign power.[153] Such new influences as there were on formal political theory took England closer to the continent and further from the 'dominium politicum et regale', the mixed monarchy of Fortescue's England.[154] As the Chancellor of the Duchy of Lancaster told Sir Robert Phelips in 1622: 'heretofore Kings

[149] Quoted by J. S. Roskell 'Perspectives in English Parliamentary History'.

[150] E. Forsett, *A Comparative Discourse of the Bodies Natural and Politique* (1606); R. W. K. Hinton, 'English Constitutional Theories from Fortescue to Sir John Eliot', *E.H.R.* 85 (1960), 423–4.

[151] J. Bodin, *The Six Bookes of a commonweale*, trans. R. Knolles (1606), ed. K. D. McCrae (Harvard, 1962).

[152] *Select Statutes and other Constitutional Documents Elizabeth and James I*, ed. Sir G. W. Prothero (Oxford, 1913), 340–2.

[153] K. M. Sharpe, 'The Intellectual and Political Activities of Sir Robert Cotton 1590–1631' (Oxf. Univ. D.Phil. thesis 1975), ch.VII.

[154] R. W. K. Hinton, 'English Constitutional theories...'. Of the pieces I have examined only the author of the dialogue between Phileleuteros and Philopolites spoke of the English government as 'pollitique and mixtly regall'. Tanner MS. 84, fo. 226.

tempered and applyed themselves to theyr people the tyde was
now turned and people must now observe theyr princes and
so comply with them.'[155]

It might be objected that formal political theory in no way
reflects rapid development in attitudes amongst those engaged
in governing. Professor Pocock has argued that the early
modern period was one in which the individual's awareness of
himself 'as social being and political actor—as humanist counsellor or as puritan saint was on the increase', and that this
'entailed changes in the structure of political thought'.[156] There
may be something in this: M.P.s do seem to have become
conscious of their role as representatives of the people and
aware of the unique survival of active representative institutions
in England.[157] But members of parliament were often anxious
to deny their personal role as conscious political actors or
theorists. In 1621, at his examination, Phelips considered himself incapable of commenting upon the liberties of parliament.[158] Sir Thomas Wentworth advised the Commons against
any theoretical statements about privilege: 'in arguing we
rather loose ground then inlardge our limitts reducing our
liberties within narrow boundes which before weare in themselves att least in opinion of a large extent.'[159] Despite his
criticisms of the court in parliament, at home in Yorkshire
Wentworth reminded his neighbours that they basked in the
'beames of his Maiestie's grace breaking down upon you like a
beautiful sunshine throw a dusky cloude'.[160] If there were new
attitudes and new emphases, there was no sign that they were
preparing a spirit of rebellion.

An early seventeenth-century education in the classics was
by no means a road to republicanism. Phelips who, we recall,
'well knew that neither out nor in parliament was it fit to contend with his Majesty's prerogative', drew up under the title

[155] Phelips MS. DD/Ph. 224, fo. 157.
[156] J. G. A. Pocock, 'England', in *National Consciousness: History and Political Culture in Early Modern Europe*, ed. O. Ranum (Baltimore, 1975), 103. For a different view, see D. W. Hanson, *From Kingdom to Commonwealth* (Cambridge, Mass., 1970).
[157] D. Hirst, *The Representative of the People?* (Cambridge, 1975), chs. 8, 9; P. Zagorin, *The Court and The Country* (1969), 87; cf. James I's own comment, *The Political Works of James I*, ed. C. H. McIlwain (Cambridge, Mass., 1918), 313.
[158] Phelips MS. DD/Ph. 227/1.
[159] *Wentworth Papers*, 154.
[160] Ibid. 163.

'De Regimine Politico' notes on government from the writings of Aristotle, Cicero, Seneca, Quintilian, Plato, Sallust, Xenophon, Richard Hooker, and Jean Bodin.[161] Sir John Eliot's study of the classics and of humanist historical and political writings led him to the clearest justification of the king's emergency power in the *De Iure Majestatis*. No less, study of English law and legal history reinforced conservative attitudes. As Mr. Brooks and I have argued elsewhere, the common law in early Stuart England was expected to resolve problems, not to support positions.[162] Precedents were similarly consulted to illuminate difficulties rather than to substantiate novel claims.[163] In 1621 Sir Edward Coke found it impossible to substantiate by precedent the Commons' claim to punish non-members. My examination of Sir Robert Cotton's career does not substantiate Notestein's belief that the antiquaries 'read the rolls in manuscript and out of them forged chains to bind fast Stuart kings'.[164] Neither the lawyers nor the antiquaries were the van of a revolution against prerogative.

May we then advance as advocates of that cause the rising gentry class, the new wealthy men freer from dependence on their lords? This is no place to discuss theories about the rise of the gentry or the crisis of the aristocracy. We still await a good study of the political influence of the early Stuart nobility. But the careers of Pembroke and Arundel in the 1620s suggest no marked decline in the influence of patron over client. When the Earl of Pembroke made his peace with Buckingham, his client, Sir Benjamin Rudyerd, mirrored this change in his own behaviour in the Commons.[165] In 1624 Sir George Chaworth reflected the attitudes of his patron, the Earl of Arundel, in a house universally hostile to him.[166] Dr. Molyneux has argued that in the 1620s the power of aristocratic patrons rose and fell with events and changes of

---

[161] Phelips MS. DD/Ph. 221/38.

[162] C. Brooks and K. Sharpe, 'History, English Law and the Renaissance', *Past & Present*, 72 (1976), 333–43. See Clare to Wentworth 25 Jan. 1628, *Wentworth Papers*, 287. I owe this reference to Derek Hirst.

[163] E. R. Foster, 'Speaking in the House of Commons', 41. See, too, Brit. Lib. MS. Harl. 6283.

[164] *Winning of the Initiative*, 51. Sharpe, 'Sir Robert Cotton', *passim*.

[165] C. Russell, 'Parliamentary History in Perspective', 18–19.

[166] Below, pp. 220–1.

allegiance.[167] That was no less true of any other period.

It was indeed the dependency of some M.P.s (as well as the desire of others to court popularity) which worried the king and Council. In 1604 James exhorted the country to return only 'the principle knights and gentlemen of sufficient hability' who were free to give honest counsel.[168] Heedful of Bacon's warning against near dependants upon great persons, in 1621, the king spurned the 'men of meane qualities in themselves who may only serve to applaud the opinions of othere men on whom they attend'.[169] John Chamberlain thought there was hope for a harmonious parliament in 1624 because less attention had been paid to recommendations by great men.[170] Connection was not regarded as an instrument of royal control, but as a barrier between a dutiful subject and a gracious king who had summoned him to give his free advice. That is why the Earl of Southampton was arrested and examined for meeting with members of the Commons outside parliament.[171] It was in Sir Robert Phelip's favour at his examination that he was believed not to have 'other but general obligation to court'.[172] Despite the king's insistence that members of parliament proffered their advice freely, it is clear that some were spokesmen for greater patrons. We might well help to explain the crisis of parliament by a study of the early Stuart nobility.[173]

Since Professor Zagorin published his study of Court and Country, it has been argued that the members of parliament in the early seventeenth century represented a 'country' with its own ideology, hostile to the life-style of the court.[174]

[167] J. Leroy Molyneaux, 'Clientage Groups in the English Parliaments of the 1620's' (Univ. Virginia Ph.D. thesis 1968). Dr. Molyneaux argues for a decline in the power of the aristocracy. In my view, however, much of the interesting evidence he presents contradicts that argument. See V. Rowe, 'The Influence of the Earl of Pembroke on Parliamentary Elections 1625–1641, *E.H.R.* l (1935), 242–56.

[168] *Stuart Royal Proclamations*, i. 66–8.

[169] *Letters and Life of Bacon*, viii. 127; *Stuart Royal Proclamations*, i. 493–4.

[170] *C.S.P. Dom. 1623–5*, 156.

[171] *C.S.P. Dom. 1619–23*, 269.

[172] Phelips MS. DD/Ph. 224, fo. 156. 'he [the chancellor] replyed . . . that he never sawe me to carye myselfe factiously but as a discreete impartiall man . . .'

[173] We await a good study of the patronage wielded by the old nobility and of the influence and importance of the many new creations of nobles in the early seventeenth century.

[174] P. Zagorin, op. cit. See Hirst, below, pp. 105–137.

'. . . The Country was honest, the Court corrupt, the Country was chaste and heterosexual, the Court promiscuous and homosexual . . .'[175] In this volume Dr. Hirst has shown that we cannot identify any such supposed 'country' ideology with the politicians in parliament, many of whom sought court offices and some of whom (Wentworth and Noy, for example) obtained them. In a speech of 1610 defending his own pro-digality, James I poignantly reminded the members of the Commons: 'I can looke very few of you this day in the face, that have not made suits to me, at least for something either of honour or profit.'[176] Few leaders of parliament can be neatly categorized as members of 'Court' or 'Country'. Rather, Janus-like, they balanced loyalties to both.

It may be that during the 1620s this became more difficult, as the men of the localities became a more vocal pressure group. Frequent elections, wider publication of national and continental affairs and preparations for war acquainted a wider world with the business of parliament and Council. This was in some ways as unwelcome to parliament as to the king. Parliament men made no protest against the proclamation of 1621 forbidding public debate of royal policies, because they believed that it did not include them.[177] In *The Representative of the People?* Dr. Hirst has shown that M.P.s were at times sent up to the House with detailed instructions from the localities and were expected to account to them at the end of the session.[178] When M.P.s then argued that they were representatives of the people, they might have been sincerely anxious to justify themselves to the king rather than to make claims for the power of parliament. In 1614, Sir Thomas Wentworth believed that many members were 'unwilling to undertake that grant of supply for others, which for themselves they would readily have performed.'[179]

Undoubtedly, some M.P.s, as James I complained, had courted popularity in the country before pursuing the king's

---

[175] L. Stone's summary of an interpretation, *The Causes of The English Revolution*, 105–6.

[176] *Political Works of James I*, 320.

[177] See 'A Discourse by way of Dialogue betweene a counsellor of state and a Countrey gentleman . . .', Phelips MS. DD/Ph. 227/16.

[178] D. Hirst, op. cit., chs. 8, 9.

[179] *Wentworth Papers*, 80.

service.[180] But by the 1620s an aroused and informed opinion in the countryside had to be considered by all M.P.s.[181] As early as 1610 James had told the Lower House that they should not grant him too much money, for they would bear the blame when they returned home.[182] A decade or so later it was more than money which concerned the country. And for all M.P.s a fear of reprisals from the court for hindering the king's business was then balanced by apprehension concerning the reaction of the country to a too ready compliance with the court. The point of decision came at the time of the forced loan in 1626. Then, a 'faithful friend' advised Sir Robert Phelips to consider the problem carefully before refusing the loan. If he believed that the greater part of the country and parliament would refuse to pay it, he should remain a recalcitrant. 'But if I were not sure of a major part, I would by no meanes draw more displeasure upon myselfe by shewing a willingnesse to cross those ends wch I should foresee would take effect nevertheless but I would rather seem readie and forward to concurre in ye doing . . . *I should not in this case judge ye middle a good way* . . .'[183] Phelips, along with most deputy-lieutenants and J.P.s, acquiesced in the loan. The realm still had to be governed and they had their positions to protect. As the breach between the court and the country widened, members of parliament, especially men like Sir Thomas Wentworth, William Noy, and Sir Dudley Digges, increasingly threw in their lot with the court. If it had ever had one, the country now lost active political leadership. Had it had a leadership, the personal rule would not have lasted for eleven years.

It has been argued that members of parliament were most representative of the country when they reacted with hostility to the royal policy of a Spanish marriage, which they thought to be unpatriotic. Parliament after 1621 demanded a Protestant crusade for the recovery of the Palatinate. Close examination of the evidence does not support this picture. In 1621 most

---

[180] *Parliamentary Diary of Bowyer*, 42.

[181] e.g. Sandys's comment, *Commons Debates 1621*, ii. 399.

[182] *Political Works of James I*, 317.

[183] Phelips MS. DD/Ph. 219, fo. 67–67ᵛ. The author of 'A True Presentation' spoke of the double obligation but urged that 'No relation to the Country . . . should bee soe pr[e]valent w[i]th them as to make them forgett or neglect there great relation of aleagance & subiection wch they have to there soveraigne . . .'

members debated the grant of supply for the recovery of the Palatinate only because they thought it was their duty to do so. Firstly, in such emergencies an extraordinary grant was the usual course.[184] Secondly, many M.P.s thought that the motion for war put by Sir George Goring, a courtier and known client of Buckingham, was an official signal for the Commons to offer a grant. Sir Robert Phelips twice mentioned the 'proposition from Sr. Geo[rge] Gor[ing] at the rising of the house wch induced me to think that something sayed to that purpose might conduce to his Ma[jest]y ends...', 'as if his Ma[jes]ty had the purpose to break w[i]th Spayn...'.[185] The Chancellor accepted Phelips's explanation of his speeches in 1621, and 'assured himself that had not Goring made that proposition, they had not bin by me [Phelips] at the tyme spoken'.[186] In 1624, it was the king who invited the two Houses to debate the Spanish match. Given the mood of the country and the pressure from the war-hawks led by the prince and Buckingham, the response from the Commons was surprisingly lacking in zeal for a crusade. Both houses advised the king to break off negotiations, but the money offered was inadequate for a war. Once again rhetoric outstripped effective action. A Councillor of State in the dialogue with an M.P. dismissed parliamentary expressions of support for Elizabeth as 'but meere flourishes, for when the overture for her assistance was propoinded unto them, they then shrunk backe...'.[187] As Conrad Russell once put it, many members were anti-Spanish for almost 'ritualistic' reasons,[188] because the survival of England in 1588 was part of the living legend of the great days of Elizabeth. Sir Edward Coke may have felt seven years younger at the declaration of a breach with Spain, but neither he nor his colleagues revealed the activity of new-found youth. After Easter 1624 the House of Commons was 'thin'.[189] In May, 'the apprehension of the closing of parliament *makes a crowding of private bills and hinders*

---

[184] G. L. Harriss, below, p. 77.

[185] Phelips MS. DD/Ph. 224, fos. 145, 156. I would like to thank Conrad Russell for drawing my attention to this episode.

[186] Phelips MS. DD/Ph. 224, fo. 156.

[187] Phelips MS. 227/16.

[188] In an interesting paper on 'English foreign policy 1621–8' delivered at Oxford 1976.

[189] *C.S.P. Dom.* 1623–5, 209.

business.'[190] John Chamberlain thought it would be impossible to raise 6,000 men without pressing.[191] So much for Protestant fervour. Even in 1625 after the vote for supply for war and constant vacillations by the Council, Phelips thought it best, 'Not to advise the king to a warr but to leave it to himself and councell'.[192] Foreign policy remained essentially the business of king and Council. Only divisions within the Privy Council and at court brought the royal marriage policy into parliament. As Dr. Adams demonstrates in this volume, divisions within the Houses of Lords and Commons reflected personal rivalries and disagreements at court. From 1621 to 1628 there was no one official foreign policy to support or oppose.[193]

This itself, it might be said, directs us to the main political problem of the early seventeenth century—to the inadequacies of James I and Charles I. The charges against James are familiar: he lacked the common touch, he misunderstood the nature of English government, he spoke rashly and too much, and he failed to ensure that his views were represented by councillors in the House of Commons. By these failings, he converted issues into conflicts which his intractable son hardened into war. There is something of truth in these charges. But many contemporaries saw James in a much more favourable light. Sir Roger Wilbraham, Master of Requests 1593–1616, thought the new king more decisive than Elizabeth.[194] The country gentleman in a dialogue with a councillor thought that in 1621 James had shown himself well acquainted with the art of winning affection. In fact, when James was present in parliament, or even in London, his will usually prevailed.[195] Roger Munden argues below that, at the time of the debates on the Union, James showed remarkable patience with the petty, selfish vacillations of the Commons.[196] He was always ready to distinguish loyal critics of his policies from ambitious politicians. The biographer of John Williams argued that to

---

[190] Ibid. 237 (my italics).
[191] Ibid. 267.
[192] Phelips MS. DD/Ph. 216, fo. 16.
[193] Below, pp. 139–72.
[194] *Journal of Wilbraham*, 59.
[195] *C.S.P. Venet. 1603–7*, 479; *Ambassades*, i. 93, 100–1.
[196] Below, pp. 62–65.

trace the origins of the Civil War from James I's reign of peace and mildness would be to argue 'out of long spun deductions'.[197] As late as 1624, James stands out of Ruigh's frame as a king of sense and vision. Had he died three or four years earlier, he would certainly have enjoyed a better reputation. Had he lived three years longer he might have left his son a better legacy—the legacy of a reinvigorated Privy Council, freer of factions and favourites.

V. THE CRISIS OF COUNSEL?

The problems which I have surveyed—problems of finance, of religion, and of foreign affairs—were problems for the government. They were then problems for parliament (that is, King, Lords, and Commons) rather than problems created by it, because parliament was thought to be an essential part of the king's government. Government was the king's, but he was expected to listen to advice. It was the duty of the Privy Council, and of parliament when it met, to give the king advice which would assist him with governing. Successful government, then, depended upon good counsel.

Early Stuart commentators rarely defined 'good counsel'. When they used the term 'counsel', they thought of the men who provided it: they employed the terms 'counsel', 'council', and 'consilium' interchangeably and indiscriminately.[198] Sir Walter Ralegh spoke of counsel only in connection with men; Francis Bacon thought 'counsel', 'the greatest trust between man and man'.[199] They were clearer about the type of men who made good counsellors. In 1626 William Walter thought that they should be men of breeding and courage free from the temptations of corruption and independent enough to shun sycophancy.[200] James I looked to men who had experience and dismissed the many 'that never went out of the compasse of Cloisters and Colledges', who yet would freely wade by their

---

[197] J. Hacket, *Scrinia Reserata: A Memorial Offered to the Great Deservings of John Williams* (1693), i. 227.

[198] E. R. Turner, *The Privy Council 1603–1784*, i. (Baltimore, 1927), ch. VIII, 55, 57, 60.

[199] Ibid. i. 69; F. Bacon, 'Of Counsel', in *The Works of Francis Bacon*, ed. J. Spedding (7 vols., 1857–9), vi. 423.

[200] Bodl. MS. Rawl. 674, fo. 9. Cf. 'Speaking in the House of Commons', 45.

writings in the deepest mysteries of government.[201] Edward Forsett scorned the 'nimble headed Pragmaticks' who lacked both learning and experience.[202] Sir Thomas Wentworth echoed Bacon when he contrasted 'yonge gentlemen' with 'grave councillors of estate'.[203] Counsel was a concept definable in terms of the men who gave it.

The most important source of good advice was the king's Privy Council; not only in theory did it consist of great men who were experienced in government, it met daily in term time. Francis Bacon thought the Council was 'Rex in Cathedra, the King in his chair or consistory where his will and decrees which are in privacy more changeable are settled and fixed'.[204] Sir Julius Caesar echoed Sir John Fortescue when he depicted royal councillors as 'watchmen for the preservacon of that great bodie of his wholle kingdome from all oppression from abroade & from all confusion at home'.[205] Where many gave advice freely, unanimity could not be expected. But Bacon insisted that when the Council publicized and advanced the king's business —especially in parliament—it should do so united.[206] For the early part of James I's reign, for the most part this was realized. Robert Cecil, Earl of Salisbury, and Henry Howard, Earl of Northampton, co-operated, despite their rivalry, to prosecute the king's affairs—for example, to secure supply or to advance the bill for Union with Scotland. In 1612 Cecil died, followed two years later by Northampton. The Overbury scandal (and subsequent disgrace of Suffolk in 1618) dethroned the Howards, leaving a void at court. After 1614 James I's Council was recruited from men of lesser social standing who also lacked the experience of their predecessors. The rise of Buckingham was a symptom of this larger problem. As I have tried to show in my own essay, James I did not allow Buckingham to eclipse the Privy Council. Most of the proclamations issued by James I were drawn up with the advice of the Council,[207] but the dearth of able men and the

---

[201] *Stuart Royal Proclamations*, i. 243–4.
[202] Forsett, op. cit. 85.
[203] *Wentworth Papers*, 78; *Letters and Life of Bacon*, vii. 124–8.
[204] Ibid. iii. 178.
[205] Quoted in E. R. Turner, op. cit. i. 70.
[206] *Letters and Life of Bacon*, vi. 232.
[207] *Stuart Royal Proclamations*, i, p. viii.

divisions and personal disagreements which were a consequence of Buckingham's promotion made it difficult to work
with the Council. The active political participation of the
Prince of Wales after 1621 erected two royal administrations.
The last years of James I's reign, unique to the seventeenth
century and a preview of the eighteenth century, saw a
political crisis of division within the royal family and administration contemporaneous with a dangerous situation abroad.[208]
It was the collapse of the Council as an independent source of
advice that persuaded James in 1624 to turn to parliament for
counsel.

The parliaments of early Stuart England were ill equipped
to offer sound counsel. Francis Bacon had outlined clearly the
qualities necessary for those M.P.s whose duty it was to
proffer advice to their sovereign. They should be: 'experienced
parliament men; wise and discreet statesmen, that have been
practised in public affairs...grave and eminent lawyers', not
'young Men that are not ripe for grave consultations'.[209] On
nearly all counts, they failed. Contemporaries, M.P.s and
others, complained of new members who were green to the
problems of government and rash in their bearing.[210] A messenger advised Secretary Conway in 1624 to recall the
Parliament of 1621 rather than issue writs for the election of
new members who would be ignorant of the situation in
Europe. 'The old continewers have amonge other thinges
learned more advisedness.'[211] Experienced parliament men
knew how to criticize without offence. The author of "A
Present View" believed that free speech would never have been
an issue had discreet men been elected to the House of Commons.[212] Lack of continuity of membership often meant that
business advanced in one session had to be recommenced the
next. Phelips admitted that other questions had led to the

[208] Sir Cavalero Maycote thought 'All the worldes turned upside down' when James
apparently devolved power on the prince. *C.S.P. Dom. 1623–5*, 199. We await a study
of the political role of Charles as prince.

[209] *Letters and Life of Bacon*, vii. 124–8, 172.

[210] Bodl. MS. Ashmole 1149 speaks of 'our moderne parliamts...where the silliest
burgesse of a corporacon or a fishe towne that neither understands lawe nor latine
scarce letters or his w[orshi]pps eldest sonnes housekeeper in his county ...'

[211] *C.S.P. Dom. 1623–5*, 145.

[212] Bodl. MS. Ashmole 1149, fo. 171; cf. Bodl. MS. Tanner 84, fo. 237; 'Speaking
in the House of Commons', 45–6.

shelving of the grievance of impositions.[213] New sessions
brought new grievances, and often new grievances pushed to
the fore new leaders. Sir Edwin Sandys and William Hakewill
fade from the leadership of the House after 1621. John Selden,
Sir John Eliot, and John Pym emerged from backbench
obscurity only in the later 1620s. There was as little continuity
of counsel in the Commons as in the king's Privy Council.

Secondly, Jacobean parliaments seemed at times afraid to
give advice. The first decade of the seventeenth century was a
period of great change and turmoil which was partly a product
of new scientific discoveries that undermined a whole world
view.[214] Members of parliament themselves reveal a fear of the
passage of time, a fear of the changed circumstances that the
future might bring. In 1610, they feared that proclamations
might *in time* overthrow law, that prerogative might *become* a
tyranny over liberty and property.[215] William Hakewill expressed the more general insecurity, 'we live in a happier state,
but that commonwealth is best which is framed for all tymes.'[216]
This fear of change (and the dearth of able men prepared to
act according to the needs of the time) produced a reluctance to give advice which altered circumstances might undermine. M.P.s looked to rules and laws which would prevent
alteration. In 1621 Sir Edward Coke expressed a preference to
'rather live under severe laws than under any man's
discretion'.[217] He expressed the fear of an age which had lost
confidence, an age in which none had appeared with the
experience and flexibility which the Elizabethans were thought
to have displayed.[218]

From a Council which was divided within itself, James I,
prompted by Buckingham, appealed to a parliament which
offered little hope of confident and constructive advice. The

[213] Phelips MS 216/27.

[214] J. E. C. Hill, *The Intellectual Origins of the English Revolution* (Oxford, 1965),
Introduction.

[215] *Parliamentary Diary of Bowyer*, 258, Brooks and Sharpe, art. cit. 341.

[216] *Parliamentary Debates in 1610*, 139. Cf. *C.J.* i. 659, and Chamberlain's comment
in *Letters and Life of Bacon*, iii. 180–1.

[217] *Commons Debates in 1621*, i. 257.

[218] Knolles stressed the need for experience in counsellors (*Six Bookes of a commonweale*,
'To the Reader'). Forsett echoes both the fear of change and the need for counsellors
with learning and experience who might 'applie … cogitations to the discrepancies of
occasions …' (Forsett, op. cit. 86–94).

House of Lords was divided by faction, and the prestige of the old aristocracy was tinselled by the new creations of the 1620s. As one member noted, no public bills came down from the Upper House in 1624: 'See what care they have for the commonwealth who were wont to be the chief statesmen and should be pillars of the commonwealth.'[219] The House of Commons, managed by Buckingham as an instrument by which he could promote his policy and defeat his rivals, proffered the programme of a faction, not the counsel of the realm. It failed the king. But at least James I had clung to a belief in the need for counsel. Buckingham, however, survived the death of James. With the accession of Charles I, Buckingham ruled and the Privy Council was virtually eclipsed.[220]

Buckingham failed the parliament which had followed his counsel. He failed to prosecute the war; new abuses appeared in church and state; old problems of government remained unattended. Parliament urged Charles in 1625 to take other counsel. 'Actions not to be judged by the event but if they have bin undertaken w[i]thout councell the partys to be called in question.'[221] In 1626 Sir William Walter moved that 'the cause of all the grievances is that all the King's Council ride upon one horse, therefore the Parliament shall advise the King to take unto him assistants.'[222]

The king paid no heed. Parliament faced a situation that had not existed under James I and had no answer to the problem. Because James had permitted parliamentary judicial proceedings against his advisers, the House of Commons had no need to formulate a theory of ministerial responsibility— a theory which anyway would have offended their own belief and trust in the king's choice of his own counsellors. Only the leadership of Buckingham's enemies in the Lords brought him to the point of impeachment. Without that leadership, the House of Commons could only exhort him to act more responsibly. When the members of the Lower House recognized

[219] Ruigh, op. cit. 42, 393; *C.S.P. Dom. 1623–5*, 211, 256, 278–9; *The Diary of Walter Yonge*, ed. G. Roberts (Camden Soc., 1848), 76. Below, pp. 221–5.

[220] D. H. Willson, 'Summoning and Dissolving Parliament 1603–1625', 300.

[221] Brit. Lib. MS. Harl. 6645, fo. 6.

[222] *C.S.P. Dom. 1625–6*, 389. Cf. Walter's statement 'where there is abundance of counsell there is peace & safety', Bodl. MS. Rawl. 674, fo. 9, and the gentleman's belief 'Counsell and armes protecteth states', Phelips MS. DD/Ph. 227/16.

their inability to act as the king's counsellors in the absence of an active Privy Council, they left Buckingham the sole adviser to Charles I.

Buckingham's ascendancy need not have shut the door on advice. In the period of his ascendancy, Buckingham had enjoyed the counsel of Francis Bacon, Bishop John Williams, Sir Robert Phelips, and Sir John Eliot. He had considered their advice before determining his course. But confident of his position with King Charles in a way in which he had not been sure of his standing with James, Buckingham shunned all advice which ever questioned his will. Without counsel, he conducted many affairs rashly and others not at all. Even in 1626, Sir William Walter thought that the Duke could have been a responsible minister had he been careful not to 'abound in his own sense'.[223] As Bacon had predicted, if matters 'be not tossed upon the arguments of counsel, they will be tossed upon the waves of fortune, and be full of inconstancy, doing and undoing like the reeling of a drunken man'.[224] Buckingham was a man uncounselled. In that he epitomized the problem of early Stuart government.

It was a problem which Sir Thomas Wentworth and William Noy understood clearly. The king needed able counsellors in order to govern well, and the parliaments of the 1620s had been unable to provide good advice. They joined the court in order to provide a counsel which was needed to tackle the problems of government. As Mr. Thompson shows, the session of 1629 justified their decision and bore out their analysis.[225] A disorganized, divided, and undisciplined House of Commons proved unable to give counsel for the governance of the realm. The crisis of counsel had been, perhaps, the central crisis of early Stuart government. As such it had also been the crisis of parliaments.

---

[223] *C.S.P. Dom. 1625–6*, 389.
[224] *Bacon Works*, vi. 423.
[225] Below, pp. 245–85.

II.   James I and 'the growth of mutual distrust': King, Commons, and Reform, 1603–1604

R. C. Munden

Perhaps one of the most striking features of the problems that beset James I is the speed with which they materialized. Opening his first session of parliament in March 1604, James recalled how, twelve months earlier, on his arrival in England, 'the people of all sorts rid and ran, nay, rather flew, to meet me; their eyes flaming nothing but sparkles of affection; their mouths and tongues uttering nothing but sounds of joy.' His closing speech, however, less than four months later, was of a quite different character. Joy and hope were replaced by disappointment and reproach. In that short 'honeymoon period' there had developed between king and Commons what S. R. Gardiner described as 'a complete lack of sympathy'. Furthermore, it seems that a prominent factor in this failure of *rapport* was the frustration of what some of the Commons' members described as a widespread desire for reform and for 'ease ... of those burdens and sore oppressions under which the land did grown'.[1]

It is not difficult to find an explanation for this change and the role that reform played in it. A whole generation of scholars has laid the blame squarely on the shoulders of James himself. For Professor D. H. Willson, for example, James was the monarch who 'as everybody knows was quite unfit to guide the Commons at a most delicate moment in their history'. What is more, it seems that he was 'a man who gave no serious study' to the problems of his new kingdom because 'he was

---

[1] *C.J.* (all references are to vol. i), 142; P.R.O. S.P. 14/8/93; S. R. Gardiner, *The History of England from the Accession of James I to the Outbreak of the Civil War, 1603–1642* (10 vols., 1895), i. 193; P.R.O. S.P. 14/8/70. I am deeply indebted to Professor Robert Ashton and Mr. Conrad Russell for their helpful comments and suggestions during the preparation of this piece.

inclined to think that England was exactly as it should be, with little need of reform'. In this way, James's personal failings have come to be regarded as the key factor in a deteriorating political situation from the very outset of his reign.[2]

In recent years some doubt has been cast on such views by work on the Hampton Court Conference. The work of Professor Curtis, Professor Collinson, and Dr. Tyacke has reconsidered James's personal role at that meeting. As a result, the clumsy exponent of divine right, confusing puritan and presbyterian and upholding a *iure divino* episcopacy at all costs, has gone. Rather, it seems that James was not unreasonable, that he was prepared to countenance some measure of reform, and that the anti-puritan character of the early Jacobean church owed far more to Bancroft than to the king.[3] Similarly, this essay will seek to question the traditional view of James's behaviour in other areas. By an examination of his response to pressure for reform—other than religious reform—in the months before parliament assembled and a reconsideration of his role in the handling of some of the principal issues during the session of 1604, it is hoped to challenge the idea that the personal culpability of the monarch was the prime factor in the difficulties attending James's first eighteen months in England. In short, it will be argued that James's ability and his conduct have both been seriously misrepresented.

REFORM WITHOUT PARLIAMENT: THE PETITIONS OF 1603.

Both on his journey south and in the months that followed, James was bombarded with an assortment of petitions. Many were merely requests for recognition or advancement, but amongst those there were others of an altogether more serious and public nature. One such was the Millenary Petition: the request for ecclesiastical reform that was in large part responsible for the summoning of the Hampton Court Conference. There

---

[2] D. H. Willson, *The Privy Councillors in the house of Commons, 1604–1629* (Minneapolis, 1940), 13; idem, *James VI & I* (1956), 173–4. In the same vein, see also W. Notestein, *The House of Commons, 1604–1610* (New Haven, 1971), 59–60; M. Prestwich, *Cranfield*, (Oxford, 1966), 10; and C. Russell, *The Crisis of Parliaments* (1971), 257–8.

[3] M. H. Curtis, 'The Hampton Court Conference and its Aftermath', *History*, xvi (1961), 1–16; P. Collinson, *The Elizabethan Puritan Movement* (1967), 455–63; N. R. N. Tyacke, 'Arminianism in England in Religion and Politics, 1604–40' (Oxford Univ. D. Phil. thesis 1968), 19–31.

were, however, others, less well known and more concerned with secular reform but suggestive of a well-considered and possibly concerted movement for reform on some scale. The royal amateur theologian might have been expected to take some sort of interest in requests for church reform, but his supposed predilection for absolutism should perhaps have been a barrier to any 'popular' demands for reform in the state. However, from the very first his attitude was extremely conciliatory.

While still at Newcastle on his journey south, James wrote to the English Privy Council concerning complaints and pleas for reform he had already received. The complaints were serious (including ministerial corruption) and, though he refused to be stampeded into action on issues he knew little about, he suggested that the Council announce his intention: 'to hold our parliament at our city of Westminster as soon as conveniently may be after our coronation . . . and that the same *shall be chiefly assembled for the relief of all grievances of our people*'.[4] The Council decided against publishing this intention, so that particular statement remained private, but six weeks later a more public forum for the king's views was found. In a Star Chamber 'sermon', or address to the Assize judges before their departure on circuit, the Lord Keeper, Sir Thomas Egerton, delivered his Majesty's opinion that 'it cannot be but that in government of states there will be abuses', and his determination to see them redressed. Again, less than six months later, though in the context of religious reform, a royal proclamation acknowledged that 'the imperfections of men . . . do with time, though insensibly, bring in corruptions'.[5] Another metaphor used by James in making the same point was that of bodily sickness. On the first day of the Hampton Court Conference (7 January 1604) he rebuked the bishops for their opposition to the conference with the words: 'There is no state either ecclesiastical *or civil* whereunto in 40 years some corruptions might not creep, and that it was no reason that because a man had been sick of the pox forty years, therefore he should not be cured at length.' Similarly, in his *Counterblaste of Tobacco* (pub-

---

[4] Bodl. MS. Ashmole 1729, fos. 68–9 (my italics).

[5] J. Hawarde, *Les Reportes del Cases in Camera Stellata*, ed. W. P. Baildon (1894), 161–2; *Stuart Royal Proclamations*, ed. J. F. Larkin and P. L. Hughes (Oxford, 1973), i. 60–3.

Analysis of complaints and grievances voiced in contemporary sources *c.* 1603/4

Subject of complaint	Sources[a]	Action taken before Parliament	Action in Parliament[b]
Ministerial Abuses (inc. bribery, plurality, and mismanagement)	1,2,4,5,6,7,8	No known action	
Legal Maladministration (inc. plurality, delay, excessive fees, etc.)	1,2,4	Proclamation A[c]	**
Government Policies:			
i. Monopolies	1,2,4,7	Proclamation A	**
ii. Purveyance	1,2,3	Proclamation A	**
iii. Stalling of, and protection for, debts	1	Proclamation A	**
iv. Sale of Crown Lands	1		**
v. Export of Ordnance	1,2		**
vi. Over-taxation	1,2,3,6,8	Discussion of long-term financial problems by Council[d]	**
vii. Local Government	1	General exhortation to J.P.s by Lord Chancellor in 1604[e]	
Miscellaneous:			
i. Packing in Parliament	1	Proclamation B[f]	**
ii. Treatment of maimed soldiers	2		**
iii. Against advancement for Ralegh and the Earl of Lincoln	2	Neither received the advancement but the suggestions were unrealistic.	

a Sources: 1. 'Thinges grievous and offensive to the Commonwealth which maie be reformed by your highness or by a Parliament', P.R.O. S.P. 14/1/68.

2. 'The Poore Man's Petition to the King', P.R.O. S.P. 14/1/28 (and many copies elsewhere).

3. The 'booke' and 'project', P.R.O. S.P. 14/11/216.

4. 'A speech delivered to the king's most excellent Majesty &c.', *Harleian Miscellany*, i. 128–32.

5. Hawarde, op. cit. 178.

6. *Original Letters Illustrative of English History*, ed. H. Ellis (3 vols., 1824), i. 195–6.

7. Bodl. MS. Ashmole 1729, fos. 68–9 (Letter of James I to the Privy Council, 10 Apr. 1603).

8. *Manningham's Diary*, ed. W. Tite (Camden Soc., 1868), 148.

b Topics marked ** received attention in the parliamentary session of 1604 either in bills, debates, or conferences, though few were the subject of statutes.

c 'A Proclamation inhibiting the use and execution of any Charter or Grant made by the late Queen Elizabeth of any kind of Monopolies &c.', 7 May 1603, *Stuart Royal Proclamations*, i. 11–14.

d Wilbraham's Journal, 63.

e Inner Temple Petyt MS. 538.51, fos. 262 ff.

f 'A Proclamation concerning the choice of Knights and Burgesses for the Parliament', 11 Jan. 1604, *Stuart Royal Proclamations*, i. 66–70.

lished in 1604) James wrote of the 'naturally inclined corruptions' of even the best-governed states and of the specific duty of the king as 'physician of the body politic' to purge it of disease 'by medicines meet for the same'.[6] James accepted therefore, not only the possibility of a need for reform and a duty on his part to see it carried out, but also, when convenient, the involvement of parliament in that reform.

Such statements were clearly not designed to discourage the idea of reform. However, it might be argued that they were only good intentions and no guarantee of action. James was making no promises except that he would listen to what his new subjects had to say. For an estimate of the extent of James's response to such calls for reform we must look more closely at what reforms were actually sought. The table of grievances included here (page 46) was drawn up from a wide range of sources including private memoirs, letters, and a public oration —a range that gives some idea of the extent to which it was hoped that James would play the part of 'new broom'. Of these sources the most important and comprehensive are the two petitions entitled 'Thinges grievous and offensive to the Commonwealth which maie be reformed by your highness or by a Parliament' and 'The Poore Man's Petition'. Though we know that the latter was presented to the king, and internal evidence suggests that the former was known to him, these petitions have received far less attention than the campaign for ecclesiastical reform that centred on the Millenary Petition. Yet these petitions provide us with evidence of a parallel and probably not unrelated campaign for secular reform of some importance.[7]

In the main, those secular complaints centre on the established government of the day—its personnel and policies. Inefficient administration; high fees; corruption in high places; burdensome taxation; the over-exploitation of 'fiscal-feudal'

---

[6] R. G. Usher, *The Reconstruction of the English Church* (2 vols., New York, 1910), ii. 342 (my italics); James I, 'A Counterblaste to Tobacco', (1604), reprinted in E. Arber, *English Reprints* (1869), 96–7.

[7] P.R.O. S.P. 14/1/68; 28; Hawarde, op. cit. 182, records the delivery to the king of a document 'called the poore's petition'. That James knew of the 'Thinges Grievous' is indicated generally by the response its complaints evinced (see above, p. 46) and specifically by the correlation between its call for reform of electoral malpractice and his proclamation of 11 Jan. 1604 on the same topic—*Stuart Royal Proclamations*, i. 66–70.

sources of revenue—these were the main points at issue. None of this is very surprising. Complaints against excessive taxation may be accounted for by the war with Spain. The expensive and inglorious war of attrition which had replaced the life-and-death struggle of 1588 had been directly responsible for annual collections of subsidy since 1588 and had necessitated an increasingly efficient exploitation of any royal rights and privileges that might yield extra revenue.[8]

The attacks on personnel were perhaps even more predictable. For some two years prior to Elizabeth's death, the government had been controlled by a small group dominated by Robert Cecil. As a result, there must have been many who saw in James's accession an opportunity for humbling the 'old guard' and advancing, or simply restoring, their own fortunes. The survivors of the Essex group; Lord Henry Howard and the Earl of Northumberland, all spring easily to mind. Even amongst those in power there were some who, like Cobham and Ralegh, hoped to improve their position, and Cecil had taken out political insurance before Elizabeth's death in the form of secret communication with James.[9] In such uncertain times any prominent (or aspiring) courtier might have espoused the cause of reform as a means of bringing himself and his ability to the king's attention, and the facility with which the petitions reached the king's ear and references by the petitioners to contacts with 'some [persons] of credit and near to his Majesty' suggest that someone (or some group) was doing just that.[10] There is insufficient evidence to make any identification, but it seems that pressure for reform in 1603 was as much a matter of 'high politics' as of 'popular' discontent, and the manner of James's response is therefore even more important.

When assessing that response we must bear in mind that James was restricted in what he could do. The extent to which, legally, the king could interfere in the workings of the common law (a popular target) was severely limited; a cash crisis in the

---

[8] F. C. Dietz, *English Public Finance, 1485–1641* (2 vols., 1932), ii. 86–99, 389 n.17; J. Hurstfield, *The Queen's Wards* (Rev. edn. 1973), *passim.*

[9] Lord Hailes, *The Secret Correspondence of Sir Robert Cecil with James I* (Edinburgh, 1766) and *The Correspondence of King James VI with Robert Cecil and others in England during the reign of Queen Elizabeth*, ed. J. Bruce (Camden Soc., 1860), both *passim.*

[10] Usher, op. cit. ii. 358. P.R.O. S.P. 14/11/216 also speaks of 'some near about his Majesty'.

Exchequer during the summer of 1603 meant there was little possibility of any action being taken that might involve a major reduction in revenue; one of the worst outbreaks of plague for many years thoroughly disrupted both court and administration throughout the summer and autumn months; and besides, until parliament could be summoned, James could advance reform only by proclamations (the enforcement of which he could not guarantee) or by personal appeals and injunctions (which might be ignored).[11] Nevertheless, his record is a good one.

Some indication of how many problems were tackled is given in the Table. As a whole, the response was positive; encouraging to those who sought reform of specific grievances, without in any sense being a *carte blanche* for change. In this way the response may be compared with that given at Hampton Court, and, though we have no accounts of how those reforms were put into effect, we do have an unsolicited contemporary tribute. In a manuscript commonplace book John Hawarde wrote of these first months that 'his Majesty's chiefest study and care would seem to be for reform', Furthermore, he substantiated his claim by reference to a royal proclamation of 7 May 1603.[12]

Entitled 'A Proclamation inhibiting the use and execution of any charter or grant made by the late Queen Elizabeth of any kind of Monopolies &c.', it was not concerned only with monopolies.[13] Purveyors, cart-takers, and saltpetre men were all warned to execute their offices fairly and with care. Lawyers, their associates, and subordinates at all levels were warned against the extraction of excessive fees. The practices of issuing assignments on the royal revenue for fictitious debts and protections and exemptions for real debts were condemned. Finally it contained a strong injunction for a more reverent

---

[11] For evidence of the cash crisis see: Dietz, loc. cit.; E. Lodge, *Illustrations of British History* (3 vols., 1791), iii. 21 and 30–1; *H.M.C. Buccleuch MSS.* (hereafter *H.M.C. Bucc.*), I. i. 44; *The Journal of Sir Roger Wilbraham*, ed. H. S. Scott (Camden Soc., 1902), 62, 63; *Miscellaneous State Papers* (1778), i. 385. For the disruption caused by the plague, see e.g. Lodge, op. cit. 20, 32, 33, 35–6, 54, and 57, and, generally, F. P. Wilson, *The Plague in Shakespeare's London* (Oxford, 1927).

[12] Hawarde, loc. cit. That this attack on monopolies continued to be seen as a positive gesture of goodwill is indicated by references to it in the preamble to the Subsidy Act of 1606—*Stat. Realm*, IV. ii. 1109.

[13] *Stuart Royal Proclamations*, i. 11–14.

keeping of the Sabbath day. All these grievances were complained of in one or more of the petitions mentioned. Without the provisions concerned with monopolies, therefore, this proclamation would constitute a considerable tribute to James's goodwill in respect of grievances. With them it becomes even more impressive.

The distribution and administration of monopolies had been a grievance for many years before 1603. Increasingly intense parliamentary activity in the sessions of 1597 and 1601 had culminated in the extraction from Elizabeth of a proclamation revoking a dozen grants as illegal and referring others to the common law for a test of their validity.[14] Though a considerable achievement, this was apparently less than the complainants had hoped for. In particular, it had not condemned patents as *malum in se*. Thus, those patents referred to trial at law were to be regarded as valid until such time as a test case could be brought. This, the authors of 'Thinges grievous' complained to James, put the aggrieved to great charge and might lead to the continuance of an abuse simply because the large sums necessary to bring such a case before the courts were not forthcoming.[15]

James's response was all that the petitioners could have hoped. With the exception only of grants to 'any corporation ... company ... art or mystery, or for the maintenance and enlargement of any trade of merchandize' all patents were suspended forthwith, in order that they might 'be examined and allowed of by us with the advice of our council'. What is more, though lack of evidence prevents us following the story any further, it should be pointed out that, three days before this proclamation was issued, a Privy Council commission had been appointed for that very purpose.[16] It is also perhaps worth mentioning that, though the issue of monopolies was raised in parliament in 1604, the only patents to which exception was

[14] J. E. Neale, *Elizabeth I and her Parliaments* (2 vols., 1953), ii. 352–6, 376–88; *Tudor Royal Proclamations*, ed. P. L. Hughes and J. F. Larkin, iii. 235–8. That Elizabeth's famous parsimony also affected questions of reform is perhaps suggested by the motion in 1601 that Elizabeth's promise of action in respect of monopolies should be written in gold, 'lest that which is now meant may ... be altered and perhaps not so happily effected': Sir S. D'Ewes, *The Journals of all the Parliaments during the reign of Queen Elizabeth &c.* (1682), 656.

[15] *C.S.P. Dom. 1601–3*, 210; P.R.O. S.P. 14/1/68, para. 1.

[16] Brit. Lib. Add. MS. 11402, fo. 88ʳ.

taken were those affecting the very trading corporations the
proclamations had excluded.

In this way, James supported his proclaimed attitude to
reform with positive action. No doubt much of this was inadequate. We do not know, for example, just how much notice
royal officials took of threats of royal displeasure. However, the
state of the law on proclamations was not of James's making
and, even if these actions are regarded simply as a gesture,
that gesture can have been scarcely less than encouraging.
Besides, the proclamation against monopolies was not the only
such gesture. To that proclamation must be added those
concerned with the reformation of pricing in the markets, the
reform of weights and measures, the reform of election abuses,
and the positive steps (in the form of letters to the Justices of
the Peace, few of which, unfortunately, survive) taken to see
that such reforms were actually implemented.[17] Thus, it is clear
that James's achievement in secular affairs was no less than that
in ecclesiastical affairs. That is to say that the hopes of
Hawarde were as justified as those of the moderate puritans,
and that, whatever the reason for the eventual disappointment
of those hopes, it can hardly be attributed to unwillingness on
James's part to give the question of reform any consideration.
By March 1604, therefore, the outlook for the first parliamentary session of the reign must have been good as far as those
who sought reform were concerned.

JAMES AND THE HOUSE OF COMMONS: REFORM IN PARLIAMENT, 1604

They were not—initially at least—to be disappointed. On
the first full day of business Sir Robert Wroth put before the
Lower House a list of seven topics for consideration: the confirmation of the Book of Common Prayer, wardship, purveyance, monopolies, the dispensation of penal statutes, the export
of Iron Ordnance, and abuses in the Exchequer.[18] These were
all topics with which Wroth's audience would have been
familiar. Most had been the subject of debate in later
Elizabethan parliaments and all, in one form or another, are

---

[17] A. Everitt, 'The Marketing of Agricultural Produce', in *The Agrarian History of
England and Wales* (1967), iv. 578–9; *Stuart Royal Proclamations*, i. 23–7, 37, 66–70;
H.M.C. Rutland MSS. i. 391; Holkham MS. 684, No. 46.

[18] *C.J.* 151a.

to be found in the petitions of 1603. What is more, it would seem that the audience shared Wroth's opinion of their significance, for five of the topics were treated in some detail during the session and two of those (wardship and purveyance) were to achieve a particular significance as major reform issues. What makes Wroth's initiative particularly important, however, is evidence that, far from being unilateral, it had powerful official backing. Dr. N. R. N. Tyacke suggests that, in the simultaneous presentation of reform programmes in both Lords and Commons, Wroth was actually working with Robert (then Lord) Cecil.[19] If so, it must have seemed that the good intentions of 1603 had survived into 1604 and that parliament was going to be able to tackle the problem of grievances with more or less official backing. However, despite this promising start, all consideration of reform was brought to a halt, within a week, by the Goodwin *v.* Fortescue dispute.

Though not strictly a question of reform, it will be necessary to treat this issue in some detail because of the extent of James's personal involvement in it and the strategic importance of its position. As the first 'issue' in the first session of the first parliament of a new monarch, its handling was bound to have an effect on the judgement and reactions of both contemporaries and historians. It is particularly unfortunate therefore that the nature of that handling has been so misconstrued.

In particular, this issue has been regarded as a prime example of James's tendency to interfere in parliamentary affairs in general, and the affairs of the Lower House in particular, with high-handedness and lectures on constitutional and political theory. James's assertions that he was acting only on the advice of his councillors and his denial of any interest in favour of Fortescue have been either ignored or discounted. However, there is evidence that he spoke the truth; that the most serious blunders in handling were the responsibility of his councillors; that James was personally involved in all the positive initiatives taken; and that this *fracas* did not seriously sour the attitude of the Commons towards their new king or prejudice him against them.

[19] N. R. N. Tyacke, 'Wroth, Cecil and the Parliamentary session of 1604', *B.I.H.R.* (forthcoming). I am indebted to Dr. Tyacke for allowing me to consult a proof copy of this important article.

In the first place the technicality of the case makes it difficult not to believe that the quashing of Goodwin's election was the work of his councillors rather than of James himself. The arguments used by both sides were very complicated and peculiar to English law.[20] It must be doubted therefore whether James would have been capable of instigating such an action. He must have relied, as he claimed he did, on the advice of his councillors. Equally, there is no reason to doubt James's denial of a personal interest in Fortescue's election. For reasons that are not entirely clear, Fortescue did not get on well with the new king. In the first year of the reign he had lost two powerful offices—Chancellor of the Exchequer and Master of the Great Wardrobe—to the Scots favourite, Sir George Home. What is more, he does not seem to have been well liked by Lord Henry Howard who was then very much a rising star at court.[21] This is important because, if James held no brief for Fortescue, what has been described as clumsy hectoring and interference may be seen rather as a genuine attempt to solve a difficult problem; a problem that had not been of his making, that he did not fully understand and which was unnecessarily complicated by the inept behaviour of some of his advisers.

The opening stages of the dispute in parliament are a case in point. Having decided to challenge the Commons' decision to support Goodwin's election, the Council's first initiative came in the form of a request from the House of Lords for an explanation of the Commons' proceedings. The very idea of such an approach was foolhardy in the extreme. Whatever the merits of their claim to judge returns, the Commons were unlikely to concede any duty to explain their proceedings to the Upper House. Nor did they. Their indignation at the suggestion

[20] For a discussion of the problems involved in the reconciliation of English and Scots law, see B. P. Levack, 'The Proposed Union of English Law and Scots Law in the Seventeenth Century', *Juridical Review* (1975), part ii, 97–115 (*N.B.* esp. pp. 99–100). For an interesting parallel in which many of the same precedents were cited see Fitzherbert's case in the Parliament of 1593—Sir S. D'Ewes, *The Journals of all the Parliaments*, 478–518. Of special note is Coke's opinion that whether 'a man [be] outlawed, attainted or excommunicated, or not lawfully elected, if he be returned, out of all doubt he is a lawful burgess', ibid. 482a.

[21] Belvoir Castle, Rutland MS. xiv. fo. 205; *D.N.B.*, 'Fortescue, Sir John'; *H.M.C. Salisbury MSS.* xv. 171, 199; *H.M.C. Mar and Kellie MSS.* i. 59. For a reconsideration of the motives involved in Fortescue's defeat at the election see R. C. Munden, 'The defeat of Sir John Fortescue: Court vs Country at the Hustings?', *E.H.R.* (forthcoming).

was loud and vigorous. They refused to account to the Lords, but agreed to report to the king if he desired it. This brought a change of tack. A further message sought an explanation on behalf of the king. The Commons agreed and, at the audience for the receipt of that explanation, James was personally involved for the first time.[22] It was hardly an auspicious beginning. The Commons had been put on the defensive, and James was therefore in the position of having to defend an already unpopular viewpoint on the basis of highly technical arguments that probably meant little to him.

The speech James delivered at that audience has long been a source of misunderstanding. On the face of it, the main body of the speech might have been written for his critics. It is pompous, didactic, and even contains the customary biblical allusion, but it should not be accepted at its face value. Whoever actually wrote that part of the speech, the arguments were not those of James. They were a complex and technical defence of the quashing of Goodwin's election, and were probably based on the precedents and ideas which Cecil and Lord Chief Justice Popham had culled from the judges.[23] What is significant, however, is the dichotomy between the main body of the speech and its conclusions. The arguments set out in the former allow of no rebuttal. If they were correct, the Commons did not have a case, but James did not pursue the logic of the arguments he had delivered by dismissing the Commons' plea out of hand. Rather, he asked only that they should produce an accurate account of their proceedings; debate the matter further and reach a conclusion; confer with the judges; and report their proceedings in these first three to him via the Privy Council. Despite the preamble, therefore, the speech ended by furthering rather than smothering discussion and recognizing, implicitly (as the main body had not), that the Lower House might have a case.

This was a positive initiative and the Commons responded to it. They devoted most of a whole day's sitting to further argument and discussion and they produced the detailed account they had been asked for, reiterating in it, point for

---

[22] *H.M.C. Bucc.* iii. 83; *C.J.* 156a, 937a; Brit. Lib. Cotton MS. Titus FIV, fo.7; Rutland MS. XIV, fo. 204.

[23] *C.J.* 158; L.C.J. Popham to Cecil, 24 Mar. 1604, *H.M.C. Salis.* xvi. 43.

point, their previous position.[24] A stalemate had been reached and clearly the king had to intervene again. But before he did so, the resolve of the Lower House was further hardened by a particularly clumsy piece of interference. James's request for a conference with the judges was rejected on Friday 30 March on the grounds that the Commons were in no doubt about the legal position. However, despite this, the Speaker tried to raise the matter again the following Monday. The response of the House was emphatic. Not only would they not confer, they also introduced a procedural rule prohibiting the repetition of any question on which a decision had once been taken. That the Speaker was acting on instructions can hardly be doubted, but the only result was greater intransigence on the part of the Commons.[25] Like the initial inquiry via the Lords, this was a foolish move and one for which James, some fifty miles away at Royston, cannot fairly be blamed. Indeed, when he returned, he responded once again with a positive initiative.

At a two-hour audience with the Speaker, James admitted that, having heard both sides of the case, he was 'distracted in judgement'. Furthermore, he could see no way of resolving the problem other than open discussion. He therefore 'commanded as an absolute king' that a committee from the Commons should meet the judges and argue the case before himself and his Council.[26] Far from being an early sign of incipient absolutism, this was an astute initiative, worthy, and indeed reminiscent, of his predecessor. The Commons could not possibly refuse such a command and so the meeting could take place without any loss of face on their part.

At that meeting James tempered the firmness of his command with moderation and conciliation. After offering to leave the meeting if it was felt that he was too interested a party, he went on to concede that the Lower House was indeed a court of record and the proper judge of election returns. There remained only the question of the disputed seat in parliament, and for his handling of that too James deserves credit. At a point when the Lord Chief Justice, according to one observer, 'was

[24] *C.J.* 159–60, 162–4.
[25] *C.J.* 162a.
[26] *C.J.* 166b; *H.M.C. Bucc.* iii. 85. As an example of how limited a meaning the term 'absolute' (omitted in the Buccleuch MS.) could have for contemporaries, see Coke's report on Cowdrey's case (1591) in G. R. Elton, *The Tudor Constitution* (1960), 226–7.

about to disprove by another reason that Sir Francis Goodwin was not duly chosen . . . the king, desirous to compromit the matter, made offer to the lower house to be contented that Sir Francis should not be also' and that a new writ should be sent out for an election of 'neither of them both'. The compromise was quickly accepted by all concerned. The Commons addressed a vote of thanks to James for his handling of the problem and this, the first major issue of the session, was brought to a successful conclusion, leaving a not unfavourable impression of the king's political ability.[27]

Certainly there is no real evidence that this affair, in itself, unduly soured relations between king and Commons. The day after the presentation of their vote of thanks, the suggestion from a courtier (Sir George More) that the bill for the recognition of his Majesty's title be committed was rejected on the grounds that 'the fervent zeal of the house was such that they would suffer no delay'. As a result, the bill was accorded the unusual honour of three readings 'within an hours space', at the end of which it was 'passed with great shouts'.[28]

For his part, James's attitude at the end of this dispute was conciliatory. At the audience for the delivery of the Commons' letter of thanks James made what was almost a second 'opening' speech. Once again he outlined what he hoped for from the session, the subjects for discussion and their priorities. He seems to have wished to put what he described as a mutual misunderstanding behind him and make a fresh start. It was perhaps an obvious gesture, but there is no reason to doubt its sincerity. On the contrary, the addition to the list of priorities of 'religion and reformation of ecclesiastical discipline' suggests that it was indeed genuine. Although it is not now clear quite what was intended by this, it was a substantial concession and one that the Commons would not have expected from his predecessors.[29]

Despite this, however, religion did not receive the attention that might have been expected. The next six weeks of the session were dominated by consideration of the more secular problems of wardship, purveyance, and the king's scheme for Union—

[27] *C.J.* 168; Rutland MS. XIV, fo. 208; Titus FIV, fo. 9ʳ, *H.M.C. 7th Report*, i. 526; H.L.R.O. MS. 3, fo. 113.
[28] Titus FIV, fo. 8; *H.M.C. Bucc.* iii. 83.
[29] *C.J.* 171; *H.M.C. Bucc.* iii. 85. For Elizabeth's reluctance to sanction discussion of ecclesiastical affairs, see: Neale, op. cit., *passim*.

three issues that were crucial both to the session itself and the development of James's relations with the Commons. This was the period during which there was most contact between the king and the Lower House and it is especially important because that exercise in co-operation failed. This period was both the zenith and the nadir of the session. During it important and radical schemes were floated: the abolition of the king's right to wardship in return for a 'certain' revenue levied on all landowners; the suppression of purveyance in favour of a country-wide composition that would not so unfairly burden the home counties; the adoption of a new name — Great Britain — for both England and Scotland as the first step towards what some saw as a 'perfect' Union;[30] and co-operation on questions of church reform between the bishops and the more 'tender-conscienced' members of the Lower House. Yet, by the end of the first week in June the whole programme lay more or less in ruins. Composition for wardship was rejected as not becoming his Majesty's dignity; that for purveyance had simply petered out in a series of sterile debates; the new name of Great Britain was flatly rejected; and the opportunity for mutual reform of the church had been wasted. This failure brought disappointment and frustration to both king and Commons. James made his disappointment clear in a speech on 30 May in which 'many particular actions and passages of the house were objected unto them with taxation and blame'. The Commons responded with a decision to prepare a 'form of satisfaction to be offered to his Majesty . . . as may inform him of the truth and clearness of their proceedings'.[31] However, if it is clear that there was failure, James's responsibility for it is by no means as obvious.

The first issue to receive extensive discussion in this session was the reform of purveyance. Encouraged by the House of Lords, the Commons had begun their campaign against this grievance with a bill condemning the administration of purveyance, but the end of the Goodwin *v.* Fortescue dispute saw a 'fresh start' in this as in other areas. The committee considering the bill, for reasons that are not clear, recommended that procedure by bill be dropped in favour of procedure by

---

[30] On the implications of, and the problems involved in, the idea of a 'perfect' Union, see Levack, art. cit.

[31] *C.J.* 193; *H.M.C. Bucc.* iii. 93.

petition. It is possible, however, that this change of heart came as a result of an official initiative, for the committee was dominated by members with court and administrative connections, but certainly, the change was accompanied by a readiness on the part of the administration to offer quite extensive reform. In place of reform of administrative abuses, the Commons were offered the abolition of purveyance in return for a composition. Procedure by petition also meant the direct involvement, in an issue on which he had a good record since his accession, of James himself.[32]

Understandably, the interest of the administration in such 'root and branch' reform was not entirely altruistic. On 13 April, the Speaker had reported James as saying 'that his occasions were infinite and much beyond those of his predecessors: and therefore that in his first Parliament we should not take from him that which we had yielded in others'.[33] Stringent reform of the existing administration would have resulted in a decrease in the yield from purveyance and, consequently, in an additional strain on an already depleted Exchequer. Composition, if set high enough, would avoid that *and* eliminate a substantial grievance. However, if not entirely altruistic, the attitude was not thoroughly cynical either. The steps taken in 1603 suggest that purveyance was recognized as a genuine grievance and, whilst the matter was still under discussion, James demonstrated his goodwill in a practical fashion. In a message to the Commons on 28 April, he reported that, having become aware of the abuses of a particular purveyor, he had ordered the man's imprisonment and trial at commom law.[34] As a gesture of sympathy and a recognition that the abuses of purveyors should be a matter for due process of law rather than for 'special' consideration by the Court of Green Cloth, this message must have been received as a source of encouragement. Certainly, procedure by petition was adopted on 14 April and,

---

[32] *C.J.* 155–6, 171–2. For the committee and its disposition, see R. C. Munden, 'The Politics of Accession: James I and the Parliament of 1604' (University of East Anglia M.Phil. thesis), 282.

[33] *C.J.* 171b.

[34] On purveyance in general in this period see: A. Woodworth, 'Purveyance under Elizabeth', *Transactions of the American Philosophical Society*, xxv (Philadelphia, 1945), 1–89, and G. Aylmer, 'The last years of Purveyance, 1610–1660', *Ec. H.R.* 2nd series, x (1957), 81–93. *C.J.* 189a.

despite other business, the petition was presented on 28 April. Equally, the king's behaviour at that audience does not suggest that the hopes of the Lower House were misplaced.[35]

From the beginning of the audience James declared his readiness to effect reforms where he found them necessary. He would not, he said, like Rehoboam, be unresponsive to the voice of his people. He recalled his attempts to improve the situation the previous summer and expressed sorrow that 'the general expectation of relief was frustrate' by misconduct of the purveyors. He was apparently unmoved by defensive protests from members of the Board of Green Cloth present at the audience, and, at the beginning of the following week, he sent word to the Commons that he had referred the case of another errant purveyor to the Lord Chief Justice, with the additional injunction that, if necessary, he should hang. Though undoubtedly a further gesture of encouragement, this was the last occasion on which James was directly involved in the issue. Thereafter, until the whole question was 'let sleep' on 2 June, the Commons dealt with a Lords' committee.[36] James was not, therefore, directly involved in the demise of this particular scheme. However, if the handling of this issue materially affected the nature of the relations between king and Commons at all, it seems more likely that the behaviour of the Lower House should have upset the king than the other way about.

Petitions, both public and private, had assured James that his new subjects desired reform of the system of purveyance. In response to that desire, an injunction by proclamation in 1603 had been followed by the offer of extensive reform in parliament. However, in the face of that offer, the enthusiasm for reform had apparently evaporated. Not only had the amount of composition been questioned, there had also been considerable division in the Lower House over the desirability of the reform itself. To James it must have seemed that reform was not as popular as he had thought and/or that those who did desire reform wanted, in a sense, to have their cake and eat it. That is, that they wanted substantial administrative changes without paying the compensation to the Exchequer without which James would have been a fool to sanction such

[35] *C.J.* 946a; and for the petition and James's response to it, see *C.J.* 190–3.
[36] *C.J.* 193 and 200–49 *passim*; *L.J.* (all references are to vol. ii), 290, 292a, 295–6.

reform. It must also have seemed that time was being wasted and initiatives were being disregarded to no effect. No doubt this reflects on James's understanding of English parliamentary procedure, but it would hardly be surprising if such an impression had made the king doubt the seriousness of the Commons' intentions. Besides, although a full explanation of the failure of this scheme may never be possible, conflicting regional interests almost certainly played a part. Whereas the committee that recommended composition was dominated by members from the Home Counties, the house as a whole—in which the idea was 'talked out'—was not.[37] However, if James had grounds for feeling frustrated and annoyed over purveyance, it would seem that the Commons were very much the aggrieved party in respect of the other major attempt at reform—the case of wardship.

In some ways the two cases have much in common, apart from the fact that both are examples of 'fiscal feudalism'. In this case too, the scheme for reform was extensive and turned on the abolition of the right itself in return for a composition; and once again the Commons received direct encouragement from the Upper House (and in particular from Cecil) that must have seemed like an official blessing. However, though agreement was reached with the Lords on a joint request to be put to the king for leave to discuss wardship as early as 28 March, progress was soon halted. At the same conference that reached that agreement, Cecil first raised the question of the Goodwin *v.* Fortescue case and, as a result of that and of the subsequent discussions of purveyance and the Union, no more was heard of wardship for some seven weeks when, once more, the Commons sought a conference with the Lords. However, this initiative proved no more successful. Though a conference was arranged for 24 May, the meeting was completely abortive. Apparently on behalf of the king and his ministers, the Lords rejected the whole idea of composition out of hand.[38]

On the face of it, it might seem that the Commons had every reason to feel angry and misled. The initial impetus for composition of wardship had apparently come with official backing and, only eighteen days before that conference, the Lords had

---

[37] See above, p. 59 n. 32.
[38] *C.J.* 153a, 155–6; *L.J.* 301b, 309b.

been responsible for the suggestion that the bill against purveyors be replaced by composition. For the Lords' committee
to suddenly suggest that composition implied a diminution of
the royal prerogative must have seemed a volte-face of considerable proportions.[39] It may be, however, that this rejection
did not come as a complete surprise, for the parliamentary
political situation at the end of May was fraught with tension.

We have already seen that the offer of reform for purveyance
had (from James's point of view at least) met with argument
rather than the anticipated enthusiasm, and by 28 May it was
already well on its way to the stalemate in which it died. But
that was not all. On 26 May an attack was begun in the
Commons on a book by the Bishop of Bristol, John Thorn-
borough. Ostensibly the attack was concerned with a breach of
the parliamentary privilege of secrecy of debate, but the book
was a defence of the king's scheme for Union, and the privileged
material leaked was the list of objections the Lower House had
used in its emasculation of the scheme less than a month
previously.[40] This attack must therefore have reopened an old
wound and a dangerous one. For, it can be argued that of all
this session's problems the one that most contributed to the
growth of distrust between king and Commons was the question
of Union. As such, James's handling of that issue is of particular interest to this study.

The scheme for Union was very much James's personal
brainchild and he was no doubt unduly attached to it for that
reason alone. Rejection, therefore, and especially a rejection
that might be regarded as carping or narrow-minded, could not
do other than make James profoundly distrustful of the persons
or institution responsible. Why should James accommodate or
meet half-way the requests of those who would not do as much
for him? Yet, despite its obvious importance, James's actions
and intentions have perhaps been more seriously misunderstood and misrepresented by historians in respect of this issue
than of any other.

Whilst the arguments of the scheme's opponents have been
seen as careful, judicious, and objective, the king's response has

[39] See above, p. 53; *L.J.* 295–6.
[40] See above, pp. 58–61; *L.J.* 226b; *Harleian Miscellany*, ix. 95–105 for the Bishop's pamphlet, and *C.J.* 188 for the list of the Commons' objections.

been described as 'typically Jamesian'; as motivated by a feeling that he was '*en rapport* with the Supreme Being'; and as ignoring what are described as the 'real' difficulties and the 'real' issues.[41] Such a picture represents a gross caricature and is extremely unhelpful. James's actions were not entirely unreasonable, nor were his opponents' arguments intrinsically more rational.

In the first place it is not true, as Professor D. H. Willson seems to suggest, that James attempted to stampede the whole project through in a single session. No doubt, in the early months of his reign, his enthusiasm for the scheme might have led him to think it could be finalized swiftly, but in fact no such mistake was made when the scheme was actually presented to parliament. Consistently, James sought only three things in 1604: agreement in principle to the general idea; the adoption of one name for both kingdoms as a practical expression of that agreement; and the appointment of commissioners to investigate the problems that might accompany a full or 'perfect' Union, who should report their findings to the next session of parliament.[42] This can scarcely be described as browbeating. Apart from the adoption of the name, the Lower House was not being asked to *do* anything positive for the Union except nominate a commission of inquiry, all of whose recommendations would be subject to subsequent parliamentary review and veto. From James's point of view, therefore, all that the Commons was being asked for in 1604 was a display of goodwill towards a general idea, but it was precisely that general goodwill that was lacking. Whereas James was undoubtedly too sanguine about his scheme, his opponents' prejudices prevented it from ever having a fair trial.

The specific objections employed by those opponents were not, on the whole, objections to the name as much as to the whole idea of a Union. What is more, they were permeated by fear, hatred, and a national pride that verged on racial intolerance.[43] There was fear of a 'flood' of Scots who would consume offices and honours that were the birthright of Englishmen; fear that

---

[41] Willson, op. cit. 250; Notestein, op. cit. 83, 85.

[42] Willson, op. cit. 251. For James's aims see P.R.O. S.P. 14/7/74 and *C.J.* 953, 180b. On the idea of a 'perfect' Union, see above, p. 58 n. 30.

[43] For these objections and what follows, see *C.J.* 172–94 and 950–1.

the succession might pass to a Scot with no English blood; and fear that the precedence of England over Scotland might be lost. Such objections, together with a natural, conservative, attachment to the old name, provided the basis of a campaign that was altogether more emotional than rational. This is not a criticism of the campaign. National pride, even when inelegantly expressed, is an important factor and one that James was inclined to overlook too easily. However, it must serve as a counter to the view that one side in the discussion had a monopoly of reason or fairness.

This point is perhaps highlighted by the nature of the general argument on which the scheme's opponents chiefly relied. On the basis of a doctrine of 'essences', this argument rejected the possibility of separating the new name from a fuller Union. The change of name, it ran, would change the very nature of the relationship between England and Scotland anyway and would thereby prejudge the commissioners' deliberations.[44] Whatever the merits of this argument in terms of logic and philosophy, politically it was little less than a direct challenge to the king; for, from a roughly similar philosophical standpoint, he had argued that the adoption of the name would help to reconcile two traditionally hostile peoples. Thus, the attack on the name was little more than a thinly veiled attack on the general scheme. However, despite determined opposition, James remained reasonable. Indeed, on the question of the name he showed that, when absolutely necessary, he was prepared to make considerable concessions.

Amongst the objections to the name on which much stress was laid were those described by Professor Notestein as 'the real issues as to laws and writs'. Briefly, these arguments suggested that a change in name would throw many, if not most, aspects of the English legal system into complete chaos. What, it was asked, would be the status of writs returnable in an 'English' court; what relation would statutes of an 'English' or a 'Scottish' parliament have to the subjects of 'Great Britain'; how could *Coram Rege Angliae* be reconciled with *Coram Rege*

---

[44] See e.g. speech of 19 April at *C.J.* 177–8 (attributed to Sir Edwin Sandys—*C.J.* 950) which refers to the philosophical doctrine that 'Nomen signum Rei' and Sir Edward Mountague's report of a later Sandys speech—Northampton Record Office, Montague MS. XIII, fo. 71, p. 4.

Britanniae?[45] Certainly these were very real issues and ones to which James had to pay some, albeit belated, attention. His response, however, has received little notice. In Professor Notestein's account it is not even mentioned although it was a course of action at variance with the traditional picture of James as an intrasigent despot *manqué*.[46] When it became clear that arguments against the name were threatening the progress of the whole scheme, James agreed to put the legal aspects of the case to the judges for arbitration, adjuring them 'on their consciences to God and their alleigances [to him] to declare the truth if I may not at this time use the name of Britain'. According to Cecil it was the judges' unanimous decision 'that the first hour wherein the Parliament gave the king the name of Great Britain there followeth necessarily by our laws . . . an utter extinction of all the laws now in force'. Though, understandably, he did not find this palatable, James accepted the decision and the proposal for a new name was withdrawn. The Commons received the news of this 'victory' on 28 April, but they continued to drag their feet. Only the appointment of commissioners remained, but a list of names was not agreed until 12 May. Even D. H. Willson admits that 'the commissioners were voted only with obvious reluctance', and this despite the fact that they had only to investigate and report.[47]

It is surely understandable that James should have felt that his new subjects had not given his project a fair hearing. Whilst the Commons may have felt that an important national identity was being wilfully abandoned, to James it must have seemed that a perfectly reasonable and desirable scheme was being wrecked by prejudice and inconsequential bickering. As a result, he did on occasions lose his temper. In a 'sharp' letter of 1 May to the Commons he made it quite clear that he felt ill used in respect of the Union.[48] Such outbursts were, no doubt, unwise, but they are also understandable and it is perhaps unfortunate that they should have received so much more attention than the fact that proposals for reform continued to be sponsored and discussed, despite them.

The day after the Commons heard of James's capitulation over the name and the day before the 'sharp' letter was

[45] Notestein, op. cit. 85; *C.J.* 186–7, 958. [46] Notestein, op. cit. 83–4.
[47] P.R.O. S.P. 14/7/38, 14/7/85; Willson, op. cit. 252.
[48] *H.M.C. Bucc.* iii. 93; *C.J.* 193–4.

delivered, for example, they received a third, quite different, message from the king. This was the message concerning the second errant purveyor; a message which, we have seen, in the context of the debates on purveyance, was a positive gesture of good faith.[49] In the context of these concurrent issues it is perhaps even more remarkable. Similarly, disappointment over the Union did not stop James promoting something close to the hearts of many of the Lower House—a project for church reform.

First raised at the beginning of the session by Sir Edward Montague, the question of church reform had received a tremendous boost from James's remarks at the end of the Goodwin *v.* Fortescue case, as a direct result of which a committee was appointed in the Commons with a brief that included a specific injunction to consider the points James had raised.[50] Unfortunately, after such a promising start, further progress was delayed by one of those errors of judgement on James's part so much beloved of his detractors. In order (as he saw it) to facilitate discussion between the clergy and the laity over reform, James suggested a conference between representatives from both the Commons and the Convocation in session at St. Paul's. In the Lower House the mere suggestion provoked a storm of opposition because it seemed to imply a parity between the two institutions. However, having created the situation, James was quick to take action to defuse it. In two messages to the Commons (sent on consecutive days) he acknowledged that there was no question of the two bodies being equal and accepted a Commons' proposal that they should confer with the bishops, but as Lords of Parliament rather than as members of Convocation.[51] This compromise was accepted by both sides, but, though the Commons sought such a conference on 18 April and received an agreement in principle, the actual meeting was postponed four times and did not actually happen until 17 May. When it did meet, it was addressed by James.[52]

The month during which the meeting had been postponed had been a busy one. James had received the Commons'

[49] See above, p. 60.
[50] *C.J.* 151a, 171, 173a; *H.M.C. Bucc.* iii. 80–1, 91.
[51] *C.J.* 173a, 176, 178.
[52] *C.J.* 189–204 *passim; L.J.* 286a, 287b, 294b, 300b.

petition against purveyance; dealt with the second purveyor; dropped the idea of the name of Britain; and sent his 'sharp' letter to the Commons. This was also the month in which the Lords had first suggested composition for purveyance. But from James's point of view perhaps the most important factor was the Union, for his address to the conference on religion was delivered barely a fortnight after the sending of the letter he had written on the failure of the name.[53] There were, however, no recriminations, only the offer of a new initiative. The suggestion was that there should be a joint committee of both Houses to consider the legislation the church required in 1604; that which might be required in future sessions; and the nature and extent of the royal supremacy.[54] For the Commons this meant the recognition of the supremacy, in ecclesiastical affairs, of king-in-parliament over Convocation and High Commission, and for the king it meant the retention of control over the Commons' reforming zeal. For, by committing the whole scheme to discussion (which could be interminable) and legislation (which could be vetoed), James could hope for the 'reformation by degrees' that had always eluded Elizabeth. If so, he must have been encouraged by the committee's first meeting on 24 May.

The members for the Commons raised three issues at that meeting: the planting of a learned ministry; the abolition of pluralities; and the articles of religion. For the first, it was agreed that the Lower House should continue with the bill it already had in hand; the state of the ministry was referred for discussion at the committee's next meeting; and the potentially volatile issue of the articles was postponed indefinitely.[55] Unhappily, this cautious progress was soon interrupted, not as a result of dissatisfaction on the part of lay puritan gentlemen or clumsy interference by the king, but because of pressure from within the church itself.

At the committee's second meeting, before discussion of the ministry could begin, Bancroft presented the representatives of the Commons with a document (known as the 'Instrument') from Convocation. This accused the Lower House of having 'prejudged the liberties of the church' and ordered the bishops

[53] See above, p. 65.
[54] *C.J.* 214a, 975a.
[55] *C.J.* 224b.

to break off the discussions, threatening, if they did not, to appeal to the king against them.[56] At a stroke, any goodwill or spirit of co-operation that might have been generated by James's initiative was destroyed and the question of church reform became, for that session, virtually a dead letter.

So too did any serious attempts at large-scale reform in general. The Instrument was presented to the committee on 4 June. On 2 June the scheme for composition of purveyance had been officially 'let sleep'. On 1 June, in two reports of earlier meetings, the Lower House had heard of the Lords' rejection of composition for wardship and of a speech from James in which their proceedings on a variety of issues had been subjected to severe criticism. The nadir had, apparently, been reached, and it was as a result of the reports of 1 June that the Commons had decided to prepare their 'Apology' or explanation of their previous proceedings. This, however, was the end neither of all direct contact between king and Commons, nor of royal initiatives. Two further incidents show that, despite the set-backs, James continued to create and exploit political opportunities for maintaining his credibility with the Lower House.

Though small, the first incident was particularly significant. The decision to write the Apology had been taken on a Friday. The following Tuesday the Speaker came to the Lower House with a message from the king in which he tried to explain why he had earlier given vent to his feelings. He admitted that he had felt frustrated by the time that had been wasted and the little that had been achieved, but he denied feeling that they were disloyal. He claimed to understand, and to be grateful for, their desire to explain their proceedings to him, but said it was not necessary. He remarked on the 'greater expedition in those things desired [by him] to be effected' since his speech of 30 May and concluded with what was, in terms of the parliamentary procedure of the time, a generous gesture. In the words of the Speaker, 'he giveth what time we desire, for finishing the matters of importance depending.'[57] Since Elizabeth had generally been keener to curtail than to extend parliamentary activity, this must be seen as an open-handed

[56] *C.J.* 235a.
[57] *C.J.* 232–3; *H.M.C. Bucc.* iii. 89.

and conciliatory move. Furthermore, there is evidence that, in some circles at least, the gesture was appreciated. Sir Edward Montague, the 'puritan' member for Northamptonshire, described the speech as 'comfortable'.[58] Whatever the motives for such gestures, it is difficult to see them as attempts to precipitate confrontation or as, in any way, clumsy or hectoring.

The second incident is no exception. As a result of some highly unreliable soundings in the Lower House, the idea that a subsidy should be granted in this session was mooted in the Commons on 19 June. This was then followed by a more direct approach, from the Lords, at a conference on the Bill for Tonnage and Poundage two days later. Since the final instalment of the 1601 subsidy still remained to be collected, it is not surprising that the mere suggestion met with a storm of protest and the idea had to be abandoned.[59] However, James seems to have seen a political opportunity and seized it. Since he could not avoid conflict without withdrawal, he could at least try to turn that withdrawal to his own advantage. In a matter of days he had sent a letter to the Lower House categorically rejecting the whole idea.[60]

Referring to his speech at the opening of parliament, James claimed that he had never had any intention of overburdening his subjects with another subsidy (nor of accepting one if it were offered!), but that he had been assured by 'divers members of that House [i.e. the Commons] that were otherwise strangers to our affairs' that he *ought* to accept such a grant. As a result, he said, he had made some inquiries, but had nevertheless reverted to his original position and therefore did 'desire them at this time not to meddle any further in that question'. In this way, a rather delicate situation was turned to the king's personal advantage. For, whether the incident was genuine or contrived, the desired effect—that of a display of magnanimity—was achieved. In the Commons, one motion that 'the King's letter might be recorded here for an everlasting memory of his

[58] *H.M.C. Bucc.* loc. cit. Though he had powerful contacts at court (one brother—Henry—was appointed Recorder of London at James's request, another—James—was a Royal Chaplain), he was a sincere supporter of church reform and seems to have been a fairly 'independent' member of the Commons—*D.N.B.*, 'Montague, Sir Edward'.

[59] *C.J.* 242a, 995; P.R.O. S.P. 14/8/69.

[60] For this letter and what follows, see *C.J.* 246–7.

Majesty's grace' was followed by another, 'that all Knights of Shires may take a copy of it and publish it in their countries', and a resolution, 'That Mr. Speaker at the end of this session should present thanks to his Majesty in the name of the House for his grace expressed in his letter'.[61] The Speaker did as he was bid, but the Knights of the Shire were relieved of the more onerous aspects of their duty by a further piece of public relations work emanating, presumably, from the court. The whole letter was printed and put on sale 'in Paul's churchyard at the sign of the Swan'.[62] Once again, the worst consequences of an inept overture had been avoided by a positive initiative on James's part. There was no hectoring in the letter and no appeal to abstract constitutional ideas. It was simply a straightforward (if rather obvious) attempt to make political capital and generate goodwill, in an otherwise dangerous situation. Here, as elsewhere, there is more to be said for James's position—and indeed his political ability—than it has been customary to acknowledge in the past.

In none of the cases we have examined can it reasonably be maintained that full responsibility for any ill-will or failure lay with James. The growth of distrust—at the beginning of the reign at least—was a complicated process which cannot be explained in terms of a single personality. James's methods and motives in parliamentary affairs in particular, and his role in politics generally are, therefore, in need of fundamental revision. Both that revision and the alternative explanation it might offer are beyond the scope of a present essay, but, in conclusion, a suggestion may be made.

POSTSCRIPT: DISTRUST AND 'MISINFORMERS'

The suggestion is that, if anyone should bear a particular responsibility for the failure of this session, it is the king's principal advisers, the great lords at court and in the Council. For, though the misunderstandings of this session were mutual and owed something—especially in the cases of the Union and purveyance—to irresponsibility on the part of the Lower House, it is difficult not to feel that something more positive

---

[61] *C.J.* 247a.

[62] *C.J.* 253. Printed copies of the speech may be found at P.R.O. S.P. 14/8/78 and H.L.R.O. MS. 3 between fos. 324ᵛ and 325.

was involved. Certainly contemporaries thought so, and there is some evidence that they believed that what was involved was the deliberate 'misinforming' of the king about the Commons' intentions and that some courtiers and counsellors played a leading role in it.[63]

On the crucial issue of the Union, for example, the Venetian ambassador reported to the Doge and Senate that the House of Lords was as opposed to Union as the Commons, but that 'though they do not openly display their sentiments they privately urge the Commons to stand firm, and furnish them with arguments'; a view that is largely borne out by the private testimony of the M.P. for Nottinghamshire, Sir John Holles.[64] In a letter to Lord Burghley he complained of the way in which the Lords used the Commons in respect of the same issue; 'wherein we [the Commons] put on the one and they [the Lords] the other skin of Lysander, we like countrymen plainly, they like statesmen more covertly and with ceremony, whence though proceeding one and the same effect, I mean the adjournment of resolutions till further debate, yet they clad angel-like were received into Abraham's bosom while we fried in the furnace of the king's displeasure.' His claim is verified by the distinction James was to make in his closing speech between the activities of the two Houses.[65] Further, though this was a particularly important issue it was by no means the only one in which members of the Lords played, or seemed to play, what the Commons might have regarded as a negative role.

The mishandling of the Goodwin *v.* Fortescue dispute, following the election itself, was more conciliar than royal in origin; one of the reasons for the failure of the negotiations surrounding purveyance was the size of the composition suggested, presumably with official prompting, by the Lords; the demise of the wardship debates was presided over by a Lords' committee dominated by privy councillors; in a similar way, the principal overtures for a subsidy came from the Upper

---

[63] Misinforming was one of the principle complaints of the authors of the 'Apology': P.R.O. S.P. 14/8/70.

[64] *C.S.P. Venet. 1603–10*, 151. Sir John Holles went on to become a successful Stuart courtier and politician: *D.N.B.*, 'Holles, Sir John'. For the letter that follows see *H.M.C. Portland MSS.* ix. 11–13.

[65] P.R.O. S.P. 14/8/93.

House; and there can be little doubt that Bancroft was involved in blighting the progress of the joint committee on ecclesiastical reform in the same way that, the year before, he and Whitgift had led the attempt to prevent James making any concessions to the 'puritan' lobby at all.[66]

Of course, this may all be purely coincidental, and there is certainly no evidence for a concerted attempt to sour relations between king and Commons. However, the suspicions of contemporaries like Holles deserve consideration and, even if they were only partly true, they suggest that an explanation for the 'growth of distrust' between James and his subjects in parliament should perhaps be sought in a better understanding of the 'high politics' of the day than in James's political inability or craving for absolutism.

---

[66] See above, pp. 53–7; *H.M.C. Portland*, loc. cit.; *L.J.* 303a, 323a; *C.J.* 235a; P.R.O. S.P. 14/8/69; above, p. 67; Munden, thesis cit. 114–17. It may also be noted that though it was a busy time, the Lords' reasons for postponing the conference on religious affairs were not always entirely convincing—above. p. 66 n. 52.

III. Medieval Doctrines in the Debates on Supply, 1610–1629

G. L. HARRISS

THE 'ANTIQUARIANISM' of members of parliament in the early seventeenth century has for the most part aroused derision or reproach. That the appeal to the past could be polemical, pedantic, and anachronistic, and that it could impede rather than assist the search for solutions to the current problems of the state, are charges that undoubtedly have some substance.[1] But to condemn is not to explain, and it may be worth considering whether practical men turned to medieval records not merely as a political armoury but for guidance on the urgent problems of government. It is not difficult to see why some historians have been reluctant to believe that they did, for it would imply that the political structure and mentality of early Stuart England remained essentially medieval, and call in question that transformation of medieval into modern England which has been identified either with the 'New Monarchy' or with the creation of a national sovereign state at the Reformation.[2]

In constitutional terms the identity of the period from the fourteenth to the seventeenth century is clearly defined as one

---

[1] Complaints that members of parliament 'dredged up' medieval precedents with the implication that these were irrelevant and misleading will be found in L. Stone, *The Causes of the English Revolution, 1529–1642* (1972), 93; R. E. Ruigh, *The Parliament of 1624* (Cambridge, Mass., 1971), 253; J. E. Neale, *Elizabeth I and her Parliaments, 1584–1601* (1957), 304–5. Contemporaries were, of course, keenly critical of the use of precedents, as to both their accuracy and their relevance. Thus Sir Humphrey May in 1625 could admonish: 'let no man despise ancient presidents, no man adore them. Examples are powerfull arguments, if they be proper, but tymes alter' (*Debates in the House of Commons in 1625*, ed. S. R. Gardiner (Camden Soc., 1873), 110).

[2] The influence of this conceptual barrier may be seen in two examples: M. A. Judson noted that in the debates members 'wandered back in their ideas along many paths to the Middle Ages...ignoring the fact that those older ideas had developed at a time when the state hardly existed...' (*The Crisis of the Constitution*, New Brunswick, 1949, 8); J. P. Kenyon castigates 'the incorrigible antiquarianism of the Commons, and their belief that the precedents of the Hundred Years War were immediately applicable to modern conditions' (*The Stuart Constitution, 1603–1688*, Cambridge, 1966, 56).

of mixed monarchy. The seventeenth-century crisis marked the death-knell of this political system which the early Renaissance of the thirteenth and fourteenth centuries had produced.[3] In England Fortescue, Smith, and Hooker are equally its apologists.[4] Moreover, the striking similarities in the political crises of the late medieval and early seventeenth centuries show that —as J. S. Roskell has convincingly argued—the constitutional relationship of king and parliament remained essentially unchanged over this period.[5] For Whig historians the catalogue (stretching from 1250 to 1650) of kings deposed, ministers impeached and executed, taxes refused or removed from royal control, and accounts demanded, all betokened a continuing struggle between liberty and prerogative ending with parliament's predestined victory over the crown. Whatever value this has as a story of constitutional progress, it has been discarded as an analysis of political motives. The political crisis of the seventeenth century is now commonly regarded as the unlooked-for failure of a normally balanced and ideally harmonious partnership. King and parliament were its unwilling victims, not its agents. This failure has in recent years been variously ascribed to a lapse in parliamentary management, to profligacy in public finance, to the cankerous growth of patronage bureaucracy, or to the tensions between the localities and the centre; in social and economic terms it is seen as a struggle between groups and classes which the old political structures could not contain. Multiple causes are preferable to single ones, and of these flaws in the traditional system contemporaries were anxiously aware. But since that system had shown a marked resilience throughout four centuries of political and social turmoil, any explanation of its crisis and ultimate failure must also take account of its long survival. Here is a problem which the medieval historian should not evade and to the solution of which he may be able to contribute. He may

[3] Cf. H. R. Trevor-Roper, 'The General Crisis of the Seventeenth Century', in *Crisis in Europe, 1560–1660*, ed. T. H. Aston (1965), 63–4; Gaines Post, *Studies in Medieval Legal Thought* (Princeton, 1964), chs. x, xi.

[4] R. K. Hinton, 'English Constitutional Theories from Sir John Fortescue to Sir John Eliot', *E.H.R.* lxxv (1960), 410–21.

[5] J. S. Roskell, 'Perspective in English Parliamentary History', in *Historical Studies of the English Parliament*, ed. E. B. Fryde and E. Miller (2 vols., Cambridge, 1970), ii. 296–323.

take courage from the evidence that it was the consciousness of past troubles survived and problems overcome that impelled men in the seventeenth century to look back to history in their present dilemmas.

I do not pretend that a discussion restricted to the debates on supply can encompass, let alone solve, the problem of the collapse of mixed monarchy. Yet supply was not merely one of the most contentious themes in early Stuart parliaments, evoking a repeated appeal to precedent, but was a focal point of the rights and obligations of the crown and its subjects; it was the cynosure of mixed monarchy. Although it was only in the early seventeenth century, under the pressure of political crisis and conflicting legal theories, that mixed monarchy achieved the stature of a conscious constitutional system, its roots lay three centuries back in the practical need of reconciling the growing authority of national kingship with the rights of subjects. Its first and proudest achievement (as Fortescue makes plain) had been to define the authority by which the crown could tax a subject's property for the common good of the realm. Moreover, of all aspects of early Stuart government, the system of public finance remained most evidently medieval in both its mechanism and outlook.[6] Thus when men debated the problems of supply they did so within a framework of conventions governing the terms on which taxes were demanded, granted, and spent, which by long and enduring practice had become central to their constitutional relationship with the crown. We must therefore review this medieval legacy in a little more detail.[7]

In medieval political doctrine the crown was the symbol of the identity and perpetuity of the state. By his coronation the king became responsible for the welfare and preservation of the state, being by virtue of his office both sovereign over it and minister to its needs. To maintain the estate and dignity of the

---

[6] R. Ashton, 'Deficit Finance in the Reign of James I', *Ec.H.R.* x (1957), 15–18; C. Russell, 'Parliament and the King's Finances', in *The Origins of the English Civil War*, ed. C. Russell (1973), 91–3.

[7] The following paragraphs summarize arguments advanced in my book *King, Parliament and Public Finance in Medieval England, to 1369* (Oxford, 1975) and in 'War and the Emergence of the English Parliament, 1297–1360', *Journal of Medieval History*, 2 (1976), 35–56. My debt to the work of Gaines Post and E. H. Kantorowicz is acknowledged in both of these.

perpetual crown the king enjoyed the hereditary and inalienable fisc, that complex of lands, revenues, and rights which was commonly designated his 'own'. Here his authority was sovereign, not shared, though he was to exercise it for the support of the dignity of the crown, not for his private pleasure. For while the realm had a duty to ensure that the fisc was sufficient to maintain the crown, the king had a duty not to alienate or impair the fisc so that it became insufficient for this purpose. Subjects could thus claim a legitimate concern with the management of the king's 'own', but that concern stopped short of the power to determine or constrain the king's use of it.

Normally, then, the king had no claim on his subjects' wealth to maintain the dignity of the crown; but a clear and inescapable obligation bound them to contribute to the preservation of the state in times of exceptional need. The 'case of necessity' had to be laid before subjects in parliament and accepted by them as genuine ('evident and urgent'). Parliament's grant of taxation to meet such a designated and acknowledged necessity of the realm was (along with legislation) the foremost of those acts of shared government that characterized a mixed monarchy. By common assent subjects were deprived of their individual goods for the common good. Thereafter the tax was levied and spent by the king's regal authority (though for its designated purpose) and parliament had no power to supervise expenditure or require account. If subjects refused to grant taxation in a legitimate necessity, the king might be held to have a residual obligation to impose a tax for the preservation of the realm by regal authority alone. Indeed, such a refusal of common obligation might be held to spell a renunciation of mixed government. Perhaps for this reason such a situation was carefully avoided in the Middle Ages. The dualism of the medieval system was thus designed to protect the rights of both king and subjects in their 'own', while enforcing their corresponding obligation to employ it for the common good.

Because the plea of 'necessity' was so compelling, its application came to be closely defined. The most obvious necessity of the realm was a war which threatened its existence. Originally this was thought of as an exceptional emergency and taxation as an unusual occurrence; but the prolonged state of war between England and France in the late Middle Ages, and the need to maintain armies along the northern frontiers and garrisons in Ireland and France, created the demand for permanent taxation to meet a continuing emergency.

This threatened to undermine the right of assent. In England the dilemma was met from the middle of the fourteenth century by the recurrent grant in parliament of indirect taxes, mainly on wool exports. This debarred the king from prerogative impositions on grounds of necessity, it permitted the customs to be reserved (with varying degrees of stringency) for the permanent charges of defence, and it enabled parliament to restrict grants of direct taxation to open war and thus preserve their occasional character. The solution was more readily acceptable since much of the burden of this indirect taxation was borne by foreign consumers.

As well as being for an exceptional need, taxation had to be for the common good of the realm. It should not spring from the king's mere interest, ambition, or incompetence. Although the baronial opposition had successfully challenged Henry III's demands on these grounds, the development of national wars in the following two centuries gave little scope for similar refusals. Nevertheless, the requirement for subjects to adjudicate and accept the plea of necessity in parliament provided opportunities to examine and criticize the king's plans and achievements, particularly if these appeared to threaten the destruction or impoverishment of the realm rather than its preservation.

Even so taxation could not be confined wholly to open war. It could be justified by the maintenance of a defensive posture in time of truce, by preparations either for war or to prevent war, and even by the cost of embassies to avert war or bring it to an end. Beyond this again, taxation could be asked—if more exceptionally—for non-military expenditure provided this was extraordinary, and exceeded the king's own resources, and was for the common good. Such might be the suppression of rebellion, or the symbolic renewal of the royal authority at a coronation, this latter being habitually the occasion for a grant of taxation in the first parliament of the reign. The dignity of the crown, and thus the safety of the kingdom, might also be thought to be imperilled by royal debts; but while parliament was ready to discharge the debts of the king's predecessor on this ground, recurrent debt could only reflect either a disparity

between the crown's own resources and expenses, or the fruit
of royal extravagance and incompetence. In either case the
crown faced the likelihood of inquiry, criticism, and reform.

Such were the doctrines and conventions which governed
taxation in England at the beginning of the sixteenth century.
Grounded in the precepts of lawyers and theologians, they
articulated a generally acknowledged philosophy of the state as
the vehicle of the common good, and provided firm definitions
of the rights and obligations of ruler and ruled, while permit-
ting the interplay of their respective interests and the expression
of both loyalty and loyal criticism. This was widely recognized
as a political achievement of no mean order and as the corner-
stone of an increasingly venerated constitution, which must be
defended when threatened (as in 1525). For the 'dualism' of
the financial system—that the crown should meet ordinary
expenses from its own revenues and only approach subjects for
extraordinary needs—preserved both the independence of the
crown, which retained absolute control over its hereditary
revenue, and the independence of the subject, whose obligations were strictly limited to accepted cases of necessity. It
meant that the crown could not demand taxation, nor the
Commons refuse it, merely at will. Hence taxation was not, for
the most part, a weapon in their struggle for power but a
recognition of their common interest and obligation for the
preservation of the state. This did not preclude tensions or
pre-empt debate between crown and parliament, but it meant
that such debate was conducted within a framework of ancient
conventions. Taxation had to be related to the extraordinary
needs of the realm, but the less urgent and evident the danger
the greater was the scope for excuses by subjects, for pleas of
goodwill and promises of redress of grievances by the king, and
for hard bargaining over the abuses of royal government.
Ultimately the size of the grant might reflect parliament's
assessment of the king's plea of necessity, his accommodation
of its interests, and the degree of trust and popularity in which
the monarchy was held.

All this remained true for the sixteenth century, though the
fact that in the century preceding 1581 there were long periods
without foreign wars limited, if it did not eliminate, the need for
direct taxation. Indeed the traditional doctrine of the just war

no longer had to be distorted in the service of the secular and aggressive English claim to the French crown, but could be invoked to preserve the schismatic and Protestant English state, and the commerce which was its life blood, against papal imperialism. Moreover the establishment of an anti-papal church served to identify the defence of that church with that of the realm, and also invested the medieval role of the crown as the symbol of the perpetuity of the state with the charisma of the defender of its true faith. The crown therefore had little difficulty in justifying in traditional terms the repeated, though never heavy, grants of taxation for the maintenance of defences on which the continued peace and prosperity of the realm depended.[8]

In the last twenty years of Elizabeth's reign, however, parliaments met more frequently and the rate of taxation more than doubled. The grants of triple and even quadruple subsidies, unprecedented since the reign of Edward III, partly reflected their decline in real value even since her father's reign.[9] But the reality of the danger to the Queen, the realm, and its religion enabled the plea of necessity to be urged with a cogency that could not be gainsaid. Even though the Commons expressed their anxiety that such grants should not set a precedent, and the Queen professed her reluctance to take their gift did not necessity compel her,[10] this renewed primacy of parliamentary taxation in public finance and the almost mystical devotion to the Queen as the incarnation of the realm, which danger had engendered, both became significant elements in James I's inheritance. There are also signs of the emergence of the doctrine—which had flourished on the continent but never in England—that necessity gave the sovereign an overriding right

[8] Cf. G. R. Elton, 'Taxation for war and peace in early-Tudor England', in *War and Economic Development*, ed. J. M. Winter (Cambridge, 1975), 33–48 for a different view, which I believe to be mistaken.

[9] For the historical parallels with the fourteenth century cited by Mr. Heyle in 1593 and Sir Thomas Egerton in 1597, see Simonds D'Ewes, *The Journals of the Parliaments of Queen Elizabeth* (1682), 494, 525.

[10] At the request of the Commons the subsidy acts of 1593 and 1598 embodied a protest that 'our intencion is, that this whiche wee have nowe doon upon so extraordynarie and urgent a necessitie to so good and graciowse a Pryncesse, be not drawen a president for the tymes to come', and the 1601 Act had a similar clause (*Statutes of the Realm*, ed. T. E. Tomlins *et al.* (Record Comm., 11 vols., 1810–28), 1819, iv. 867, 937, 992). For the Queen's response see the passages quoted by J. E. Neale, op. cit. 320, 411.

to tax without consent.[11] This was spurned by parliament, but influential voices were raised there in support of a permanent tax for defence.[12] None of these suggestions was pursued, perhaps because of the Queen's dislike for any but traditional means of supply and her confidence that parliament would fulfil its obligation to grant what was needed.

But if the sixteenth century brought no essential change in the theory of parliamentary taxation, it did see a greater emphasis on taxation by regal prerogative. Fiscal feudalism was not 'unconstitutional'; indeed, it appeared to fulfil the doctrine that the king should live of his own. Subjects were spared the expense of coming to parliament and monarchs the criticism that taxation often stimulated. Yet to tax by prerogative was to expose the royal dignity to the reaction of subjects without the shield of representative assent; for it was every bit as unpopular as direct taxation and far more unpopular than indirect taxation.[13] In this the Tudors (like the Angevins before them) set a course the ultimate perils of which they hardly foresaw. More immediately, the reinforcement of the wealth of the monarchy from the monastic and chantry lands decreased the willingness of its subjects ('of all nations not subject, base and taxable') to shoulder the fiscal burdens of the state.[14] This was perhaps one reason for the failure to reinvigorate mercantile taxation which changes in the pattern of trade had reduced to half its mid-fourteenth-century level, and which inflation rendered virtually useless for meeting the permanent charges of defence. Significantly when, under Mary, ecclesiastical wealth could no longer be plundered, the first step towards making the customs revenue realistic was not by assent but by prerogative imposi-

[11] Neale, op. cit. 415–16.

[12] Ibid. 361 for Sir Edward Hoby's proposal in 1597 for an annual grant to the Queen for life. In the 1593 Parliament there were proposals from Sir Henry Knyvet for an annual land tax to the sum of £100,000, and other tax proposals from Sir Edward Stafford and Sir Francis Drake, while Francis Bacon had a suggestion for a levy or imposition as a better manner of supply 'when need doth arise' (D'Ewes, op. cit. 491–3).

[13] As Bacon saw it, 'inventions of suits and levies of money' would fill empty coffers but alienate the people: *The Letters and Life of Francis Bacon*, ed. J. Spedding (7 vols., 1862–74), iv. 50. Any legislation to extend or facilitate the crown's fiscal prerogatives invariably excited fierce opposition from the propertied classes in the Commons, as over the Statute of Uses (J. M. W. Bean, *The Decline of English Feudalism*, Manchester, 1968, ch. 6) and the extension of wardship in 1584–5 (J. E. Neale, op. cit. 91). Parliamentary taxation shifted more of the burden on to the poorer classes.

[14] The quotation is from Bacon's speech in 1593 (D'Ewes, op. cit. 493).

tion. Elizabeth returned to the exploitation of episcopal lands and imposed new customs rates, but foreign danger increasingly dictated the resort to parliamentary taxation.

It is thus easy to see why, with the accession of James I, public finance raised urgent issues of principle. The king and others saw his reign as an epoch of peace; not the peace of an armed and watchful defence as under the Tudors, but a permanent release from the traditional fear of encirclement by enemies in Scotland, France, and Ireland. Subjects expected relief from the demands of war taxation while the court turned with eagerness from the frugality of the old queen's regime to the open-handedness of her successor. How were the costs of court and government to be supported? Early Tudor government had established a reliance on prerogative finance in time of peace, but to resume this policy now that the crown's landed capital built up by 1540 had been severely diminished must mean a sharpening of legal prerogatives which would discomfort the landed and mercantile classes. Yet to seek taxation from parliament on the scale of Elizabeth's latter years but without the justification of open war not only lacked any constitutional basis but would predictably encounter resistance from a body freshly alerted to its rights, history, and political role. It was this dilemma which provoked debate on the fiscal obligations of king and subjects and turned attention to the principles and practices of the past.

Nevertheless James met his first parliament as heir to a remarkable sense of unity between the monarchy and its subjects which bore fruit in the first grant of the reign, of three subsidies and six fifteenths in 1606. Granted to discharge the debts for James's entry and coronation as well as those for Ireland, and justified by expressions of gratitude for his deliverance from the Gunpowder Plot, for the common kingship with Scotland, and for the abolition of monopolies, it followed medieval and Tudor precedents in all but size. Parliament was being generous, even lavish, and the grant got through with the barest majority.[15] It was almost the worst possible example

[15] Similar expressions of gratitude for their accessions occurred in grants to Henry IV in 1399 (*Rot. Parl.* iii. 425) and Elizabeth in 1559 (*Stat. Realm*, iv. 384), but, as the Commons noted, the present one was unprecedented 'in proportion and speed of payment... the times of peace considered' (*Stat. Realm*, iv. 1109). For the majority of one, see W. Notestein, *The House of Commons, 1604–1610* (New Haven, 1971), 208. The

to set the new king, for it not merely excited his prodigality but confirmed his mistaken belief that the benefits of royal government conferred a right to receive liberal grants of taxation. It encouraged the crown to look to parliament for supply while doing nothing to affirm the traditional limits of subjects' fiscal obligations.

It is possible that by frugality and political tact constitutional disputes over finance could have been avoided. Once the debts of the previous reign had been discharged—and for these the subsidies granted in 1601 and 1606 were broadly sufficient—the financial prospects of the crown were far from discouraging.[16] Peace brought a dramatic drop in the costs of defence to a level where they could be virtually supported from the customs.[17] On the other hand the cost of the household doubled and grants of favours and annuities quintupled since Elizabeth's day, so that the deficit on the ordinary account with which ministers confronted parliament in 1610 and 1614 was bound to excite charges of extravagance.[18] Three remedies were available: domestic expenditure could be reduced, the hereditary and prerogative revenue could be increased, and parliament could be asked for taxation.[19] Much intellectual effort and historical research was invested in plans for the first two, but as a practical programme the first was undermined by the king and the court, while the one striking increase achieved in prerogative revenue—from impositions—though it appeared to have the simplicity of genius in 1608, had by 1610 and 1614 become a millstone around the necks of ministers who were arguing for supply. For amongst ministers the influence of the late Elizabethan polity was still so strong that a parliament seemed 'the

grant yielded £453,000 (J. P. Cooper, 'The Fall of the Stuart Monarchy', in New Cambridge Modern History, iv, Cambridge, 1970, 544).

[16] M. Prestwich, *Cranfield: Politics and Profits under the Early Stuarts* (Oxford, 1966), 7–9.

[17] In 1607 it was reckoned that since Elizabeth's reign defence costs had decreased by £386,920 p.a. and, excluding charges for embassies, now stood at around £130,000 p.a. Brit. Lib. Add. MS. 36970, fos. 7, 29.

[18] R. Ashton, art cit., *Ec. H.R.* x. 18–19; M. Prestwich, *Cranfield*, 7, 247–51; R. H. Tawney, *Business and Politics under James I* (Cambridge, 1958), 138–9. Brit. Lib. Cotton MS. Cleopatra F.VI, fo. 77, 'A table of the Meanes to Repair the King's Estate', shows the cost of the household to have increased from £57,000 to £94,000 and that of pensions and annuities from £16,000 to £80,000.

[19] That is leaving aside the short-term debt reductions discussed by R. Ashton, art. cit.

ordinary remedy to supply the king's wants', 'the ancient and royal way of aid and provision for the King with treasure'.[20] Even so, Salisbury's proposal in 1610 for £600,000 supply mainly to discharge the king's debts, and £200,000 per annum 'to maintain and support his yearly charge' introduced the wholly new principle that parliament should meet the ordinary peacetime costs of the crown.[21]

Was parliament under any obligation to do so? This was the question on which debate centred. Traditionally subsidies were granted for a necessity of the realm, and although Salisbury acknowledged that 'the king is not in warres nor in action' he was able to enumerate the charges for Ireland, the Low Countries, the Navy, and the other fortresses with some confidence that these would be regarded as legitimate grounds for supply, and even to deploy the familiar argument that military preparedness was necessary to safeguard peace, to advance diplomacy, and to meet emergencies.[22] Even in the days of the embattled Tudor state, parliament had not granted more than a half subsidy and a fifteenth per annum for these defensive charges, whereas now, in different circumstances and for debts on the ordinary account, James was asking much more.

Ministers thus had to resort to an interpretation of necessity that went beyond the obligation to provide for common defence or to reimburse extraordinary expenses to that of simply meeting the king's needs. Salisbury 'took it as pro concesso that the king's necessities must be relieved by subjects', and saw it as 'a necessitie of the commonwealth to supply the king's needs'.[23] This readiness to interpret the king's needs as those of the state doubtless drew strength from current absolutist theory,

[20] *Letters and Life of Bacon*, iv. 152, 365; v. 176, 194–207. Sir Julius Caesar in 1610 clung to the 'hope which, in the late Queenes tyme, and hitherto in his, never failed; which hathe bene to relieve the King with subsidies and fifteenths uppon all occasions moved in Parliament' (*Parliamentary Debates in 1610*, ed. S. R. Gardiner (Camden Soc., 1862), 178).

[21] Salisbury himself acknowledged that the precedent was rare: *Parliamentary Debates, 1610*, 6–7, 14; and see T. M. Coakley, 'Robert Cecil in Power', in *Early Stuart Studies*, ed. H. S. Reinmuth Jr. (Minneapolis, 1970), 87–9.

[22] *Parliamentary Debates, 1610*, 3–4; *Proceedings in Parliament in 1610*, ed. E. R. Foster (2 vols., New Haven, 1966), i. 14–15, 22, 218, 269–70; ii. 11, 15, 34. For similar arguments in 1614, see *C.J.* i. 461–2; *H.M.C. Downshire MSS.* (1940), iv. 366–7.

[23] *Proceedings in Parliament, 1610*, ed. Foster, i. 12, 70. Bacon too spoke of 'the strait obligations which intercede between the King and the Subject in case of the King's want': *Letters and Life of Bacon*, iv. 234.

but it was not wholly alien to medieval doctrine, provided that such needs were extraordinary and that they did indeed concern the commonwealth and were not the product of the king's wilful greed or folly. This distinction emerged in an exchange between James I and Sir Henry Neville after the failure of the Great Contract. To James's question 'whether it belongeth to you that are my subjects to relieve me or not', Neville gave the reply that 'where your Majesty's expense groweth by Commonwealth we are bound to maintain it; otherwise not.'[24] James learned the lesson at least to the extent of claiming in 1614 that 'my greate necessitie that lookes me in the face' arose not from expenditure 'on my own affections but for my owne, yours, and the countrey's honour'.[25] One of the best analyses of the respective obligations of the king and parliament was made by Sir Julius Caesar. While he acknowledged as fundamental law Fortescue's dictum that 'as the king oweth the people defence and justice so the people are to furnishe all the king's necessities', Caesar maintained that the reduction of the ordinary deficit must remain the king's responsibility; as for the extraordinary deficit, he drew a distinction between those 'wants for necessary defense in time of war, or for necessity, conveniency or Honour of the King or Kingdom in time of peace' which pertained to the wisdom of parliament to supply, and those extraordinary 'wantes in expenses of pleasure or bountie' which should be left to the king's discretion.[26]

But if parliament was ready to acknowledge an obligation to meet extraordinary expenses of the commonwealth in time of peace, it was all the more incumbent on the crown to demonstrate and justify these. Monarchists like Bacon vehemently disapproved when Salisbury produced an elaborate statement of revenue and expenditure, because it opened the *arcana imperii* to public gaze and stimulated wanton criticism.[27] But even if

[24] *Letters and Life of Bacon*, iv. 230–1.

[25] *H.M.C. Hastings MSS.* iv, (1947), 239.

[26] *Parliamentary Debates 1610*, 173, citing Fortescue, *The Governance of England*, ch. viii (Plummer ed., Oxford, 1885, 173); Brit. Lib. MS. Lansdowne 165, fos. 138–9. Nathaniel Bacon likewise opposed any grant for the ordinary charges: 'No extraordinary cause: the wants of the King are not extraordinary but ordinary. I wish they were not so ordinary' (*Proceedings in Parliament, 1610*, ii. 144).

[27] *Letters and Life of Bacon*, v. 26.

Salisbury's example was not in general followed, royal spokes-men still needed to anticipate criticism of the king's prodigality. Protesting that the king's wants were 'not of wantoness' but expenses of necessity and magnificence, Salisbury had yet to admit that James's first three years had been 'his Christmas'; subjects had been 'most importune and unmannerly of asking', and the best defence that could be offered was the king's traditional obligation to reward and encourage faithful ser-vice.[28] The difficulty in drawing the line between politic liberality and culpable prodigality in the distribution of patron-age was no easier than when it had exercised late medieval theorists like Fortescue or the baronial opposition to the favourites of Henry III and Edward II. The king might also forestall criticism by claiming to have used his own resources for the public good. Monarchs from Edward I to Elizabeth had told their subjects, as did the Earl of Northampton in 1610, that the king 'had of necessity to depart with more of his own [by sales of land] than that which the subject hath bestowed on him'.[29]

Thus, as debate centred on the king's prodigality with his own, so the language and precedents of the late Middle Ages were revived. Thomas Wentworth and Samuel Lewknor asked that the king should resume his pensions and reduce his charges, and a bill of resumption actually appeared in committee in the early stages of the 1610 Parliament.[30] Wentworth was the most strident of these radical medievalists, echoing the articles of deposition of Richard II in demanding that the king 'diminish his charge and live of his owne without exacting of his poore subjects, especially at this tyme when wee have no warre', and citing precedents from 1386 and 1402 for a conciliar restraint of royal grants and an inquiry into royal revenues and ex-penses.[31]

In the Council chamber identical remedies were proposed. Following the failure of the 1614 Parliament, the Council

---

[28] *Proceedings in Parliament, 1610*, i. 5–6; ii. 23–5; *Parliamentary Debates, 1610*, 13, 134; Notestein, *House of Commons, 1604–10*, 274. In 1621 James was still promising that 'he would no longer make every day Christmas' (Prestwich, *Cranfield*, 290).

[29] *Proceedings in Parliament, 1610*, i. 269. For Edward I, see *Foedera*, Record Comm., i (1816), 872–3; for Elizabeth, see Neale, op. cit. 411, 427.

[30] *Parliamentary Debates, 1610*, 10–11, 135; *Proceedings in Parliament, 1610*, i. 23; ii. 71.

[31] *Parliamentary Debates, 1610*, 11–12.

debated 'how the king could repair his estate out of his own means'. Sir Edward Coke argued for a stay of pensions until the king was out of debt, and this, with the reduction of expenses to the level of income, emerged as the first of the Council's recommendations.[32] Both had been tried under the Lancastrians and raised the old problem whether the king could be constrained if he failed to restrain himself. The Council sought a declaration from James that 'in excess of his gifts as of his ordinary expenses he is resolved to be a good husbandman in both hereafter' and 'to stay his hand from all manner of gifts, till his own estate be redressed'. But James had made such promises before without effect and was largely to frustrate attempts at retrenchment by the Treasury Commission in 1618.[33] Short of formal constraints with all their political consequences, such as had been imposed on Henry III, Edward II, Richard II, and Henry IV, the strictest means of control was through the surveillance of royal warrants by the Lord Chancellor or Lord Treasurer. Yet Salisbury's entail of crown lands had failed, and when Cranfield ultimately secured such authority in 1622 his attempt to exercise it only brought him the same fate as had befallen Simon the Norman in 1240, Sir Richard Scrope in 1382, and Bishop Lumley in 1449.[34] James did not like comparisons with Henry III and Henry VI whom he described as 'a sillie weake King', but to his councillors and critics the faults of his kingship, like the remedies they prescribed, came to seem wearisomely similar.[35]

To justify the king's needs from his accounts was, as Bacon saw, to invite dangerous criticism of royal government; but on

---

[32] *Letters and Life of Bacon*, iv. 372; v. 199, 206.

[33] Ibid. v. 196; *Proceedings in Parliament, 1610*, i. 23; Prestwich, *Cranfield*, ch. v.

[34] Prestwich, *Cranfield*, 32–3, 158–61, 272, 341, 360–4; Tawney, *Business and Politics*, 205. Cranfield's suspension of annuities for one year had a direct precedent in 1404. For Simon the Norman, see F. M. Powicke, *King Henry III and the Lord Edward* (Oxford, 1947), 772–83; for Scrope, see T. F. Tout, *Chapters in Medieval Administrative History*, iii (Manchester, 1928), 401; on Lumley I have a forthcoming article.

[35] See, for instance, the schedule of medieval precedents for repairing the king's estate prepared by Cotton for the Earl of Northampton, in *Cottoni Posthuma* ed. James Howell (1651), 163 ff. For James's 'I scorne to be likened to the times of some Kings. Henry 6 was a sillie weake King...' see R. Zaller, *The Parliament of 1621* (Berkeley, 1971), 69. Similarly Sir Julius Caesar repudiated Wentworth's analogies with the reigns of Richard II and Henry IV as 'not fitt for theise tymes' since the first was 'a dissolute and profuse prince who had no respect of his estate and therefore was deprived of his crowne and kingdome; and the other was an usurper' (*Parliamentary Debates, 1610*, 12).

what other basis could subjects be obliged to contribute? To James himself it might appear axiomatic that the realm should maintain the dignity of the crown, and Northampton openly challenged the prevailing dualism which required the king to bear all ordinary charges and his subjects the extraordinary.[36] But neither was prepared for the logical consequence, namely that if the crown was to be supported by its subjects it would advance either towards absolutism or to limited monarchy. Justification for the former might indeed be forthcoming from the doctors of the church. Dr. Cowell believed that the king's needs gave him a right to subsidies without consent, and among the episcopate Harsnett of Chichester held that all goods and money belonged to Caesar, while Lancelot Andrewes urged that subjects be instructed that relief to their sovereign in necessity was *iure divino*, no less than was their allegiance and service.[37] No one as yet argued for the other extreme, of a monarchy reduced to the status of a paid official of the state. Ministers were divided rather between those who favoured Salisbury's approach or Bacon's.

Both were attempts to avoid the problem of obligation, Salisbury's by a free bargain, Bacon's by a free gift. Bacon condemned Salisbury's bargaining of the crown's prerogatives for a recurrent grant as unworthy and dangerous. Rather, he urged an appeal to subjects' gratitude and goodwill. The king should be 'rather willing to rest upon their affections than to conclude them by necessities'.[38] This was mere wishful thinking. For although it was a traditional aphorism that a king's strength and wealth rested upon the affections of his people, and grants of subsidies had been adorned with such sentiments from the fourteenth century, rarely if ever had they rested on goodwill alone.[39]

[36] See James's speech in 1614 (*H.M.C. Hastings MSS.* iv. 240) and Northampton's speech in 1610 (*Proceedings in Parliament, 1610*, i. 267). Ministers also invoked the common belief that an impoverished crown was a threat to the safety of the realm: see *Letters and Life of Bacon*, iv. 73 and Caesar's speech in *C.J.* i. 461–3.

[37] *Proceedings in Parliament, 1610*, ii. 52; *Letters and Life of Bacon*, v. 202; F. D. Wormuth, *The Royal Prerogative, 1603–49* (Ithaca, N.Y., 1939), 56.

[38] *Letters and Life of Bacon*, v. 26.

[39] As the Commons told Henry IV in 1401, 'The greatest treasure and wealth in the world is for a king to have the heart of his people; for if he has their heart he will truly have their wealth when he needs it' (*Rot. Parl.* iii. 456). Compare Winwood's speech in 1614: 'for wherein doth consist the might and majesty of a kingdom and

To bargain for supply had equally long and respectable precedents. The redress of grievances arising from abuses by royal officials and illicit extensions of the prerogative was often eased by the grant of taxation. But the connection between grievance and supply, fashioned during the Hundred Years War, was subtle and pragmatic, and did not represent a free interplay of interests. For although the king was morally bound to redress injustice, any waiving of his prerogative was a matter of pure grace; by contrast his subjects had a strict political obligation to grant taxation when circumstances required. Thus in war, at least, the king bargained from a position of strength, though royal concessions might indeed increase the grant or deflect criticism. It was quite otherwise in peacetime when the Commons were under no obligation to grant a tax and could set their demands so high that the king might find it impolitic to bargain.[40] Bacon appreciated this; hence his recommendation to James to offer graces and concessions first and thus win a grant of supply by gratitude, not as a bargain but as an 'interchange of affections'.[41] Alternatively the king could bargain on the basis of threats. Subjects might be warned that if they did not succour him with a modest grant now, the king would have to sell his lands and thus become a greater burden to them in the future, or even that the king might take all lawful courses for making the best of his own.[42] Nobody doubted that the prerogatives of the crown could be exploited to yield new revenue, but ministers recognized that the political repercussions of so doing would frustrate the search for a parliamentary grant. Salisbury's exploitation of wardship and his introduction of new impositions foreshadowed a revival of prerogative taxation. It was a dangerous path, and his Great Contract was an attempt to avoid further steps along it by reaffirming the traditional dualism of the medieval system on a more realistic and acceptable basis.[43] Salisbury proposed that

wherein his safety and security ... but in the dutiful affections of his subjects?' (*H.M.C. Downshire MSS.* 367).

   [40] For a discussion of the medieval practice, see Harriss, *King, Parliament, and Public Finance*, chs. xv–xvii.

   [41] *Letters and Life of Bacon*, iv. 366, 370; v. 28, 37–8. James followed this advice in 1614 (*H.M.C. Hastings MSS.* iv. 238–41; T. L. Moir, *The Addled Parliament of 1614*, Oxford, 1958, 89) and won over some members, e.g. Brooke (*C.J.* i. 463).

   [42] *Letters and Life of Bacon*, v. 29, 184.

   [43] Even those like Caesar who argued that the king should live of his own by

parliament would purchase the abolition of these prerogatives by a recurrent annual grant; but the king would not be dependent on parliament for this, he would merely exchange a right over one type of revenue for a right over another. When, in 1660, his scheme was revived, the intention and effect was to reconstitute the endowment of the crown as a guarantee of both traditional mixed monarchy and popular liberties.[44]

It was easier to reaffirm faith in traditional monarchy after the Interregnum than to reform it in 1610. Both king and parliament had their reservations. On the king's part the inelasticity of the new grant, the uncertainty as to how it could be levied as an annual tax, and the dislike of surrendering the prerogatives of the crown ultimately induced James to withdraw his support.[45] Within parliament members were also unclear how the levy could be raised and feared it would be unpopular, but more fundamentally they doubted whether the king could be restrained from wastefully alienating this new endowment as he had the old.[46] Here was the crux of the problem, for it raised the question whether the new financial arrangements would fundamentally alter the relationship between the crown and its subjects. Medieval writers in stressing the inalienability of the fisc had likened it to the soul of the state, or seen it as its dowry, emphasizing that the king was a trustee of it for the realm. Men still thought in these terms: Bacon could speak of 'investing the crown with a more ample,

---

exploiting his resources were insistent that 'care must be had that nothing be offered either contrary to the lawes now in force or justly distastefull to the people' (Brit. Lib. MS. Lansdowne 165, fo. 138). He acknowledged the argument that the Contract would 'prevent the stretching of the King's prerogatives which would prove unsafe bothe for himself and his State' (*Parliamentary Debates, 1610*, 173). James in 1614 disclaimed any intention to 'stretche his prerogative like other of my predecessors . . . if a prince would stretch his prerogative it would cause his people to bleed' (*H.M.C. Hastings MSS*. iv. 232). For the fears aroused by prerogative in 1610, see R. W. K. Hinton, 'Government and Liberty under James I', *C.H.J.* xi (1953), 55–63.

[44] C. D. Chandaman, *The English Public Revenue, 1660–1688* (Oxford, 1975), esp. 77–9, 265, 275–80; Tawney, *Business and Politics*, 140; G. E. Aylmer, 'The last years of purveyance', *Ec. H.R.* x(1967), 91–3. That the Contract was designed to eliminate peacetime taxation is evident from Sir Julius Caesar's words: 'this Contract passed, the King maie undoubtlie resolve to receive noe nore subsidies or fifteenths from his subjects in tyme of peace' (*Parliamentary Debates, 1610*, 178).

[45] *Letters and Life of Bacon*, iv. 170, 223–4.

[46] See the remarks by Sir Roger Owen in *Parliamentary Debates, 1610*, 127. Likewise R. Winwood, *Memorials*, ed. E. Sawyer (3 vols., 1725), iii. 194: 'with what cords shal we bind Sampson's hands?'.

more certain and more loving dowry than this of tenures', and Wentworth described the fisc as 'a piece of Holy Land assigned to the Prince so that he should not tax his people'.[47] But whereas these concepts from Roman law stressed that the fisc had a public function for which the king was merely the trustee, in feudal terms the fisc was the king's demesne; he was lord of his own to do with it what he willed. Even though he should not alienate it (for it sustained his dignity and rule), he could not be prevented from so doing. Yet if he was now to receive a new endowment by annual levy from his subjects, some assurance of its inalienability and proper use, and hence some restraint on the king's prerogative, was inescapable.

This dilemma the Middle Ages had likewise faced and never satisfactorily resolved. Fortescue, who similarly sought to remedy the crown's poverty by a new endowment, had proposed that this new livelihood be 'amortysed' to the crown, never to be alienated without the assent of parliament.[48] This was a radical solution, for to restrain the king's liberality not by an advisory Council but by a coercive parliament was to move finally from quasi-feudal mixed monarchy to limited constitutional monarchy. Fortescue's tract was widely studied at the time, though whether any applied the logic of his argument to these current debates is impossible to know.[49] Certainly James and others sensed the danger, and his instinctive retreat from any surrender of the prerogative accorded with the dominant theme in Tudor kingship. Salisbury realized that prerogative taxation had become less acceptable than in the previous century, but his political wisdom was the victim of his own expedients. For opposition to the impositions of 1608 prejudiced consideration of the Great Contract and negated the king's pleas for supply in the parliaments of 1610 and 1614. Moreover it ruled out the only escape from the impasse into

---

[47] E. H. Kantorowicz, *The King's Two Bodies* (Princeton, 1957), 173–92 for the quasi sacred character of the fisc; 217–18 for the fisc as dowry of the *respublica*; *Letters and Life of Bacon*, iv. 170; S. R. Gardiner, *History of England, 1603–1642* (10 vols., 1883–4), ii. 241.

[48] *The Governance of England*, 154.

[49] That Fortescue realized very well the import of his proposal is shown by his attempt to gloss it as conveying to the king 'a greater prerogative'. The Governance itself had not been printed in the early seventeenth century, but numerous manuscripts were in circulation and Sir Julius Caesar cites it three times in his 'debate' on the Contract (*Parliamentary Debates, 1610*, 167–76).

which prerogative finance had led the monarchy, namely by an extension and rehabilitation of mercantile taxation through parliamentary assent. It is instructive to recall that in the later fourteenth century the recurrent grant by parliament of the wool subsidies had met the need for a *de facto* permanent tax to meet the growing expenses of government, thereby avoiding either a surrender of the prerogative or resort to the wilder excesses of fiscal feudalism. Such a solution was present to some minds in the early seventeenth century, but it was blocked irretrievably by the judges' verdict in Bates's Case and only became politically feasible with the Restoration.[50] Instead, the failure of the 1614 Parliament led to Cranfield's sustained but never more than partially successful application of the medieval devices of restraint and retrenchment. By the time this had ended in predictable failure, war reopened the prospect of parliamentary supply on the traditional basis, and the decision in favour of an unequivocal and thorough exploitation of fiscal feudalism was postponed for a decade.

The debates of the first half of James's reign had centred on whether the king could use the plea of necessity to secure taxation for his ordinary expenses; in those of the decade 1619–29 necessity was invoked, as was more customary, to demand taxation for war, although finally it served to justify prerogative taxation without assent.

The very frequency of parliaments in this decade marks its analogy to the period of the Hundred Years War and the last twenty years of Elizabeth, and indicates the renewed hope of a fruitful co-operation of king and parliament in war. In their passionate commitment to the defence of Protestantism and their expectation that a war against Spanish shipping would prove profitable, members of the Commons were ready to give generously and submerge their grievances, and the crown had the chance to unite factions, bury past quarrels, and recover its leadership of parliament.[51] It was a classic pattern: Edward

---

[50] A tax on merchandize was canvassed in 1610 (*Parliamentary Debates, 1610*, 129), and C. Russell has drawn attention to the interesting scheme of Bedford, Pym, and St. John in 1640 for a parliamentary farm of the customs ('Parliament and the King's Finances', 111–15).

[51] Zaller, *The Parliament of 1621*, 136–7; Ruigh, *The Parliament of 1624*, 193–5. Caesar had noted in 1610 that people were 'willinger to part with muche in time of warr then

III had done so after 1343; Henry V after the disputes which had worn down his father; even Elizabeth had been able to disarm opposition by appeals for unity in the face of common danger. In the event war compounded the crisis of Stuart parliaments and encouraged the reversion to extra-parliamentary modes of government in the next decade.

One reason for this was the continued criticism of prodigality and corruption in court and government. At the height of his influence Cranfield could meet the Parliament of 1621 with evidence of a successful attack on administrative costs, but after his fall royal spending, royal debts, and royal bounty remained stumbling-blocks to liberal grants of aid and the confidence that these would be used for war expenses.[52] In 1621 and 1624 James still claimed that parliament was obliged to meet his debts and showed greater anxiety to secure money for these than for war.[53] The statement of royal debts in Charles's first parliament initiated the demand for an investigation of the king's finances and the attack on those 'who had brought him to this state', which was to continue for the next three years. In that parliament Coke, now alienated from the court, dealt with the king's plea of necessity by citing Bracton's threefold distinction between affected necessity, invincible necessity, and improvident necessity. He exculpated the king from an affected or pretended necessity but found the king's plea not invincible (and hence obligatory), but arising from improvidence.[54] In consequence subjects were at liberty to repudiate it (as they had under Henry III) or to inquire into its causes. In 1625 the burden of criticism was directed at the deficit on the ordinary account caused by pensions, grants of land, and household extravagance. Coke was clear that subjects had no obligation to meet this deficit: 'ordinary charges the Kinge should beare alone; but *ubi commune periculum, commune auxilium*'.[55] Sir Thomas Wentworth and Sir Robert Phelips urged measures to regulate the revenues of the crown 'that they might hereafter bear some

with litle in tyme of peace' (*Parliamentary Debates, 1610*, 173), a remark which echoes the observations of Philippe de Commynes (Harriss, art. cit. 52; *Memoirs*, trans. M. Jones, Penguin, 1972, 225).

[52] Prestwich, *Cranfield*, 286.
[53] Zaller, op. cit. 32; Ruigh, op. cit. 211–14.
[54] *Commons Debates, 1625*, 84–5.
[55] Ibid. 32; and cf. Phelips, ibid. 12.

part of the public charge', and Coke and Seymour listed a series of these (including a resumption) for which there were medieval precedents.[56] Eliot cited the commission of 1386 to investigate the king's estate 'for the advantage it would render to the Kinge that would remove all need to press supplies from us'.[57] This distrust of the integrity and competence of the court was extended in 1626 and 1628 to its management of the war, and 'improvident necessity' was held to be a valid plea for denying the crown the means of war until by the dismissal of Buckingham, and reform, it could urge the case of 'invincible necessity' with conviction.

Secondly neither James nor Charles prosecuted war with sufficient determination to override these criticisms by the invincible plea of common peril. James, like Elizabeth, shrank with good reason from the costs and risks of war, preferring diplomatic pressures and inducements to a Protestant crusade. In so far as he exerted military pressure, James chose to subsidize the land operations of continental allies and clients rather than initiate action by his own fleet. This was a policy which Englishmen traditionally distrusted and for which they had never willingly paid. Thus while James detailed his debts, the costs of embassies and the subventions to allies, even under extreme pressure in 1624 he refused to commit himself to a declaration of war; yet until he did so he could not expect subsidies at a wartime rate.[58] Moreover, by seeking to use the war frenzy in parliament to induce Spain to withdraw from the Palatinate, James only lost credibility with parliament when Spain called his bluff. Equally, his attempts to persuade Spain to comply by alliance and even marriage aroused the profoundest mistrust and hostility in England and called in question his commitment to the defence of Protestantism.[59] In short, the confusion and distrust about James's intentions, coupled with the king's own vacillations and ineptitude, and the traditional reluctance of parliament to make large grants for

[56] Ibid. 31–2, 86–7, 111. Coke's proposal that royal servants should be rewarded with offices and honours and not the inheritance of the crown recalls Fortescue (*Governance*, 144).

[57] Sir John Eliot, *Negotium Posterorum*, ed. A. B. Grosart (1881), 162–3.

[58] Ruigh, op. cit. 204–8. As Sandys pointed out, war was still a future contingency; there was no *casus belli*.

[59] Zaller, op. cit. 18, 30; Prestwich, *Cranfield*, 332–4.

a prospective rather than actual war, all combined to blunt the obligation upon subjects to contribute to the defence of the realm in time of need. Far from proclaiming the necessity in terms which would compel assent (as political practice required), James discountenanced a sense of national danger and emotive involvement and reduced the defence of the Palatinate to a diplomatic and dynastic issue from which subjects could disengage.[60]

Faced with this abdication, the Commons themselves made half-hearted attempts to define the purposes of taxation: in 1621 Phelips suggested an approach to the Lords, and in 1624 Savile put a motion that they 'handle first the thing to be done and the necessity of it, the charge it will ask, and the means to raise that charge'—all steps which should properly have been taken by the crown.[61] James's own reluctance to receive taxes for war led him to prefer a mere two subsidies in 1621 'for love' (rather than for the defence of the Palatinate) and in 1624 to suggest three (rather than six) subsidies which would be tied to specific expenditure on the defence of England and the Low Countries under Treasurers of War accountable to parliament.[62] Although this proposal reflected the distrust of each others' intentions which existed between king and parliament, it cannot rightly be described as 'an unprecedented infringement on the executive powers of the crown'.[63] The medieval precedents, which Coke noted, suggest that it had always been more effective as a government device to disarm criticism on expenditure than as a restriction on the crown's spending of the subsidy, and so it proved now.[64]

With the new reign, the initial goodwill of the Commons towards Charles and Buckingham as advocates of war with

---

[60] Cf. Zaller's comment, op. cit. 148–9. Pym's view that wars in which the subject was not involved were merely the king's litigation takes us back to the barons' detachment from Henry III's dynastic-feudal commitments (Harriss, *King, Parliament, and Public Finance*, 34–9).

[61] Zaller, op. cit. 48; Ruigh, op. cit. 220.

[62] Zaller, op. cit. 48; Ruigh, op. cit. 223–31; Gardiner, *History of England*. v. 197–207.

[63] Prestwich, *Cranfield*, 432; for a similar comment on it as an advance towards parliamentary sovereignty, see Ruigh, op. cit. 253 n. 182, 390. By contrast see C. Russell, 'Parliamentary History in Perspective, 1604–1629', *History*, 61 (1976), 7–8.

[64] James was able to secure large payments for Mansfeldt's troops from the Treasurers (Gardiner, op. cit. v. 265, 271). The disputes which this engendered may be compared with those of 1378; each produced similar official replies from Sir John Coke (*Commons Debates, 1625*, 56–9) and Sir Richard Scrope (*Rot. Parl.* iii. 36), which glossed foreign expenditure as defensive.

Spain faded into distrust as the same secretiveness over royal policy, the increasing subsidies to Denmark and Mansfeldt, and the unpopularity of the French alliance took their toll. Although Charles claimed that parliament was obliged to support a war with Spain undertaken 'by your entreaties, your engagements', it was in fact for the vast cost of unauthorized subventions to continental allies that money was needed. With justice his critics like Phelips and Sir Nathaniel Rich could protest that the tax was asked for a contingent war: 'the promises and declaracions of the last Parliament were in respect of a warr; wee know yet of noe warr nor of any enemy'; 'there is a necessitie that his Majestie should declare the enemy'.[65] In consequence the subsidy granted in 1625 was merely the traditional accession tax: two subsidies, not for war but 'as the first fruites of the springinge love of his subjectes'.[66]

Although the Commons' reluctance to grant supply for a contingent war encouraged them (as in 1376) to criticize the court and its foreign policy, over which confusion and disagreement existed in both Houses, they were not consciously seeking to determine that policy themselves.[67] They were exercising their traditional right to discuss and approve a policy for which they supplied the money: as Coke said, 'if the king demand aid he must be advised'. The Commons had always had a duty to their constituents to ensure that subsidies were spent for the common good, their representative character empowering them to endorse the king's plea of necessity as well as to grant the tax. Moreover as judges of the necessity in terms of the common good they claimed also to judge the enemies of the common good, the authors of an improvident necessity.

This was the burden of Phelips's attack on Buckingham in 1625 for which he cited precedents from the reigns of Henry III, Richard II, and Henry VI.[68] Eliot too in 1626, citing the impeachment of Michael de la Pole in 1386, invited the House to 'observe the extraordinary likeness of some particulars to the present case'.[69] But these precedents gave no clear legal justifi-

---

[65] *Commons Debates, 1625*, 31, 139. For the precedents of Edward III's reign there cited, see Harriss, op. cit. 320–7.

[66] *Commons Debates, 1625*, 32; Gardiner, op. cit. v. 368.

[67] Cf. Ruigh, op. cit. 220–1, 388–9, and Gardiner, op. cit. v. 425.

[68] *Commons Debates, 1625*, 109.

[69] *Negotium Posterorum*, 161; Gardiner, op. cit. vi. 81.

cation and hardly any consistent procedure for an attack on a
trusted minister of the crown. As Dr. Tite has stressed, it was
'a complex inheritance'. How could it be otherwise? For impeachment spelt out the irresoluble conflict between the claims
of the common good and those of the royal prerogative—
irresoluble, that is, within the contest of mixed monarchy. In
such a situation we may well believe that 'when men looked
over their shoulders or studied the records, they were not doing
so merely to search out convenient excuses for their present
actions', but to seek practical guidance from the past.[70]
Parliament's attempt to procure Buckingham's impeachment
in 1626 by agreeing on four subsidies but deferring the bill
until grievances were redressed led to its dissolution before
either subsidy or impeachment could proceed. From this point
the king began to seek ways of raising taxes without parliamentary assent. Those ways were all based upon the doctrine
of necessity, but this was now invoked in a different context and
with different consequences from when taxation was sought in
parliament.

Medieval theory accorded the king an overriding power to
levy taxation for an evident necessity of state if the normal
means had failed or could not be used.[71] Further, a refusal by
parliament to endorse a legitimate plea of necessity, for the
common safety, could be construed as dissolving *dominium
politicum et regale*, leaving regal power as the residual legitimate
force for maintaining the state. To avoid this, medieval
parliaments rarely or never refused taxation outright, but made
offers and promises conditional on reform. Those of the early
Stuarts did likewise, though Charles I saw such conditions as
factious and unacceptable, and not until 1628 was he prepared
to follow the respectable precedents of the Plantagenets in
disarming opposition by accepting a charter of liberties or
reforms which he could subsequently disavow.[72] In 1625–6 he
was provocatively sticking to the letter of the theory. At the
very end of the 1625 session Buckingham had sought further

---

[70] C. G. C. Tite, *Impeachment and Parliamentary Judicature in Early Stuart England*
(1974), 52–3.

[71] For the medieval doctrine of reason of state, see G. Post, *Studies in Medieval
Legal Thought*, ch. v. Wormuth, *Royal Prerogative*, 55 n. 15 cites Crawley's judgement
in Hampden's case; see also p. 106.

[72] As in 1297, 1301, 1311, 1341, 1386.

subsidies for the fleet 'merely to be denied', and Sir John Coke was hinting that the expenses of war must be met if not by parliament, then by 'some new waye'.[73] In 1626 the Convocation of Canterbury endorsed the king's paraphrase of Thomist doctrine: that the refusal to support the king in a war undertaken on the persuasion and promises of parliament was a sin, since aid and supply for the defence of the kingdom and like affairs of state were due to the king from his people by the laws of both God and man.[74] As for practical measures, one contemplated in 1626 and advocated by Bacon in 1614 had already been tested in 1337.[75] This was to lay the case of necessity before assemblies of freeholders in each shire to obtain a grant (or at least a promise) from them. If this had the spurious attraction of appealing beyond 'extremists' in parliament to the loyal men of the shires, it was bound to be seen, and resisted, as an attack on the authority of parliament, and was rightly abandoned. Instead the gentry were approached through the J.P.s with a request for a gift to the subsidy, on the model of the Amicable Grant. The failure of this, precisely on the ground of parliament's omnicompetence in taxation, led directly to the forced loan. Here again, the basis of the king's approach was rooted in medieval doctrine, for the plea of necessity obliged subjects to lend as well as to grant money. But obligation supposed free consent and the grounds for excusal were numerous and well practised.[76] In resorting to imprisonment of those who refused, Charles overstepped medieval precedents, though he claimed to do so by reason of the necessity which parliament's illicit refusal of taxes imposed on the crown.

At this point a confrontation clearly loomed. Charles called the Parliament of 1628 to meet the common danger; if it failed in this duty 'he must in discharge of his conscience use other means which God had put in his hands'.[77] To parliament,

[73] *Commons Debates, 1625*, 58; Gardiner, op. cit. vi. 368–71.

[74] Wilkins, *Concilia*, iv. 472, cited by Gardiner, op. cit. vi. 143; for Laud's identical view, see ibid. 263 n. 1.

[75] Gardiner, op. cit. vi. 125; *Letters and Life of Bacon*, v. 81; Harriss, op. cit. 96, 235.

[76] For the conditions under which medieval and Tudor loans were 'practised', see G. L. Harriss, 'Aids, Loans and Benevolences', *H.J.* vi (1963), 1–19, and for the continuance of these into the seventeenth century, Mainwaring's sermon cited by Wormuth, *Royal Prerogative*, 97–8.

[77] Gardiner, op. cit. vi. 231. And see his minutes to the Privy Council in February

on the other hand, it appeared that Charles was using his prerogative 'not for the safety but for the destruction of the community'.[78] Nevertheless the tradition of co-operation for the common good was strong. Wentworth, Coke, and Rudyerd were all for granting a large subsidy for defence to be associated with the redress of grievances and guarantees of the liberties of subjects. Charles at length found that he could accept the Petition of Right. The subsidies were duly granted, but the House was adamant that taxation should give no encouragement to a fresh and disastrous expedition, and it was the renewed attack on Buckingham that brought the session to a precipitate close. In the event it was only Tonnage and Poundage that Charles then levied by virtue of his prerogative, recognizing parliament's right to grant it but levying it 'for the necessity by which I was to take it till you had granted it to me'.[79] It is interesting to reflect that he could have found precedents for so doing from the reigns of Richard II, Henry IV, and Edward IV.[80]

It would be difficult to claim that any of the disputes over supply during these twenty years either raised new constitutional principles or resulted in more politically damaging conflicts than those of earlier centuries. Already in 1297 the king's plea of necessity had been challenged on the grounds of the common good,[81] while on at least four occasions (1340–1, 1386, 1406, 1450) parliamentary opposition to the crown had produced a crisis in which the crown had been forced to yield. Such conflicts reflected the tensions of mixed monarchy and may be seen as redressing a temporary imbalance. Even so I do not think that we should dismiss those of the early Stuarts as contributing nothing to the onset of civil war. For even if direct

---

1628 to consider ways of raising money by impositions or otherwise 'in a case of inevitable necessity wherein form and substance must be dispensed with rather than the substance be lost or hazarded' (ibid. 228).

[78] The fifth of the Lords' propositions in 1628 (cit. Gardiner, op. cit. vi. 260).

[79] Gardiner, op. cit. vii. 33.

[80] Under Richard II token suspensions of the wool subsidy occurred for periods of a few months in 1381–2, 1386, and 1397–8; Tonnage and Poundage was not granted to Henry IV until 1401 and this and the wool subsidies were not granted to Edward IV until 1465; yet on nearly all these occasions they continued to be levied.

[81] H. Rothwell, 'The Confirmation of the Charters, 1297', *E.H.R.* lx (1945), 34; Harriss, *King, Parliament, and Public Finance*, 58–70.

taxation was of decreasing value in the crown's budget,[82] the granting of subsidies retained considerable political significance as the principal act in which ruler and ruled co-operated for the common good. It was not an opportunity to bend the crown to the will of parliament. For just as the king had no right to levy taxation without parliamentary authorization, so parliament had no right to refuse taxation when evident and urgent necessity required it. King and parliament were jointly the judges of that necessity, consulting not their particular interests but the common good of the state. Taxation symbolized co-operation, not conflict; it was the cynosure of mixed monarchy. For the Commons to excuse themselves from granting taxation therefore implied at the very least their lack of confidence in the integrity and competence of royal government (and thus the need for reform so that the tax when granted could be effectively spent) and at worst a repudiation of their obligations to the crown and kingdom. While outright refusal of taxation was rare, the fact that taxation was demanded for the common good made it the natural vehicle for criticism. The occasion and size of the grant and the conditions to be attached to it were all legitimate matters of debate and served as bargaining counters for the redress of political grievances and the advancement of political interests. Debates provided the opportunity to demonstrate the strength of feelings but were intended to be the prelude to agreement and common action.

Yet precisely because parliament was seen as an instrument of co-operation in government and not of confrontation, the failure to reach agreement was cumulatively damaging to its purpose and repute, and not least so when the crown broke off negotiations before agreement on taxation had been reached. A prematurely dissolved parliament brought alarm and heart-searching to the Commons no less than reproaches from the king. The dissolution of parliament in March 1629 thus marked the end—for the moment at least—of a conviction that had sustained king, ministers, and Commons for the past twenty years, that a parliament was the proper instrument to meet the common needs of the realm and would produce union between crown and people.[83] Within that short span nearly every medi-

[82] C. Russell, 'Parliamentary History in Perspective', 12–13.
[83] In 1612 Bacon had seen the two purposes of a parliament as 'the one for the

eval conflict had been re-enacted, nearly every medieval remedy tried. So traumatic an experience—fed and partly guided by the appeal to precedent—could not fail to produce the sense that the system of mixed monarchy was itself in crisis. The resort to prerogative government and the final attempt to restore the traditional system by the first civil war followed logically from the cumulative frustrations of 1610–29.

If we view the disputes of these two decades against the background of similar arguments in the late Middle Ages, it is apparent that whereas the latter had contributed to the establishment of the system of mixed monarchy and had helped to produce a political consensus under the stimulus of war,[84] those of the seventeenth century were expressions of frustration (by both king and subjects) against the limitations and failure of a well-defined system. Medieval conflicts were often creative and led to adjustments in the system; those of the seventeenth century more frequently produced a barren confrontation and the rebound to an ideological stance. Reasons for this may doubtless be found in the atrophy of the administrative system, the shifts in wealth and political power in society at large, and the unnerving background of inflation, but it was also the fruit of a longer historical pattern.

The establishment of mixed monarchy in the era of the Hundred Years War had been followed by an almost equally long period—from 1460 to 1580—of peace and consolidation during which government became more regal than mixed in character. It is misleading to talk of this as despotic. The mode of royal government was largely determined by the business in hand. War, which called for the active involvement of the realm, demanded an active role from parliament, and so too did the great changes in the religion of the state at the Reformation, and any attempts to legislate on social and economic ills. All these might enhance the role of parliament. Nevertheless the general trend of this period was to strengthen regal authority and government. Only in the last quarter of the century did

supplying of your estate; the other for the better knitting of the hearts of your subjects unto your Majesty; for both which, Parliaments have been and are the antient and honourable remedy' (*Letters and Life of Bacon*, iv. 280). See likewise James I's proclamation dissolving the Parliament of 1610, *Stuart Royal Proclamations*, ed. J. F. Larkin and P. L. Hughes (Oxford, 1973), i, n. 14, p. 258.

[84] Harriss, 'War and the emergence of the English parliament'.

open war again demand a more continuous involvement of parliament in royal policy. As practised in England 'regal' and 'mixed' government were not stark opposites, but differences of emphasis within the same system, to meet different situations. Precedents suggested that the more regal mode was suited to government in time of peace, the more mixed and parliamentary mode to time of war.

The paucity of parliaments in the years 1610–20 and their increased frequency in 1620–30 broadly reflect this rule. Yet it was becoming far less easy for the Stuarts to adapt their mode of government to the changing needs of policy than it had been for their predecessors. In Europe, the crisis of Estates and the burgeoning debate on rival doctrines of government were polarizing the choice between monarchy and parliament. In England, both traditions had been reinvigorated. Tudor government had made prerogative a far more potent instrument, in legal and administrative terms, than it had ever been for the Plantagenets or Lancastrians. This bred among subjects a corresponding unease and truculence over their rights and a consciousness of parliament as the historic defender of them. As heirs to a mature system of three centuries' growth, both sides could appeal to historical precedents with entire sincerity but increasing obduracy. Thus historical and idealogical developments led *dominium regale* and *dominium politicum* to oppose each other as rival modes of government instead of being correlative and exchangeable facets of a composite system. This was certainly assisted by the intrusion of religion into policies and factions, and was to be consummated by outside intervention.[85]

The inadequacy of the traditional revenues for the Stuart style of government precipitated this confrontation of prerogative and parliament. James, as we have seen, tried both to secure additional parliamentary taxation through an extension of the doctrine of necessity to embrace all the needs of the king and kingdom,[86] and at the same time to develop further the Tudor

[85] As suggested by H. G. Koenigsberger, 'Dominium Regale or Dominium Politicum et Regale', Inaugural Lecture, King's College, London (1975).

[86] Thus in 1621: 'You are the authors of sustenance also to him, to supply his Necessities. This is the proper use of parliaments: Here they are to offer what they think fit to supply his wants; and he is in lieu hereof to afford Mercy and Justice. All people owe a kind of tribute to their kings by way of thankfulness to him for his love to them' (cited by Ruigh, op. cit. 2).

exploitation of the crown's fiscal prerogatives. He thereby threatened the medieval dualism which guaranteed the limit of his subjects' fiscal obligations; hence they in turn revived the traditional demand that he fulfil his own obligations and spare them by living within the limits of his own. Salisbury's attempt to remodel the medieval system to embrace some form of permanent taxation for ordinary expenditure was a move in the right direction in that it looked to the co-operation of crown and parliament. It failed to win acceptance, because by abolishing the crown's prerogatives it could offer no guarantees (as did the medieval dualism) against limited monarchy on the one hand and absolutism on the other. The much older solution of how to extend the king's ordinary revenue while preserving the dimensions of the prerogative, namely by recurrent parliamentary grants of indirect taxation through which prerogative itself might be kept under control, might well have been revived in the early seventeenth century if it had not been prejudiced by the decision to extend impositions. In this sense the Tudor revival of fiscal feudalism proved indeed to be the *damnosa hereditas* of the Stuarts. However profitable, it was an antiquated and abrasive system of taxation, inconsistent with the further development of mixed monarchy.

Nevertheless, to suggest that the system in its decline was separating into its component parts is not to say that there was as yet a conscious struggle for power between them. Late medieval kingship, let us repeat, served the common good of the state, which was secured in some aspects of government by the king acting regally and in others by him acting with parliament. The system precluded by definition a struggle between the crown and parliament for sovereign power, though they could and did struggle over the exercise of their respective powers and even over the extension (within strict limits) of these powers. Medieval crises were about how authority should be exercised rather than who should exercise it. Because the system collapsed in a struggle for supreme power, it does not follow that its history had been a perpetual struggle of this kind; if that had been so it is doubtful whether it could have survived for so long.[87] This, in essentials, seems to me still to be true of men's

[87] On this I differ from Koenigsberger and find myself in agreement with Russell (art. cit.).

attitudes up to 1629 and even a decade later. It is difficult to detect in the speeches either the consciousness of or the desire for a struggle over sovereignty, only the growing uneasy recognition that dispute was leading to this. And that, I believe, is why men looked back to the past. Their citation of precedents was at times defensive, triumphant, and nostalgic; but the basic impulse to search was an appeal for help in a predicament which seemed familiar in character but frighteningly novel in its implications. To call their attitude antiquarian is as misleading as it is to call the ideas of Peter de la Mare or Sir John Fortescue precocious. Each responded to the problems of his age, and these problems were essentially similar. We must recognize that the history of the period 1250–1650, and of the institutions of government within it, cannot be read as a linear progression from 'medieval' adolescence to 'modern' maturity, but as a single phase of political development—that of mixed monarchy—within which men were naturally conscious of 'continuing or recurrent constitutional and political realities and situations'.[88]

The appeal to history could thus validate and even prescribe men's actions and attitudes. Did it also narrow their vision and impede a clear analysis of the problems of their changing world? Perhaps so, but this is a more difficult and subjective judgement and not one which I feel competent to make. Both in the concepts and in the techniques of government the temper of the age was conservative and men foresaw change with fear and reluctance. Their preoccupation with history was characteristic of the general intellectual climate; but though it failed to avert the 'crisis of the constitution', may it not be said to have laid the basis for that cautious, controlled, and historically minded revolution which Burke was to celebrate in retrospect, at a time when the Middle Ages had finally ceased to be part of a 'recurrent political situation' and had become a romantic dream?[89]

---

[88] Roskell, 'Perspectives in English Parliamentary History', 322.

[89] Even so Burke could remark, apropos of the chivalric treatment of the French king after Poitiers, that 'four hundred years have gone over us; but I believe we are not materially changed since that period. Thanks to our sullen resistance to innovation, thanks to the cold sluggishness of our national character, we still bear the stamp of our forefathers' (*Reflections on the Revolution in France*).

IV. Court, Country, and Politics before 1629

Derek Hirst

A GENERATION which is experiencing its own loss of faith in central institutions has appropriately rediscovered localism in seventeenth-century England. Confidence that laws passed by sovereign law-makers are automatically enforced has given place to an awareness of factors akin to our own 'credibility gap' and 'community politics' in affecting willingness to see laws executed. While we lose ability to appreciate the religious preoccupations of the time, we gain in the understanding of such other areas as law-enforcement; or perhaps in the capacity to recognize the dilemma of those who were aware of the nation's economic problems but were not anxious to be in the forefront of those making the requisite sacrifices. Reinterpretations are necessary, but they do have their difficulties, and one of these is the question of balance. Historians anxious to revise orthodoxies make their cases strongly and sometimes in so doing overlook nuances or complexities. The reader is then left with what is effectively old thesis and new antithesis, whereas the intent of the critical historian had perhaps merely been to remodel.

This failure to assimilate and synthesize adequately has been evident in assessments of the relations of 'court' and 'country', and the allied, though separate, question of centre and locality, in early modern England. Some years ago Professor Trevor-Roper asserted the importance of the 'mere' country gentry who were angrily reacting against the increasing interference and cost of the court and thereby administered a corrective to the temptation to search exclusively at the political centre for the causes of the Civil War. Professor Everitt went further,

---

[1] This argument has benefited from profitable discussions with Conrad Russell stretching over a period of years: I am also grateful to him and to Kevin Sharpe for criticism of this essay in draft form.

repeatedly emphasizing the degree to which the rest of the country was distanced from, and almost oblivious of, London and the court: to his mind, 'national' politics and events may have barely rippled the placid waters of the localities where the bulk of England's population lived.[2] The effect of this salutary historiographical shift away from London has been marked, and one of the major recent interpretations of the causes of the war has based itself on, and taken its title from, the polarity of 'court' and 'country'.[3] Most other recent studies have attributed to the mutual distaste of these two supposed entities a large role in the breakdown of the early Stuart polity, with the 'court' taking little heed of the concerns of the country, and the 'country' dissociating itself, by refusing supply or collaboration, from an abhorrent 'court'.

This new departure has not lacked wrong turnings. One of these is that two rather separate issues have been confused. Everitt's introspective provincialism is not Trevor-Roper's parliament-centred movement for reform and retrenchment.[4] There are obvious connections between the two, most practically at parliamentary elections and in recesses, but the failure of historians to distinguish the tendency to use the term 'country' for each has bred some unnecessary confusion. The second, and more serious, error is, conversely, that certain other lines have been too sharply drawn. The contention that frictions and animosity existed between the court and men outside it who have been named both by contemporaries and by historians as 'the country' is unchallengeable. But it should be remembered that before the Civil War the central government had virtually nothing in the way of physical force with which to enforce its will. The manifest hostility directed towards the court, as personified by Buckingham, in the impeachment proceedings of 1626, or in the developments culminating in the Petition of Right in 1628, might in that

---

[2] H. R. Trevor-Roper, 'The Gentry 1540–1640', *Ec. H. R. Supplement*, no. 1, and 'The General Crisis of the Seventeenth Century', in *Crisis in Europe 1560–1660*, ed. T. Aston, (1965); A. M. Everitt, *The Local Community and the Great Rebellion* (Historical Association pamphlet, 1969), *Change in the Provinces: the Seventeenth Century* (Leicester University, Dept. of English Local History, Occasional Papers, ser. 2, no. 1, 1969), and 'The County Community', in *The English Revolution 1600–1660*, ed. E. W. Ives (1968).

[3] P. Zagorin, *The Court and the Country* (1969), 32: 'In the strife of the Court and the Country ... the English revolution had its origins.'

[4] I am most grateful to Dr. Clive Holmes for stressing this point to me.

context have entailed the paralysis of royal rule. Non-co-operation might have been expected from those involved in the parliamentary storm when they went home to the localities and faced the unwelcome task of resuming their other role as unpaid agents of that regime which they had just attacked so vehemently. But the court had a not wholly catastrophic record, even in the apparently black days of Buckingham's last three years. In parliament subsidies were often granted—not enough, certainly, but equally certainly without that redress of grievances which then and now was claimed as the *sine qua non* of such grants[5]—and in the country men were raised for service in unpopular causes abroad, and the militia mustered, armed, and drilled—not as much nor as effectively as the court wanted, but more than had been the case since the war years of the 1590s, and more than the country wanted.[6] If what was done, and by whom, is examined, instead of just what was said in the excitement of the parliamentary chamber, then the apparent polarities might not seem quite so marked, or so destructive.

This is not to say anything new, merely something that has sometimes been overlooked. Professor Everitt himself observed that in the seventeenth century loyalty to the nation-state was growing in train with that loyalty to the locality which he has so sympathetically depicted (although he subsequently asserted that the latter was the stronger in this period, which seems dubious). Professor Stone still more sensitively argues that 'the conflict between loyalty to the particularist locality and loyalty to the nation was fought out within the mind of each individual gentleman', and this suggestion is surely well founded. It is, as he observes, part of the natural order of things in all political societies where there is tension between pressures for centralization and decentralization. But elsewhere, when surveying the broad political scene rather than analysing the notion of 'country', he forgets the complexity he points to, and argues that 'by the reign of Charles I, the concept of harmony and co-operation within the Commonwealth had almost completely broken down, the two words Court and Country having

[5] C. Russell, 'Parliament and the King's Finances', in *Origins of the English Civil War*, ed. C. Russell (1973), 103; C. Russell, 'Parliamentary History in Perspective, 1604–1629', *History*, lxi (1976), 1–27: I am most grateful to Mr. Russell for allowing me to read a draft of this article.

[6] L. Boynton, *The Elizabethan Militia* (1967), 165–269.

come to mean political, psychological and moral opposites.' He can even speak, as Professor Zagorin tends to do, of 'the Country' as 'the beginning of a formal opposition', under whose banner a purposive ideological struggle was waged in the 1620s. But such polarized, ideological combat is not easy to reconcile with his other reference to an instinctive localism, or with the internalized conflict he points to. The works of Zagorin and Stone both bear witness to the problems contained within the notion of 'country'. Only by remembering that Everitt's use of the word is distinct from that of Trevor-Roper, and only by a development of the notion that internal contradictions were as much in evidence as political polarization can we understand why parliamentary attacks on the court at this period were so indecisive, why the crown did repeatedly receive subsidies, and why there was nothing remotely like a localist assertion of independence or even the determined obstructionism which might be inferred from Professor Everitt's likening of the seventeenth-century English counties to the states of either of the North American federations.[7]

If we consider the major parliamentary confrontations of the period, at least up to the Petition of Right, we may find it difficult to uphold the use of the labels 'court' and 'country' as worthwhile analytical tools. In most of them the polarities were not much in evidence. Thus, as important as antipathy to the court in the disruption of the 1614 Parliament appear to have been the divisions within the court, and particularly those between the pro- and anti-Spanish factions, the Howards and their enemies.[8] And while the role of the court in that instance warrants examination, conversely the 'country' grouping lacks solidarity. If there was one vocal member of the 1614 Commons who deserved the label it was Sir Roger Owen who, early in the session, outspokenly attacked the sitting of the Attorney-General in the House, alleging that the king's livery he wore would blind him to the ills of the country. Yet when the final confrontation of that unhappy parliament came, Owen was pointedly put down by his colleagues for going too far, and the Clerk of the House took the unusual step of putting a

---

[7] Everitt, *Local Community and Great Rebellion*, 5, 8; L. Stone, *Causes of the English Revolution* (New York, 1972), 108, 86, 92–3; cf. Zagorin, op. cit. 74–118.

[8] T. L. Moir, *The Addled Parliament* (New York, 1958), esp. 134–49.

memorandum in the Journal to the effect that he had been stopped in full flight—hardly a sign of collective determination.[9] The crisis was occasioned by a speech by Bishop Neile in the Lords virtually charging the Commons with sedition for daring to question the king's power to levy impositions on trade—a power which, were it to go unchallenged, would fatally weaken the Commons' hold on the crown's purse-strings. Despite the fundamental importance of the substantive question involved, of which many members were fully aware, it became evident that what members objected to, if anything more than the claim that impositions were a 'Noli me tangere', was the bishop's imputation of disloyalty to the House. If the king were to become convinced of this, then members realized there might be no more parliaments.[10] So, ironically, the final squabble of this parliament was characterized not by an onslaught on impositions, but by attempts to persuade the king of the House's love and affection towards him. Purposive opposition activities were not much in evidence, nor, at this stage, was much destructive alienation from the court. Obviously, there was antipathy, for otherwise impositions, the presence of the Attorney-General, or the favour shown to the Scots would not have been raised: but it had not yet degenerated into hardened bitterness.

More interesting are the later parliaments when we might expect firmer polarization. The clashes in the 1620s are well known, and the case for crisis in the relations between crown and parliament does not need to be made here: the revival of impeachment, the attacks on foreign policy and on Buckingham, and on the crown's religious policy after 1625, all leading to a reluctance to grant supply, warrant no rehearsal. The genesis of all these confrontations, however, casts doubt on the claims that have been made for the alignment of politics in this crucial decade, for as in the case of the Howards in 1614, courtiers were heavily involved. It was a privy councillor, Coke, who was in large part responsible for the revival of impeachment in 1621; Lord Chancellor Bacon was effectively destroyed by the combination of two councillors, Coke and Cranfield;

---

[9] *C.J.* i. 456, 498.
[10] Russell, 'Parliament and Finances', 100; *C.J.* i, esp. 496. I am grateful to Mr. Russell for discussions on this theme.

Cranfield fell in 1624 because Buckingham turned on him; the attacks on Buckingham in 1626 were strongly supported, or perhaps even led, by important councillors, most notably the Earls of Pembroke and Arundel. Almost every parliament of the early Stuart period displayed similar peculiarities. In 1624 the attack on the king's foreign policy was led by the *de facto* head of government, Buckingham, and by the heir to the throne: in such circumstances, courtier coherence in parliament was virtually non-existent.[11] The causes of the 1624 foreign policy reversal are well known, but the implications of Professor Zaller's discussion of the equally momentous foreign policy debate of late 1621 are perhaps not fully appreciated. It seems possible that the disastrous debate and criticism of the crown's peace policy, which provoked James's angry attempt to stop it, the consequent cry of free speech in the Protestation, and then the bitter dissolution, was initiated by Buckingham who was apparently 'flying a kite' for his own devious purposes.[12] In affairs such as these, where was the 'court' interest? And if that question cannot be answered without major qualification, then 'country' too must be devalued.

Now it would obviously be folly to argue that factions and hostilities at court, flowing over into parliament, destroyed political harmony in England. Without indigenous resentment at the activities of monopolists and patentees, the machinations of Coke and Cranfield against Bacon would have been in vain; without indigenous desires for war, Buckingham's 1624 volte-face would not have found such support; and so on. 'Country' feeling in Professor Trevor-Roper's sense was present and was important, but that is no sufficient condition for an anlaysis of politics in two-party terms. A crucial factor here is the character of the court. Scholars of the Elizabethan political scene have emphasized the value of a factious court, balancing opposing groups (whether Cecil and Dudley or Cecil and Devereux), which allowed opinion in the country access to the corridors

---

[11] For the events of 1621, see R. Zaller, *The Parliament of 1621* (Berkeley, 1971), revised in certain respects by J. S. Flemion, 'Slow Process, Due Process, and the High Court of Parliament', *H.J.* xvii (1974), 3–13; for 1624, see R. E. Ruigh, *The Parliament of 1624* (Cambridge, Mass., 1971); and for 1625 and 1626, see J. N. Ball, 'The Parliamentary Career of Sir John Eliot, 1624–1629' (Cambridge Univ. Ph.D.thesis 1953).

[12] Zaller, op. cit. 150–4.

of power, as one faction sought support against another. Several historians have pointed out that while the presence of men like Leicester, Walsingham, and Bedford in Elizabeth's Council might mean that puritan activists in the country could not be effectively repressed, it also meant that they would not become dangerously alienated. There was always the hope that their court patrons might get the upper hand in the struggle going on around the throne, that reform would come from above, and that alternative organization would therefore be unnecessary. Professor MacCaffrey concluded that 'so long as the Privy Council retained a broadly representative function . . . there would be some protection against a dangerous rift between the rival foci of loyalty and action.'[13]

The rule of Buckingham clearly violated the maxims of statecraft which dictated balance at court. It was not just the absence of an heir to the throne as a rallying-point for the discontented under the early Stuarts which drove men like the Earl of Southampton to dabble in parliamentary opposition, as has been suggested elsewhere, but rather Buckingham's overpowering hold on the court. It is arguable that the notorious divisions amongst the courtiers of Elizabeth and Charles II were more characteristic of the political workings of early modern England than were the parliamentary clashes of the 1620s. But in that decade it became exceptionally difficult to advance alternative policies at court. Buckingham's clients might, admittedly, be variegated in their ideological colouring—his ability to befriend both Laud and John Preston is an indication of this—but those on whom the favourite did not smile would nevertheless find great problems in gaining a hearing for their advice. Thus, for much of the 1620s the Duke was faced with opposition within the Council; at times this was even in a majority, and yet, especially after the crisis in the Council of 1623–4, his promptings were those which were heeded on all issues. Hopes of changing policies at court were further diminished by increasing evidence of Charles I's blind religious commitment in the later years of the decade, and by

---

[13] W. T. MacCaffrey, *The Shaping of the Elizabethan Regime* (Princeton, 1968), 484–5; P. Collinson, *The Elizabethan Puritan Movement* (1967), *passim*; Russell, *Origins of the Civil War*, 17–18; see also R. A. Marchant, *The Puritans and the Church Courts in the Diocese of York 1560–1642* (1960), 204; Stone, *Causes of the Revolution*, 85–6.

the ousting of the Duke's enemies, such as Bristol or Bishop
Williams. The only recourse for those in disagreement (as
Pembroke, Warwick, Roe, Digges, Rich, and others, over
foreign policy) was to parliament as a means of applying
leverage. Resistance, whether by favourite or king, to such
unwonted parliamentary pressures could then generate crisis.
A grave error of James and Charles was to misunderstand the
purposes of the court and to allow personal preferences to over-
rule politics in their dealings, as Elizabeth had by and large
refused to do (for example, in her relations with Leicester and,
though less surely, with Essex).[14]

Nevertheless, while the court under James and Charles
evidenced an unhealthy imbalance, it was not yet fatal: until
perhaps the very end of the 1620s when Charles's religious
prejudices became clear, the court still possessed a degree of
heterogeneity. Buckingham's desire to insure himself by playing
off all sides and using men like Preston meant that discontented
gentry were able to find friends at court, and vice versa (as the
parliamentary attacks on the Duke show), and this presumably
helped to limit alienation from the regime.[15] It was not until
the end of the 1620s that the danger signs became fully evident.
By that time the religious policy of the king was having its
effect in the ominous upsurge of emigration: after having
become an attorney in the Court of Wards as late as 1626,
John Winthrop left his place in 1629, debating long and hard
with himself about whether to make the journey to New
England. One of the considerations he noted was the dangerous
conclusion that 'The fountains of learninge and Relig[ion] are
so corrupted, as . . . most Children, even the best wittes and of
fayrest hopes, are perverted, corrupted and utterly over-
throwne by the multitude of evill examples and the licentious
government of those seminaryes.'[16]

---

[14] MacCaffrey, op. cit. 93–116, 120; G. E. Aylmer, *The Kings' Servants* (1961), 61. I
am also grateful to Professor G. R. Elton for conversations on this matter.

[15] It appears that most of the privy councillors in the Commons were opposed to
Buckingham's request for a second supply in 1625. Ball, 'Parliamentary Career of
Eliot', 86. For the position of Preston, see I. Morgan, *Prince Charles's Puritan Chaplain*
(1957), *passim*; and C. Thompson, 'The Origins of the Politics of the Parliamentary
Middle Group, 1625–1629', *T.R.H.S.* 5th ser., xxii (1972), 74–5.

[16] Winthrop's arguments also passed through Hampden's and Eliot's hands: *The
Winthrop Papers*, ed. S. E. Morison *et al.* (Massachusetts Historical Soc. 1929–), ii.
106–49.

Perhaps as important as religious despair in producing a more rigid estrangement from the court was the political monopoly acquired by the Duke. If we want to understand the reasons for the efforts of certain influential puritans to establish what were virtually the organs of an alternative foreign policy in the Carribbean companies, and the startling readiness of prominent and basically conservative gentlemen to move outside the conventional political channels in such measures as circulating the Petition of Right in the country, we have to realize the extent to which those channels had become clogged up. When Buckingham made the difficult transition from father to son in 1625, thwarting hopes of his fall, and then in his new security proceeded to deal with his court opponents by silencing men like Bristol and Williams, following this in 1628 with a reconciliation with Arundel and Pembroke, then there was little hope for aid from above as all courtiers were forced to acknowledge the omnipotent Duke. What this might effect can be seen in Wentworth's appeal to public opinion by means of a veiled attack on the Duke at the York assizes in 1626 when earlier hopes that he might be toppled at court had failed, and when Savile's addresses to Buckingham had achieved Wentworth's dismissal from the *custos*-ship. A similar sense of hopelessness about the prospect of change coming from the working of the due processes must be presumed to have underlain the parliamentary and foreign policy developments of the end of the decade. But before that dangerous stage was reached, Buckingham's own irresponsible use of parliament in 1621 and 1624, and the realization of his courtly enemies that some of the conventional ways of gaining the king's ear were being closed, served to provide encouragement or leadership for inchoate resentment in the Lower House, and thus to avert dangerous alienation.

Conclusions derived from the crises are supported by the careers of the men concerned, for the ambiguities of 'court and country' politics are personified by those whom Professor Zagorin regarded as the leading 'country' activists in the

---

[17] Thompson, 'Origins of the Parliamentary Middle Group', 71–86; *The Earl of Strafforde's Letters and Dispatches*, ed. W. Knowler (2 vols., 1739), i. 20, 36: I am grateful to Mr. Russell for the first reference.

Commons.[18] His list is distorted by hindsight, by judging the 1620s by what happened in 1640, for it includes Oliver Cromwell and John Hampden, who only achieved prominence in the Long Parliament, and Denzil Holles and William Strode, of whom much the same could be said, although they attained a certain notoriety in the final débâcle of 1629. If we exclude them, we are left with Sir Edwin Sandys, Nicholas Fuller, William Hakewill, Edward Alford, Sir Dudley Digges, Sir Robert Phelips, Sir John Eliot, Sir Thomas Wentworth, William Mallory, Sir Walter Erle, Sir Edward Coke, John Pym, and Sir Francis Seymour. A 'country' opposition seems a strange way of describing some of these men, if by that phrase is meant a distrust of and opposition to the court. Professor Zagorin concedes that some 'abandoned the Country', but the relations of some to such an entity were never less than ambivalent. Mallory, Erle, Seymour, Alford (despite his closeness to Bedford) probably pass muster as countrymen; Phelips, possibly as complex a figure as Wentworth, son of a Master of the Rolls, close contact of Buckingham in 1623–4, might also be included, though he might perhaps have had a court career in the 1620s had he been luckier: his convoluted history certainly seems to bear out the notion of a conflict 'within the mind' to which Professor Stone referred. But the others could as easily be described as intelligent and frustrated courtiers as 'country' politicians. The problems of deciding whether a man was a countryman who abandoned his commitment, or a frustrated courtier, are well illustrated by a confidential letter from Wentworth on the death of James: in it he declared that his 'pretences and hopes' were 'at Court', and that he had to consider how to play his 'cards upon this new shuffle of the packe', and yet *in the same letter* he commented that the saltpetre-men 'straine the prerogatiue to the highest'. Judging by his light-hearted tone, Wentworth does not seem to have thought his current ideological position particularly remarkable, and when—if ever—he changed 'sides' must be an open question. The most prominent in the politics of the 1620s of the men on Zagorin's list were Sandys, Coke, Wentworth, Digges, and Eliot, and it is perhaps worth including Pym for the anachronistic reason of what he became—and they all

---

[18] Zagorin, op. cit. 79–80.

reveal much the same difficulties of categorization, for they all personally straddled whatever gap there was between court and 'country'. Pym, client of Bedford, receiver of Crown lands, was, it has recently been shown, fully prepared to give positive consideration to the crown's financial problems; furthermore, lacking as he did any genuine local base, his career emphasizes the dangers inherent in a confusion of Everitt's 'country' with that of Trevor-Roper. Eliot, a client and confidant of Buckingham until well into 1625, gradually became convinced of his patron's destructive role and clearly had as his major goal between 1626 and 1628 the removal of the Duke; Digges, an ally of Buckingham in the 1624 Parliament, and a client of Archbishop Abbot, was often subsequently a mediator between a group of councillors and the Commons, aiming like his master at the removal of the Duke; Wentworth dramatically achieved his career at court; Coke, displaced Chief Justice, and still Privy Councillor in 1621, retained his hopes and his contacts long afterwards, and Sandys had as idiosyncratic a career in politics as he did in religion, becoming a client of Buckingham in the later 1620s when some of his allies were detaching themselves.[19]

It is a measure of the disastrous achievement of the early Stuarts that this should appear strange, that it should be thought improper and remarkable that aspiring courtiers should be politically at odds with current policies. But service to the crown did not have to mean, as Owen had alleged in 1614, time-serving and rigid discipline. The courtiers of Henry VIII and Elizabeth had been divided in their religious affiliations as well as personally, and had worked at court and at the Council Board to advance their ends; what Professor Elton found remarkable and Elizabeth objectionable was when their divergent preferences were expressed in parliament, and it was on this that she took action against some of them.[20] As Elton

---

[19] Russell, 'Parliament and Finances', 106–7; *Wentworth Papers 1597–1628*, ed. J. P. Cooper (Camden Soc., 1973), 229–30; Ball, 'Parliamentary Career of Eliot', *passim*; *Notes and Queries*, 4th ser., x (1872), 326: I am grateful to Conrad Russell for this reference; *D.N.B.*, *sub* 'Coke'; Brit. Lib. Add. MS. 37819, fo. 11^v; Bodl. MS. Rawl. A 346, fo. 226. A similar point is made by Professor G. R. Elton in his essay, 'Tudor Government: the Points of Contact: I. Parliament', *T.R.H.S.* 5th ser., xxiv (1974), 199–200. See also Thompson, 'Origins of the Parliamentary Middle Group', 71–86.

[20] G. R. Elton, 'Sir Thomas More and the Opposition to Henry VIII', *B.I.H.R.* xli (1968), 19–34; C. Russell, *The Crisis of Parliaments* (Oxford, 1971), 246; J. E. Neale, *Elizabeth I and her Parliaments*, 2 vols., 1953–7), ii. 267–74.

recently stressed, where there is a centralized monarchical government, and where parliaments are at best irregular, the court and the Council should represent and give a hearing to as many grievances as possible. When they fail to do so, those grievances may be expressed outside the court.[21] This had happened rarely in the sixteenth century, but became habitual in the early seventeenth, especially after Buckingham had crushed opposition at court after 1625, with the silencing of men like Bristol, Williams, and Arundel. That men like Wentworth, Sandys, and Coke, with close ties to and hopes of the court, should be apprehensive of the direction of the crown's policies was not new, for many of Elizabeth's courtiers had had similar doubts over religion; but the channels of communication, and therefore of hope, had on the whole then remained open. What was new was that men in the early Stuart Commons and, as we have seen, men like Pembroke and Arundel, should be driven to voice their fears in parliament repeatedly in default of a hearing elsewhere. James's angry attacks on those who courted 'popularity' by opening the 'mystery' of government to a wider audience were unfair, for it was now only thus that pressure could be brought to bear on a doting king.

The significance of such men as these is of course that they provided the leadership. 'Country' feeling was manifest in the Commons, most obviously in the resentment directed at the fiscal demands of the crown: but without the collaboration of those playing a more subtle game, it might not have been effective, merely leading to negative protest and speedy dissolution. As we have noted, it was Coke who headed the impeachment proceedings in 1621, and it was he and Cranfield who brought the House back from the minor monopolists and patentees on to the Lord Chancellor; it was Pembroke's agents who first dared to name Buckingham in 1626, and Eliot and Digges were perhaps the leaders in the impeachment campaign; and it was Wentworth and Coke who were most prominent in the Petition of Right struggle in 1628.[22] The

---

[21] G. R. Elton, 'Tudor Government: The Points of Contact. II. The Council', *T.R.H.S.* 5th ser., xxv (1975), 195–211; and 'Tudor Government: the Points of Contact. III. The Court', *T.R.H.S.* xxvi (1976), 211–28. Professor Elton's important articles appeared after this essay was substantially complete.

[22] F. H. Relf, *The Petition of Right* (Minneapolis, 1917).

corollary was that it was partly the presence of such Janus-like men as these in the van of the protesters in the House of Commons that ensured that at least some money would go through. Mr. Russell has demonstrated the intelligent and positive stands of Sir Nathaniel Rich and John Pym on this issue, but even the supposedly more negative and short-sighted Eliot was capable of saying in 1626, 'Cutt of the king's revenewes, you cutt of the principall meanes of your owne safeties, and not only disable him to defend you, but enforce that which you conceav an offence, the extraordinary resort to his subjects for supplies, and the more than ordinary waies of raising them.'[23]

So if the leadership of the attack on current court policies was not quite what we have commonly been led to believe, what of the general notion of 'the country'? Here we must go back to the suggestions of Professors Everitt and Stone that national allegiance was increasing in train with localist loyalties, and indeed we might suggest a causal connection between the two. Professor Tilly argued perceptively in his work on the Vendée that aggressive localism is only likely to occur when local integrity is under threat, for, as he says, 'two groups which never meet cannot fight'.[24] Royal centralization and the clearer emergence of a nation-state in the sixteenth century are thus necessary conditions for the vocal espousal of the old ways and local rights. As Professor Stone succinctly indicated, each gentleman experienced the tug of court and country, or rather of nation and locality, within himself. By bearing that in mind, the apparently wayward courses of some early Stuart politicians might become rather more comprehensible.

Those like Wentworth, Sandys, Rudyerd, or Digges who aspired to success at court were not the only ones to operate under conflicting pressures, for the gentry in the counties also felt opposing loyalties, to a greater or lesser degree. This again is not a novel assertion—several local historians have made the point strongly; but it is one that has not been absorbed sufficiently by those studying the national scene. The ambivalence of localism, very different from the complacent provincialism

---

[23] Russell, 'Parliament and Finances', 106–7; Ball, 'Parliamentary Career of Eliot', 133–4, and see also Dr. Ball's argument below, pp. 173–207.

[24] C. Tilly, *The Vendée* (1964), 61.

described by Professor Everitt, is admirably revealed by Dr. Hassell Smith's work on politics in Elizabethan Norfolk, in which he showed the inroads that Elizabeth's military, fiscal, and social policies were making into the powers and independence of the county élite. The old county families protested fiercely through a variety of channels, making just those claims that Professor Everitt might have us expect, appealing to the old ways and autonomy against this novel interference from above. But merely to complain and grumble achieves little, unless the complaints are addressed to those with the power to change things. And just as Wentworth and others came to realize later that it was the court and not the parliament that had the power, so the paradoxical but thoroughly typical spectacle arose of protests of localist independence being addressed to the court, from which the Norfolk gentry might have been thought to be shutting themselves off. In order to make those protests heard, the 'country' tried to find friends at court, exploiting friends and relations and making contacts. Just as in so many parliamentary confrontations, so in this local affair, alliances between members of the 'court' and members of the 'country' interests developed.[25]

While the courtiers in parliament are difficult to characterize as a solid group, so the need to present an effective case by means of addresses to the centre undermined the coherence of localism. Thus, Sir Henry Montague wrote from London to his brother at home in Northamptonshire in 1613 assuring him that he need not worry about the outcome of a local quarrel, for his opponent 'finds not himself maintained as perhaps he hoped'. From a correspondent retailing London and court news, the message must be taken as emphasizing the constructive nature of the links between court and the localities. What might happen if no links with the centre were retained is revealed most clearly in the war years, in Dr. Morrill's study of Cheshire, where Sir William Brereton, the radical 'centrist', is shown to have triumphed in most of his disputes against the local establishment solely because he had the ear of the central power. Admittedly, war brought more sanctions into

---

[25] A. Hassell Smith, *County and Court* (Oxford, 1974), 229–304. See also Professor Elton's invaluable stress on the court as the centre of power, in 'Points of Contact. The Council', 211–28.

operation, but the parallel still probably holds good: pure localism might be self-defeating.[26]

The non-viability of an unmitigated espousal of the 'country' position is reinforced by the factor of office. Dr. Hassell Smith has shown how valuable local office was, enabling the holder to help his friends and hurt his enemies in the locality by action or inaction in the justice's round or by partisanship in tax-rating: a Star Chamber suit against a Wiltshire justice alleged he had used his position to 'induce ignorant people to believe that he had absolute power and authority in himself', thus exalting himself above his colleagues.[27] For, like the gentry, the meaner sort needed access to those with power and influence. But the crown was the ultimate arbiter of local office-holding, and therefore care had to be taken by the country gentleman that he should not be known to tread too blatantly an anti-court road. Failure to abide by such elementary rules could have repercussions, as Sir Robert Phelips found when, in punishment for his obstreperousness in a number of parliaments, he was removed from his local offices in Somerset in the later 1620s and suffered a consequent diminution in his local standing. As Professor Barnes observed, he even lost much of his control over the town of Ilchester, of which he retained his stewardship. Despite his earlier support for the forward Protestants in the House of Commons, he was in 1633 one of the few gentlemen to back Archbishop Laud's anti-puritan policy in favour of churchales in the county in the anxious attempt to regain favour at court and thus restore his local position. Professor Barnes's conclusion on the dilemma of Phelips and his fellows was that their position 'was based in both Court and country'. Despite his career in the House of Commons, or perhaps in relation to it and its apparent inconsistencies, Phelips cultivated contacts at court assiduously.[28]

---

[26] *H.M.C. Buccleuch MSS.* i. 244; J. S. Morrill, *Cheshire 1630–1660* (Oxford, 1974), 139–79.

[27] Hassell Smith, op. cit., 51–86; compare the Earl of Hertford's complaints in 1605: *The Earl of Hertford's Lieutenancy Papers 1603–1612*, ed. W. P. D. Murphy (Wiltshire Record Soc., 1969), 103; J. Hurstfield, 'County Government, c. 1530–c. 1660', *V.C.H.* Wiltshire v (1957), 102.

[28] T. G. Barnes, *Somerset 1625–1640* (Oxford, 1961), 22–4, 43, and 'County Politics and a Puritan Cause Célèbre: Somerset Churchales 1633', *T. R. H. S.* 5th ser., ix (1959), 103–22; compare J. P. Cooper's similar verdict on the situation in Yorkshire at the same time, in *Wentworth Papers*, 5.

Standing in the county and at the centre were bound together, and the local gentry could not afford to set themselves against the will of the centre too thoroughly. Phelips, as an important parliament man, is not typical of Professor Everitt's 'country', but his case is suggestive. A localist gentleman could certainly drag his feet, but if he became too assertive he could suffer. The history of the social descent of office-holding in the Civil War and Interregnum and again in the 1680s makes this point still more clearly; the state need not be blocked by local non-compliance, but could find other agents. Recalcitrant gentry thus ensured they suffered doubly, from the objectionable policy and from being displaced. There was normally someone who, hating someone else, could be relied on to combine the crown's business with his own, or who would be reluctant to ignore the crown's lest his own should suffer at the hands of another. That, after all, was what a system of unpaid voluntary local officials was all about. While there were obviously many leading gentry who were unwilling to do the crown's bidding in the years of fiscal expedients 1626–27, Wentworth's friend Wandesford pointed to the other side of the coin slightly lower on the social scale in Yorkshire when he observed 'everyman praing that the safe shelter of collectorship may cover and protect him. And for my pert I should be glad of the service.'[29]

The contortions induced in Phelips over the churchales affair by the loss of office were matched by those of some of the Yorkshire gentry over the privy seal loans of 1626, through a similar agency. The victimization of Sir Thomas Wentworth in that year, for the same reasons as that of Phelips, was accompanied by the appointment of his arch-enemy in the county, Sir John Savile, to the Privy Council, and this occasioned something of a purge of Wentworth's friends locally. One of these, Sir Henry Savile, wrote sourly to the Chancellor of Exchequer that Sir John had lessened the sum due to the crown from the county on the privy seals 'to make him popular in the cuntrey

---

[29] *Wentworth Papers*, 276. Considerations of *noblesse oblige* might also contrive to keep the dispirited gentleman in office, as can be seen in Wentworth's attempt to dissuade Sir Gervase Clifton from resigning office in *c.* 1630: 'When you think better of it, less inwards upon your own ease, more outward upon the duties we owe the public, I assure myself you will not desire it.' Quoted in C. V. Wedgwood, *Thomas Wentworth first Earl of Stafford: A Revaluation* (1961), 86.

to the disseruice of his Maiestie'; he had also had Sir Henry
and his brother-in-law put out of local office. The dispossessed
then claimed that they could have raised more for the crown
and more equitably—all with the aim of their own restoration.
A courtier was thus doing the county's business for it in order
to make himself friends at home, while men with links to
Wentworth and thus to the 'country' claimed that they could
do the work of the court more competently.[30]

Courtiership, as we have noted, did not necessarily entail
isolation from the country at the centre, and the same case can
be made for the position of courtiers locally, although
obviously with diminishing effect as the court of the early
Stuarts, particularly that of Charles, became more of a closed
world. Just as the country gentlemen needed to retain links
with the court, so the reverse, for the court ideally was composed not only of sycophants and careerists but also of men
important in their own right, who could add strength to the
government of the country. That is the point of the comments
that were made even under the less than perceptive James and
Charles that election results in the localities were taken note of
'above', as evidence of a man's standing and suitability for
employment.[31] What Savile performed for Yorkshire over the
loans was no different from what Burghley had earlier done
for Hertfordshire in the field of the militia, despite his avowed
concern to curb favouritism and consequent inefficiency elsewhere; and friends at court likewise achieved a lessening in
Caernarvonshire's load under Charles's fiscal expedients.[32] The
epithet 'Janus-like' was applied earlier to some of the 'country'
politicians, but it is applicable also to some who were the paid
servants of the crown, for it was only a matter of degree that
separated them. Wentworth during the recess of the 1621
Parliament went home and defended the county's election of
his partner, Secretary of State Calvert, by recounting what he
had won for the country: given Calvert's exceeding of his brief
from the king in the early crisis over freedom of speech in the
first session, in an apparent attempt to build bridges between

---

[30] *Wentworth Papers*, 249, 254.

[31] Ibid. 144; *Strafforde's Letters*, i. 13; *H.M.C. Buccleuch MSS.* iii. 75.

[32] Boynton, *Elizabethan Militia*, 168, 178; A. H. Dodd, 'The Pattern of Politics in
Stuart Wales', *Transactions of the Honourable Society of Cymmrodorion* (1948), 32.

the crown and those who were apprehensive of its intentions, then Wentworth's plea had some justice.[33] The position of the unpaid servants of the king in the locality was seen as being 'as well for the advancement of the King's service as for the ease and good of the country'.[34] This balance of course became difficult to preserve as the advancement of the king's service ran increasingly counter to the ease of the country with the heavy exactions for war in the 1620s. But the role of many courtiers, even in this period, was not *in principle* dissimilar, for had it been so, and had they also lacked the favour of the unpredictable Duke, then they could have fallen. A client system, such as still functioned in the seventeenth century, is by definition a two-way relationship, and while feuds at court could reverberate in the country,[35] the reverse was also the case. A squabble over office in Northamptonshire in 1613 set the courtly contacts of the local principals at odds; at a point slightly further removed from the centre, the relations of Wentworth and Savile were worsened by a dependant's grievances. It was, and had to be if the patron were to remain effective, in the power of 'meane fellowes [to] sow such tares betwixt gentlemen of qualety'.[36] Personal standing dictated that men pay heed to what happened outside the immediate circle, and therefore courtiers needed to stay in touch with those at home.

While there are abundant instances of local electoral hostility to courtiers,[37] alienation was not and could not be anywhere near total, for reasons discussed above. If the crown's demands were increasing, then there could be all the more cause to cultivate someone close to the king in order to divert those pressures—even a cursory reading of the Essex Lieutenancy

[33] D. Hirst, *The Representative of the People?* (Cambridge, 1975), 174–5; *C.J.* i. 522; *Commons Debates, 1621*, ed. W. Notestein, F. H. Relf, H. Simpson (7 vols., New Haven, 1935), vii. 575–6; iv. 55. James declared in his letter to Calvert that he had no intention of abridging that liberty of speech 'which appertaines unto' the Commons. Calvert seems to have expanded this into a concession to the House of jurisdiction over words spoken in it; he was at least understood as having said this, and Smyth noted that the King 'granted (in effect) as much as was petitioned'. Ibid. ii. 83 n. 11; v. 256, 463; vi. 290.

[34] *Hertford's Lieutenancy Papers*, 135.

[35] Hassell Smith, *County and Court*, 26, 66, 303–4, 340–1.

[36] *H.M.C. Buccleuch MSS.* i. 243; *Wentworth Papers*, 218: I am grateful to Conrad Russell for this reference.

[37] Hirst, *Representative of the People*, 137–53.

Book shows the importance attached to the Essex-born Chancellor of the Exchequer, Sir Richard Weston, as a hedge between the troop movements of the later 1620s and the county. The cynical observation that there was a strong neighbourly attendance at the Northamptonshire christening of Sir Edward Montague's son in 1616, only because the father had just been seen to be on good terms with James and the new favourite, is one that might at that date have been expected. But nearly twelve years later Montague could be most anxious that 'the country' should not see he was in any 'disfavour' with the king, and at about the same time the new Earl of Worcester was spurned 'as a Jack out of office' by his neighbours in South Wales who showed themselves increasingly 'alienated and disaffected' from him because he had not been appointed to his father's offices. The apprehensions of Wentworth's friends in 1628 that Savile's recent elevation to the Council would prove disastrous to his own electoral hopes in Yorkshire because of men's 'servile adoration of any temperary greatness', while ultimately unfounded, were not unjustified.[38]

The segregation of court from 'country' whether at Westminster or in the counties poses more problems than many recent historians have been prepared to admit. Their relationship is so integral that if they can be identified as opposed entities then government has reached a stage of major crisis, and even breakdown.[39] When the crown was so isolated (or so ill informed, which amounts to the same thing) at the end of the 1630s that it pricked some staunch opponents of the tax as Ship-Money sheriffs, with unfortunate results in certain counties, then what the polarization of court and country could entail was clearly visible, and the administration of important areas of policy was effectively paralysed.[40] But in more 'normal' times governments had few policies offensive enough to drive the gentry into such intransigence, and the gentry would be unwilling to run the risks entailed, both to local society and to their own personal standing. Court and 'country' depended on

[38] Bodl. MS. Firth C4; *H.M.C. Buccleuch MSS.* i. 250; ibid. iii. 321; Dodd, 'Politics in Stuart Wales', 40; *Wentworth Papers*, 283.

[39] *Pace* Professor Trevor-Roper, who, rather confusingly, asserted quite the opposite. Aston, *Crisis in Europe*, 114–15.

[40] B. W. Quintrell, 'The Government of the County of Essex, 1603–1642' (London Univ. Ph.D. thesis 1965), 89–90; Dodd, 'Politics in Stuart Wales', 37.

each other for their mutual well-being, and, what is more, both tended to appreciate this. Intellectual historians have often criticized the period for the 'poverty' of its ideology, for the mental blockage its thinkers and politicians displayed when, in an age of apparent constitutional conflict, they were not able to come up with conflicting ideologies which made sense of their conflicting positions. The constant harping of contemporaries, whether members of the court or of the 'country', on 'unity', 'balance', and 'harmony' accorded ill with the presuppositions of a generation of historians nurtured on Whiggish ideas of a momentous conflict between prerogative and the ancient constitution. But if the notion of inexorable constitutional confrontation is defused, then the ideology begins to make sense. Contemporaries knew what they were talking about when they stressed unity and a myriad of correspondences linking the various members of the body politic, for that was the way of their world.[41] It was certainly a normative picture, for they were only too well aware of what might come were those links broken and that unity dissolved. But talk of harmony was more than just a nostalgic appeal to the good old days of Queen Elizabeth: it was still in the 1620s a descriptive rhetoric, albeit idealized. There were still links between the centre and the periphery, between members of the 'opposition' and the court: the Archbishop of Canterbury was still a Calvinist and the gentry were willing to do unpaid and often unprofitable service, beyond merely keeping the price of their grain down in order to supply the markets of the poor, and thus preserving social stability.

There are signs of organization of the parliamentary 'country', it is true—the meeting of the opposition leaders before the parliamentary disasters of 1629 is well known,[42] but not so well known are the evident electoral arrangements made between at least Wentworth and Seymour, if not more of the disenchanted, in 1626.[43] But more common and harmless

---

[41] M. A. Judson, *The Crisis of the Constitution* (New Brunswick, 1949), 8–9; C. Hill, *Intellectual Origins of the English Revolution* (Oxford, 1965), 1–2.

[42] I. H. C. Fraser, 'The agitation in the Commons, 2 March 1629', *B.I.H.R.* xxx (1957), 86–95.

[43] Wentworth at the end of March 1621 promised to find a seat for Sir Richard Wynne in an unnamed borough: at that date it could only have been Pontefract, which Wentworth was having restored to parliamentary status. Wynne eventually sat for

manifestations of 'country' feeling are contacts between members for constituencies in a certain county: and neither kind of contact, whether between 'opposition' leaders or lesser members, precluded close and constructive dealings with courtiers. Thus, while Buckingham's parliamentary alliance with the 'opposition' was no longer in evidence in 1625, not all bridges seem to have been burnt. He was co-operating with the Warwick–Barrington group in the 1625 Essex election, and the lists of deputies chosen by the two Lords Lieutenant of Essex, the Earls of Warwick and Sussex—very different political characters—reveal a marked absence of division. Warwick nominated Lord Maynard, and Sussex Sir Francis Barrington and Sir Harbottle Grimston, although Warwick was later to be in alliance with Barrington and Grimston against Maynard.[44] Political historians of the period have understandably used the correspondence of the Secretaries of State, and other prominent men's collections, as major sources, and in these it is natural that the upsets and the confrontations should have been a subject of comment. The daily and undramatic compromises were not thought newsworthy, just as in today's newspapers, and our understanding has been distorted in consequence. Only by means of detailed studies of both central and local events and alignments can the balance be redressed.

One of the weaknesses of the label 'country' is that it connotes an integral community (a notion explicitly developed by Professor Everitt, and also hinted at by Professor Zagorin, when he implicitly contrasts loyal friendships in the country with rather different ones at court).[45] But of course county societies were internally divided too, and these personal hostilities could cut across the major alignments. Members of the court collaborating with the 'opposition' because of their dislike of Buckingham had their equivalents at the other end of the political axis. Compared with Norfolk or Yorkshire, Northamptonshire appears to have been a relatively unfactious county,

---

Ilchester, for which Phelips was doing the same. Wentworth and Seymour in 1626 discussed the possibility of exchanging seats in order to circumvent Charles's attempt to exclude them from parliament by pricking them sheriffs, and it is evident that Sir Arthur Ingram, the Earl of Clare, and perhaps also Coke and Phelips, were involved in the consultations. *Strafforde's Letters*, i. 14, 30–1.

[44] Hirst, *Representative of The People?*, 200; Bodl. MS. Firth C4, p. 154.
[45] Zagorin, *Court and Country*, 45.

and yet there too, just as in the Yorkshire quarrel of 1626, internal fissures could give the centre a point of entry and a way of finding allies. Sir Edward Montague, having previously been taxed by the crown with his laxity in enforcing the recusancy laws, was stimulated into vindictive activity in 1613 by a feud with one of the major Catholic gentry of the shire over a local office: the crown's will was done for very private and local reasons. A few years later, Dr. Williams (the future Bishop of Lincoln and Lord Keeper), who very much depended on court favour for his elevation to local office, became involved in a squabble with Montague over the implementation of the King's Declaration of Sports, and promptly sought revenge by hindering Montague's work as a Deputy-Lieutenant: here again we see personal rivalries disrupting the superficial considerations of court and 'country'. It seems likely that many counties, if examined, would provide some parallels to the Phelips–Poulett feud in Somerset, allowing the crown to find one ally or another as local circumstances dictated — the most remarkable aspect of the Somerset situation may merely be the long-term nature of the dispute.[46] Again, at another level, municipal privileges, always a barrier to the crown's attempt to organize the militia, might be overridden readily enough by gentry Deputy-Lieutenants whose relationships with their local towns were not always wholly amicable. One long-suffering town clerk warned all other towns to beware the gentry, 'who make no other use of them but as they doe of their stirops to mount to their horse'. Conflicting particularisms, especially where they were exacerbated by jurisdictional disputes (as for example in the case of York and the Ainsty, which fell under a plethora of powers), could give some leverage to the centre — as well as providing an exceptionally favourable environment for the growth of *intra*-court and *intra*-'country' friction.[47] While we normally only consider an aspect of the latter phenomenon, the refusal of one locality to co-ordinate activity with another,

---

[46] *H.M.C. Buccleuch MSS.* i. 240–4, 253–4; ibid. iii. 156–7; *H.M.C. Report, MSS. of Lord Montagu of Beaulieu*, 94–5; Barnes, *Somerset 1625–1640*, 281–98.

[47] *Hertford's Lieutenancy Papers*, 189, 191–2, 193–4, 196–7; Hirst, op. cit. 211. York and the Ainsty came under the jurisdiction of the Council in the North, the High Commission of the Northern Province, the other ecclesiastical courts at York, the Lord Mayor and Corporation, the J.P.s of the West Riding (claiming jurisdiction over the Ainsty), and the Assize Judges.

it is plain that there was ample scope for a perceptive government to divide and rule.

It needs to be stressed, after all, that England continued to
be governed adequately until 1639–40, though the tales of
disaffection to be met in the great crisis debates of the 1620s
or in the State Papers might lead us to think otherwise. Dr.
Boynton concluded that, on balance, the pressure for a more
competent militia applied by James and Charles was relatively
effective. Certainly there was a noticeable re-equipment of the
county trained bands with the expensive musket, and the
military performance in the European crisis of 1619 and in the
invasion scare at Harwich in 1625 seems impressive—not up to
the level of 1599, true, but after years of peace and supposed
alienation not grotesquely inferior.[48] Subsequent deterioration
seems to have owed almost as much to the incompetence of
the Privy Council—failure to carry out its dire, and necessary,
threats to punish defaulters, crass failure to keep its word,
general dilatoriness when it was trying to persuade the country
of an emergency[49]—as to intransigence in the country.

Local intransigence is a phenomenon remarkably absent in
this and other periods. In part, this must be for reasons already
touched on, as when Sir Edward Montague eventually suc-
cumbed to royal pressure to make a fuller apology for
presenting the 1604 Northamptonshire petition in behalf of the
persecuted puritan ministers because he 'would not be singular,
and could not tell how it might be taken'. Again, while we are
only too aware of the massive attacks mounted on the forced

[48] Boynton, *Elizabethan Militia*, 237–57; *The Montagu Musters Book A.D. 1602–1623*,
ed. J. Wake (Northamptonshire Record Soc., 1935), xxxvi; Bodl. MS. Firth C4.

[49] The Essex Lieutenancy Book abounds in instances of these failings: in 1627 the
Council wrote sternly to the Commissioners for the Loan, saying that the king had
resolved to punish defaulters, who 'shall finde what itt is to bee divided from theire
kinge and the better part of the whole kingdome', but this was followed by a memorandum 'that after the writinge of the aforesaid Letter there was nothinge more
done . . .'; in the invasion scare of 1625, the king's instructions to Warwick as commander at Harwich included the disingenuous clause that if people were reluctant to
pay the charges he should 'mingle with the remonstrance of the lawe, and theire
duties, the opinion or assurance that yf the law and practice hath not beene such [as
to warrant the contributions] . . . they shall have a reambursment out of the exchequer.'
The county was trying for years to recover its outlay. Bodl. MS. Firth C4, pp. 383,
152 ff. See also A. Fletcher, *County Community in Peace and War: Sussex 1600–1660*
(1975), 194, for continuing efficiency in Sussex till 1640. For a further discussion of
this issue, see my forthcoming article, 'The Privy Council and problems of enforcement
in the 1620s', in the *Journal of British Studies*.

loan in parliament in 1628, the fact remains that it had been
implemented in the localities, and Sir Francis Seymour in the
House bitterly scorned those Deputy-Lieutenants and Justices
of the Peace who for fear of dismissal had done the crown's
grievous work for it.[50] Seymour clearly realized that while
considerations of vested interest could hamper the court, they
could also aid it by preventing the expression of opposition. But
we must also, and as so often in discussion of this complex
subject, return to the contention of Professors Tilly, Everitt, and
Stone that local and national awareness and allegiance develop
in train. The product of this was that while objections to the
crown's demands might be made, few objections *in principle* were
ever voiced. The rating grievance, the complaint that the
relative distribution of demands was unfair, was the commonest
form of protest. This was on the one hand merely a safe form
of obstructionism, offering resistance to the state without risking
martyrdom, particularly when the crown was so slow to re-
taliate.[51] But such a cynical analysis fails to explain certain
episodes which suggest that at any time, the court, with little
state apparatus, was not quite so powerless in face of the
country. For all men accepted that it was proper for the state
to command, and improper for the subject to disobey—a
manifestation of this being the scaffold confessions of Tudor
traitors. Not until September 1640 was any justification of
resistance heard in England. Opposition to the will of the
crown often crumbled when that will was expressed in the form
of a clear command—and this not necessarily for reasons of
pusillanimity. Perhaps the best instance of this is provided by
Dr. Holmes's demonstration of why the Eastern Association in
the Civil War succeeded and why all other associations failed:
largely because parliament willed and unambiguously commanded that it should succeed, which it neglected to do in
other cases. By leaving no loopholes for rating disputes and
particularist quibbles, it averted them, and there were few men

---

[50] *H.M.C. Montagu of Beaulieu*, 46; Relf, *Petition of Right*, 31. But Seymour was already
a Deputy-Lieutenant and later became a local agent of the crown; P.R.O. S.P.
16/19/51; Hurstfield, 'County Government', 82; and Birmingham Reference Library,
Coventry MSS., Commissions of Depopulation, no. 6, 11 July 11 Car. I: I owe these
references to Mr. Russell.

[51] See for example Professor Barnes's verdict on the Council's failure to act against
William Strode over his reluctance to pay Ship-Money: *Somerset 1625–1640*, 224.

ready to question parliament's *right* to command.[52]

The same was largely true of pre-war England in its relations to the crown. Professor Hurstfield commented on the surprising willingness of men, at the lowest level, to accept the utterly thankless task of being parish constable, and the reasons for this are worth considering. Or again in this humble realm, the behaviour of the pressed men in the Harwich mutiny of 1627 is evidence as much of apparent willingness to obey orders as of insurrection. Although the affair caused distinct perturbation amongst both local and central authorities, it became clear that at least the articulated focus of the protests was the fear that the levies were to be sent to join the king's enemies, and resentment at confinement in the squalid conditions on board ship for some time before they were to sail for the continent. After the mutineers had been satisfied on both these scores, the Deputy-Lieutenants reported to the Council that 'they have behaved themselves with as much obedience as wee Can wish.'[53] The violence of these men does not seem to have represented a major challenge to the constituted authorities.

Amongst the gentry the same pattern of behaviour is evident. The legitimism and deference of protest are patent in the storm that blew up against payments to the muster master in Wiltshire in 1605–6, which included a major onslaught on the Lord Lieutenant, Hertford, in the House of Commons. In his Lieutenancy of Somerset, Hertford appointed an able and competent soldier as muster master, whereas in Wiltshire he appointed his secretary, a man of no military experience. In Somerset, where Hertford had less personal influence than in Wiltshire, the payments came in without too much trouble, while in Wiltshire they were fiercely resisted—but when Hertford appointed a more suitable man his problems apparently ceased.[54] It was clearly the person, not the principle or the turbulence of Wiltshire men, which created the dif-

---

[52] See Stone, *Causes of the Revolution*, 101–2; Zagorin, *Court and Country* 197; C. A. Holmes, *The Eastern Association in the English Civil War* (Cambridge, 1974).

[53] Hurstfield, 'County Government', 105; Bodl. MS. Firth C4, pp. 339, 346, 358.

[54] *Hertford's Lieutenancy Papers*, 10, 12, 25–8, 31, 33–5, 40–2, 63–4, 68–71, 103–4, 134–5, 177. Such compliance is perhaps all the more remarkable in view of the fact that scruples about the legality of the burden in peacetime and with the repeal of the covering statute in 1604 did exist: see *The Parliamentary Diary of Robert Bowyer, 1606–1607*, ed. D. H. Willson (Minneapolis, 1931), 130, 154.

ficulties. Historians of the militia have made much of the efforts
of one of the Northamptonshire Deputies to delay the musters
in 1613, and of his reference to them as 'this Maye game', but
it is not often noted that when the Lord Lieutenant finally
commanded him to act, he obeyed, and even made suggestions
as to how to improve communications; and three months
earlier that same apparent obstructionist had advised that the
county should 'give away to the Purveyance, in respect [of the
King's] extraordinary necessities', of which 'we are bound to
take knowledge'.[55] Attitudes such as this, closely akin to passive
obedience, had major political significance. Seymour alleged
in 1628 that the execution of the forced loan had been mere
time-serving on the part of those involved, but it may have owed
something to the dictates of obedience to a legitimate command.
When Charles attempted to collect the subsidies which had
failed to materialize in the 1626 parliament as a 'benevolence',
he was met by the frequent and disastrous reply of the
subsidy-men that they could only give through a parliament.[56]
But when the Council changed the name of the game and
commanded a loan instead of requesting a benevolence, it was
remarkably successful, bringing in the equivalent of five subsidies far more quickly than if they had been gathered through
parliament.[57] It was claimed in Northamptonshire that the loan
was only a success because the government stressed that it
would not be used as a precedent for further demands, this
message being relayed to the public,[58] and this might put it in
the same category as Ship-Money, devastatingly successful at
first but doomed were it to be repeated and its implications
realized. It is impossible to judge the validity of this allegation,
for the loan was not followed by another: but the success of
the loan can be compared with the vehemence of the protests
in the succeeding parliament. Many of those protesting were,
as Seymour unkindly hinted, just those who had done the work,

[55] Boynton, *Elizabethan Militia*, 213–14; *Montagu Musters Book*, liv, 232; *H.M.C.
Buccleuch MSS.* iii. 154.

[56] *C.S.P. Dom. 1625–1626*, 393, 397, 398, 404, 407.

[57] F. C. Dietz, *English Public Finance 1558–1641* (1932), 238. Professor Dietz also
noticed the undynamic character of much of the opposition to the loan, observing that
when the crown allowed the money to be used locally, for billeting payments or for
coastal defence, the opposition often ceased. Ibid. 236; and Fletcher, op. cit. 195–6.
See also Aylmer, *Kings' Servants*, 450.

[58] *H.M.C. Buccleuch MSS.* i. 265.

and the significant point then is that they had not made their demonstrations in the country, but had with few exceptions more or less efficiently gone about their business.[59]

The correct place for dissent was clearly not in the locality, where an unfortunate precedent for questioning commands might be given to those below.[60] Opposition-minded gentry, unlike some modern historians, did not on the whole confuse the parliamentary and local arenas. Emphasis on this distinction was most strongly expressed by the crown in its attacks on those seeking 'popularity', and it came to the fore in the years 1640–2 when the quest for public support began in earnest, but it seems to have been tacitly accepted by many. Professor Elton described parliament as 'the point of contact' between government and governed, between centre and locality, and this phrase seems most appropriate. Protests could be made there, but afterwards, when members went home, the country had to be governed. Wentworth's comment to his confidant Wandesford in December 1625, as he was in the process of being victimized by the crown, is a significant pointer to this realization: '...my Rule, which I will not transgress, is, Never to contend with the Prerogative out of a Parliament; nor yet to contest with a King but when I am constrained thereunto, or else make Shipwreck of my Integrity and Peace of Conscience.'[61] In the light of this attitude, the greater degree of political tranquillity which can be observed in the early years of the 1630s when parliament was discontinued becomes more comprehensible.

The hypothesis also helps to explain the otherwise strange behaviour over the subsidies granted in 1624 'for the maintenance of that Warre that may hereuppon ensue'. Fierce complaints were made in the Parliaments of 1625 and 1626 that the money had been used for the expedition of Count Mansfeld,

---

[59] Compare the way in which Essex was commanded to provide troops in 1627: the magistrates went into action and *then* protested that the county had borne too many burdens recently. Bodl. MS. Firth C4, p. 332.

[60] See Montague's misgivings when magisterial divisions were made public, or, earlier, Archbishop Parker's horror that 'principles be spread into men's heads... referred to the judgment of the subject ... what master shall be sure in his bedchamber?' *H.M.C. Buccleuch MSS.* iii. 210, 264; J. Loach, 'Pamphlets and Politics, 1553–8', *B.I.H.R.* xlviii (1975), 44.

[61] Hirst, *Representative of the People?* 181–8; Elton, 'Points of Contact: Parliament', 183–200; *Strafforde's Letters*, i. 33.

whereas it was alleged that it had been made quite clear in 1624 that the Commons at least did not contemplate a land war to regain the Palatinate, and aimed merely at a naval, diversionary campaign. But those involved, many of them former or future parliament men, in pressing and supporting locally the men the Privy Council made perfectly clear were destined for Count Mansfeldt, had evidently been only too happy to take the money from the subsidy collectors, presumably in order to lessen the local burdens.[62]

Until the disastrous error of trying to run counter to prevailing religious opinion in England and Scotland at the same time as imposing disturbing new taxes had been committed, the court retained considerable assets; for other than in the field of religion, its positive goals were few,[63] and with these there might be disagreement in detail but not normally in principle. The county gentry had an equal interest in the preservation of peace and in military security. Nevertheless, the differences should not be dismissed, for 'country' sentiment was a fact of life. Local sources reveal an increasing preoccupation with hostile gossip about Buckingham and the religion of the court in the 1620s;[64] and in face of growing resentment at recurring military charges, Charles was forced to save his face by abandoning the planned general muster of the nation's horse on Hounslow Heath in 1628.[65] 'Country' feeling, a possibly stronger, certainly less sophisticated version of that expressed in parliament, was real and could not be ignored, although its cohesiveness has, probably unwittingly, been exaggerated.[66]

[62] 21 Jac. I, c. 33, s. 1; S. R. Gardiner, *History of England under the Duke of Buckingham and Charles I* (2 vols., 1875), i. 230, 274–5; ibid. ii. 17; Bodl. MS. Firth C4, pp. 112–15, 122–3. One of those most vocal in parliament was Edward Alford, member for Colchester, a part of Essex apparently quite happy to get whatever was going.

[63] On the other hand, such lack of purpose could be yet another sign to the zealot of the iniquity of the government. *The Diary of Walter Yonge, Esq.*, ed. G. Roberts (Camden Soc., 1848), 76.

[64] See, for example, *Diary of Walter Yonge, passim*; *The Diary of John Rous*, ed. M. A. Everett Green (Camden Soc., 1856), 1–31; J. S. Morrill, 'William Davenport and the "Silent Majority" of Early Stuart England', *Journal of the Chester Archaeological Society*, lviii (1975), 119–21; and the letters collected in *Court and Times of Charles I*, ed. R. F. Williams (1849).

[65] Boynton, *Elizabethan Militia*, 252–3.

[66] The unwittingness of this tendency, and the need for synthesis, is made clear in the disparity between the admirable provisos of chapter 2 and the analysis and narrative of chapter 4 of Zagorin's *Court and Country*, or in the apparent disjuncture in the statements of Stone cited earlier.

There were, however, novel and disruptive factors which increasingly invested 'country' with firmness, and one of these was, of course, Buckingham. The importance of the Duke here is suggested retrospectively by the evident diminution of political tension soon after his death, which ought to be attributed at least in part to it and not just to the easing of strains which came with peace and the cessation of parliaments. Lord Treasurer Weston appears to have thought that the removal of the Duke must bring an alteration in, and a greater political responsibility to, the role of courtiers, for he commented, 'It is said at Court there is none now to impute our Faults unto; I say the like . . . "[67] The last years of Buckingham's dominance indicate why his absence should have had such a large impact. Not only did his domination of the court drive frustrated courtiers into unprecedented activity in parliament: a parallel development occurred elsewhere and this was perhaps just as ominous. The Duke's grasp on central politics caused his opponents to move outside the conventional channels, but a distortion of the normal relationships at the centre must, if there is a connection with the localities, have similar effects there. It has been argued that right-thinking gentry did not normally take the dangerous step of expressing publicly forcible disagreement with current trends, but the hegemony of Buckingham witnessed disturbing developments as the normal functioning of local politics was often disrupted and ousted patrons at court were found to be powerless to redress the balance. Wentworth's response to Savile's riding on Buckingham's coat-tails into the Yorkshire *custos*-ship in 1626 has been noted: a vindicatory speech to the assizes was not proper, but then, there was clearly no hope of aid from the court. Far more ominous were events in Somerset, where a near-treasonous address to the Grand Jury by Hugh Pyne in 1626 about the evils of Buckingham and the foolishness of Charles seems to have been related to a challenge to Pyne's local position engineered by the Duke and, presumably, the inability of Pembroke to protect him.[68] The rule of Buckingham saw national politics taken outside Whitehall and Westminster

---

[67] *Strafforde's Letters*, i. 47.
[68] See above, p. 113; P.R.O. S.P. 16/36/46: see also Nicholas's endorsement of the letter revealing his interpretation of what was happening.

and being aired in the country. At a time when the financial exigencies of war were making the Westminster stage rather more important this was most unfortunate, for a wider audience was being appealed to and informed of the iniquities of the court when the political role of that audience was anyway expanding.

War required taxes, and taxes had to be approved. The constitutional maxim that consent must be accorded to all grants of tax was not an empty principle, and there is abundant evidence of subsidy grants occasioning consultation between members of the Commons and their constituencies in this period. Such exercises in addressing a larger community were not limited to parliamentary subsidies, but seem to have extended to all forms of exaction. Dr. Hassell Smith discussed the arguments taking place at quarter sessions over purveyancing in Elizabethan Norfolk, although he seems to have been unable to adduce evidence for the *public* broadcasting of those conferences. But at the end of our period, the Essex Grand Jury repeatedly presented the alleged increasing excesses of purveyancing as a grievance.[69] More important than the activities of the Board of Green Cloth were Charles's military demands of the 1620s, which led grand juries across the country to discuss and present those increasingly heavy burdens as oppressions.[70] It appears that most forms of levy led to some sort of consultation between the local governors and at least some of the governed: when faced with a novel demand for Ship-Money in 1627 the Essex magistrates told the Privy Council that, as considerations of time had not allowed 'our usuall proceedinges in the like Cases, which hath bee[n] purposlie to assemble the Countie together to receive theire resolutions, wee have ... Communicated your Lordshipps Letters with the Grand Jurie beinge the representative body of this Countie and drawne together from all partes thereof.' The Grand Jury replied that, having 'Considered thereof amongst our selves, as alsoe with all the Pettie Juries of this sessions And many other Freeholders warned to appear for the whole Countie', they had concluded that the county could not pay.[71]

[69] Hirst, *Representative of the People*, 166–77; Hassell Smith, *County and Court*, 277–332, 335; Bodl. MS. Firth C4, pp. 520–1, 523, 539, 577–8.

[70] Boynton, *Elizabethan Militia*, 290–1; *Hertford's Lieutenancy Papers*, 177; Barnes, *Somerset 1625–1640*, 70; Bodl. MS. Firth C4, pp. 415, 432, 434.

[71] Bodl. MS. Firth C4, pp. 323–4.

The magistrates' message was that a wider consultation than this was usual on all occasions of novel levy—and such occasions were multiplying in the 1620s. The common people were being told in a public place by those above them that they had legitimate grounds for discontent and protest.

The pressure of public opinion on the local governors was clearly genuine. Sir Edward Montague, who presented enclosure and conversion in parliament in 1604 as one of the county's grievances 'enjoined' on him by 'the cry of the country', was unlikely to have been merely rhetorical in his claim, for he himself and many of his friends were enclosers;[72] the Deputy-Lieutenants of Essex in 1627 were forced to raise money on their own credits for the troops, for they dared not make any new demands of the county, and by the next year they, supposedly the servants of the crown and not of the county as were parliament men, were also giving an account and justification of their doings to the country.[73]

It was thus unfortunate for the court that at a time when public opinion was becoming 'distasted' by rumours of Buckingham and religious change, financial problems springing from war-induced military activity should create the occasions (as at the more frequent parliamentary elections) and the need (to obtain new levies) for the local governors to consult that opinion. While the prominent parliamentary gentry might be sophisticated or even sophistical in their relations to court and 'country', their lesser neighbours were more simple. The ambivalence of the former continued throughout the decade, but by the middle years dangerously skewed perceptions of the court were becoming evident in the country. The court clearly was not as degenerate, irresponsible, or proCatholic as the rumours collected by diarists like Yonge or Rous, or the newsletter-writers, held, but that was not wholly the point.[74] Such prejudices perforce exerted novel and disruptive pressures on the likes of Wentworth, Phelips, or Coke when their holders came to troop through the division lobbies, to vote at the hustings, or to respond to the demands of the local governors.

---

[72] *H.M.C. Montagu of Beaulieu*, 42, 85; *H.M.C. Buccleuch MSS.* iii. 76–7; I am grateful to Conrad Russell and Ms Julie Lansdown for this information.

[73] Bodl. MS. Firth C4, pp. 332, 447; for parliament men, see Hirst, *Representative of the People*, 157–88.

[74] See above, p. 132, n. 64.

Electoral reactions against courtiers in early Stuart England are too common to be enumerated. But something of a shift seems to have occurred in the first three decades. Initially, rejection of courtiers seems to have owed a great deal to their inaccessibility, to the fact that they were not local men, whereas in the course of the 1620s more ominous signs appeared. A local politician increasingly had to keep his distance from the attractions of the court lest his local standing should suffer amongst his neighbours. The degree to which this was a subject of matter-of-fact acceptance is revealed by Sir Robert Phelips's evident intention of complaining to *the Privy Council* in 1628 that his local rival, Poulett, had smeared him in 1624 as one who had 'turned Courtyer', 'uppon designe to withdrawe the good opinion of the country from me'; the corporation of Bury St. Edmunds asserted with reference to the county election of 1626 that 'in Generall they wolde giue no voise to any Cortier espetialy at this time of all others'. The defeat of Sir Edwin Sandys in Kent in 1626 gives point to this.[75] If a man wanted electoral accolades, he had to follow an anti-court path, and while the political principals might not be anti-court, an increasingly important element in their world was becoming so.

But as we have seen, there were dangers in going too far in that direction. The essential circularity, or at least the real interconnections, of the relationship between court and country are seen here. Favour at court increased a man's standing (as evidenced by Wentworth's concern about the prospects of the newly elevated Savile in 1628), too much favour could wreck it; for electoral success a man ought to tend against the court, but an ingredient in favour at court was electoral success as evidence of local standing. A delicate sense of balance might be needed for political survival. Simple labelling of 'court' and 'country' thus seems insufficient in an analysis of the breakdown of the early Stuart polity. Historians of the early eighteenth century tend to describe political alignments almost in terms of boxing the compass: and when feuds like that of Wentworth and Savile cut across apparent political assumptions, with both sides making approaches to Buckingham and both sides appealing to anti-court prejudice in the county, it does not seem that

[75] Hirst, op. cit. 137–53, 174, 180; E. Farnham, 'The Somerset Election of 1614', *E.H.R.* xlvi (1931), 599 n. 5.

navigation of some areas of the early seventeenth-century
terrain was much more straightforward.[76] But as the court
became more and more distorted, at first through the agency
of Buckingham and subsequently with Charles's gratification of
his conscience at the expense of political good sense, and as
recurring elections and fiscal novelties allowed the voice of the
country more expression, the proper bonds between court and
country began to break. Members of the Commons might not
want to set themselves intransigently against subsidizing the
court, but they might have to answer for it to an increasingly
aroused country when they went home if they did not. A
recognition that the country included men outside the ranks
of the parliamentary gentry helps to explain some of the
careers of the latter, as does a recognition that the court
included men with minds of their own as well as the creatures
of Buckingham.

[76] That Yorkshire was not alone in such peculiarities can be seen in the confused
Northamptonshire election of 1626, where Sir Lewis Watson and the Fanes, both with
ties to Buckingham, were very much at odds—like the rest of the county gentry.
J. K. Gruenfelder, 'The Parliamentary Election in Northamptonshire, 1626', *Northamptonshire Past and Present*, iv (1968), 159, 162.

V. Foreign Policy and the Parliaments of 1621 and 1624

S. L. ADAMS

FEW STUDENTS of Stuart History would deny the concern of members of parliament in the 1620s with the foreign policy of the realm. In 1621 and 1624 few M.P.s were not aware that parliament had been summoned specifically because the foreign policy of James I had collapsed. Profound issues of ideology and politics were involved; but the actual debates on foreign policy were complex and confusing, both to contemporaries and to future students. Many of the issues of greatest import were not, in fact, debated directly, though they were present in the background. The purpose of this essay is to make some sense of the debates and to expose their central concerns. I also hope to make certain specific points. First, that the debates were not concerned with whether or not England should enter the Thirty Years War, but with the method and purpose of military intervention. Secondly, that James I did not restrain parliament from a foolish crusade, but rather that parliament rejected proposals from the crown that were either militarily, politically, or financially absurd. Thirdly, that in 1624 the Duke of Buckingham did not make an alliance with a parliamentary war-party, but rather that the inspiration for the proposals actually carried in parliament probably emanated from the Earl of Pembroke. The discussion of the parliamentary debates will be left to a concluding section of the essay: in the first two sections I shall examine the wider ideological and political debate over foreign policy in the early 1620s and then the role played by the Duke of Buckingham in the formulation of foreign policy.

I

It is misleading to confine the ideological debate over foreign policy within the context of 'government' or 'court' policy on the one hand and 'opposition' or 'country' on the other, for the debate extended into the Privy Council and councillors were by no means a united body. Nor did James I adopt a clear-cut position. The debate was conducted between men who saw contemporary events as part of a pattern of Protestant apocalyptical history and men who, fearing the revolutionary implications of such an ideology, sought a policy more conducive to the stability of the political and social *status quo*. The debate was an inheritance from the reign of Elizabeth but had become deeply embedded in Jacobean politics, partly as the result of the growth of semi-puritan Protestantism in England and partly through the emergence of a more self-conscious conservatism, inspired by the subversive effects of radical Protestantism in England and on the continent in the late sixteenth century. Labels are always controversial; but at the risk of crudity of argument the first position may be termed 'puritan', the second 'Spanish'.[1] The politics of the Duke of Buckingham were quite distinct as was the foreign policy he pursued between 1623 and 1626, and these, therefore, will be subject to separate consideration.

The implications of the puritan and Spanish policies and their significance to the debate of the 1620s can best be discussed in the context of an analysis of the balance of political forces and the specific issues of foreign policy. It would be impossible to catalogue the political opinions of all M.P.s, but a discussion of the opinions of leading political figures does provide some guide to wider attitudes. The Spanish party of early Stuart politics has long deserved a serious study. The legends of bribery and secret Catholicism connected with the 'Spanish Faction' have tended to obscure much of the significance of support for an alliance with Spain. The Catholic issue may well be a red herring, for the attitude taken to the Roman Church by such important members of the Spanish party as Sir George Calvert, Sir Richard Weston, and Sir Francis Cottington in the early

[1] Since the debate was carried on within an ostensibly Protestant context, to label the first position 'Protestant' would be misleading. Moreover, the growing anti-Calvinist and anti-puritan wing of the Church of England was increasingly unwilling to identify the church with the wider Protestant cause. For a more detailed discussion of this point, see my unpublished D.Phil. thesis, 'The Protestant Cause: Religious alliance with the West European Calvinist Communities as a Political Issue in England, 1585–1630' (Oxford, 1973), 21–3.

1620s is far from clear.[2] The political significance of the Spanish alliance is far more revealing. The House of Habsburg represented social order and monarchical legitimacy and stability in a world threatened by Dutch and presbyterian republicanism.[3] The 'Instructions Additional' given to Sir John Digby on his embassy to Spain in 1617 expressed the hope that an Anglo-Spanish alliance would halt 'a creeping disposition to make popular states and alliances to the disadvantage of monarchy'.[4] While it was not necessary to be a Catholic to support an alliance with Spain, it was impossible to be a puritan. The Spanish policy was also a peace policy, offering the chance to avoid the crippling cost of military support for continental Protestants and possibly a means of curbing the commercial expansion of the Dutch.

The policy of alliance with Spain therefore commended itself to men who wished to construct a stable monarchical government in England. Both James I and Charles I saw it to some degree in their interests. Owing to James's desire to balance faction at his court and the Duke of Buckingham's anti-Spanish policy in the years 1623-8, it was only during the personal rule of Charles I that the Spanish policy became clearly a 'court' policy. But because the puritan members of his court and Council refused ay involvement with the Spanish alliance, James was forced to create what amounted to a separate administration to conduct negotiations with Spain. Between 1614 and 1625 there was a 'Spanish' secretary of State, Sir Thomas Lake, and after 1618 Sir George Calvert. The diplomatists most closely involved in the negotiations with Spain, Sir John Digby, later Earl of Bristol, and Sir Francis Cottington, were Spanish as were the advocates of economical government, Lionel Cranfield, Earl of Middlesex, and Sir Richard Weston.[5] It is also interesting that the two 'keepers of the king's conscience', Lord Chancellor Bacon and Lord Keeper Williams, supported

---

[2] On Cottington, see M. J. Havran, *Caroline Courtier: The Life of Lord Cottington* (1973), 77. On Weston, see M. V. Alexander, *Charles I's Lord Treasurer: Sir Richard Weston, Earl of Portland (1577–1635)* (1975), 29–30.

[3] Cf. J. V. Polischensky, *The Thirty Years War* (1971), 8.

[4] *The Letters and Life of Francis Bacon*, ed. J. Spedding (1861–74), vi. 157–9.

[5] For Cranfield's views, see M. Prestwich, *Cranfield: Politics and Profit under the Early Stuarts* (Oxford, 1966), 425–6.

the Spanish policy while in office.[6] The Earl of Arundel, head of the premier family of the nobility and the obvious leader of a conservative party on the council, also supported the Spanish alliance, but owing to strained relations with Buckingham could not be considered a reliable 'courtier'.

During the final phase of the negotiations over the Spanish marriage between mid-1621 and 1624, the Spanish party was clearly the most influential at court. During 1621 a number of its members were advanced to key positions. In January 1621 the 'puritan' secretary of state, Sir Robert Naunton, was suspended from office and Calvert acted as sole secretary until the appointment of Sir Edward Conway in January 1623. In October Cranfield was appointed Lord Treasurer, Weston Chancellor of the Exchequer, and Cottington secretary to Prince Charles. In 1622 Bristol was sent as ambassador to Madrid to conclude the negotiations, and Weston, Cranfield, Williams, Calvert, and Arundel were appointed to the junta of twelve privy councillors created to conduct foreign relations. The strength of support for this party in the Commons is difficult to compute, owing to the fact that in 1621 their policy was largely subsumed in that of the crown, while in 1624 they were under steady attack from the Duke of Buckingham. Thomas Wentworth, the future Earl of Strafford and a good friend of Calvert's, provides a good example of 'backbench' support in 1621 but he did not sit in 1624. Only one M.P. in 1624, Sir George Chaworth, a follower of Arundel, openly opposed rejection of the alliance with Spain.[7]

The puritan party is more diffuse and, since its position at court was steadily declining, less easy to identify among officers of state. It was largely composed of descendants, both lineal

[6] Neither was necessarily committed wholly to the Spanish policy. Bacon was concerned about the failure of the crown to respond to public sympathy for Frederick in October 1620. *Letters and Life of Bacon*, vii. 123–4, Bacon to Buckingham, 18 Oct. 1620. Williams apparently supported the Spanish policy because he believed it to be the king's desire. R. E. Ruigh, *The Parliament of 1624: Politics and Foreign Policy* (Cambridge, Mass., 1971), 33. Williams's views on foreign affairs do not appear to have been of major importance in his appointment as Lord Keeper in July 1621, though Archbishop Abbot's opinions may have eliminated him as a rival candidate. See G. W. Thomas, 'James I, Equity and Lord Keeper John Williams', *E.H.R.* xci (1976), 524.

[7] For Wentworth in 1621, see below, p. 163. For Chaworth's stand in 1624, for which he was expelled the House, see Ruigh, op. cit. 224–5; K. Sharpe, below, pp. 222–3.

and ideological, of the puritan coalition of Elizabeth's reign but during the 1620s discovered a new focus in the cause of James's daughter Elizabeth, Electress Palatine and Queen of Bohemia.[8] At court the leading members were the 3rd Earl of Pembroke and Archbishop Abbot, spiritual heir of Archbishop Grindal. Pembroke's public prestige and personal power were extensive, but the fact that he continued to operate within the court indicates the limits of his political radicalism. There was little secret as to his views. 'Nothing makes him so sad or merry as the success of their [the King and Queen of Bohemia] affaires.'[9] But Pembroke was also aware that James was 'unwilling to be engaged in a warr, if by any way, with his honour, he may avoid it' and thus closely appreciated the limits of acceptable political activity.[10] In the House of Commons the most important of his associates was Sir Benjamin Rudyerd, surveyor of the Court of Wards, who acted as his mouthpiece.[11]

Pembroke also acted as adviser to the Queen of Bohemia on English politics.[12] So did the Queen's girlhood friend Lucy Harington, the Countess of Bedford, a close friend of Pembroke.[13] Since her husband, the 3rd Earl of Bedford, was an

---

[8] During most of the 1620s, the King and Queen of Bohemia were heirs to the throne in the event of Charles's death and their 'party' may have represented a reversionary interest. The importance of their possible succession to the politics of the 1620s is unclear, however.

[9] P.R.O. S.P. 81/18/155, Sir Benjamin Rudyerd to Sir Francis Nethersole (agent with the King and Queen of Bohemia), 27 Sept. 1620.

[10] P.R.O. S.P. 14/110/81, Pembroke to Sir Dudley Carleton (ambassador at The Hague), 24 Sept. 1619.

[11] The closeness of the friendship between Pembroke and Rudyerd may be gauged from the fact that they wrote a volume of poetry together, *Poems written by the ... Earl of Pembroke ... many of which are answered ... by Sir Benjamin Ruddier* (1660). See also Ruigh, op. cit. 178. In his account of the parliament of 1625, Sir John Eliot is quite explicit that Rudyerd was expected to speak on Pembroke's behalf. *An Apology for Socrates and Negotium Posterorum*, ed. A. B. Grosart (2 vols., 1881), i. 69. My interpretation of Rudyerd's role in the Parliament of 1624 differs from that of Conrad Russell, who considers him a 'government spokesman', see C. Russell, 'Parliamentary History in Perspective, 1604–1629', *History*, lxi (1976), 8. For a further discussion of this important point, see below, p. 165.

[12] See, for example, P.R.O. S.P. 14/152/89, Pembroke to Carleton, (?Mar.–Apr.) 1624.

[13] Only one letter of the correspondence between the Countess of Bedford and the Queen of Bohemia has survived, *H.M.C. Supplementary Report on the Manuscripts of the Duke of Hamilton*, 9, Elizabeth to the Countess of Bedford, 3/12 Mar. 1620. The content is revealing. See also *The Private Letters of Lady Jane Cornwallis*, ed. Lord Braybrooke (1842), 41–3, Countess of Bedford to Lady Cornwallis, 12 July 1621 (misdated 1616).

invalid, she controlled the Russell interest, probably in Pembroke's favour.[14] Her sister was married to Arthur Chichester, Lord Belfast, whose father Sir John Chichester had been an intimate of the 2nd Earl of Bedford. Belfast was appointed to the Privy Council in 1622. Rudyerd was married to one of her cousins. She and Pembroke also cultivated the leading Scottish peers at the English court, the Duke of Lennox and the Marquess of Hamilton. The two Scots, Pembroke, and Belfast sat on the junta for foreign affairs and voted as a group in the important vote on the manner of rejecting the Spanish treaties in January 1624. In the autumn of 1624 Sir George Goring warned Buckingham of the 'ill councils of Bedford House'.[15] After the death of Hamilton and Belfast at the beginning of 1625, the Countess of Bedford wrote to a friend that Pembroke was the 'only honest hearted man imployed [at court] that I know now left to God and his cuntrie'.[16]

Two other political factions which supported the puritan policy to a greater or lesser degree during the 1620s can be identified, though neither was as influential as the group around Pembroke and the Countess of Bedford. One was led by the 3rd Earl of Southampton and included the 3rd Earl of Essex, Edmund, Lord Sheffield (later Earl of Mulgrave), Lord Cavendish, Sir Edwin Sandys, Sir Thomas Roe, the Danvers brothers, and possibly Sir Robert Phelips. To a certain degree this group still had associations with the 2nd Earl of Essex and definitely acquired a reputation for radical politics. Both Southampton and Sandys were accused at various times of republican sympathies.[17] Southampton had his own contacts with the King and Queen of Bohemia and in 1620 tried to

---

P.R.O. S.P. 14/130/15, 14/140/57, 14/143/63, Countess of Bedford to Carleton, 4 May 1622, 28 Mar. 1623, 24 Apr. 1623.

[14] Pembroke held Bedford's proxy in the Lords in 1621, 1624, and 1625. *L.J.* iii. 3–4, 205, 431.

[15] Brit. Lib. Harl. MS. 1580, fo. 445, Goring to Buckingham, 4 Oct. 1624. For the vote of the junta in January 1624, see below, p. 156.

[16] *Letters of Lady Cornwallis*, 125–31, Countess of Bedford to Lady Cornwallis, 12 Apr. 1625.

[17] For Southampton's 'popularity', see *C.S.P. Venet. 1619–21*, 275 and H. G. R. Reade, *Sidelights on the Thirty Years War* (3 vols., 1924), i. 284, quoting the Tuscan ambassador, Gabaleone. In January 1624 Sir Nathaniel Rich accused Sandys of trying to create a Brownist republic in Virginia. *H.M.C. VIIIth Report*, Part II (Manuscripts of the Duke of Manchester), 45.

raise a volunteer force on their behalf.[18] He and his friends were noticeably outspoken during the first session of 1621 and as a result he and Sandys were imprisoned and Roe sent into virtual exile as ambassador to Constantinople.[19] In 1624 their politics were less clear. There were some associations with Pembroke, who with Hamilton prevented Sandys from being sent to Ireland at the beginning of the session, and many members of the faction joined Pembroke after Southampton's death at the end of 1624.[20] However, during the parliament Southampton, Sandys, and Phelips assisted certain manœuvres of Buckingham's, giving rise to suggestions that they had entered into an alliance with the Duke, though the evidence is not entirely clear.[21]

The second group was composed of East Anglian puritans led by Robert Rich, Earl of Warwick, and his half-brother Sir Nathaniel Rich. During 1624 they were in fact allies of Buckingham and estranged from Southampton and his followers as the result of bitter disputes over control of the Virginia Company. Their alliance with Buckingham has been attributed to the activities of the puritan divine John Preston and their breach with the Duke to the York House Conference of 1626. It is worth noting, therefore, that Sir Nathaniel Rich was still regarded as a partisan of the Duke's in May 1627, while the evidence for Preston's importance is not entirely convincing.[22] The real con-

[18] See 'Protestant Cause', 300–1.

[19] In the examination of Southampton and Sandys after the first session of the Parliament of 1621, the Privy Council was particularly interested in their contacts with the King and Queen of Bohemia. See T. Tyrwhitt, *Proceedings and Debates of the House of Commons in 1620 and 1621* (2 vols., Oxford, 1766), ii., Appendix; Brit. Lib. Harl. MS. 389, fo. 105.

[20] *C.S.P. Venet. 1623–5*, 419–20. The number of Southampton's followers who were associated with Pembroke in 1625 and 1626 is revealing. Dr. Samuel Turner, who sat for Pembroke's borough of Shaftesbury and proposed the articles of impeachment against Buckingham in 1626, had extensive contacts with the Wriotheslevs in 1623 and 1624. Sheffield gave his proxy to Pembroke in 1625. The 5th Earl of Huntingdon gave his proxy to Southampton in 1624 and to Pembroke in 1625 and 1626. Sir Edwin Sandys may have owed his seat at Penryn in 1625 and 1626 to the Earl, who was making extensive use of his electoral influence as Lord Warden of the Stannaries in those years. See P.R.O. S.P. 16/523/77, the famous letter of Sir James Bagg to Buckingham of *c.* 10 Mar. 1626 and 'Protestant Cause', 382–3.

[21] See below, p. 166.

[22] For Nathaniel Rich and Buckingham, see Bodl. Tanner MS. 72, fo. 198, William Bedell to Samuel Ward, 18 May 1627. Preston's role in the alliance between Buckingham, the Riches, and other puritans is discussed in J. F. Maclear, 'Puritan Relations

tact between Warwick and Buckingham may well have been his
brother Henry Rich, Viscount Kensington (later Earl of
Holland), who played a key role in Buckingham's negotiations
with France in 1624.[23] It is not irrelevant that in December
1624 Warwick was considered a supporter of the French
alliance.[24]

The proportion of M.P.s included in these groups and factions cannot be fully computed, but there can be little doubt
that they set the tone for both parliaments and that there was
little dissent from the general lines of policy they proposed. For
this reason the 'puritan' policy may be considered 'parliamentary' without implying a necessary commitment to further
reform of the church. This policy was based ultimately on the
Protestant apocalyptical conception of history, within which
the Bohemian revolution of 1618 and the acceptance of the
Bohemian crown by the Elector Palatine were seen as the great
revolution that would usher in the final struggle between the
godly and the papal Antichrist. 'The apparent way His pro-
vidence hath opened to the ruine of the papacy,' commented
Sir Edward Herbert, the future Lord Herbert of Cherbury,
ambassador in Paris in 1619.[25] Frederick's apocalyptical mission figured prominently in his propaganda.[26] The response of
Archbishop Abbot to the news of Frederick's acceptance of the

with Buckingham', *Huntington Library Quarterly*, xxi (1958), 113–14 and C. Thompson,
'Origins of the Parliamentary Middle Group, 1625–1629', *T.R.H.S.* 5th ser. xxii (1972),
74–5. Much of the argument is derived from the evidence of the apologetical biographies of Williams (J. Hackett, *Scrinia Reserata* (1693), 202–6) and William Laud (P.
Heylen, *Cyprianus Anglicus* (1668), 118–19). Since both biographers saw their heroes as
the victims of puritan conspiracies, the prominence they assign to Preston should not
be accepted uncritically.

[23] For Kensington's role in the French negotiations, see below, p. 157.

[24] *C.S.P. Venet. 1623–5*, 419–20.

[25] *Letters and Documents illustrating the Relations between England and Germany . . . 1618–
1620*, ed. S. R. Gardiner, Camden Soc. xcviii (1868), 12–13, Herbert to Sir Robert
Naunton, 9 Sept. 1619. It is unfortunate that the growing body of research into
apocalypticism and millenarian thought in seventeenth-century England has tended to
emphasize apocalyptical thought as a response to the disasters suffered by the Protestant
cause in the Thirty Years War, rather than to examine the role of apocalypticism in the
outbreak of the war. See, for example, C. Hill, *Antichrist in Seventeenth-century England*
(Oxford, 1971), 20 and C. Webster, *The Great Instauration* (1975), 1. In *The Rosicrucian
Enlightenment* (1972), chs 2 and 4, F. A. Yates discusses some aspects of Frederick's
millenarian appeal.

[26] See, in particular, the works of John Harrison: *A Short Relation of the Departure of
the Most High and Mighty Prince Frederick* (Dort, 1619) and the dedication of *The Messiah
Already Come* (Amsterdam, 1620).

Bohemian crown provides an eloquent example of this interpretation of events.

> And methinks I do in this, and in that of Hungary, foresee the work of God, that by piece and piece, the Kings of the Earth that gave their power unto the Beast (all the work of God must be fulfilled) shall now tear the whore, and make her desolate, as St. John in his revelation hath foretold . . . Our striking will comfort the Bohemians, will honour the Palsgrave, will strengthen the Union, will bring on the States of the Low Countries, will stir up the king of Denmark, and will move his [Frederick's] two uncles the prince of Orange and the Duke of Bouillon, together with Tremouille (a rich prince in France) to cast in their shares; and Hungary I hope (being in that same cause) will run the same fortune.[27]

England together with all Protestant countries had a duty to support Frederick in his godly work. Moreover, since the 'cause of religion' was involved, engagement in the struggle was inevitable and neutrality could only be purchased at the price of apostasy.[28] In the parliamentary context, however, the belief in a predestined struggle inspired an important spirit of compromise, especially in 1624. So long as the king was engaged in the war convincingly, the precise terms of the engagement did not matter. This spirit underlay the willingness of parliament to drop the declaration that the war was one of religion from the subsidy bill in 1624 in deference to the king's wishes. The reasoning behind the gesture was well expressed by the Earl of Pembroke. It did not matter that the war 'be styled rather a particular war for the kingdom of Bohemia, then a war for religion . . . I know in consequence they can not be severed'.[29]

In neither parliament were the ideological issues debated openly, though a debate might have occurred if the impeachment of Richard Montague, who denied the pope was Anti-

---

[27] Bodl. Tanner MS. 74, fos. 221–2, Abbot to Sir Robert Naunton, 12 Sept. 1619.

[28] In his essay 'The Fast Sermons of the Long Parliament', H. R. Trevor-Roper comments on the use of the 'Curse of Meroz' (Judges 5: 23) by Civil War preachers as an example of divine displeasure at neutrality. *Religion, the Reformation and Social Change* (1967), 307–8. For an example of the employment of this text in the context of support for the Protestant cause in the Thirty Years War, see T. Gataker, *A Sparke toward the kindling of Sorrow for Sion* (1621), 36.

[29] P.R.O. S.P. 14/176/34, Pembroke to Carleton, 9 Dec. 1624. Cf. ibid. 14/164/11, George Carleton, Bishop of Chichester, to Carleton, ? May 1624: 'These warres will turn from the quarrell betweene the Emperor and the Palsgrave, to the quarrell for religion . . .'

christ in the *Appello Caesarem*, had gone forward in 1625.[30]
James I himself had no desire to precipitate such a debate
because his own opinions were in flux. In earlier years he had
been outspoken on the subject of the papal Antichrist, though
his most celebrated statement, in the *Premonition to all Most
Mighty Monarchs* of 1609, was not perhaps as unequivocal as it
appeared at first.[31] By the 1620s, though he never publicly
denied Calvinist orthodoxy, James became increasingly disenchanted with the idea of an apocalyptical struggle and never
accepted that Frederick's actions in Bohemia were part of the
divine plan.[32] The king's equivocation caused great confusion
in England as well as on the continent, for it was impossible to
believe that he could remain neutral. His failure to act was attributed for a time to a secret grand design, but then more generally to a deliberate campaign of deception by Spain, master-
minded by the Conde de Gondomar.[33] By 1624 the belief in 'Spanish practice' had become so widespread that when the Duke of
Buckingham gave his relation of Spanish duplicity during the
negotiations in Madrid he was preaching to the converted.

In the absence of a debate over the deeper ideological issues,
the most controversial subjects of debate were policy toward
Spain and the United Provinces and the closely related issue of
the strategy to be employed in the defence or recovery of the
Palatinate. The Conde de Gondomar and the Spanish party had
carefully fostered James's belief that Philip III of Spain did not
share the pretensions of the papacy and that an Anglo-Spanish
entente for the preservation of the *status quo* from religious ex-

---

[30] *Appello Caesarem* (1625), 141–3. See also Hill, *Antichrist*, 33–6.

[31] The key passage in the *Premonition* can be found in *The Works of the Most High
and Mighty Prince James*, ed. C. H. McIlwain (Cambridge, Mass., 1918), 149–50. At
the York House Conference in 1626, Richard Montague claimed that this passage did
not prove that James believed in the papal Antichrist. See J. Cosin, 'The Summe and
Substance of the Conference', *The Works of . . . John Cosin, Lord Bishop of Durham*, ed.
J. Sansom (5 vols., Oxford, 1843–55), iii. 80–1.

[32] There are at least two examples of James's denying that he considered the pope
Antichrist during the Spanish Marriage negotiations. C. H. Carter, *The Secret Diplomacy
of the Habsburgs 1598–1625* (New York, 1964), 243–4, Gondomar to Philip III, 6/16
Feb. 1621; and Bodl. Tanner MS. 73, fo. 297, James to Charles and Buckingham,
25 Mar. 1623.

[33] The pamphlet attack on Gondomar as deceiver of the king was led by Thomas
Scott. See *Vox Populi* (1620) and *The Second Parte of Vox Populi* (1624) and S. L. Adams,
'Captain Thomas Gainsford, the "Vox Spiritus" and the *Vox Populi*', *B.I.H.R.* xlix
(1976), 143.

tremists of all kinds was possible. The policy of the crown was therefore based on two postulates: that the continental wars were separate 'quarrels' and not part of a general ideological struggle, and that the King of Spain could be persuaded to remain neutral in the dispute between Frederick and the Emperor. Despite the blow this policy received through the invasion of the Palatinate by the army of Flanders in the autumn of 1620, it was still expounded by Lord Digby in his relation to the conference of Lords and Commons at the beginning of the second session of the Parliament of 1621, the only full-scale exposition of the foreign policy of the crown given in either parliament.[34]

Relations with the United Provinces were as important as relations with Spain. A close alliance with the United Provinces was essential if England was to partake in the defence of the Protestant cause on the continent. Effective assistance to Frederick was impossible without it. Such an alliance would, however, involve England in the revived war between Spain and the Netherlands after the Truce of Antwerp expired in April 1621. The forthcoming expiration of the Truce had an important effect on reactions to the Bohemian crisis of 1619–20, for the Bohemian Revolution was to a large degree the product of the cold war between Spain and the Netherlands during the Truce. Both the Dutch government and the Spanish saw Frederick's cause and the Dutch cause as identical.[35]

The main target of Spanish diplomacy in England was therefore the Dutch, and Gondomar achieved considerable success in his efforts to inhibit English assistance to the Netherlands owing to James's unhappiness with both the leading parties in Dutch politics. James never lost his distaste for Dutch republicanism and had therefore supported the Stadtholder Maurice against Oldenbarneveldt; but on the other hand Maurice was too closely involved with schemes to advance the Protestant cause. Like John Chamberlain, James probably believed that Frederick's Bohemian adventure was a plot instigated by

[34] See below, p. 162.
[35] The disagreement between the Archduke Albert in the Netherlands and the Madrid government over the decision to renew the war in the Netherlands was over timing rather than aims. Albert wished to delay war in the Netherlands until victory in Germany was achieved. P. Brightwell, 'The Spanish System and the Twelve Years Truce', *E.H.R.* lxxxix (1974), 286.

Maurice and others 'to drawe in our king, *nolens volens*'.[36] James did not intend to be drawn into the Hispano-Dutch war as the result of Frederick's 'rashness'. Frederick's legitimate rights in the Palatinate were to be protected but not at the expense of good Anglo-Spanish relations. James hoped that he would receive the assistance of Spanish diplomacy in negotiating a surrender of Frederick's pretensions in Bohemia in exchange for a recognition of his rights as Elector Palatine. But he never ruled out the defence, or in 1624 restoration, of Frederick's rights by force.

Since a military commitment to the Palatinate was never denied, the main subject of debate between crown and parliament was the strategy to be pursued. Here both king and a consensus of parliament had distinct opinions, while a third option was promoted (though not in parliament) by the Duke of Buckingham in 1624. The king's strategy was concerned solely with the defence or recovery of the Palatinate. The purpose of parliament was to provide sufficient funds to enable troops to be sent there, or, it was hoped, for the threat alone to add weight to James's diplomacy. This strategy was, however, immensely expensive and fraught with military and political difficulty. On 13 January 1621 James appointed a council of war of experienced military and naval officers and instructed them to compute the size and expense of an army strong enough to defend the Palatinate. The council reported a month later that 25,000 foot and 5,000 horse would be necessary and would cost £258,370 to raise and equip and £912,768 yearly to maintain.[37] One million pounds annually was considered during most of the 1620s to be the cost of an adequate expedition to the Palatinate.[38] Equally controversial were the

---

[36] *The Letters of John Chamberlain*, ed. N. E. McClure (Philadelphia, 1939), ii. 262–4, Chamberlain to Carleton, 11 Sept. 1619.

[37] P.R.O. S.P. 14/119/21 and 14/119/93.

[38] There is some confusion over the significance of this figure. S. J. Houston, *James I* (1975), 78 refers to £900,000 p.a. as being the cost of a 'war of intervention' or a 'protestant crusade'. In 'Parliament and the King's Finances', in *The Origins of the English Civil War*, ed. C. Russell (1975), 103, Conrad Russell comments, 'For a successful war, something over a million in a year was necessary.' A million pounds a year was solely the cost of an expedition to the Palatinate and did not include any other military or naval expenses. Given the dubious chances of such an expedition, the unwillingness of the Commons to entertain this level of expenditure becomes more understandable.

military and political constraints on the expedition. It would be composed of largely untrained troops and have to operate deep in Germany without a firm base or secure lines of communication. It would also have to operate independently of the Dutch. Nor was it to be used against Spanish troops, which left its role in those parts of the Palatinate occupied by the Army of Flanders unresolved.

The dubious nature of the proposed military operation and the king's refusal to accept that the German war and the Hispano-Dutch war were in any way related made his strategy impossible to accept. If nothing else, it promised immense expenditure for uncertain ends. Yet opponents of the king's strategy did not, as many historians have argued, reject all military intervention on the continent. The desired strategy of parliament was that of the 'war by diversion'. The key to the war by diversion was an alliance with the United Provinces under which an Anglo-Dutch army would attack the Spanish Netherlands while Anglo-Dutch naval forces attacked Spanish commerce. Such a strategy, it was hoped, would force Spain on to the defensive and force Spinola to evacuate the Palatinate and cease assisting the Imperial forces in order to defend the king of Spain's own possessions. The withdrawal of Spinola would give Frederick the opportunity to rally his allies in Germany. At a later stage the Anglo-Dutch army could, if successful in the Netherlands, advance up the Rhine. The obvious merits of this strategy were its appreciation that war must be waged from positions of strength, regardless of its divine inspiration. 'The eternal God is in these days pleased to worke more by ordinary and aparent means than by miracles,' wrote Ferdinando, Lord Fairfax, in his tract advocating the diversionary war, 'The Highway to Heidelberg' of 1622.[39] Secondly the strategy was the one desired by England's probable allies. Both Maurice of Nassau and Frederick urged James to follow this course.[40] The officers of the council of war were also known to favour it.[41]

[39] Brit. Lib. Add. MS. 28326, fo. 20. For Fairfax's views on strategy, see fos. 18–19, 23.
[40] See Brit. Lib. Egerton MS. 2593, fos. 262–3, Frederick to Achatius von Dohna (his ambassador in England), 12/22 Nov. 1620; P.R.O. S.P. 84/93/143–4, Carleton to Buckingham, 5 Dec. 1619.
[41] *C.S.P. Venet. 1619–21*, 562–3.

The parliamentary debates of 1624 were concerned with a further important aspect of military strategy. Since the war was expected to be on a major scale, suitable preparation was vital. The disinterest of James in 1621 in any form of military preparation made his strategy doubly suspect. In 'A discourse by way of a dialogue betweene a counsellour of state and a countrey gentleman who served in the last assembly of the estates in the year 1621', a tract written after the return of Charles from Spain in 1623, both the councillor and the gentleman agreed that adequate preparation should be the first concern of the king.[42] The 'Four Propositions' specifying the purposes of the subsidy attached to the subsidy bill of 1624 all dealt with vital preparations.[43] The proposals, as I shall argue below, were not intended as the sum total of English military commitment to a continental war but as the essential first step. The seriousness of the king and Council in implementing these measures would provide evidence of their commitment to the cause.

II

Neither James I nor the advocates of the puritan strategy found it easy to fit France into their assessments of the political and military situation.[44] The reason lay in the constantly shifting balance of power at the French court and the erratic and uncertain foreign policy pursued by the French government between the death of Henri IV and Cardinal Richelieu's victory over his domestic opponents in the 'Day of the Dupes' in 1630. On the outbreak of the Thirty Years War it was unclear whether Louis XIII would follow the traditional anti-Habsburg policy of the French royal house or ally with the Habsburgs in defence of the Catholic Church—the policy of the *dévots*. Under the influence of the favourite Luynes in the years 1619–21, French policy was confessional in tone, though limited to an attempt to exploit the involvement of the Protestant world in Germany in order to crush the remnants of Huguenot political autonomy. In 1622–4 the ministry of La Vieuville, alarmed by Habsburg success in Germany, returned to a more anti-Habsburg policy. Relations with England were compli-

[42] Somerset Record Office Phelips MSS., DD/PH/227/16, fos. 2ʳ–3. I owe this reference to the kindness of Dr. Sharpe.

[43] See below, pp. 165, 168.

[44] See, for example, Fairfax, 'Highway', fos. 20ʳ–21.

cated by the problem of the Huguenots. The French government believed the Huguenots to be largely dependent on
foreign Protestant support and in December 1620 offered
James I assistance in Germany in return for a public disavowal
of the Huguenots. James could not make such a gesture, but
on the other hand did not wish to jeopardize the chances
of the support of Louis XIII in Germany by granting the
Huguenots the military assistance they requested in 1621 and
1622.[45] Ideally, James would have liked Louis XIII to join him
and Philip III in a *Dreikönigsbund* to preserve the *status quo* in
Europe; but if the French were not prepared to assist in his
negotiations over the Palatinate, they were irrelevant, though
he was unhappy about military intervention in Germany
without French support.

The advocates of the puritan policy saw the Huguenot cause
as part of the general Protestant cause and did not contemplate
sacrificing the Huguenots as the price of French assistance.[46]
In 1619 Archbishop Abbot expected that the Huguenot leadership would come to Frederick's aid, and in March 1620
Pembroke saw the threat of a Huguenot rising as sufficient to
deter Louis XIII from assisting the Habsburgs.[47] While there
was a good deal of exaggeration of Huguenot capabilities and
wishful thinking in these calculations, the course of the French
civil wars of 1620–2 suggested that Louis XIII would not be
able to play a major role in Europe one way or the other.

An alliance with France against the Habsburgs only became
a major concern of English foreign policy after the Duke of
Buckingham's return from Spain in the autumn of 1623. During
the next three years the alliance was the focus of his foreign
policy. This policy was not based on an accurate assessment of

[45] On James's policy toward the Huguenots, see S. L. Adams, 'The Road to La
Rochelle: English foreign policy and the Huguenots, 1610 to 1629', *Proceedings of the
Huguenot Society of London*, xxii (1975), 421–3. V. -L. Tapié, *France in the Age of Louis XIII
and Richelieu* (1974), 111–30, gives a good summary of French policy in the period
1620–4. C. Russell's statement that, since the '"protestant" side was largely inspired
by the French, under Cardinal Richelieu', M.P.s were mistaken in seeing the Thirty
Years War as an ideological struggle is not relevant to the early 1620s. Russell,
'Parliament and the King's Finances', *Origins of The English Civil War*, 101.

[46] Berkshire Record Office Trumbull MSS., Alphabetical Series, xvi, art. 44,
Carleton to Sir William Trumbull (agent in Brussels), 6 Nov. 1620.

[47] See Abbot's letter to Naunton, 12 Sept. 1619, quoted above, p. 147. P.R.O. 30,
53/10/66, Pembroke to Sir Edward Herbert, 20 Mar. 1620.

French intentions and abilities, nor on ideological considerations; but rather it emerged as an answer to the political difficulties in which Buckingham found himself after the return from Spain. This new foreign policy provides the key to Buckingham's attitude to the Parliament of 1624 and its evolution demands careful examination.

Despite his growing influence over patronage in the years prior to 1624, Buckingham had little real influence over the balance of power in James's Council. Only in the winter of 1624–5, when tension with both the Spanish party and Pembroke made it necessary to pack the court with reliable men, did he begin to create a party of men whose primary political loyalty was to him alone. It was widely known, for example, that the appointment of Sir George Calvert as secretary of state in 1618 was not Buckingham's work.[48] During the years 1619–22 his only close ally on the Council was James Hay, Viscount Doncaster and Earl of Carlisle, and the first politically significant appointments he made in the early 1620s were those of Sir Edward Conway and Viscount Grandison to the Council in the summer of 1622 and the appointment of Conway as secretary of state in January 1623.[49] Of the members of the junta for foreign affairs, he could count on the loyalty of only Carlisle and Conway. There is no evidence that Buckingham had any formed opinions on the crisis in Europe. The war offered him the opportunity to play a more ambitious and virile role than that of royal favourite, but Gondomar and the Spanish party were prepared to bid highly for his support. During the first half of 1620, owing largely to the influence of Carlisle, Buckingham assisted the King and Queen of Bohemia, but turned against them in the summer as the result of a relatively minor, though interesting, dispute over patronage.[50] During the Parliament of 1621 Buckingham tended to support the king's policy, with the single exception of the controversial

---

[48] P.R.O. S.P. 14/105/112, Sir Edward Harwood to Carleton, 16 Feb. 1619.

[49] Sir Robert Naunton, the puritan secretary suspended in January 1620, had been advanced by Buckingham, but that was before the Bohemian crisis.

[50] The dispute concerned the appointment of a commander for the English troops sent to the Palatinate after Southampton had been refused permission to go. Buckingham claimed that under a prior agreement the command should go to his client Sir Edward Cecil; the King and Queen of Bohemia wanted, and obtained, Sir Horace Vere. See 'Protestant Cause', 300–2.

motion proposed by his follower Sir George Goring in the Commons on 29 November.[51] There is evidence that he was growing restive with the Spanish negotiations during 1622, and the promotion of Conway, a puritan and partisan of the Dutch, was seen as a sign that Buckingham was tending more towards a war policy.[52] It is possible that the voyage to Spain was the product of his frustrations and his desire to see the negotiations with Spain concluded quickly and clearly.

The difficulties Buckingham faced after deciding to repudiate the Spanish alliance on his return to England in the autumn of 1623 have not, perhaps, been fully appreciated. He had to woo and cajole James away from a policy on which he had set his heart. He had to isolate and disarm the Spanish party, who could, with information supplied by Bristol, argue that he had ruined the negotiations by his impulsive actions in Madrid.[53] He had to prevent Gondomar from returning to England and winning James back to negotiation. Hostilities with Spain and a new bride for Charles were, therefore, essential; only when war was declared and Charles married would he be really safe. Moreover, the break with Spain had to be made with speed; if he lost the initiative his enemies might be given the opportunity to rally.[54]

The need for a speedy resolution to his difficulties governed Buckingham's attitude to parliament. Parliament was important in his calculations because without a parliamentary grant the war policy would lack credibility. But parliament must be prevented from frightening James with its demands or from setting out a course of foreign policy which the king would reject. Buckingham's initial scheme was to create a new foreign policy before parliament met. At the end of 1623 embassies were prepared or were sent to the Netherlands, the King and Queen of Bohemia, Denmark, and Savoy to propose that a grand alliance against the Habsburgs be created and that James be invited to lead it. Here Buckingham met with a set-back, for

---

[51] See below, p. 163.

[52] See *C.S.P. Venet. 1621–3*, 370–1.

[53] Brit. Lib. Harl. MS. 1581, fo. 379, Lord Rochford to Buckingham, (? Aug.–Sept.) 1623. *C.S.P. Venet. 1623–5*, 130–1, 167–70.

[54] Cf. Ruigh, op. cit. 40. Buckingham was successful in destroying the influence of the Spanish party in 1624–5. He received the enthusiastic support of Sir Robert Phelips. See *Cabala sive Scrinia Sacra* (1691), 313–14, Phelips to Buckingham, 21 Aug. 1624.

the general response was that James should make a gesture to prove his seriousness before negotiation of the alliance began.[55] The effects of this set-back were twofold: first Buckingham now lacked a foreign policy to present to parliament and, secondly, parliament became more important as the obvious source for a 'gesture of intent'. In January 1624 his efforts to create a policy before parliament met received a second set-back. In order to prevent parliamentary discussion of the Spanish negotiations, which offered an opportunity for an attack on himself as well as the risk of alienating the king, Buckingham proposed in the junta for foreign affairs that the treaties with Spain be repudiated by the Council before parliament met. Of the twelve members, only two, Carlisle and Conway, voted with him. The five members of the Spanish party (Williams, Weston, Middlesex, Arundel, and Calvert) opposed the motion, while Pembroke, Belfast, Hamilton, and Lennox abstained.

The news that Pembroke refused to repudiate the Spanish treaties caused a considerable stir, but he made it clear to the Bohemian and Venetian ambassadors that he wished to see Buckingham questioned in parliament about the negotiations and that he wanted the treaties repudiated in parliament and not beforehand.[56] This manœuvre was crucial to the course of the parliament. It deprived Buckingham of his last chance to create a new foreign policy before parliament met and left him vulnerable to attack. It also suggests that Pembroke had definite measures he wished to see passed in parliament. Nothing is known about later discussions between Buckingham and Pembroke, but the course of the debate on foreign policy suggests that some form of compromise was reached. Buckingham was not interrogated about the Spanish negotiations, and a detailed series of proposals was introduced in the Commons at the beginning of the debate by Pembroke's spokesman, Sir Benjamin Rudyerd.[57] Buckingham himself, as his actions

---

[55] P.R.O. S.P. 84/115/151–2, Carleton to Buckingham, 18 Dec. 1623; S.P. 84/116/20, Buckingham to Carleton, 9 Jan. 1624; S.P. 84/116/41, Carleton to Conway, 15 Jan. 1624; S.P. 84/116/62, Carleton to Buckingham, 24 Jan. 1624.

[56] *C.S.P. Venet. 1623–5*, 216. *Mémoires et Négotiations de M. de Rusdorff*, ed. E. Cuhn (2 vols., Leipzig, 1789), i. 190, Rusdorff to King of Bohemia, 22 Jan./1 Feb. 1624. *Chamberlain Letters*, ii. 541–4, Chamberlain to Carleton, 31 Jan. 1624. For a different interpretation of the disputes in the junta, see Ruigh, op cit. 39–42.

[57] See below, p. 165.

during the parliament showed, preferred an open grant of supply without strings, but since he could not afford an unsuccessful session, he was prepared ultimately to accept whatever he could get. The course of the negotiations with France reveals that he had no intention of allowing Rudyerd's proposals to inhibit his foreign policy.

To a certain degree the alliance with France was part of the policy of a grand anti-Habsburg alliance, but it was also crucial to the campaign to woo James away from Spain. James did not consider a minor German or Scandinavian princess of sufficient dignity to be a bride for Charles, only a French princess could provide an alternative to Spain. Only with an alliance with France would James contemplate military operations. Buckingham's contacts with the French court originated with Carlisle and informal correspondence was well under way by the beginning of 1624.[58] Buckingham's feelers met with an encouraging response, largely because the French desired to see the threatened Anglo-Spanish *entente* disrupted. The initial negotiations were entrusted to Kensington in February 1624 and he, carried away by a carefully staged reception, reported that there would be little difficulty in making both a marriage and an alliance.[59] While there was little doubt of the desire of the French to prevent the Spanish marriage by a marriage to one of their own princesses, by April 1624 it was becoming obvious that Kensington's optimism about a military alliance was unfounded. Sir Edward Herbert, the resident ambassador, warned that great care must be used in the negotiations because he felt that, in the event of a war between England and the Habsburgs, the French 'would render themselves neuters and in the meantime settle their affairs at home to the sure detriment of those of the Religion'. Carlisle, who had been sent to join Kensington in negotiating the marriage and alliance, was also sceptical.[60] But, since neither success in parliament nor the break with Spain was assured at this point, Buckingham could not

[58] *C.S.P. Venet. 1623–5*, 124. Bodl. Add. MS. D. 111, fo. 434, Roger, duc de Bellegarde [a follower of the duc d'Orléans] to Buckingham, 30 Dec. 1623/9 Jan. 1624.
[59] Brit. Lib. Harl. MS. 1581, fos. 26–7, Kensington to Buckingham, 26 Feb. 1624. P.R.O. S.P. 78/72/50, Kensington to Buckingham, 4 Mar. 1624; S.P. 78/72/52, Kensington to Buckingham, 9 Mar. 1624. Cf. Tapié, op. cit. 147.
[60] P.R.O. 30, 53/6/73, Herbert to James, 13/23 Apr. 1625; P.R.O. S.P. 78/72/89–90, Conway to James, ? Mar. 1624.

afford a set-back to the alliance with France.

To retain the initiative, Buckingham made perhaps his most disastrous error in foreign affairs by employing Ernest, Count von Mansfeldt. Mansfeldt enjoyed a certain reputation as Frederick's general in 1620–2, but since then he had been largely discredited. In 1623 he had been briefly retained by the French, and in April 1624 arrived in England with a scheme for a jointly financed Anglo-French army, operating from French territory, to regain the Palatinate. It would cost James only £40,000.[61] The limited and economical scale of the operation appealed to James, while the apparent French involvement suggested that Mansfeldt's expedition might become the basis for the Anglo-French military alliance. In May Mansfeldt returned to France with an advance of £20,000 as a gesture of English intent.[62] The negotiations over Mansfeldt's expedition continued throughout the summer, only to reach a major set-back in August when La Vieuville was dismissed and replaced by Cardinal Richelieu as chief minister to Louis XIII. Richelieu made it clear from the start that he intended to revise both treaties with England. Carlisle wished to withdraw from the negotiations completely but Buckingham was too committed to the alliance to do so.[63] If the French policy collapsed, he would once again be at the mercy of the Spanish party, and now the money advanced to Mansfeldt had to be justified. Moreover, he was already trying to use Mansfeldt's expedition as the basis for a revival of the Grand Alliance he had tried to create at the end of 1623.[64] To save the alliance he began the steady series of concessions to Richelieu which led to the final débâcle of his French policy in 1625.

The course of the negotiations with France provides a clear guide to Buckingham's attitude to parliament in 1624. He had no intention of making foreign policy in parliament, or even of taking parliamentary opinion into account. While it was

[61] *C.S.P. Venet. 1623–5*, 294, 303; *Négotiations de Rusdorff*, i. 289, Rusdorff to King of Bohemia, 26 Apr./6 May 1624.

[62] P.R.O. S.P. 14/165/67, [Conway] to Attorney-General Coventry, 31 May 1624; *Négotiations de Rusdorff*, i. 287–8, Rusdorff to King of Bohemia, 24 Apr./4 May 1624.

[63] P.R.O. S.P. 78/73/1–3, Carlisle to Buckingham, 6 Aug. 1624; S.P. 78/73/40, Charles to Carlisle, 13 Aug. 1624.

[64] *C.S.P. Venet. 1623–5*, 434–6, 473–4; P.R.O. S.P. 84/120/269, Sir Robert Anstruther [Ambassador in Denmark] to Carleton, 24 Oct. 1624.

fairly widely known in February and March 1624 that approaches were being made to France, the negotiations were kept a close secret and the nature of the treaties not appreciated until 1625–6.[65] The money spent on Mansfeldt's expedition, £62,000 by the end of 1624, was taken from the subsidy in direct violation of the terms of the Subsidy Act.[66] At no time was parliament consulted on the decision to employ Mansfeldt. The Duke's cavalier attitude towards the Subsidy Act can only suggest that he never had any real interest in its terms. It was important that some form of subsidy be passed; but Buckingham had no intention of compromising his freedom of action as a *quid pro quo*.

III.

The debates on foreign policy in both parliaments had many similarities. In both cases the foreign policy of the crown had collapsed. Parliament was summoned in 1621 because James had been unable to prevent Philip III from assisting the Emperor by invading the Palatinate in September 1620. It was summoned in 1624 because Buckingham wished to terminate the negotiations with Spain. Only in the second session of the Parliament of 1621 did the crown have a course of action to propose. During both parliaments the real aim of the crown was to retain as much freedom of manœuvre in foreign policy

[65] P.R.O. S.P. 14/176/16, Dudley Carleton the younger to Carleton, 4 Dec. 1624; *H.M.C. Report on the Manuscripts of the Earl of Mar and Kellie*, ii. 216, Earl of Kellie to Earl of Mar, 15 Dec. 1624. How much Pembroke knew or approved of the French negotiations is an interesting question. He was aware of the need to make the war palatable to James (see P.R.O. S.P. 14/176/34, Pembroke to Carleton, 9 Dec. 1624) and after an interview with Buckingham, Williams, Arundel, Pembroke, and Hamilton early in October 1624, the Venetian ambassador reported that the English were unwilling to enter a war against Spain without a French alliance (*C.S.P. Venet. 1623–5*, 452–3). How much this reflected personal opinions is not clear, for at the same time the ambassador was recording the hostility of both 'Spaniards' and 'puritans' to both the match and the alliance with France (*C.S.P. Venet. 1623–5*, 443–5, 455–6, 473–4). In December Buckingham excluded Pembroke, Hamilton, Arundel, and Weston from the signing of the marriage treaty (*H.M.C. Mar and Kellie MSS.*, loc. cit.). In 1625 Pembroke expressed his scepticism about the alliance to Buckingham openly (Brit. Lib. Harl. MS. 1581, fo. 386, Pembroke to Buckingham, 31 May 1625). During the Parliament of 1626, Pembroke declared that he had never been involved in the initial negotiations in the winter of 1624–5 over the loan of ships for use against La Rochelle (Bodl. Tanner MS. 72, fo. 86).

[66] P.R.O. S.P. 81/31/173, Francis Nethersole to John Woodford [secretary to Carlisle], 22 Nov. 1624; 'Protestant Cause', 360.

as possible, though a grant of supply was necessary to provide English diplomacy with credibility. In 1621 James dissolved parliament rather than make any real concessions to parliamentary opinion. In 1624 he was far more successful in avoiding concessions, on the issue of the declaration of war against Spain, for example, than is often appreciated.[67] The attitudes of M.P.s were also similar. They did not deny the responsibility of king and Council to make foreign policy, nor did they deny the duty of parliament to provide the financial support expected of loyal and patriotic subjects. But in the absence of concrete or realistic proposals, they were unwilling to write a simple blank cheque. In both parliaments the Commons made greater concessions to the crown than they are often credited with, but they were highly suspicious of attempts to manœuvre them into open-ended financial commitments. They were not taking the initiative or trying to challenge the prerogative, but rather were frustrated and unhappy at the failure of the crown to provide leadership in a critical situation.

The king's opening speech to the Parliament of 1621 made it quite clear that despite the set-backs of the previous year the policy of the crown was basically unchanged. James denied that the alliance with Spain posed a threat to the security of the realm or to religion. He accepted no responsibility for Bohemia but reaffirmed a commitment to the Palatinate and requested an immediate supply for its defence. This was estimated at £300,000 by Sir George Calvert on 5 February. James did, however, take the unwise step of invoking the cause of religion in the defence of the Palatinate, 'the cause of religion is involved in it, for they will alter religion where they conquer'. This made it less easy for him to persuade M.P.s later that a war for religion had not occurred.[68]

The king's speech and the question of supply were not debated until 15 February, when reassurance had been given that the proclamation of 24 December 1620, 'Against excess of lavish speech in matters of state', was not intended to abridge parliamentary privilege.[69] There was general agreement in the

---

[67] Cf. Ruigh, op. cit. 385.

[68] For James's speech see *The Commons Debates for 1621* ed. W. Notestein, F. H. Relf, and H. Simpson (7 vols., New Haven, 1935), i. 9–11. For Calvert's, ibid. ii. 19.

[69] P.R.O. S.P. 14/187/207. The proclamation prohibited discussion of the Spanish

House that immediate measures should be taken to defend the Palatinate. Calvert now claimed the cost of an expedition would be £500,000 a year, but was contradicted by Sir Robert Phelips who stated that it would be nearer a million and urged that a conference with the Lords be held to discuss strategy and finance.[70] This suggestion was rejected by Calvert who declared that the crown did not have to discuss strategy with subjects, and moreover that such a discussion was unnecessary since James still intended to negotiate a settlement in the Palatinate. This more or less destroyed the case for a supply and the debate concluded on a suggestion by Sir Edwin Sandys that two subsidies be granted as a gesture of goodwill. Sandys recognized that this sum was 'no proportion' of the expense of defending the Palatinate, but felt that the question should be reopened when the crown put forward more solid proposals. According to the Venetian ambassador, the Commons expressed a strong desire for the diversionary strategy, but the parliamentary diaries record only allusions to it.[71] Further proposals from the crown were not forthcoming and foreign affairs were not debated during the rest of the session. The Commons were, however, greatly concerned when parliament was adjourned on 4 June without a decision having been taken. On the advice of Sir James Perrot, they drew up a declaration that they would finance any military operation James should undertake for the defence of 'the true professors of the same Christian religion professed by the Church of England in foreign parts'. This description was deliberately chosen, so Sir Nathaniel Rich later declared, to include not only the Palatinate, but also Bohemia, the Low Countries, and the Huguenots.[72]

---

alliance and threatened exemplary punishment for first offenders. It was widely believed to be a response to Thomas Scott's *Vox Populi*. See above, p. 148 n. 33.

[70] On both the 5th and the 15th Calvert claimed that his estimates were based on the report of the council of war. This was untrue. It is possible that Phelips knew of the true estimate in the report, though it had not been made public.

[71] *C.S.P. Venet. 1619–21*, 589–90. For the debate of 15 February, see *Commons Debates 1621*, ii. 84–91; iv. 56–8; v. 464.

[72] *Commons Debates 1621*, iv. 415–16. Text, ibid. v. 203–4. Rich's comment, in the debate of 27 November, can be found ibid. iii. 470. See also Sir William Herrick's letter to the Mayor of Leicester, ? June 1621, in *Records of the Borough of Leicester*, ed. H. Stocks (4 vols., Cambridge, 1899–1923), iv. 195. Perrot had close connections with Pembroke, though there is no evidence that Pembroke was involved in the Declaration. It is interesting that Edward Alford opposed the Declaration as 'too great an engagement'.

During the autumn, a fresh set-back to James's diplomacy forced him to recall parliament for a second session in November. While on embassy to Ferdinand II Digby had discovered that the Emperor had already assigned the Palatinate and its electoral dignity to Maximilian II of Bavaria. Any hope for a negotiated settlement now rested on a successful defence of the Palatinate, and financial support from England was vital if Frederick's army was to survive the winter. This situation did at least provide James with a straightforward motive for appealing to parliament and there was a notable change in his tactics. At the beginning of the session (21 November) three privy councillors, Williams, the new Lord Keeper, Digby, and Cranfield, the new Lord Treasurer, outlined the crown's policy in some detail to a conference of Lords and Commons. Williams began by requesting that the Commons provide an immediate supply for the defence of the Palatinate, which they had promised under the Declaration of 4 June. Consideration of grievances was to be postponed to a further session to be held after Christmas. Digby then gave a report on the diplomatic and military situation in Germany. He urged that parliament supply Frederick's army during the winter. This would be a more economical policy than the dispatch of a fresh expedition from England, which he conceded would cost nearly a million a year. But he then went on to argue that Anglo-Spanish relations were in no way compromised by the current crisis. 'For the state of the warre, the question is only betweene the Emperor and the Palsgrave; all the rest are but of the by.' Cranfield's contribution was equally controversial, for he declared that the supply should not only cover future military expenses but also those incurred by James's diplomatic missions over the past year.[73]

The implicit invitation for the Commons to examine foreign affairs produced from 26 to 29 November an intense debate on foreign policy. Inevitably M.P.s concentrated on the relationship between the war in Germany and the wider crisis. Phelips countered Digby's bald statement that Spain was not concerned in the Palatinate with the equally bald pronouncement that Spain was the 'Great Wheel' and Germany but the 'Little

---

[73] *Commons Debates 1621*, iii. 421–5; iv. 423–8; vi. 414–18.

Wheel'. During the debates of the 26th a series of speakers, Perrot, Sir Dudley Digges, Sir Edward Giles, Sir George Hastings, and Sir Miles Fleetwood, seconded Phelips and called for the full Anglo-Dutch diversionary war, both in Flanders and on the sea. By the end of the day deadlock had been reached, with Phelips proposing that supply be delayed until James declared a wider war, while Calvert argued that the parliament should only be concerned with the Palatinate.[74] On the following day Pym proposed a compromise. A 'free gift' was to be offered for the defence of the Palatinate and the remainder of the session devoted to grievances. The proposed third session could be used for a full supply, once war had been declared. Calvert, with the assistance of his friend Thomas Wentworth, tried to prevent the full supply being delayed to the third session, but by the end of the debate on the 28th, Pym's proposal had received general approval. One subsidy was to be offered immediately for the defence of the Palatinate, while full supply would await the declaration of war.[75]

On the 29th, however, the debate took a more dramatic turn, following the most mysterious episode of the session. Sir George Goring, speaking on instructions from Buckingham, proposed that the Commons petition the crown to declare war on Spain if Philip IV (who came to the throne in April 1621) did not respond to James's request that he cease his support for the Emperor.[76] Buckingham's motive has never been satisfactorily explained. Goring's motion may have reflected dissatisfaction with the Spanish policy. It may have been an attempt to add weight to James's diplomacy, or it may have been a cynical manœuvre to provoke a conflict between king and parliament.[77] The response of the Commons was equally curious. There was considerable surprise at the obvious origin of the motion, but Phelips later claimed that he thought Buckingham's involvement indicated the king's approval. At his prompting a subcommittee was nominated to draft the peti-

[74] Ibid. iii. 445–58; iv. 435–41; v. 195–9; vi. 210–14.

[75] For the debate of the 27th, ibid. iii. 454–73; iv. 441–6; v. 214–20. For that of the 28th, ii. 461–7; v. 221–4; vi. 206–9, 326–31.

[76] Brit. Lib. Harl. MS. 1580, fos. 401–2, Goring to Buckingham, 29 Nov. 1621; *Commons Debates 1621*, ii. 474–6.

[77] Cf. R. E. Zaller, *The Parliament of 1621. A Study in Constitutional Conflict* (Berkeley, 1971), 152–3.

tion.[78] No record of its deliberations has survived, but the Petition and Remonstrance presented to the House on 1 December was outspoken to the point of bluntness. James was requested to declare a war for the defence of the Protestant religion immediately and to employ the diversionary strategy. Charles was to marry a Protestant princess. A subsidy was granted 'for the present relief of the Palatinate only'.[79] Further financial support was not mentioned but it was implicit in the request for a full-scale war.[80]

The dispatch of the Petition to the king initiated the chain of events which led to the dissolution. In his reply of 4 December to the Petition James declared that discussion of 'deep matters of state, and namely . . . our dearest sons match with the daughter of Spain, the honour of that king, or others our friends and Confederates' was an infringement of the prerogative.[81] The Commons replied in their defence of the Petition on 9 December that 'although before this time we were in some of these points silent, yet being . . . invited' to discuss the Palatinate by the three privy councillors on 21 November, they could not overlook the fact that 'the lower Palatinate was seized by the army of the kinge of Spaine as executor of the ban there in the quality of Duke of Burgundy', and that 'the king of Spaine, at his own charge, hath now at least five armies on foot'.[82] Once the issue of the prerogative had been raised, however, the debate over foreign policy was at an end.

In the Parliament of 1624 the central issue was the policy to be pursued after the treaties with Spain had been repudiated. Still trying to retain his freedom to negotiate with Spain, James provided no guidance on this issue in his opening speech on 19 February. Parliament was asked to give its advice; but there was no assurance that it would be accepted. Nor did Buckingham in his relation of the negotiations with Spain suggest much more. Parliament should advise the king whether the negotiations should be terminated or not. Neither of these gestures towards consultation was genuine; but they mollified

---

[78] See K. M. Sharpe, above, p. 35.

[79] Text in J. Rushworth, *Historical Collections* (1659), i. 40–3.

[80] In the 'Dialogue between the Counsellor and the Gentleman', fo. 8ᵛ, the gentleman states explicitly that James would have received 'satisfaction' in the third session.

[81] Rushworth, op. cit. i. 43.

[82] Ibid. 44–5.

parliament without committing either the king or the Duke to any particular course of policy.

Sir Benjamin Rudyerd opened the Commons' debate on the Duke's relation on 1 March. His speech is worth some attention.[83] He urged that the Commons should join with the Lords to petition the king to break the treaties with Spain immediately: 'For until it be done, his friends will hold him in continual jealousie.' This was an accurate description of the failure of Buckingham's diplomatic efforts at the end of 1623, whether Rudyerd knew it or not. James should then 'enter into a confederacy with his friends abroad' and revive the Protestant cause in Germany. At this point parliament should provide a supply for four purposes: the defence of Ireland, the coastal defences of England, outfitting the fleet, and providing reinforcements for the English troops in the Dutch service. When James went to war to recover the Palatinate, he should wage it 'neare hand, to save charges . . . there the Low Countries will be ready to assist us for their own interest'. The crucial part of the speech was the specification of the immediate purpose of supply—the future Four Propositions of the Subsidy Act. These military preparations would give the crown the opportunity to prove its *bona fides*, yet not bind parliament beforehand to any particular course of strategy, though Rudyerd's preference for the diversionary war and a Dutch alliance was clear. Mr. Conrad Russell and Dr. J. N. Ball have argued that Rudyerd was a 'government spokesman' in this parliament, on the grounds that Rudyerd introduced the scheme for parliamentary treasurers.[84] The parliamentary treasurers were in fact first proposed by James, on the advice of Buckingham, and later adopted by Rudyerd, but this first speech cannot be said to embody government policy. The Four Propositions implied a wider war and the diversionary strategy, which James never accepted, while Buckingham did not want supply tied to specific proposals. It is probable that these proposals came from Pembroke's circle, and Pembroke may have reached some form of agreement with Buckingham, but there is no evidence that

[83] There are several texts: see P.R.O. S.P. 14/160/8 and Brit. Lib. Harl. MS. 6799, fo. 182.

[84] Russell, 'Parliamentary History', loc. cit. Professor Ruigh is less sure, Ruigh, op. cit. 178–9.

Rudyerd spoke either for the king or for the Duke.

Rudyerd's speech dominated the day's debate and received general approval.[85] On one important issue, that of religion, he had not, however, been explicit. He did not specify whether the alliance James should form with 'his friends abroad' should be a confessional one. This ambiguity may have been deliberate, for Pembroke, if he sponsored the speech, knew James would not agree to a war for religion. The Commons included the danger to religion among the reasons for breaking the Spanish treaties, but on 5 March Archbishop Abbot announced to the Lords that the committee of Lords and Commons drafting the joint petition had decided to omit this reason because it was 'necessarily included' among the others. The concession caused some soul-searching among puritans of the stamp of Edward, Lord Montague and Sir Robert Harley, but the majority in both Houses were prepared to compromise.[86] The Commons did so once again on 20 March, when they deleted the cause of religion from the final resolution to supply at the king's insistence.[87]

The favourable response to his relation and the willingness of the Commons to consider financing a war caused Buckingham to seek a supply on more favourable terms than those proposed by Rudyerd. On 4 March, Southampton in the Lords, and Sandys, Phelips, and Digges in the Commons on the 5th, suggested that parliament make an open offer of supply to the king if he accepted the 'Advice' to break the treaties. This appears to have been organized by Buckingham, for on the 4th he advised James that he should respond to an open offer by allowing expenditure to be overseen by parliamentary treasurers. This was the one occasion in the foreign policy debate on which some form of alliance between Buckingham and 'opposition' M.P.s appears to be at work. Buckingham's source for the idea of the parliamentary treasurers is not known, but it may have been suggested by his 'allies' as the price of their co-operation.[88]

---

[85] P.R.O. S.P. 14/160/33, Dudley Carleton the younger to Sir Dudley Carleton, 5 Mar. 1624.

[86] *H.M.C. Report on the Manuscripts of the Duke of Buccleuch and Queensberry*, iii. 232; Ruigh, op. cit. 195.

[87] P.R.O. S.P. 14/161/36, Nethersole to Carleton, 25 Mar. 1624.

[88] Brit. Lib. Harl. MS. 6987, fo. 202, Buckingham's advice to James. See Ruigh, op. cit. 193–5, 199.

The Commons discussed the proposal of an open offer on the 5th and rejected it. But the receipt on the next day of the king's answer to the Advice, delivered on the 5th, placed the financial debate in an entirely different context. While making the concession of the parliamentary treasurers, James demanded at this point that the crown be restored to financial solvency before he accepted the Advice or changed his foreign policy. In the course of his answer he cited several of Rudyerd's propositions, the defences of Ireland and the state of the navy, as areas where money was needed.

The response to the Advice was the first occasion in the parliament when James had publicly to declare himself and to reveal how little he was prepared to concede. His answer was debated on the 11th and 12th. Initially, three financial proposals were under discussion. Cranfield in the Lords argued the king's case, that the existing debts of the crown be repaid before a new foreign policy was undertaken. Southampton, Sandys, and Phelips continued to support the open offer of supply. Rudyerd returned to the Four Propositions, which he now claimed the king had accepted in his answer, with some concession on the repayment of debts. Buckingham was undoubtedly concerned at this point that an open clash might occur, for it was doubtful that parliament would agree to repay James's debts, while James might not accept anything less. A compromise was essential. Charles undercut Cranfield by denying that repayment of the crown's debts was necessary, while Buckingham, through Conway and Phelips, tried to persuade the Commons on the 12th to offer something 'real' as part of the open offer. This was rejected, however, and by the end of the debate on the 12th, the Commons decided that a simple open offer, which they had opposed on the 5th, would be a sufficient concession.[89]

The king's answer on the 14th to the open offer of supply if the Advice was accepted came near to shattering the whole edifice of compromise. He declared that while the Advice implied that war would follow the breaking of the treaties, it

---

[89] For Cranfield's speech, see *Notes of the Debates in the House of Lords . . . A.D. 1624 and 1625*, ed. S. R. Gardiner (Camden Soc., 1880), 23–5. For the Commons' Debates, see Brit. Lib. Harl. MS. 159, fos. 80–82ᵛ and Ruigh, op. cit. 204–9. Rudyerd was supported in this debate by Sir Robert Mansell, another of Pembroke's followers.

did not commit him to a declaration of war. Even if he
accepted the Advice, he still retained the freedom to go to war
on terms of his own choosing. He also outlined his financial
demands in forbidding detail. He would need a supply of five
subsidies and ten fifteenths for immediate military purposes
together with a recurrent annual grant of one subsidy and two
fifteenths for his debts. Only one concession was added to that
of the parliamentary treasurers: a second session at Michaelmas
and a third in the spring of 1625. It was, considered Simonds
D'Ewes, 'an unpleasant answer full of uncertaintie for any-
thinge to be done and yet required a great sum of money'.[90]
The king's answer dashed whatever optimism there may have
been about a successful conclusion to the parliament and was
largely responsible for the caution and uneasiness which permeated the remainder of the session. Sandys, Phelips, Digges,
and the other M.P.s who had advocated an open offer were
now gravely compromised. If the session was to be preserved
from disaster, Buckingham had to persuade the king to
ameliorate his demands. After considerable effort he was able to
cajole James into withdrawing the demand for recurrent
subsidies in exchange for an immediate supply of six subsidies
and twelve fifteenths—later estimated by Sir Edward Coke to
be worth £900,000.[91]

The debate on the king's answer of 19–20 March was widely
regarded as crucial. Rudyerd once again opened the discussion
and proposed that the full sum be granted because it would be
useful for propaganda and provide the king with security on
which to borrow. But he also suggested that it be paid in
increments over a long period with the first increment devoted
to the Four Propositions. By the end of the 19th there was
general agreement that the supply should be divided into one
immediate and several later increments—termed the specific
and general supply.[92] On the 20th Sandys opened and supported the idea that the specific supply be devoted to the Four
Propositions. Sir Robert Killegrew and other followers of the
Duke tried to obtain a commitment to the general supply, but
without success. At the end of the debate the Commons decided

[90] *The Diary of Simonds D'Ewes, 1622–1624*, ed. E. Bourcier (Paris, 1974), 186.
[91] Brit. Lib. Harl. MS. 6987, fo. 200, Buckingham to James, *c.* 15 Mar. 1620.
[92] Brit. Lib. Harl. MS. 159, fos. 87ᵛ–92.

to offer £300,000 (three subsidies and three fifteenths) to be dispensed by parliamentary treasurers on the Four Propositions within a year of the repudiation of the treaties. The resolution embodying the offer carefully glossed over the question of the declaration of war by stating that the grant was contingent on the

dissolution and utter discharge of both the said Treaties ... in pursuit of our advice thereto, and towardes the support of that war *which is likely to ensue* [my italics].

Upon such a declaration of war

we your loyal and loving subjects will never fail in a parliamentary way to assist your Majesty in so royal a design, wherein your own honour ... the welfare of your noble and onely daughter and her consort, and their posterity, the safety of your own kingdom and people, and the posterity of your neighbours and allies are so deeply engaged.[93]

The caution underlying the resolution was made explicit by Coke, who, when Sir John Savile queried the purpose of the resolution, stated that supply was granted only for the Four Propositions and did not commit parliament to 'future possibilities'.[94]

James accepted the resolution on 22 March with little enthusiasm and took the opportunity to re-emphasize that diplomacy and strategy remained within the prerogative and that he still intended to concentrate on the Palatinate and not wage a general or confessional war against Spain. Nor did he expedite his part of the agreement. No open declaration of the dissolution of the treaties was made. Only on 17 April, after parliament had become restive, did he allow his instructions to his agent at Madrid to be revealed. At the end of April Richard Knightley warned Buckingham that 'the disturbance is mens thoughts are [*sic*], that soe much duty really showne should not produce a speedy dispatch, the time of year requiringe noe dallyinge.'[95] The final drafting of the subsidy bill in May was a difficult

---

[93] Text in Rushworth, op. cit. i. 135–6.

[94] Brit. Lib. Harl. MS. 159, fo. 94ᵛ. Ruigh, op. cit. 217–27, gives a somewhat different interpretation of this debate.

[95] Bodl. Add. MS. D. 111, fo. 443, Knightley to Buckingham, ? Apr. 1624. See also P.R.O. S.P. 14/136/16, Carleton the younger to Carleton, 19 Apr. 1624.

process. A new council of war had been created in April to advise the parliamentary treasurers on disbursement of the subsidy, but there were few precedents on which to base the spheres of responsibility. The relationship between the Council, the treasurers, and parliament was not defined to anyone's satisfaction.[96] At the last minute, on 14 May, Conway requested in the king's name that the subsidy bill be rewritten to include recovery of the Palatinate as one of the Four Propositions and to limit assistance to the Dutch to that necessary for them to participate in a campaign in the Palatinate.[97] The request was rejected, but it was also clear proof that, whatever else had been accomplished in the parliament, a new foreign policy had not emerged.

The course of events that followed the conclusion of the session provided further proof that neither the king nor the Duke was prepared to accept parliament's suggestions regarding a new foreign policy. No declaration of war against Spain had been made by the time the Parliament of 1625 met. Under the treaty of Southampton of May 1624 four new regiments of foot were added to the British troops in the Dutch service, but the Anglo-Dutch alliance progressed no further.[98] The difficulties of the French negotiations made it impossible to recall parliament at Michaelmas.[99] At the same time Buckingham was pouring men and money into Mansfeldt's expedition and in April 1625 agreed to subsidize Christian IV of Denmark's intervention in Germany with £30,000 a month. It was doubtful that the next parliament would be as amenable to concession as that of 1624.

Although he was aware of the risk he was running in

[96] See Ruigh, op. cit. 253–4. Ruigh's statement that the Subsidy Act converted the Council of War into 'a body responsible to the House of Commons' is not strictly accurate, for in 1626 when the Commons wished to question members of the Council over their disbursement of the subsidy during the impeachment of Buckingham, the Privy Council denied parliament's right to do so without the king's permission. See 'Protestant Cause', 386–7.

[97] Ruigh, op. cit. 254–5. Conway probably had Mansfeldt's expedition in mind. He wished the advance of £20,000 made to Mansfeldt issued in a form which would bring it under the Subsidy Act. See P.R.O. S.P. 14/165/67.

[98] A Dutch embassy had been in England since February 1624 and was antagonized by the lack of interest shown towards them. P.R.O. S.P. 14/163/16, Carleton the younger to Carleton, 19 Apr. 1624.

[99] *The Earl of Strafford's Letters and Dispatches*, (2 vols., 1739), i. 24, Wentworth to Sir George Calvert, 12 Oct. 1624.

employing the subsidy on Mansfeldt's expedition, Buckingham was gambling on success providing its own justification.[100] He cannot, however, be accused of violating an agreement with parliament, because he never recognized that one existed in the first place. Tying supply to specific purposes was never his idea; he accepted it because he could not get a supply on any other terms. Buckingham played a major role in the Parliament of 1624; he persuaded James to summon it, he was the vital intermediary between king and parliament, and it was probably only as a result of his cajoling that James accepted the resolution of 20 March. But he did not make his foreign policy in parliament.

In this context the Subsidy Act of 1624 does not represent an innovation, or an invasion of the prerogative instigated by the Duke. It was a desperate attempt to create a compromise war policy on which both king and parliament could agree. The Parliament of 1621 had revealed the wide difference of outlook between them. Parliament would not support an expedition to the Palatinate; James would not undertake any other form of military operation. The positions were little altered in 1624. The difference in outlook on foreign affairs reflected a growing ideological tension in England, as the Stuart court more and more openly rejected a puritan conception of the world which had become embedded in English politics in the late sixteenth century. It is significant that the Earl of Pembroke probably played a leading role in the compromise, for he was the last member of the Elizabethan aristocracy to occupy an important position in the Jacobean court. As a compromise the Subsidy Act of 1624 was a failure; the political consensus it depended on for its success no longer existed.

---

[100] P.R.O. S.P. 14/181/50, Buckingham to Mansfeldt, 12 Jan. 1625. Brit. Lib. Harl. MS. 7000, fo. 179, Buckingham to the Earl of Nithsdale, n.d. (? Oct. 1624).

VI.   Sir John Eliot and Parliament, 1624–1629

J. N. BALL

THE MOST recent biography of Sir John Eliot[1] throws much new light on his career as Vice-Admiral of Devon and on his relations with other politicians of the south-western counties. It also considerably modifies our view of his leadership in the parliaments of the later 1620s, by showing that his hold over the House of Commons was less sure and less pre-eminent than had previously been supposed. It advances our understanding of parliamentary groupings to a lesser extent, so that in this area much remains to be done. In its fundamental interpretation of Eliot's political objectives it remains firmly within the boundaries set over a century ago by S. R. Gardiner. For Hulme, perhaps even more than for Gardiner, Eliot was deeply confused, and eventually torn apart by his divided loyalties to the crown and the House of Commons. For both historians, the theoretical works which Eliot composed during his final imprisonment in the Tower were totally irreconcilable with his parliamentary practice. Without presupposing a degree of consistency abnormal amongst political men, it is to this problem that the present essay is primarily directed.

Over the last fifty years historians have mostly come to see the conflict between crown and parliament in the early seventeenth century less in terms of a struggle for sovereignty, conscious or unconscious, and more in terms of tensions within a single corpus of rules and precedents inherited from the remote or recent past.[2] Those who are interested in the evolu-

---

[1] Harold Hulme, *The life of Sir John Eliot, 1592 to 1632* (1957).

[2] This change of perspective stems largely from the work of C. H. McIlwain, e.g. *Constitutionalism and the Changing World* (Cambridge, 1939). See also, F. D. Wormuth, *The Royal Prerogative. 1603–49* (Ithaca, N.Y., 1939); Margaret Judson, *The Crisis of the Constitution, 1603–45.* (New Brunswick, 1949). The present writer derived much stimulus and guidance from Mr. B. H. G. Wormald, of Peterhouse, Cambridge, in preparing the doctoral thesis upon which this paper is based

tion of 'constitutional' ideas are more inclined than those whose concern lies with the group of survivors who led the Long Parliament to emphasize the great mutation between the 1620s and 1640. At the same time, the distillation of constitutional principles from the imperfect surviving records of debates is a more delicate process than many historians of political ideas have appreciated. Each statement needs to be studied in its context of the debates and related to the evolution of short-term tactics before its full meaning can be understood. In addition, whilst the nature of the sources restricts attempts to penetrate from what was said in debate to the 'real' intentions of the participants, there is an equally difficult problem standing in the way of those who might seek to prove that those intentions were essentially different from what was said in debate.

In Eliot's case, the existence of late theoretical works has seemed an impediment to the interpretation of his political career. One of these works, it now appears, was not original; the other was ethical rather than political in intention. The *De Iure Majestatis* is a translation, or a full English summary, of a Latin treatise published in 1610 by Henningus Arnisaeus of Halberstadt. It is perhaps unsafe to use it as evidence of Eliot's conception of the state, though C. H. McIlwain, who first recognized it for what it is, rested his discussion of Eliot's political ideas upon it.[3] *The Monarchie of Man*[4] is certainly Eliot's own. It exploits the analogy of the government of society as a model for the government of the inner self. Its annotations include many references to Arnisaeus's works, and it contains nothing which is in conflict with the *De Iure Majestatis*. Its discussion of the role of representative assemblies grants them considerable rights as counsellors to monarchs, but reserves, without apparent irony, 'mysteries of state' and *arcana imperii* to kings. It asserts the objectivity and independence of law and subjects' rights whilst recognizing the necessity for a prerogative power in the monarch 'to prevent those evils which the law by power or terrour cannot reach, be it either foreign or domesticke'. Eliot's friend

[3] *De Iure Majestatis*, ed. A. B. Grosart (1882). For McIlwain's analysis, see *Constitutionalism and the Changing World*, 78–9.
[4] Edited by A. B. Grosart (2 vols., 1879).

Richard James wrote that he thought the author had been too kind to the prerogative. It is most unlikely that Eliot was hoping to prepare the way for his release by redefining his attitudes. He could probably have gained his liberty by con-ceding the right of the Privy Council or other courts to judge his behaviour in the Commons at the time of the 'Three Resolutions' of 1629; his refusal to do so gained him his martyrdom in the cause of parliamentary privilege.

There is clearly, at least prima facie, a serious difficulty in reconciling such statements with his role as a leader of the Commons between 1626 and 1629. Nor do some of his earlier speeches help to resolve the paradox. He first entered the Commons in the Addled Parliament of 1614 and, though he did not sit in that of 1621, he offered an explanation of the breakdown of both to the Parliament of 1624 which is in many ways in line with what he was to write at the end of his life about assemblies and the prerogative;

The greatest doubts, (as I conceive), the kinge had of the Parlia-m[en]t [of 1621] concerned his prerogative; his Ma[jes]tie being perswaded that theire liberties did entrench vpon him; the feares the Parliaments had of the Kinge were that by his prerogative he sought to retrench and block up the antient priveledges and liberties of the house. This made the insistence stronge on both sides; the Kinge mayntayning his royall power, the howse pretendinge for their priviledges, whereas, being well distinguished, both might freely have inioyde theire owne w[i]thout impeachment of the others right; for the King's prerogative no man may dispute against it, it being an inseparable adiunct to regalitie, and exampled in the first, and greatest monarch the Kinge of Kinges, who reserves to himselfe beyond his lawes a power to save w[hi]ch Seneca calls *proprium regis* and we his prerogative.[5]

Such an analysis of the reasons for the breakdown of the Parliament of 1621 seems remarkably objective. Yet it throws

---

[5] Printed from Port Eliot MS. by A. B. Grosart as an appendix to his edition of Eliot's fragmentary parliamentary narrative, *Negotium Posterorum* (1881), i. 130–9. Eliot sat for St. Germans, Cornwall, in the Parliament of 1614; for Newport, Cornwall, in those of 1624 and 1625; again for St. Germans, where his house Port Eliot was situated, in 1626. In the Parliament of 1628–9 he was elected as one of the Knights of the Shire for Cornwall. For details of the dispute concerning this election between Eliot, Coryton, and Sir Richard Edgcumbe and John Mohun, see Hulme, op. cit. 173–81.

light on the future as well as upon the past. The phrase 'his Ma[jes]tie being perswaded that theire liberties did entrench upon him' takes on new meaning when it is placed alongside Eliot's more explicit reference to the cause of the breakdown:

The rocks were not naturall on which you then stroke, but were cast in the waie by some subtill arte to prevent the passage of your duties to the Kinge...fals glasses that reflected not the trew sence of the obiect but with colours and illusions wrought deceipte.

Speaking of the Parliament of 1614, Eliot said:

Our ielosie...was the advantage of the ill-affected, who made it the instrument of their designs to dissolve that meetinge...which (as we have since felt) trencht more upon the priviledges and liberties of this Kingdome than the uttermost undertakings in Parliament can ever doe.

The seeds of Eliot's later conviction that a true understanding between king and Commons was being prevented by sinister manœuvrings by persons with private interests at heart are here clearly visible. In the circumstances of 1624, it is most unlikely that he saw the Duke of Buckingham as one of these. He was the Duke's subordinate and servant, indebted to him for his knighthood, and was to play a part in the judicial process against Lord Treasurer Middlesex which Buckingham organized. The speech from which these extracts are taken also contained proposals for secrecy of debate which were tactfully buried in a subcommittee, but which were not inconsistent with the tactical needs of Buckingham. The indirect defence of 'undertakers' was timely, as a rumour was circulating that some of the opposition men of 1621 had reconciled themselves to Buckingham and were helping to manage the new parliament for him. Management was needed, as Buckingham and Prince Charles were determined on war against Spain, but realized that parliamentary enthusiasm must be carefully controlled if the king's doubts and suspicions were to be removed. The management was to permit the Commons a new freedom to discuss foreign policy, on the invitation of the king, and to employ the techniques of parliamentary judicature against a major officer of state whom the king did not protect against the designs of his son and his favourite. Apparently on the king's initiative, clauses were written into the Subsidy Act broadly defining the objects on which the money was to be spent, with accountability of the Treasurers to a future parliament. Eliot's real parliamentary apprenticeship was served during a session when freedom of speech was no longer limited in practice except by the need to preserve the king from personal criticism. What James had refused in 1621 was invited in 1624, and was to be taken as of right by the Commons in future. Equally significantly, the session saw the heir to the throne and the royal favourite working in close collaboration with the Commons.

By the time of the accession of Charles to the throne in the spring of 1625, the alliance which he and Buckingham had struck with the Commons' leaders was already weakening. Most of the subsidy money of 1624 had been wasted on aid to Denmark and on Mansfeldt's futile expedition to recover the Palatinate for James's son-in-law, but there was no sign of the naval action against Spain which was the popular aspect of the war policy. A Catholic marriage with France was about to replace the discarded Catholic marriage with Spain and rumours of its likely consequences for domestic religious policy were soon to be confirmed by the release of several priests and Jesuits. Though Charles's accession was followed by some signs of naval preparations, it was rightly suspected that experienced commanders were in short supply. When the first parliament of the new reign met in June 1625, those who had remained aloof from the war fever of 1624 were easily able to seize the initiative in restricting the grant of new subsidies to two, in limiting the traditionally lifetime offer of Tonnage and Poundage to one year only, and in pursuing religious grievances.

Buckingham's insistence on calling a second session of the Parliament at Oxford, after London had been hit by plague, intensified opposition to the point of hardly veiled threats of impeachment against him. In the face of this, any hope of a further grant was abandoned and a dissolution was ordered on 12 August. The fleet eventually sailed for Cadiz in September, only to return defeated and demoralized, the ships and crews in poor shape. Gloomy forecasts of inadequate preparations, poor leadership, and ill-discipline were fully confirmed.

Despite the existence of Eliot's own narrative of the Parliament of 1625, there are many difficulties in the way of an interpretation of his part in it. He emerged into prominence during the Oxford session by defending Buckingham, laying the blame on lesser officers for the slowness in fitting out the fleet. He set a complicated historical puzzle, however, by inserting in his account of the debate on 10 August a speech which, if it was his own and was in fact spoken, means that within four days he had swung completely round to join those who were attacking the Duke. It is most unlikely that the speech was delivered in the House, and improbable that Eliot was the author of written versions which circulated amongst members of parliament.[6] We also have his own evidence that he was active behind the scenes in these few days in trying to dissuade Buckingham from persisting in the demand for a further grant of subsidies, and from sending out the fleet that autumn.[7] There is no independent evidence that Eliot was connected with the speech. Leaders of the attack on Buckingham, including Sir Edward Coke and the antiquarian Sir Robert Cotton (who had almost certainly provided the long list of medieval precedents for the impeachment of royal favourites), were excluded from the next parliament, but Eliot took his seat and stepped into their shoes.

As Vice-Admiral of Devon, Eliot was well placed to be aware of the inadequate preparations of the fleet and was an eyewitness of its shameful return. He had already blamed Sir John Coke, chief of the Admiralty Commissioners, as part of his defence of Buckingham, and probably resented Coke's promotion to a Secretaryship of State in September 1625. Coke had sat for St. Germans, where Eliot's influence was naturally strong, in the Parliament of 1625, but despite the intervention of the Bishop of Exeter, was passed over in favour of Sir Henry Marten, a judge of Admiralty, as Eliot's fellow-member in the Parliament of 1626.[8]

Eliot's decision to move into open opposition certainly came before parliament met again in February 1626. Even then, it

[6] See J. N. Ball, 'Sir John Eliot at the Oxford Parliament, 1625', B.I.H.R. xxviii (1955), 113–27.

[7] *Negotium Posterorum*, ii. 53–5.

[8] Letters from Valentine Carey, Bishop of Exeter, to Sir John Coke, 22 and 26 Jan. 1626, *H.M.C. Cowper MSS.* i. 251, 157.

was not immediately clear to members of the Commons that he had determined on a full-scale attack on Buckingham. His early speeches in the Commons took up several of the themes introduced by others at Oxford in 1625, but his personal attack was still formally aimed at Sir John Coke. Though one or two contemporaries expressed their suspicion that Eliot was aiming higher, it is significant that such an intention was masked. The circumstances of the parliament dictated caution. The mood of the House itself was difficult to assess. The exclusion of those who had led the attack on Buckingham in 1625 deprived the Commons of leaders of great experience and authority. Amongst the half-dozen who were pricked as sheriffs of their counties were Sir Edward Coke, Sir Robert Phelips, Sir Francis Seymour, and Sir Thomas Wentworth. In the first few weeks of the new parliament, the crown's supporters had a good chance of gaining the initiative and of rapidly persuading the Commons to discuss specific proposals for supply. Eliot certainly played an important part in transforming discussion of the king's revenues into an investigation of the expenditure of the 1624 subsidies and of the reasons for the inadequacy of the ordinary revenues of the crown. His speech of 10 February had features which linked it with those of Sir Edward Coke and others at Oxford, and with the unspoken 'Cotton' speech, but it seemed more moderate than any of these:

Cutt of the king's revenewes, you cutt of the principall meanes of your owne safeties, and not only disable him to defend you, but enforce that which you conceave an offence, the extraordinary resort to his subjects for supplies, and the more than ordinary waies of raising them.[9]

Eliot is still making judgements in harmony with his analysis in 1624 of the reasons for the breakdown of earlier parliaments. If there was to be a serious attempt to improve the financial position of the monarchy, it follows that the Commons' leaders were not yet convinced that the only hope of continuing parliaments lay in forcing the crown into per-

[9] Port Eliot MS., printed by Grosart, *Negotium Posterorum*:. 149. This version is substantially confirmed by the manuscript diary of the Parliament of 1626 once owned by Bulstrode Whitelocke, Cambridge University Library MS. Dd. 12. 20–22, I, fos. 92v–90v. The foliation of this MS. runs first backwards on the verso, then forwards on the recto.

manent dependence upon them for supply.

The context of the above quotation makes it clear, however, that Eliot considered that the acquisition of royal property by favourites and their dependants was a principal cause of the declining private income of the crown. He later cited some of the precedents of the 'Cotton' speech to show that 'the squeezing of these sponges of the Commonwealth into the King's coffers' had been an effective cure for medieval financial crises, especially when accompanied by a commission of inquiry into the king's revenues.[10] The idea of improvement of the administration of royal lands was not new. Bacon had suggested the 'disparking' of royal forests. Sir Dudley Digges had written to the king in January 1626 advising him to allow a parliamentary investigation of the revenues.[11] The whole of this part of Eliot's speech was lifted almost word for word from Sir Walter Ralegh's pamphlet, the *Prerogative of Parliaments*, of which a heavily marked manuscript copy exists in the Port Eliot collection.[12] Ralegh had argued that the use of parliamentary authority for the resumption of alienated crown lands was perfectly safe and respectable, since both Henry VII and Henry VIII had allowed such statutes. Digges's letter and Eliot's speech of 10 February both emphasized the necessity of obtaining the king's permission to proceed. That it was not simply a tactical device is suggested by its reappearance later. On 24 February Eliot again accompanied a proposal for a 'search of the expenc of those moneys which we gave before' with that for 'looking into the auncient revenewes of the crowne, if they be nott fitt enough for so great a king'.[13] The Chancellor of the Exchequer was asked to 'declare to the king the particulars of this day', passing the initiative to the crown. So it was not entirely the fault of the Commons that the matter was not mentioned again until 4 May, when Eliot

[10] In a debate on supply, 27 March, Port Eliot MS., printed in *Negotium Posterorum*, i. 156–64.

[11] P.R.O. S. P., 16/19/107.

[12] Eliot admitted under examination when under arrest in May 1626 that he had read the commission of Richard II's time in 'the treatise which passes from hand to hand under the name of Sir Walter Raleigh by way of a dialogue between a Councillor and a Justice of the Peace...out of which...he had of late taken some notes for his memory'. P.R.O. S. P., 16/27/18. A manuscript copy exists at Port Eliot, with numerous pencilled markings of important passages.

[13] Whitelocke, I, fos. 67ᵛ-66ᵛ.

proposed a request to the king which received the royal approval within a few days but was naturally neglected during the final crisis of the session. The crown itself took some action to improve the income from the royal forest of Gillingham,thereby provoking considerable popular disorder.[14]

Some outside observers commented that Eliot's opening speech was not received with much enthusiasm, and for another fortnight the privy councillors and officials seemed to hold the House well on course towards consideration of supply. Then Eliot intervened in a discussion about the defence of coastal waters against 'Turkish pirates' and Dunkirk privateers to propose that the House should first 'sett downe what the evill is, and then what remedye to be provided . . . to which the Committee agreed'.[15] As Gardiner noted, Eliot provided a framework within which a broad consideration of grievances was possible.[16] The committee for considering the king's revenues, which the councillors hoped would become a committee for supply, was converted into a committee of 'evils and causes', and only thirdly of 'remedies'. By the end of February, it had been resolved that the evils consisted of 'the diminution of the Kingdom in honour and strength, and the stoppage of trade at home and abroad'. On the 28th, the committee resolved to press for the examination of the Council of War on the expenditure of the subsidies of 1624, and the advice it had given the king.

Meanwhile, Eliot had persuaded the Committee of the Whole House for grievances, of which he was chairman, to pursue a case concerning the arrest of a French merchant ship, the *St. Peter* of Le Havre, arguing that it was the main cause of an embargo placed on English merchants' goods in Rouen. Eliot demanded the examination of the Lieutenants of the Tower and of Dover Castle for their part in the affair and secured the establishment of a subcommittee. By 1 March he reported that his fellow-member for St. Germans, Sir Henry Marten, had stated that the Duke of Buckingham had himself ordered the second arrest of the ship, five days before

[14] Ibid. I, fos. 177–8. In July 1626 royal commissioners were appointed to consider reducing the number of unprofitable royal parks and forests. D. G. C. Allan, 'The Rising in the West, 1628–31', Ec.H.R. 2nd Ser. V (1952), 78.

[15] Whitelocke, I, fo. 62ᵛ.

[16] S. R. Gardiner, *History of England . . . 1603–1642* (10 vols., 1893–4), vi. 73.

consulting Marten on the legal aspects. Marten asserted that he 'was so far from advising the second stay of this ship that he... would grant a writ of attachment if he were required against the stayers of the ship'.[17] On the afternoon of the same day, Eliot reported 'something forgotten by him this morning, viz: that the 23 bags of silver and 8 of gold taken from the *St. Peter* on its first arrest were by Sir Francis Stewart delivered to my Lord Duke'.[18] This is the first evidence we have in this parliament of the naming of the Duke in connection with a specific grievance. Pym proposed that Buckingham be examined, but the House of Lords took time to consider his request for permission to answer the Commons, only agreeing that he might decide for himself after receiving an assurance from the Commons that their original order had been modified. The Duke answered through the Attorney-General, admitting that he had ordered the rearrest of the vessel, but claiming the king's express direction.[19] On 11 March Eliot again reported from the subcommittee that Buckingham's behaviour was a grievance, but, in the debate which followed, even members of the subcommittee were divided on the question whether the rearrest had been the cause of the embargo on English merchants' goods in France, and whether, once the Court of Admiralty had ordered the release of the ship, only that court could order its rearrest. The House eventually resolved by a majority of six that it would not vote on the question whether the affair was a grievance.[20]

The 11th March administered a double blow to Eliot's parliamentary tactics, since the Commons also resolved to abandon the attempt to get the members of the Council of War to give a fuller and more satisfactory account of their advice to the king on the war, and of their trusteeship of the subsidies of 1624. At the same time the king was putting renewed pressure on the Commons to consider supply, and Eliot was defeated in an attempt to secure further delay. Though he argued that 'mighty affairs are not guided with the publique counsell which is not now such as none can

---

[17] *C.J.* i. 826–7; Whitelocke, I, fo. 54ʳ.
[18] *C.J.* i. 827. Cf. Whitelocke, I, fo. 53ʳ.
[19] *C.J.* i. 831; *L.J.* iii. 513–16.
[20] *C.J.* i. 835.

complayne',[21] the House agreed to debate supply on 13 March. Even members who had been eager to seek out grievances seemed to be admitting the urgency of financing defence— 'the *unum necessarium* of this time is the security of ourselves from our provoked enemy.'[22]

The next fortnight was critical in the history of the Parliament of 1626. It saw the collapse of the king's new initiative, and the beginnings of an open general attack on Buckingham, but this development was not achieved under Eliot's leadership. The tactical situation was delicate. The king had to be placated sufficiently to avoid a premature dissolution, whilst the prosecution of grievances would need to be accelerated if any redress was to be achieved. The matters on which Eliot had concentrated his efforts had required lengthy investigations, and some had proved to be minor matters affecting the Admiralty administration to which he still belonged. It was Sir Dudley Digges who seems to have taken charge of the tactical decisions of the House after Eliot's failure. In response to the king's request for urgent discussion of the subsidies, Digges proposed 'to take a resolution to entertayne no other business till the great matters are determined', and produced an acceptable time-table.[23] The House voted subsidies in committee on 27 March. Eliot had tried to secure yet further delay of supply until grievances had been redressed, and again it was Digges who successfully proposed 'that we may deferre the passing of the act till we have our grievances answered. When they are preferred, too soone; if we should say "after we have redresse" it would argue a distruste.'[24]

The formula which the House adopted to push on more rapidly with grievances was also Digges's work. On 11 March, after Eliot's double rebuff, a member named Dr. Turner had introduced 'six queries' whether the Duke was the 'causing cause' of the evils of the kingdom. One by one these were introduced into the committee's proceedings, most of them by Digges. Gardiner long ago noted the shift of emphasis in Dr. Turner's queries, but was unaware that they were accom-

[21] Whitelocke, I, fos. 29–28.
[22] Ibid. I, fo. 29ᵛ. (Mr Wentworth, Recorder of Oxford).
[23] Ibid. I, fos. 61–2.
[24] Ibid. I, fo. 5ᵛ.

panied by a change of leadership.[25] Hulme has shown clearly
that Eliot lost the leadership at this point, but it remains to
analyse its significance in terms of the impending impeachment of Buckingham.[26] The 'six queries' represented both a
broadening of the area of grievances under discussion and a
sharpening of the edge of the Commons' attack on one
individual. It is difficult to be certain whether Eliot's early
leadership was part of a well-masked but previously worked-
out plan. When the dramatic change of pace and tone came
in the middle of March, the initiative was certainly taken out
of Eliot's hands, at least for the critical few weeks. It seems an
open question whether Eliot had fully realized from the outset
where the laborious investigations he had sponsored would
lead, but there was no room for doubt where Turner's queries
pointed. It is also possible that Turner and Digges were
operating in closer liaison with groups of peers and disaffected
councillors than Eliot had been. Turner was a client of the
Lord Chamberlain, the Earl of Pembroke, who had used his
considerable electoral influence on behalf of members of the
Commons who were to play a leading part in the attack on
Buckingham.[27] Digges was a close associate of Sir Maurice
Abbot, brother of the sequestered Archbishop of Canterbury.
Other peers such as the Earl of Clare (father-in-law of Sir
Thomas Wentworth), Lord Saye and Sele, and the Earl of
Devonshire had connections in the Commons with men who
took an increasing part in the attack on Buckingham.

The sure delineation of parliamentary groupings is a
difficult task, and it would be dangerous to assume that Eliot
was operating independently of such a combination of peers
and Commons men. Eliot's friend William Coryton was also
a subordinate official to Pembroke as Warden of the Stannaries. Eliot himself was held by the Vice-Admiral of Cornwall,
Sir James Bagg, to have 'whollie given himself' to Pembroke.
He had moved into opposition at almost exactly the same time
as Lord Saye and Sele, and his daughter later married into
the Fiennes family. It would therefore be more prudent to

---

[25] Gardiner, *History of England*, vi. 77.

[26] Hulme, op. cit. 114. Also H. Hulme, 'The Leadership of Sir John Eliot in the
Parliament of 1626', *J.M.H.* lv (1934), 361–86.

[27] V. Rowe, 'The Influence of the Earls of Pembroke on Parliamentary Elections,
1625–41', *E.H.R.* l (1935), 242–56.

conclude that Digges's seizure of the initiative in the Commons represented a new phase of the intervention of disaffected peers rather than its beginning. Nevertheless it provided a scheme which appealed much more easily to the mass of the Commons than had Eliot's. Members were very willing to vote the 'multiplicity of offices in one man's hand', the 'not right ordering of the king's revenues', the 'anticipating of revenues', the 'exhausting of honour and buying them', the 'growth of popery' as evils of which Buckingham was the 'causing cause.[28] They required little investigation, for they were matters, in the view of most, of 'common fame'. Digges brushed aside a further attempt by Eliot to reintroduce the *St. Peter* affair, and Eliot had to wait until the House was on the brink of drawing up formal impeachment charges before he was successful in obtaining its inclusion.

By the time the House debated supply on 27 March, Eliot had resumed a more active role. His suggestion that 'there are *causae causatae* and *causa causantes* [*sic*]' led to the establishment of a subcommittee of 'causes of causes'.[29] On 25 March Eliot successfully moved that Buckingham be sent for to answer the charges. The days following the supply debate of 27 March were taken up by the intervention of the king to prohibit the questioning of his great officers of state by the Commons, and with the preparation of a remonstrance defending the Commons' right as the 'Great Council' of the kingdom to prosecute grievances wherever they might lead.

So far there had been no decision to proceed by impeachment. Parliament was in recess for Easter from 5 to 13 April, and when it reassembled, the king gradually withdrew his opposition to the presentation of charges against Buckingham. By agreeing in advance to the presentation of charges 'either to himself or to the Lords', he saved an important point of principle. Not until after the king's message had been received did any of the Commons' leaders refer even hypothetically to proceeding by impeachment. A subcommittee sat to consider whether charges might be preferred against a peer based merely on 'common fame', but whether to the king or before the Lords was still left open. The formal decision to send the charges to the Lords was not taken until 2 May, when the supporters of

---

[28] Whitelocke, I, fos. 54–6.
[29] Whitelocke, I, fo. 63.

impeachment made much of the argument that the king had already assented to this procedure.[30] During the supply debate of 27 March, Eliot had avoided creating the impression that any of the medieval favourites named in his list of precedents had been impeached. Indeed he said that in the case of de la Pole 'in 10 Richard II, the supplie demanded was refused untill upon *peticion* of the Commons . . . he was removed both from his offices and the court, and a commission likewise granted for the rectifying of the king's estate.' Others had as clearly implied that the Commons were still thinking in terms of a petition to the king.[31] We can only speculate as to

[30] Ibid. I, fos. 173–174ᵛ. Cf. diary of Sir Richard Grosvenor, Trinity College, Dublin MS. 611, p. 22. It seems clear that either the subcommittee was itself in doubt about the advisability of an impeachment charge against Buckingham until the last moment, or at least that it was concerned that a premature disclosure of its intentions to the whole House would risk its rejection. See C. G. C. Tite, *Impeachment and Parliamentary Judicature in Early Stuart England* (1974), 193–8. Tite has argued in this work that, strictly speaking, it is doubtful if any of the proceedings before the Lords against Michell, Mompesson, and Bacon in 1621, or even that against Middlesex in 1624, can be regarded as impeachments in the full sense that the Commons both presented full written charges and retained some part in the course of the case before the Lords. He recognizes, however, that the distinctions were highly technical, perhaps appreciated only by a small number of members of the Commons. It is significant that Selden's treatise *Of Judicature* was probably composed about 1626. Tite also considers it doubtful whether Charles gave assent to procedure before the Lords in 1626 consciously to avoid the creation of a precedent in favour of the unilateral action of the Commons (op. cit. 192 n.25). Whilst certainty on this and other points is unattainable, it is by no means clear that Charles was constitutionally unsophisticated, nor that he was not well advised. It is relevant to re-emphasize in this connection that the first mention of the possibility of Buckingham's being 'transmitted to the Lords' was the hypothetical one by the Chancellor of the Exchequer as early as 24 March: 'If I thought him [the Duke] the immediate cause [of the failure to guard the narrow seas], I would as willingly as any man give my voyce for the transmitting of him to the Lords.' (Whitelocke, I, fo. 16ᵛ.) When on 2 May the formal decision was taken to go to the Lords, Sir William Beecher said: 'We knowe the King hath promised that he will referre these things we shall complayne of . . . Thought the K. gave us leave to pcede against the Duke, yet rather in generall to reforme hereafter then upon these pticulars.' Coryton had argued in a way which tried to minimize the difference between transmission to the Lords and a petition to the king: 'to goe to the Lords; for after it will be left to the King' (Grosvenor, I, p. 22). Essentially, the king's apparent expressed indifference meant that the Commons could avoid an internal crisis on this question.

[31] Port Eliot MS., printed in *Negotium Posterorum*, i. 156–64. Other speakers on 27 March had clearly implied that the Commons intended only to proceed by petition to the king. Coryton said: 'lett us sett down how much wee will give and desire his Majestie for redresse of our grievances, and when it is done to passe the Acte' (Whitelocke, I, fo. 9ᵛ). Sir Francis Goodwin proposed that 'upon our petition to the King and his answer, we may passe the Acts of subsidies' (ibid. I, fo. 5ᵛ). Digges's motion was made the basis of the final resolution that 'as soon as we have preferred

whether the idea of impeachment as a practical possibility entered the minds of the Commons' leaders only after the king had dropped the hint that he would allow it; nor is it clear why the king did so. We do know, however, that efforts to strengthen the pro-Buckingham party in the Lords had been made during the parliament. It is possible that the king suggested impeachment, in the expectation that it would fail, and that a resulting breach between Lords and Commons could be exploited by the crown.

The supply debate on 27 March and the proceedings of the subcommittee of 'causes of causes' in April also suggest that there was doubt in the minds of the Commons' leaders about the kind of case against Buckingham to be presented. On 22 April the whole House debated the question which had most disturbed the subcommittee — whether 'common fame' was a sufficient basis for charges. It was finally agreed that since the Commons had no power to condemn but only to present charges, common fame was a sufficient basis, no individual witnesses being necessary because the Commons were functioning as the 'Grand Inquest' of the nation.[32]

An examination of the Articles of Impeachment, as presented by those members delegated to 'aggravate' them before the Lords, reveals considerable differences between those which had evolved from Dr. Turner's 'six queries' and those based on the cases which Eliot had pursued earlier, and which were now reincorporated into the impeachment. During the justification of the charge that Buckingham had bought offices and places of judicature, it was admitted that this was not 'against any particular law . . . yet as far as they divert the good and welfare and safety of the people, so far they are against the highest law, and assume the nature of the highest offences'. The aggravation of the charge that Buckingham had ennobled his relations to the prejudice of the king's estate, went further: ' . . . in the court of parliament . . . the proceedings are not limited either by the civil or the common laws, but matters are adjudged according as they stand in opposition or conformity with that which is *suprema lex* — *salus populi*.

---

our grievances to the King and received his answer, the bill shall be brought in' (ibid).

[32] *C.J.* i. 847–8.

Honour is a public thing, it is the reward of deserts . . . and this your lordships have seen that the sale of honour is an offence unnatural, against the law of nature.'[33]

The charges which had seemed attractive to Turner and Digges because of the ease with which the Commons accepted them had proved impossible to justify on strictly legal grounds. By contrast, the charges which emerged from the cases investigated under Eliot's leadership, at least in the way in which Eliot presented them both in the Commons and before the Lords, were made to seem of a different order. About the case of the loan of ships to the French, Eliot said:

> Even if . . . his Majesty were pleased to have consented, or to have commanded, which I cannot beleeve; yet this could no way satisfy, for him [the Duke] or make any extenuation of the fault. For he should have opposed it by his praiers, and by his intercessions to his Majesty making known the dangers and inconveniences that might follow. And if that prevailed not, must he have rested there? Noe, but should have addressed himself to your lordships, your lordships sitting in Counsell, and there have made it known, there have desired your aides. Naie, if in this he sped not, he should have entered there a protestation for himself that he was not consenting. This was the dutie of his place, that hath been the practise of his elders, and this being now neglected leaves him without excuse.[34]

For Gardiner, this represented 'the dashing into ruin of the whole scaffolding on which the Tudor monarchy had rested — the responsibility of ministers to the sovereign alone'.[35] According to Gardiner, Eliot here was being more 'extreme' than other managers of the impeachment. But there are other considerations to be taken into account. The king had consented to the drawing of articles of impeachment. The Lords, not the Commons, were the judges, in a sense on the king's behalf. Miss M. V. Clarke long ago pointed out that only in 1641, at Strafford's impeachment, did the main conduct of the trial cease to be *ex parte regis* and pass altogether under the control of the Commons.[36] Also, even if the implications of

[33] T. B. Howell, *A Complete Collection of State Trials*, (1809), ii, cols. 1326, 1352.

[34] Port Eliot MS. The version in *State Trials*, ii, cols. 1367–70 is somewhat more condensed, but substantially the same.

[35] Gardiner, *History of England*, vi. 103–4.

[36] M. V. Clarke, 'The Origins of Impeachment', *Fourteenth Century Studies*, ed. L. Sutherland and M. McKisack (Oxford, 1937), 269.

Eliot's 'aggravation' of this charge were as far-reaching as Gardiner suggested, there had been little sign of resistance to the inclusion of this kind of charge from the councillors in the Commons. The Chancellor of the Exchequer had said on 24 March: 'If I thought him the immediate cause [of the failure to guard the narrow seas], I would as willingly as any man give my voyce for the transmitting of him to the Lords'.[37]

Eliot's 'Epilogue' to the impeachment charges nevertheless went further than anything he had implied during the Commons' investigation of grievances. He had begun the inquiry into the *St. Peter* affair by attempting to prove that Buckingham had acted both illegally and without the king's authority. The royal acknowledgement of knowledge and responsibility had forced Eliot back on to the weaker argument that the responsibility was still the Duke's because he had advised the rearrest of the ship on insufficient evidence. But when Eliot persuaded the House on 2 May to include the *St. Peter* case in the formal charges, he had abandoned any attempt to connect it with the complaints of the merchants against their seizure of their goods in France, and developed it as a simple question of judicial irregularity: 'We have not this in consideration for the merchants, but propose our advise for the safety of our justice, use of our liberties and preservance of our lawes. The question is of our injustice here, but of goods unjustly stayed: may not the like be to you and us and all?'[38] Moreover Eliot reverted to his earlier position, that the Duke had acted without the king's knowledge, and it was in this form that the charge was incorporated in the Articles of Impeachment. Consequently, it was an exceptionally weak charge, already nullified by the king's acceptance of responsibility.

The case of the loan of ships to France is parallel. When challenged by Secretary Coke that the English government could not be blamed for the diversion of the ships by the French government from a common expedition against Genoa to the blockading of the Protestant stronghold of La Rochelle, Eliot had replied: 'Mysterie of state, conjunctures and disjunctures of affayres [I] will not meddle with, but the miseryes

[37] Whitelocke, I, fo. 16ᵛ.
[38] Grosvenor, I, p. 19. Cf. Whitelocke, I, fo. 173.

we suffer hereby we are all sensible of, and it is propper for the cognisance of this courte. It was never concluded [I am] confident, by the councell of state, that we should quitt our shipps and let other men have the governance of them, and to send away some of our best shipps on forrein contracts.'[39] Later, the committee of 'causes of causes' reported that they held Buckingham responsible for handing over the ships, justifying it with arguments which were embodied unchanged in the Articles of Impeachment. Buckingham was charged with the illegal impressment of merchant ships and 'by subtile means and practices, having, without order of justice and without the consent of the ... masters and owners, compelled the said masters and owners to deliver the said ships into the ... possession of the French king ... without either a sufficient security or assurance for the re-delivery ... contrary to the ... duty of the ... offices of great admiral, governor general and keeper of the said ships and seas ... contrary to the duty which he oweth to our sovereign lord the king in his place of privy counsellor.' He was further charged with knowledge that the ships were going to be used against La Rochelle, 'contrary to the purpose and intention of our sovereign lord the king, and against his duty in that behalf', and that 'to mask his ill intentions [he] did at the Parliament held at Oxford in August last ... intimate and declare that the said ships were not, nor should be so used ... in contempt of our sovereign lord the king, and in abuse of the said houses of Parliament'.[40]

The implications had been clearly expressed by Eliot in the Commons on 21 April. Buckingham was being charged with 'illegally varying from his original good instructions', 'presuming to give others of his own head in matters of state', with 'violating the duty of a sworn privy counsellor to his Majesty', and with 'abusing both houses of Parliament by a cautelous misinformation under colour of a message from his Majesty.'[41] Eliot had attempted to draw a distinction between Buckingham's private acts and those of a royal counsellor. 'He had observed a new wisdom in this house, that the faults of private men be shaddowed under secretts of state. The intention of the state was not to hand over the shipps, but to serve

[39] Whitelocke, I, fo. 58.   [40] *State Trials*, ii, cols. 1314–15.
[41] Ibid., col. 1350.

against the publique enemy in the publique cause.'[42]

In his epilogue to the impeachment Eliot certainly took a far-reaching view of the responsibilities of a sworn counsellor of the king, but it is clear that he saw that responsibility as being towards the body of the Privy Council rather than to parliament. But where it reached further forward, it was in contradiction of that distinction which Eliot had tried to maintain. Except in the epilogue, he had scrupulously tried to maintain a distinction between matters of state and things debatable in the Commons, by attempting to show that Buckingham had been acting in an unauthorized capacity contrary to the wishes of the body of the Council and of the king. It was this distinction, normally well maintained, that preserved him from 'shattering the foundations of Tudor monarchy'. It was an *evasion* of the problem of responsibility, not a revolutionary conception of it. Its weakness lay in the willingness of the king to protect his servant by accepting personal responsibility for acts complained of.

The weakness of impeachment under these conditions was revealed by the slowness of the conduct of Buckingham's trial after it passed from the Commons' control. The time of the Lords was taken up with considering charges brought by the king against the Earl of Bristol, with counter-charges brought by Bristol against Buckingham, and with the Lords' own conflict with the king concerning the Earl of Arundel's exclusion from this parliament. Grumbling in the Commons gradually crystallized into a decision to ask the Lords for a conference. At the same time the Grand Committee for Privileges was considering the implications of the temporary arrest of Eliot and Digges. On 3 June the select committee considering the agenda for a conference with the Lords recommended that its proceedings should be joined with the Committee for Privileges and that a remonstrance should be prepared for submission to the king, in which the Lords might join if they saw fit.

For Gardiner, the Remonstrance was a further step taken by the Commons, under Eliot's leadership, towards the ultimate claim of sovereignty. He saw it as a recognition that impeachment had failed, and the substitution for it of a request

[42] Whitelocke, I, fo. 148–148ᵛ.

that the 'king should abandon his minister on the grounds that the Commons could not trust him'.[43] Whilst it is possible to disagree with Gardiner's interpretation of the Remonstrance even if we accept his view that it was a substitute for impeachment, an analysis of the debates leading to it suggests it was nothing of the sort. Under renewed pressure from the king to vote supply, the Commons certainly moved on 12 June to the position that the subsidy bill would not be passed until the grievances were redressed, but Eliot made it clear on that day that he at least was not yet convinced that impeachment had failed.

that there is a hesitation with the Lords it is too true...It is but justice that wee crave, wch the king oweth us, and I am confident we shall in time receave; that the king in his honour cannot forbeare that protection of one so neare him; in this we butt desire that he may come to his tryall. 50 H. H [*sic*] the king's confessor being charged in generall by parliament the king returned his answear...that he knew no faults he was guilty of butt bicause he was impeached by all his parliament hee would not keep him from his tryall, but leave him. This much I am confident wee shall have this much [*sic*] of our king.[44]

The next day, another member, Mr. Spencer, made the point as clearly: 'The request is to desire the sequestration of the Duke from the King, he standing now accused by us in the Lords' House.'[45]

The impertinence of the threatened resolution was, in Gardiner's view, sufficient reason for Charles's decision to dissolve the Parliament, but by rejecting his interpretation of the Remonstrance, we are left with the problem of explaining the precipitate dissolution, which followed within two days. The week before, the king had warned that further delays in granting supply would be taken as a refusal. The dissolution may therefore have been a straightforward reaction to the Commons' excuse for further delay. On the other hand, it has recently been argued that it followed rapidly upon the weakening of Buckingham's strength in the Lords following

[43] Gardiner, *History of England*, vi. 120.
[44] Whitelocke, II, fo. 54–55ᵛ.
[45] Ibid. II, fo. 57.

the long-fought-for return to it of the Earl of Arundel on 8 June and Buckingham's own voluntary withdrawal from it. This is undeniably so, but we cannot be sure that, if the Parliament was dissolved to save Buckingham, it was to save him from the Commons' impeachment, for the climax of the battle between Buckingham and the Earl of Bristol in the Lords was also rapidly approaching.[46]

Nevertheless, the king had failed to obtain financial support, and money for the war had soon to be raised by the 'more than ordinary ways' which Eliot had forecast at the opening of the session. The Commons had equally clearly failed to secure the removal of the favourite, a movement which, as Eliot had also pointed out, had been 'begun at Oxford and by those that are now absent.' That Eliot had persisted for so long lends colour to the view that he was sincere in protesting that 'I am confident that uppon our declaration the kinge will be pleased to expecte the event of these councells, rightly understanding both the Duke and us.'[47] Equally, the dissolution involved the abandonment of those plans for the 'rectification' of the king's estate, also begun at Oxford.

By the time the next parliament met in 1628, the expedition to aid the Protestants of La Rochelle had failed as disastrously as that to Cadiz, and scores of gentry had been imprisoned for refusal to contribute to the forced loan levied for the war. Eliot was among the many who suffered imprisonment. He petitioned the king for his release, citing precedents to prove the illegality of the loan, some pertinent, others irrelevant, but was not one of the Five Knights who sought legal remedy. The release of the imprisoned gentry

[46] Ibid. II, fo. 54ᵛ. The wording here has been somewhat modified compared with that in J. N. Ball, 'The Impeachment of the Duke of Buckingham in the Parliament of 1626', *Mélanges Antonio Marongiu; Studies presented to the International Commission for the History of Representative and Parliamentary Institutions*, xxxiv (Palermo, 1968), 35–48. Since then Dr. Flemion has argued strongly that the return to the Lords on 8 June of the Earl of Arundel, armed with five proxy votes, seriously disturbed the balance of forces in the Lords. Flemion considers it likely that the dissolution *was* necessary to save Buckingham, and that it is possible that the last demand that the Commons pass the subsidy bill was designed to throw the blame for the dissolution upon them. J. S. Flemion, 'The Dissolution of Parliament in 1626; a Revaluation', *E.H.R.* lxxxvii (1972), 784–90.) Whether the major threat to Buckingham lay in the Commons' impeachment charges is less clear. See Kevin Sharpe, below, pp. 232–3.

[47] Whitelocke, II, fo. 55ᵛ.

came too obviously as a preparation for the new parliament to have any effect in conciliating opinion. The tactics to be followed by the Commons' leaders were possibly discussed at a meeting in Sir Robert Cotton's house. Under the influence of Sir Edward Coke and Sir Thomas Wentworth, it was agreed that the legal and constitutional aspects of the forced loan and of imprisonment without legal cause shown should be squarely faced. The renewal of the attack on Buckingham, probably favoured by Eliot, was to be postponed until satisfactory legal guarantees for the liberty of the subject had been safely secured.[48]

The complexities of the legal issues involved were greater than was initially realized, certainly by the majority of the House who were not professional lawyers, and perhaps even by the minority who were. Eliot was clearly at a disadvantage in bidding for leadership in such conditions. During the early weeks of the parliament he shared the widespread opinion that the violation of property rights by the forced loan was of greater importance than the arbitrary imprisonment by which it had been enforced. He also displayed some unwillingness to accept the primacy of the legal issues by seeking unsuccessfully further inquiries into the details of the war policy before the House agreed in committee to vote the unprecedented sum of five subsidies.

During the early weeks there was little disagreement in the Commons concerning the drafting of resolutions on the liberty of the subject. Confusion about the law of arbitrary imprisonment gave way to relief when it was discovered that neither the judgement in the Five Knights' Case nor the 'Anderson' judgement of 1592 gave unequivocal authority to the crown to imprison without cause shown.[49] To maintain a common front with the Lords was more difficult, especially

[48] Hulme, *Sir John Eliot*, 184–5. Hulme has also failed to discover the documentary evidence for this meeting which John Forster claimed existed at Port Eliot. He points out that Gardiner stated that the Venetian ambassador reported that Charles had received assurances that the attack on Buckingham would not be renewed, and had then issued writs for the elections. Hulme, however, converts Gardiner's admitted 'guess' that Pembroke offered these assurances into a certainty without presenting further evidence.

[49] Frances H. Relf, *The Petition of Right* (Minneapolis, 1917), ch. 1. It was Eliot who was able to produce for the House a manuscript copy of Anderson's Reports containing this judgement. Brit. Lib. Add. MS. 27878, fos. 87–8.

after the Upper House added a further resolution to the four proposed by the Commons, requesting the king 'not to use or divert his royal prerogative incident to sovereigntie, and intrusted him from God, to the preiudice of any of his loyall people in the proprietie of their goods or the libertie of their persons'.[50] To the Commons, this nullified the effect of the other resolutions. Differences of opinion now began to arise in the Commons, and it is from this point that Gardiner dated a fundamental distinction between 'moderates' led by Wentworth, and 'extremists' led by Sir Edward Coke and Eliot, in which 'the origins of the parties in the Civil War could be discerned'.[51] Professor Relf has shown that a closer study of the detailed proposals of the two groups between 25 April and 2 May reveals that although there was a difference between the Wentworth and the Coke-Eliot groups, it is misleading to see it in terms of a clash between moderates and extremists.[52] Essentially it was a difference about the most practical means of achieving a common objective—the prevention of the use of arbitrary imprisonment to enforce arbitrary taxation. This was the only issue on which the king and his councillors were offering stiff resistance, as it seemed to be impossible for them to compromise on it without destroying altogether the power of arbitrary imprisonment regarded as essential to the security of the state, and that power 'beyond the law' which Eliot was later to grant the monarch for the common good. It was Wentworth who first proposed a bill to explain the *lex terrae* clause of Magna Carta, Coke who chaired a subcommittee which produced a draft bill that was debated for three days. The difference between Wentworth on the one hand and Eliot and Coke on the other reduced itself to one essential point. Eliot and Coke favoured the enactment of the full Commons' resolutions of 1 April, whilst Wentworth thought that a habeas corpus bill would be a more practicable and acceptable as well as an equally effective, protection.[53] Then on 2 May, Secretary Sir John Coke intervened to deliver a

---

[50] Brit. Lib. Stowe MS. 367, fo. 144ᵛ. (MS. of Sir William Borlase). Cf. Add. MS. 27878, fo. 189, which gives 'royal prerogative intrinsecall to his soveraigntie'.

[51] Gardiner, *History of England*, vi. 272.

[52] Relf, op. cit., ch. IV.

[53] Stowe MS. 367, fo. 155–155ᵛ; Add. MS. 27878, fos. 213 214ᵛ; Grosvenor, I, p. 181.

message from the king demanding to know whether the Commons would 'rest on his royall word or noe, declared to us by the Lord Keeper', and adding that anything which the Commons desired to add to the laws as they stood was a diminution of the king's rights and an addition to those of the subject. The Secretary of State added for himself that, whatever the law said, he would be compelled to commit to prison without showing cause in cases involving the safety of the state. After the considerable silence which followed Sir John Coke's statement, Sir Edward Coke and Eliot moved an adjournment.[54]

On the face of it, the king's message provided Wentworth with an opportunity to press his own proposal home. Eliot and Coke proposed an adjournment because the king's message utterly destroyed their hope of a declaratory act. However, an analysis of the debates from 2 to 6 May suggests that Wentworth's scheme was as effectively killed as was that of Eliot and Coke. Wentworth's habeas corpus scheme involved an addition to the law, just as did that of Coke and Eliot. It involved the creation of new procedures which would have been just as fatal as would the explanatory bill. That Wentworth's scheme was in fact abandoned for exactly the same reason as the declaratory one is supported by the reference of a lawyer member, Mason, to both schemes as 'acts of explanation'.[55] Wentworth's preference for 'moderate courses' was confined to designing a bill which had some hope of receiving the assent of the Lords and the king. That it was an early sign of party alignments to come is made doubtful by the support which Wentworth received from John Pym. By 5 May the king had finally made it clear that no statutory solution of the crisis was acceptable to him, but Eliot had already abandoned hope of any bill on 3 May: 'This is noe tyme to speake of a bill. I agree we doe not enlarge, or restrain any newe thinge; the King saith he will ranke himself with the best Kings and therefore hee would have us rank ourselves with the best Subjects; wee will not incroach upon that

---

[54] Add. MS. 27878, fo. 218–218ᵛ; Stowe MS. 367, fo. 161–161ᵛ; Grosvenor, I, pp. 182–3.
[55] *Old Parliamentary History*, viii. 90.

Soveraigntie that God hath put into his hands.'[56]

The difficulty which faced Sir Edward Coke after the attempt to secure an act was abandoned was how to convince the Commons that their objective could be almost as effectively obtained without one. We know that Coke's belief in the need to have the original Commons' resolutions on the liberty of the subject recited in a public document lay at the root of his proposal to substitute a Petition of Right. Wentworth and others had earlier opposed a petition on the ground that it would remain 'wrapped in a Parliament roll'. Now Eliot and his associate Coryton seem to have joined Wentworth in requiring to be convinced by Coke that a Petition of Right reciting the grievances of the immediate past would be acceptable to the king and would guarantee the subjects' rights in the future. They seem to have clung as long as possible to the belief that once a Petition of Right had been accepted by the king, a bill should be substituted for it. Eliot nevertheless had withdrawn his motion for an immediate vote on whether or not the House was willing to rely on the king's personal promise, and accepted with the rest of the house, that 'to decline to a petition' was the best course. By 27 May, when formal action on the Petition of Right was imminent, Eliot hoped that 'the king's affections will be more to us than all lawes. The laws are in force, that is confessed, and his assent [to the Petition] will give life.'[57]

Even at this stage all difficulties had not been overcome. Coke's effort to persuade the Commons that a Petition would be nearly as good as a bill was almost too successful, for it seems to have convinced the king as well, so that his first answer to the Petition contained a 'saving' of his prerogative along the same lines as the earlier fifth resolution of the House

[56] Add. MS. 27878, fo. 226; Stowe MS. 367, fo. 171: 'we should make it appeare wee...have used noe encroaching, lay this more perspicuously before his Majesty'.

[57] Add. MS. 27878, fo. 327ᵛ. See Elizabeth R. Foster, 'Petitions and the Petition of Right', *J.B.S.* xiv (1974), 21–45, who emphasizes the importance attached to making the Petition a matter of record. The final answer was recorded on the Petition as the assent to a bill was recorded on the original, and the Clerk of the Parliaments ordered it to be printed, and also enrolled on the Parliament Roll 'where statutes are entered', but it was never entered in the *Lords Journal* (art. cit. 42–3). This does not affect the argument here that those who seemed keenest to revive the attack on Buckingham's conduct of affairs seemed the least interested in the later stages of negotiations with the king concerning the answer to the Petition.

of Lords. The majority of the Commons felt this to be entirely destructive of what they had hoped to achieve. The king was asked to give another, more acceptable, answer. In Gardiner's view, this was obtained by Eliot's renewal of attacks on Buckingham. The whole of this session of parliament had represented an interlude in Eliot's programme, and, as we have seen, it is probable that it had been agreed that he might resume his offensive after the constitutional problem had been solved. Professor Relf has shown, however, not only that Eliot's attack on Buckingham was pre-arranged, but that those who supported it were if anything opposed to any attempt to try to persuade the king to give a more satisfactory answer to the Petition, and that the second 'satisfactory' answer failed to stop the attack on the Duke.[58]

Eliot was from this point onwards to exercise a firmer control of the majority of the Commons than he had ever achieved before. On 3 June he made a long and violent speech attacking the conduct of foreign policy since 1626. Buckingham was not named for some days, and then not at first by Eliot. Eventually a Remonstrance to the king was proposed by Selden, attacking the 'excessive power' of the Duke. Eliot has provided several clues to his intentions. He made it clear that a Remonstrance allowed greater freedom in the presentation of the case than had been possible in the quasi-judicial form of the impeachment. Acting as the 'Great Council' of the king, the Commons could complain of matters which could not form the basis of criminal charges. Their function was 'truly to present to the king what he doth not know alreadie about his ministers and officers'.[59] At the same time he showed that he thought that the Remonstrance was a more moderate way of proceeding than impeachment: 'Let us deale sincerlie, there is a necessitie why wee should name [Buckingham]. If we looke to our honour or the last Parliament, was hee not then named and are not the causes now multiplied? and have wee not declared him alreadie? Wee shall bee free from his Ma[jes]t[ie's] displeasure. Wee have now brought our cause to that lownes as onlie to present him

---

[58] Relf, op. cit. 51–3.
[59] Add. MS. 27878, fos. 343ᵛ, 393ᵛ.

to his Ma[jes]tie'.[60] The Remonstrance had a further advantage from Eliot's point of view, since it required no collaboration with the Lords. It began the last phase of Eliot's parliamentary career in which no tactical alliance with the Lords was even attempted.

The change in the political situation between the prorogation of the Parliament on 26 June 1628 and the meeting of the next session on 20 January 1629 was dramatic. In August, Buckingham was finally removed from the scene by Felton's dagger, and Wentworth immediately accepted office as Lord President of the Council of the North. Yet, despite more careful attempts to prepare for the new session, the atmosphere had in many respects worsened by January 1629. Attempts to damp down religious controversy backfired. Although Dr. Montague's *Appello Caesarem* was called in, the prohibition of public controversy about the interpretation of the Thirty-nine Articles was interpreted by many amongst both clergy and laity as an attempt to suppress 'truth' along with falsehood. The appointment of leading Arminians to bishoprics at the very moment when they were being complained of in parliament heightened the fear that traditional orthodoxy was to be branded as 'Puritanism' as the Church fell under the control of a triumphant proto-Catholic minority.[61]

The long period of 'settled government' needed for the return of political peace was not made impossible by the state of the finances, but the king evidently wished to settle the question of Tonnage and Poundage which had remained outstanding since 1625. The crown had continued to levy the duty despite the lack of parliamentary approval, so the Commons now had a valuable weapon to help them in the struggle against prerogative impositions on the ordinary customs duties. At the end of the session of 1628, the Commons had again refused to grant Tonnage and Poundage, and prepared a Remonstrance, using the newly won Petition of Right as a basis. Under the open encouragement of the Commons, merchants had refused to pay the duty. In his prorogation speech, the king had shown the same tendency as the Com-

[60] Ibid., fo. 403ᵛ.
[61] See N. R. N. Tyacke, 'Puritanism, Arminianism and Counter-Revolution', in *The Origins of the English Civil War*, ed. Conrad Russell, (1973).

mons to confuse Tonnage and Poundage with impositions, and to claim that the duty was his of right. Some London merchants had goods seized for refusing Tonnage and Poundage. In November 1628, John Rolle, a Cornish M.P., suffered confiscation of goods and failed to recover them by legal means. The use of the writ of replevin was rejected by the Barons of the Exchequer as an invalid means of recovering goods held by the king.

The king's speech at the opening of the new session was conciliatory. He now denied that he had taken Tonnage and Poundage as of right, only from 'necessity'. But the Commons were not now prepared to keep Tonnage and Poundage and impositions distinct. It was widely felt that the continued existence of parliament was dependent upon preventing the king from raising revenue at will from taxes on foreign trade. The threat of 'new counsels' was being made more frequently by royal officials. Everything therefore seemed to depend on how the issues were handled on both sides. There was a considerable body of opinion in the Commons which felt that a satisfactory compromise must and could be reached. The king's speech was designed to reach out to find common ground with the group of members who had appeared to be flexible at the end of the previous session. Amongst this group Sir Dudley Digges had favoured adjournment rather than prorogation, so that a commission might sit during the recess to consider the question. William Noy had favoured the omission of a request to the king not to levy Tonnage and Poundage until approved by parliament, preferring a request that he did not take it 'as of right'.

The failure of attempts to calm fears about religion complicated matters further, and it has generally been assumed that, for most members of the Commons, religion was the prime issue in 1629. In Eliot's case, however, there is considerable reason to believe that he was primarily concerned with the issue of the customs duties. The lead in discussion of religious grievances was taken by a different group of members from those who initially raised the Tonnage and Poundage question. Sir Francis Seymour, Francis Rous, Sir Robert Phelips, and Robert Kirton were all prominent in debate on religion, whilst John Pym took his now customary place as

Chairman of the Committee of the whole House for Religion.
As far as the diarists reveal, Eliot took no part in the religious
debates until 29 January, and when he intervened he tried to
accelerate and clarify the debate. But his proposal that 'we go
presently to the ground of our Religion, and by that downe a
rule on which all may rest' showed that he failed to appreciate
the difficulties involved in reaching an acceptable definition of
orthodoxy.[62] It was resolved on 29 January that 'the Commons
... do claim, profess and avow for truth the sense of the Articles
of Religion which were established in Parliament in the 13th
year of Queen Elizabeth, which by the public acts of the
Church of England and by the general and concurrent exposition of the writers of our Church, hath been delivered unto
us, and we reject the sense of the Jesuits and Arminians
wherein they do differ from us.'[63] The ensuing debates revealed serious differences of opinion concerning an acceptable
canon of 'orthodox' interpretation of the controversial Articles.
The Commons were far from asserting the right to define
religious truth by resolution that Gardiner ascribed to them.[64]
As Eliot put it, 'it is confirmed by Parliament because it is the
truth.'[65] But what had been confirmed by parliament was not
much, and not very helpful in excluding Arminian interpretations. The Erastian lawyers in the Commons refused to
accept anything more as 'public doctrine'. Those who found
the Articles of Lambeth of 1595 a convenient gloss ran against
the criticism that these had only been the product of a Convocation. As Eliot warned, it might 'tend to the prejudice of
the truth and the Church, if soe many Bishops in another
assembly should resolve on anything contrary to those Articles
as the orthodox opinions of the Church.'[66]

Eliot's reaction to these difficulties was the same as it had
been a week earlier. He proposed to 'rely on the ground
already laid', to strike at the Arminians by charging them with
holding beliefs contrary to the Articles of Lambeth, and 'if

[62] *Commons Debates in 1629*, ed. W. Notestein and F. H. Relf (Minneapolis, 1921),
24–8; cf. 116–17.
[63] Ibid. 23.
[64] Gardiner *History of England*, vii. 42–3.
[65] *Commons Debates in 1629*, 28.
[66] Ibid. 122.

these parties will defend themselves, *then* seek for proof'.[67] We are left in doubt by what procedures the Commons proposed to charge the Arminians, and can only presume that, as most of the individuals who were attacked were by now bishops, it would most likely have been by impeachment. As in 1626, the Commons were accusers, not judge, and Eliot's short cut had the same weaknesses as the case against Buckingham.

It seems reasonable to conclude, not that Eliot had no real interest in the religious crisis, but at least that he was tactically more concerned to bring forward an attack on those officers who had seized merchants' goods before the king again dissolved parliament in despair of a solution of the Tonnage and Poundage question.

The House abandoned the attempt to attack the newly pro-moted bishops on specific doctrinal grounds, and sought other ways of reaching them. Eliot intervened little in this new phase but began to devote more time to the tax issue and its related issue of parliamentary privilege. This question too was quickly to reveal a split of more than tactical importance between Eliot and Selden on the one hand, and a group containing Pym, Noy, and Digges on the other. Eliot and Selden wanted a practical means of restoring the sequestered goods of the merchants. The Barons of the Exchequer had now informed the Commons that they had refused restoration not because Tonnage and Poundage was a legal tax, but because incorrect procedures had been used by the plaintiffs. The situation was thus re-vealed to be similar to that in the Five Knights' Case. Eliot proposed to examine the Customs farmers on the grounds that they were 'offenders in point of privilege'. This was to single out the case of John Rolle from the others, because he was a member of the House. Even for his case to be regarded as one of breach of privilege, it was necessary to create a precedent that privilege extended to a period of prorogation between two sessions of parliament. Even so it was a useless device for the interests of the mass of merchants who were not M.P.s.

Pym was quick to take issue with Eliot: 'the liberties of this

---

[67] Ibid. 34. Cf. 69: 'that for the manner of our proceedings we may not seem to make or give any jealousy to that cause we have in hand being without question, but that first we seek and fall on them which have erred from our profession, and then the Articles of Lambeth will come in against them for a constant profession of the same.'

kingdom are greater than the liberties of this House.'[68] Eliot
and Selden had indeed taken up the 'weak ground' which
Gardiner noted. It seems less logical for him to have added
that in Eliot's case it was through extremism, in Selden's from
a 'constitutional timidity'.[69] Eliot had repeated his attempt to
avoid the major constitutional issue by trying to distinguish
between the actions of individuals (the Customs farmers were
in his view 'private men') and the state. He could only do
this in the narrowly circumscribed area of breach of parliamentary privilege. Pym had wanted a course of action similar
to that adopted in 1628: 'a proceeding to take off the commission and the records that are against us'.[70] Under the
renewed influence of Digges, Phelips, and now even Selden,
the House refused to follow Eliot further, and agreed to an
adjournment until 25 February. It then agreed to the king's
request for a new adjournment until 2 March.

On that day, Eliot faced the final crisis of his parliamentary career. During the week before, at a meeting of Eliot and
his supporters, it had been decided to pre-empt a further
adjournment of dissolution by bringing forward three resolutions on religion and Tonnage and Poundage.[71] Their content
is as well known as the breakdown of order in the House
when the Speaker announced the king's expected demand for
another adjournment. It is not even certain whether the
resolutions were passed in the normal way. Certainly in the
confusion Eliot threw the paper containing them on the fire,
so that they were proposed from memory or from another
version by Denzil Holles.[72] Earlier, Eliot had launched an
attack on the new Lord Treasurer, Weston, as the heir of
Buckingham, the arch-fomenter of popery, and architect of the
continued levy of Tonnage and Poundage. To the end, Eliot
persisted in his view that a single false counsellor was at the
root of all the political troubles: 'the interest which is pretended for the king is but the interest of that person.'[73]

The Three Resolutions carried no more formal weight than

[68] Ibid. 85.
[69] Gardiner, *History of England*, vii. 60.
[70] *Commons Debates in 1629*, 222.
[71] Ibid. 239 note b.
[72] Hulme, *Sir John Eliot*, 307.
[73] *Commons Debates in 1629*, 162.

those on the liberty of the subject in 1628, but they were
clearly intended to intimidate merchants who might prefer to
pay unparliamentary taxes rather than face the ruin of their
business. As such, they represented an appeal from parliament
to the nation for support. After a few months, resistance to
payment ceased, and the merchants enjoyed the benefits of a
newly expanding commerce, whilst the crown reaped those of
buoyant Customs revenues. In the short and, indeed, in the
medium term, it was made clear that the crown held the
strongest cards. The king could dissolve parliament, and
managed to dispense with it for eleven years, at the price of a
foreign policy which was hardly less effective in the enforced
peace than it had been during the war against Spain. As on
previous occasions, Eliot had been forced into extreme
measures only when his major policy had broken down. Its
failure was inherent in its persistent refusal to face the issues
of the day in terms of genuine structural tensions instead of in
terms of personalities.

Eliot's reputation as a martyr to freedom of speech and to
the privileges of the Commons was perhaps not as great
amongst his contemporaries as it has since become. Those
who stood aloof or opposed him in the last crisis were not
only courtiers or those who were about to 'go over' to the
court. Those, including Pym, who were most seriously disturbed at the threat to traditional orthodoxy recognized that
regular sessions of parliament offered the best hope of achieving
some modification of policy. Though contemporary comment
on Eliot is limited, it is worthwhile to refer to that of Sir
Simonds D'Ewes in his autobiography. He severely criticized
those 'divers fiery spirits in the House of Commons...by
whom the truly pious and religious members of the House
were too much swayed and carried', and whose concern for
'some exemplary punishment of the Customs Farmers' was the
occasion of the breach between king and Commons, on a
cause which was 'immaterial and frivolous'.[74]

The roots of Eliot's diagnosis of the political problems of his
age and of his conception of the role of the Commons in
dealing with them were already visible in 1624. A few men

---

[74] Sir Simonds D'Ewes, *Autobiography and Correspondence*, ed. J. O. Halliwell (2 vols.,
1845), i. 402–3.

stood as 'false glasses' in the way of a right understanding between the king and the Commons. He shared with many contemporaries a strain of idealism which saw the political discords of the early seventeenth century in terms of ill-disposed individuals but for whose manoeuvrings and ambitions the political scene would have realized the state of ideal 'Elizabethan' harmony. In the 1620s, when one man so dominated the king and monopolized both 'counsel' and patronage that virtually no access to the king was possible except through him, it is understandable that many in Lords and Commons alike should have striven to secure the removal of the favourite by every political means available. As one of them, Eliot was more concerned with achieving the practical objective than he was with the constitutional implications of what he was assisting in. The limitations of what the Commons would find an acceptable procedure were as important in determining his tactics as those imposed by the Lords. It is surely significant, in this respect, that on several occasions he stopped short of demanding what the medieval precedents he cited seemed to offer him.

In order to attack Buckingham in 1626, as with the Customs farmers in 1629, he resorted to a denial that the acts complained of were truly acts of government, attempting to show instead that they were the acts of 'private men' which were being 'shadowed under secrets of state'. In every case, the king showed his willingness to protect his servants by accepting responsibility, destroying Eliot's argument in the process. Neither Eliot nor any other prominent House of Commons man of the 1620s was prepared to criticize the king personally. Eliot's behaviour after release from imprisonment during the impeachment of Buckingham showed a more than usual determination to persuade the Commons to exercise firm control over other members whose incautious language suggested that freedom of speech might become licence to criticize the king.[75]

---

[75] 3 June 1626. A member named Moore spoke hypothetically of tyrants: 'It is an impossibility for this kingdom to be brought to that wch new councells have brought these [other] kdomes to, if God should send us a tyrant, as God be thanked we have a pious and a good k. now. Eliot, joining with those who asked for Moore's punishment, said: 'Mark but ye words spoken by him (if the king will keepe his

In 1628, it was decided that the situation demanded an impersonal approach. The question of arbitrary imprisonment as a means of enforcing illegal actions was squarely faced, and a legal solution was sought which, even if it was not fully satisfactory from the Commons' standpoint, nevertheless required close collaboration between the two Houses. Eliot, however, was still anxious to resume his earlier policy, even when collaboration with the Lords was no longer practicable. There are some signs of this even before the Petition of Right had been satisfactorily agreed between Lords and Commons.[76] Certainly, before the king's second answer to the Petition Eliot led a new attack on the conduct of affairs which soon focused on Buckingham, but indicated that he considered his proposed procedure by remonstrance to the king to be a more moderate method than the impeachment of 1626: 'we have now brought our cause to that lowness as only to present him to his Majesty'. In 1629 Eliot chose to pursue Rolle's Case with greater vigour than the more general questions of Tonnage and Poundage and impositions because it offered the chance of exacting punishment for a breach of parliamentary privilege, but it lost him the support of men like Pym as well as Digges. If the final Three Resolutions bear the mark of a new extremism, it was born of a desperation to achieve something for the record in face of a final threat of dissolution, rather than of a belief in an imminent revolutionary crisis. The king's power was soon demonstrated; the official Journal contained no record of the Resolutions, the Arminians continued on their

kdome) wch are contrary to our teneurs in religion, and in any sense cannot butt be ill taken.' Whitelocke, II, fo. 34–34ᵛ.

[76] 23 May 1628. The House was discussing in committee the Lords' proposal for an addition to the Petition of Right, saving the king's prerogative. Though denying he wanted 'moderation', Sir Thomas Wentworth warned of the dangers of a failure to maintain the unity of Lords and Commons on the Petition. Eliot replied: 'that tho the Lords should not ioyne with us yet he would not hold that either our sinewes were cut, or our stamp taken of...but through the goodness of the King we shall still flourish. He misliked the last motion. would draw us on the length of more difficulty and delay the busines. that the k. was not affectionat to the addicion when he first heard it, that he held it worse for him to have it in than left out.' (Grosvenor, III, pp. 84–5.) The account in Add. MS. 27878, fos. 295–6 gives Eliot at much greater length, but is less clear on the point of difference between him and Wentworth. Eliot was of course wrong about the king's views here. As on other occasions, it is likely that he wished to get his opportunity to revive the attack on Buckingham.

triumphant course, the merchants began again to pay customs and impositions rather than face the ruin of their trade. Eliot was left to maintain his refusal to plead in any court but that of parliament for defence of his actions there. The parliament did not come, but the cutting-off of the parliamentary sources of revenue duly enforced the 'more than ordinary ways' of raising revenue which Eliot had forecast in 1626.

Eliot had been more willing than most members of the Commons to delay or refuse supply until 'grievances' were redressed, but we have no evidence to support the conclusion that he thought this a weapon powerful enough in itself to force the king to heed the 'counsel' of the Commons. Nor was Eliot afraid of the concept of sovereignty. In 1628 Sir Edward Coke said that 'Magna Carta is such a fellow he knows no sovereign', John Pym said that he knew 'how to add sovereign to the king's person but not his power'. Eliot, on the other hand, said that the Commons did not wish to 'incroach upon that Sovereigntie that God hath put into his hands'.[77] The difference, however, should not be over-emphasized, for all three were agreed that it was dangerous for the Petition itself to contain a reference to the king's sovereign power. Yet Eliot had no doubt that sovereignty existed, nor that in England it lay with the king. But he believed, as did Bodin, to whom he referred frequently in the *Monarchie of Man*, that sovereignty could be exercised in various forms. In the best (*droit gouvernement*), it normally respected its own laws, and took the advice of assemblies in framing them. There is thus a unity and consistency between Eliot's conception of the state as expressed in the heat of parliamentary debate and in the reflective calm of his last imprisonment.

[77] Add. MS. 28787, fo. 226.

VII. The Earl of Arundel, His Circle and the Opposition to the Duke of Buckingham, 1618–1628

KEVIN SHARPE

HISTORIANS CONCENTRATING on the House of Commons have all but ignored the early Stuart nobility both as individuals and as members of the House of Lords.[1] Yet as a reward for their loyal service to his mother, Queen Mary of Scots, James I restored to power and office the Howard family which, in the decades before Elizabeth's reign, had counselled kings and broken favourites. We await a full study of the patronage and influence wielded by that family at court and in the localities. This essay will investigate the activities of Thomas Howard, Earl of Arundel, head of the senior Norfolk branch of the family, and examine from the evidence of his career the alignments in the Privy Council and the House of Lords during the 1620s.[2] The first section provides a detailed narrative of Arundel's position at court, a narrative which will demonstrate that issues concerning the constitution, religion, and foreign policy cannot explain Arundel's position or the political co-operation of the diverse men who made up his circle. In the conclusion, I shall suggest that, nevertheless, these men shared attitudes and values which have yet to be recognized and studied by the historian of politics.

Though best known today as a great patron of artists, as 'The father of vertu', Arundel was prominent in his own age as one of the greatest noblemen and as Earl Marshal of

[1] Work has commenced on procedure in the House of Lords, (See especially E. R. Foster, *The Painful Labour of Mr. Elsyng* (Philadelphia, 1972), also J. Flemion, 'Slow Process, Due Process and the High Court of Parliament', *H.J.* xvii (1974). 3–17.) We still await a political study of the Lords. I would like to thank Christopher Brooks, John Cooper, Conrad Russell, and Hugh Trevor-Roper for their most valuable comments on an earlier draft of this essay.

[2] M. F. S. Hervey's excellent biography, *Thomas Howard Earl of Arundel* (Cambridge, 1921), pays little attention to the detail of political alignment. I am engaged upon a political biography of the Earl.

England. His first biographer, Sir Edward Walker, Garter King at Arms, praised Arundel's personal qualities as well as his patronage of scholars and artists.[3] The Earl of Clarendon, however, depicted him in his History with an uncharacteristically venomous pen, dismissing those qualities as a mask behind which lived a contemptible man. Clarendon's Arundel was a nobleman apparently majestic and imperious yet in reality weak and vulgar, who donned an air of scholarship to disguise a lack of understanding, who appeared hospitable, but was arrogant and aloof.[4] But Clarendon's distaste for the Earl owed much to an inherited quarrel. In the Short Parliament of 1640 when he led the attack on the jurisdiction of the Earl's Marshal's court, Hyde perhaps recalled that in 1624 his uncle had suffered at the hands of Earl Marshal Arundel.[5] In his later years as Earl of Clarendon, when he wrote his History, 'he still remembered with feeling the days when as Mr. Edward Hyde he was at cross purposes with this Earl of ancient lineage.'[6] But, whatever his own view, even Clarendon recognized the reverence held by many for Arundel 'as the image and representative of the primitive nobility and native gravity of the nobles'. We must attempt to understand the political importance of the Earl Marshal and the origins of this image during the years before Hyde encountered him.

I

Shortly after the accession of James I, Thomas Howard was restored to the earldom of Arundel, though not to the hereditary dukedom of Norfolk. Only some of his family estates came to him, while his great uncle Henry Howard, Earl of Northampton, and Charles Howard, Earl of Nottingham, enjoyed the rest.[7] He only repurchased Arundel House from Nottingham in 1607 with the aid of his wife's fortune and for some years he suffered financial hardship.[8] But Arundel soon became an important figure at court. He was frequently active

[3] Brit. Lib. MS. Harl. 6272.

[4] Edward Earl of Clarendon, *The History of the Rebellion and Civil Wars in England*, ed. W. D. Macray (6 vols., Oxford, 1888), i. 69–70.

[5] A. Wagner, *The Heralds of England* (1967), 235.

[6] D. N. Smith, *Characters from the Histories and Memoirs of the Seventeenth Century* (Oxford, 1920), 265.

[7] *C.S.P. Dom. 1603–10*, 117, 225; Hervey, op. cit. 20–3, 464.

[8] *C.S.P. Dom. 1603–10*, 390; Hervey, op. cit. 124.

in the tilts. He became intimate with Prince Henry, and friends from the prince's circle such as John Holles, future Earl of Clare, were to be his political allies in later years.[9] He earned the favour of the king and the regard of the ambassadors. When Arundel was about to embark on his first trip to Italy in 1612, the Venetian ambassador wrote to the Doge to urge that the young nobleman be shown hospitality:

> ...he is the premier Earl of this kingdom, in which there are no Dukes save the King's sons...nor Marquises save Winchester who does not come to Court. Arundel will be, through his wife, a daughter of the Earl of Shrewsbury, heir to sixty thousand crowns a year; he is nephew of Northampton who has no children and is very powerful in the government.[10]

While Arundel was absent on his second trip to Italy in 1614, Northampton died, and he returned to claim his substantial inheritance in money and land.[11] He returned, too, as the senior representative of a family which after the Earl of Salisbury's death virtually monopolized court office and royal patronage. In May 1616 the death of the Earl of Shrewsbury added (through Arundel's wife Alethea, heir and daughter of the Earl of Shrewsbury) the substantial Talbot inheritance, to the Howard legacy.[12] In the same year, having publicly expressed formal conversion to the Anglican faith, Arundel was chosen as a privy councillor and so gave evidence of his intention to follow his uncle into power and office.[13]

In 1616, it seemed that he would not wait long. The favourite Robert Carr, Earl of Somerset, fell to the machinations of a cabal of the old nobility led by the Earls of Pembroke and Southampton. There is no evidence for the Venetian ambassador's belief that Arundel, Pembroke's brother-in-law, played a part in those intrigues;[14] rather he shared with Somerset an interest in art and architecture

---

[9] J. Nichols, *The Progresses, Processions and Magnificent Festivities of King James I* (4 vols., 1828), ii. 80. 270, 307, 361; Hervey, op. cit. 465.

[10] *C.S.P. Venet. 1610 13*, 438–39.

[11] Hervey, op. cit. 102.

[12] M. A. Tierney, *The History and Antiquities of the Castle and Town of Arundel* (2 vols., 1834), ii. 553.

[13] *A.P.C. 1615–16*, 674; Hervey; op. cit. 114–16.

[14] *C.S.P. Venet. 1615–17*, 245.

which may have bound them in friendship.[15] But despite his known attachment to some of Somerset's circle, Arundel was never tainted, as were other Howards, by suspicion of involvement in the Overbury murder. The fall of Carr suggested Arundel as the natural successor to his uncle's office and influence.

The opposition to Somerset, however, was in part an expression of discontent with the policy of a marriage alliance with Spain, a policy with which the Howards were identified and sympathetic—if only because it was the royal policy. This issue may have alienated Arundel from his brother-in-law Pembroke, while resentment at the Earl of Suffolk's manipulations of family lands, which Arundel regarded as his own, estranged him from his Howard kinsmen.[16] Arundel's isolation from his family prevented the re-establishment of Howard control of patronage. Southampton's faction took advantage of the situation to promote as a candidate for royal favour a puppet, as they thought, of their policies—George Villiers.

It has not been sufficiently noticed that the years which saw the rise of Villiers to a viscountcy and intimacy with James saw the simultaneous promotion of Thomas Howard, Earl of Arundel, to membership of the Privy Council in three kingdoms and to prominence at court.[17] His estrangement from his family perhaps saved Arundel from the discredit which fell upon the Howards in 1618 with the removal of Suffolk from his post of Lord Treasurer, and from the suspicion of Villiers, Marquis of Buckingham, who ousted the Earl of Nottingham in order to obtain his office of Lord High Admiral in January 1619. Desirous now of an office which would confirm his importance at court, Arundel attached himself to Buckingham and sued through his patronage for the posts of Lord Treasurer and Lord Keeper—places which went to Buckingham's nominees Henry Montagu and Bishop John Williams respectively. Commenting on the competition for office, John Chamberlain thought 'the best plea I hear for the Earl of Arundel is his perpetual plieing the Marquis

[15] T. Longueville, *Policy and Paint* (1913), 25.
[16] Hervey, op. cit. 21.
[17] Nichols, iii. 348.

Buckingham with all manner of observance...'[18] Arundel's association with the favourite need not be ascribed to ambition alone. Though of comparatively lowly birth, in 1620 Buckingham's 'handsome presence, amiable and courteous manners, familiarity and above all his liberality seemed to promise from him something...'.[19] If he was believed to be courteous, his valuable work on the commission to reform the navy won him the regard of all who abhorred court corruption, and doubtless of Arundel whose uncle had first instigated the inquiry.[20] More particularly, Buckingham's support for a policy of a Spanish marriage pointed to an alliance with Arundel who strongly favoured it.[21] In 1620, common interest and policy suggested co-operation and friendship, not rivalry and enmity.

The events of the first session of the 1621 Parliament may serve to illustrate that alliance. When the Lower House began inquiries into the abuses of patents and monopolies, Buckingham avoided difficult questions about his own involvement by sacrificing his clients to the reforming zeal of the Commons.[22] In the Lords, Arundel played a major role on the committee for customs, orders, and privileges and served on most of the important committees of the session. During the early examinations of Mompesson's patent of gold and silver thread, Arundel displayed a cautious, exact concern for justice, urging that none be asked to accuse himself, but to give evidence only.[23] But as the Commons' investigations increasingly threatened Buckingham himself, Arundel emerged as a staunch supporter of the favourite in the Lords where some of the peers seemed anxious to pursue inquiries into Buckingham's influence. On 19 April, Arundel was chosen to investigate charges sent up from the Commons against the Lord Chancellor, Francis

---

[18] *The Letters of John Chamberlain*, ed. N. M. McClure (2 vols., Philadelphia, 1939), ii. 272, 368; cf. J. Hacket, *Scrinia Reserata* (2 parts, 1693), i. 51.

[19] A remark made by Contarini in 1626, *C.S.P. Venet. 1625–6*, 599; in 1626 Sir Robert Pye observed that those who were Buckingham's enemies then had been his friends in 1621. *H.M.C. 13th Rep.*, app. vii (Lonsdale MSS.), 13.

[20] *C.S.P. Dom. 1611–18*, 582, 586; Arundel was also appointed to it: *A.P.C. 1617–18*, 263.

[21] They received ambassadors together: *C.S.P. Venet. 1617–19*, 569; *C.S.P. Venet. 1619–21*, 372.

[22] For this parliament see R. Zaller, *The Parliament of 1621* (Berkeley, 1971).

[23] *L.J.* iii. 62, 67.

Bacon, a client of Buckingham.[24] Like Mompesson, Bacon was sacrificed, and Arundel spoke on his behalf (against the sentence of degradation) only after Bacon had been found guilty and the Commons' anger had been assuaged.[25]

The most dangerous moment for the favourite came with the examination of Sir Henry Yelverton's patent for inns and alehouses. On 30 April, defending himself in the Lords, Yelverton accused Buckingham of promoting the monopolies which he now condemned and of having threatened dismissal of those officers who would not comply.[26] Arundel immediately moved that Yelverton's speech was a dishonourable accusation against the king and Buckingham and for the next few days was adamant for his condemnation and for clearing Buckingham's name.[27] On 8 May, Lord Spencer moved that Yelverton be given a formal hearing; he reminded Arundel, who opposed the motion, that two of his Howard ancestors had suffered condemnation without the opportunity of defence. The proud Earl acknowledged that his ancestors had suffered 'and it may be for doinge the kinge and country good service, and in such time as [when] perhapps the Lords auncestors that spake last kept sheepe.' Arundel's stinging retort, an affront to the dignity of the House, caused his commitment to the Tower.[28] He remained there but a few weeks and only because he refused to apologize to Spencer. While in confinement, he was 'very much visited and courted by the Lord of Buckingham and all the grandees of that side'.[29] Buckingham with Prince Charles attempted to effect a reconciliation between Arundel and Spencer, because he needed Arundel's valuable service in the Lords. The first session of parliament came to a premature end in early June: 'some thinck yt is to enlarge the earle of Arundell the sooner.'[30]

Arundel believed that the incident had done him no harm;

---

[24] *L.J.* iii. 47.

[25] *Notes of Debates in the House of Lords 1621*, ed. S. R. Gardiner (Camden Soc., 1870), 62; *Letters of Chamberlain*, ii. 356; *H.M.C. Mar and Kellie Supplement*, 111–12.

[26] *Debates in the Lords 1621*, 47–9.

[27] Ibid. 49, 57–9. There was some sympathy for Yelverton. Ibid. 55; C. G. C. Tite, *Impeachment and Parliamentary Judicature in early Stuart England* (1974), 122.

[28] *Debates in the Lords 1621*, 73–4; *C.S.P. Dom. 1619–21*, 254, 257; *C.S.P. Venet. 1621–3*, 53.

[29] *C.S.P. Venet. 1621–3*, 55; *Letters of Chamberlain*, ii. 374–5.

[30] *C.S.P. Dom. 1619–21*, 262; *Letters of Chamberlain*, ii. 378.

rather it 'shewed the king's constancy and favor to his servants that love him truly and made me see I had some true friendes'.[31] His assessment seems to have been correct. Early in June, Chamberlain reported the court gossip that Pembroke would be made Lord Treasurer and Arundel Lord Chamberlain.[32] Though the detail was inaccurate, the spirit of the rumour was sound. On 29 August, Arundel was created Earl Marshal of England, a post which had been held by members of his family for several centuries and in which he had himself shown interest for several years. A pension of £2,000 per annum accompanied the grant of the office.[33] Buckingham evidently encouraged the appointment as a reward for Arundel's service in parliament, and it is probable that he had promised it in the spring. The release of the Earls of Southampton and Northumberland during the summer confirms the suggestion that Buckingham was anxious to strengthen himself in the Lords. Ironically, the bestowal of the Earl Marshal's office on Arundel was to be a major contribution to the restoration of Howard power and to the emergence of a group opposed to the favourite.

The new Lord Keeper, John Williams, Buckingham's protégé and mentor, was reluctant to pass Arundel's patent. He thought that the generous pension was impolitic with a new session of parliament pending. More important, he raised vital questions about the authority of the Earl Marshal's office. Firstly, Williams showed that the patent nowhere determined whether the powers of the revived Marshal's office were to be those exercised recently by the Earls of Essex, Shrewsbury, and Somerset, or those wielded by earlier Earls Marshal whose 'powers in those unsettled and troublesome times are vague uncertain and impossible to be limited'. Secondly, he drew the important distinction between the Marshal of England and the Marshal of the King's House, the power of which latter was 'to be searcht out from chronicles' and was potentially far greater. Williams assumed that the king intended for Arundel only the

---

[31] *H.M.C. Portland*, ii. 120, 5 June, 1621.

[32] On 9 June 1621, *Letter of Chamberlain*, ii. 381.

[33] *C.S.P. Dom. 1619–23*, 283, 285, 426; Arundel had been Marshal for Prince Charles's creation as Prince of Wales (*C.S.P. Dom. 1611–18*, 401), having served as commissioner for the office since October 1616. In 1617 an antiquary delivered him notes on the Marshal's office. Bodl. MS. Ashmole 862, fo. 66.

first place, 'But this new patent comprehendeth them both . . . .'[34]

Williams was worried about this great power passing irrevocably from Buckingham's control, especially at what seemed to be a difficult time. During the summer of 1621 news came of the failure to secure a truce in the Palatinate, news which hastened the recall of parliament and questioned the policy of a Spanish match. Any disagreements about foreign policy threatened to divide the tenuous personal groupings held together by Buckingham; it was no time to give power to those who might no longer be relied upon as friends. It seems likely that Buckingham seriously considered Williams's advice. In August it was rumoured that Buckingham would be made Constable of the realm, a post which would have overshadowed the marshalship.[35] In September, the Venetian ambassador reported that Williams could only be delaying Arundel's patent with the encouragement of a higher authority—an obvious allusion to Buckingham.[36] But the patent passed, either because Buckingham could not prevent it, or because he did not wish to. When the second session of parliament assembled in November, Arundel ceremonially introduced the new Lords in his capacity as Earl Marshal.[37]

The second session began on 20 November with the king absent at Newmarket. Cranfield, Williams, and the ambassador John Digby outlined the progress of negotiations and requested a supply for defence of the Palatinate. On 29 November, however, amidst the debates and acting on the instructions of Buckingham, Sir George Goring advocated not only action in Germany, but a war against Spain, if Spanish troops were not withdrawn from the Empire. The motion caused great surprise.[38] Thinking that this lead by a prominent courtier was a signal to discuss the larger question of the Spanish match, the Commons began a full debate. James sent orders to his startled councillors to put an end to the dis-

---

[34] *C.S.P. Dom. 1619–23*, 291; Williams to Buckingham, 1 Sept. 1621, *Cabala* (1654 edn.), 62–5.

[35] *Diary of Walter Yonge 1604–1628*, ed. G. Roberts (Camden Soc., 1848), 42.

[36] *C.S.P. Venet. 1621–3*, 137–138.

[37] *C.S.P. Dom. 1619–23*, 293; A. Wagner, 'The Origin of the Introduction of Peers in the House of Lords', *Archaeologia*, 101 (1967), 119–50.

[38] Zaller, op. cit. 151–2; Sir George Goring to Buckingham, 29 Nov. 1621, *Commons Debates 1621*, ed. W. Notestein, F. H. Relf, and H. Simpson (7 vols., New Haven, 1935), vii. 620–1.

cussion, and so began an unlooked-for dispute about the privileges of the Lower House. Buckingham's real intentions in this episode remain an enigma.[39] For his part, Arundel seems to have supported Digby's motion and the royal policy of intervention in the Palatinate, without discussion of relations with Spain.[40] But leaving questions of policy aside, Goring's motion wrecked the second session of parliament and suggested a rash departure from the norms of conciliar discussion of parliamentary business.

While parliament still sat, on 12 December, the king wrote to his Privy Council to defend Arundel's Earl Marshal's court against the challenge made to its authority by the recalcitrant herald, Ralph Brooke:

wee take our owne honor to bee engaged to defend the power and reputation of that court, which is of so high a nature, so auncient and so immediatlie derived from us who are the fowntaine of all honor, as also that our said cousine may receive such encouragement and favour as both his generall faith in our service and his modest course shewed by appealing unto us in this particular doth deserve.[41]

Arundel's correct and precise behaviour had already made an impression upon James and the Venetian ambassador noted his proximity to the king.[42] The royal letter of 12 December enabled him to take the course which Williams had feared and to claim the widest jurisdiction for the Earl Marshal's office. Arundel consulted his friend and client Sir Robert Cotton, the antiquary, who had earlier researched into the antiquity and authority of the offices of Earl Marshal and Constable. In the summer of 1622 Arundel claimed the right to hold the old court of the Earl Marshal and Constable when there was no Constable of the realm. [43] James accepted the authority of the precedents which Cotton had supplied to Arundel and on 1 August 1622 the Privy Council formally decided in favour of the claim. On 16 April following, Arundel

---

[39] Zaller, op. cit. 152–3; S. L. Adams, above, pp. 155, 163.

[40] *Debates in the Lords 1621*, 122, and see below, p. 238. Arundel had close personal ties with the Queen of Bohemia. Arundel Castle Autograph Letters 1617–1632, fos. 228, 292.

[41] *A.P.C. 1621–3*, 99.

[42] *C.S.P. Venet. 1619–21*, 120.

[43] P.R.O. S.P. 14/132/83; T. Hearne, *Curious Discourses*, ed. J. Ayloffe (2 vols., 1771), i. 97; ii. 65.

received the Constable's staff as final confirmation of his new authority.[44]

The decision invested Arundel with considerable power. Though not formally Constable, he exercised the authority and enjoyed the status of that office. The Constable was senior privy councillor by virtue of his office, and it is evident that great political importance was attached to the hierarchy of offices. In 1601, the Earl of Essex had sought the post in order to supplant Cecil; in 1619, the Earl of Nottingham had requested the Constable's staff in order to retain his precedence over Buckingham for whom he renounced the Lord Admiral's place.[45] Secondly, in medieval times the Constable's court had wielded near regal power and during the last four decades of the fifteenth century it had been used to attack opponents of the monarch.[46] Buckingham's advisers, moreover, reminded him of the importance of such offices: Williams was to recommend that the favourite renounce the Admiralty to become Lord Steward, while Thomas Wilson, keeper of the records, hoped that Buckingham would have himself made Earl Marshal.[47] Both posts brought those who held them close to the royal closet.

Arundel's new status certainly brought him into closer contact with the king. James perhaps raised to an appropriate position a nobleman who was a stickler for forms and proprieties to offset the developing monopoly of patronage by Buckingham. Court gossip about a new favourite, Arthur Brett, brother-in-law of Cranfield, in the autumn of 1622 suggests that Buckingham's position was not unassailable.[48] In November of that year, Buckingham sued to be Lord High Constable, presumably to reinforce his position in Council and at court.[49] Perhaps the growing influence of those devoted to the royal policy of a Spanish match induced him to send Endymion Porter to investigate the possibility of a successful

[44] *C.S.P. Dom. 1619–23*, 436, 559.

[45] *The Court and Times of James I*, ed. R. F. Williams (2 vols., 1849), ii. 159; R. W. Kenny, *Elizabeth's Admiral: the Political Career of Charles Howard, Earl of Nottingham* (Baltimore, 1970), 330–1.

[46] G. D. Squibb, *The High Court of Chivalry* (Oxford, 1959); A. Wagner, *The Heralds of England*, 229–35.

[47] Williams to Buckingham, 2 Mar. 1625, *Cabala*, 101–3; *C.S.P. Dom. 1623–5*, 561.

[48] *H.M.C. Mar and Kellie Suppl.* 140–2, 145.

[49] *Diary of Yonge*, 57.

negotiation. It may then be that Porter's optimistic reports and his own desire to reassert his position by the decisive diplomatic *coup* of a negotiated marriage were the direct motives behind the journey to Spain in the spring of 1623.[50]

In March, the Earl of Kellie reported that Lady Arundel had considered a trip to Spain, 'but that she is discharged', while, 'some say that my Lord of Arundell is in great danger that his Ladye is forbidden to go to Spaine, and that he is not to be imployed himself at this tyme.'[51] The Earl Marshal by no means approved of Buckingham's enterprise: Simonds D'Ewes believed that Arundel wanted no part in the negotiations while the prince was in Spain and the advantage was with the Spaniard.[52] Privy councillors expressed grave reservations about such 'a dangerous and unexampled experiment'. Though he had earlier been won over by the arguments of the prince and Buckingham, James was now advised of the real dangers involved and 'now upone efter thochts I cannot think but it trubills his Majestie when the hazards thaye run are laide before him'.[53] As the Earl of Kellie noted, the whole affair was 'a subject that discontented folkes maye worke upon'.[54]

In addition to his reservations about the journey, Arundel had a more personal discontent. In May it was rumoured that Arundel was to be made a duke, but that he refused all but the Norfolk title, the premier duchy of the realm.[55] The patent sent to Spain making Buckingham a duke and so senior English nobleman much offended the Earl Marshal. An informant told Buckingham, 'since your patent, the Earl Marshal is become a great strainger at the Court.'[56]

In Spain, Buckingham anxiously sought information about the English court. In March, Tobie Matthew, son of the Archbishop of York and one close to Arundel, wrote to tell

[50] S. L. Adams, 'The Protestant Cause: Religious alliance with the West European Calvinist Communities as a Political Issue in England, 1585–1630' (Oxford Univ. D. Phil. thesis 1972), 333.

[51] *H.M.C. Mar and Kellie Suppl.* 156. Kellie added, 'I know him to be wyser than to take onye exceptions at this time.'

[52] *The Diary of Simonds D'Ewes 1622–4*, ed. E. Boussier (Paris, 1975), 146.

[53] *C.S.P. Dom. 1619–23*, 495, 503; *H.M.C. Mar and Kellie Suppl.* 152–3, 175.

[54] *H.M.C. Mar and Kellie Suppl.* 157.

[55] Chamberlain to Carleton, 17 May 1623, *Letters of Chamberlain*, ii. 497.

[56] *Cabala*, 160; *C.S.P. Venet. 1623–5*, 28.

Buckingham that great men were plotting against him and advised him to hurry back lest enemies take advantage of his absence.[57] While in Spain, Buckingham quarrelled with the official ambassador John Digby, now Earl of Bristol, and removed him from all negotiations there. Attempts by Buckingham to cast aspersions on Bristol's abilities met with incredulity at the English court, while Bristol's own dispatches, critical of Buckingham's carriage of business, made supporters of the match fear that the journey would disrupt years of delicate diplomacy.[58] If, as a staunch supporter of the match, Arundel was plotting against the favourite, his own influence was curtailed by the illness and death of his son in Flanders which necessitated Arundel's departure from England in July.[59] Though he gave Arundel permission to travel, James I was said to be displeased by his absence.[60] It would seem that they had become much closer, within the limits of Arundel's reserved and formal manner, while Buckingham and the prince were in Spain. Arundel returned within a month but failed to attend at court because, as he explained to Sir Dudley Carleton, 'his extreme sorrow makes him incapable of this world's affairs.'[61] Sir John Hippesley reported Arundel's retirement from court to Buckingham for whom it was probably good news.[62] For if the enemies of Buckingham and the discontented were gathering, they would look to Arundel as a leader.

Buckingham returned in September 1623, however, and the evidence suggests that the king's relief at the safe return of his son saw the favourite secure, for the time, in his position. Buckingham had returned bent on breaking the Spanish match, while Bristol stayed in Spain, with the prince's proxy, to complete negotiations for it. The winning of the prince to his policy secured a major ally for Buckingham.[63] But James

[57] Brit. Lib. MS. Harl. 1581, fo. 60; cf. fo. 244.

[58] R. Ruigh, *The Parliament of 1624: Politics and Foreign Policy* (Cambridge, Mass., 1971), 354 n. 22.

[59] *C.S.P. Dom. 1623–5*, 20.

[60] Ibid. 33.

[61] Ibid. 81.

[62] *Cabala*, 316.

[63] Bristol claimed that he remained in Charles's favour when the prince left Spain leaving him with the proxy for the marriage. By May, however, the prince was reported to be of Buckingham's party in his quarrel with Bristol. *The Earl of Bristol's Defence of his Negotiations in Spain*, ed. S. R. Gardiner, *Camden Misc.* vi (1871), v–vii.

continued to meet with the Spanish ambassadors in the autumn, and those close to the king thought 'that it wilbe contrarye to his will if the match shall not goe on'.[64] In December it was reported that, with the Council divided, the king's will would certainly prevail.[65] Bristol continued to correspond from Madrid and was said to have in England 'a great and more powerful party in Court than you can imagine'.[66] Buckingham now turned to deal with those whom he regarded as his enemies because they had influence with the king. On 26 December a newswriter reported a rumour that Arundel would be confined to the Tower, a rumour confirmed by the Venetian ambassador's belief that Arundel was in danger while James I vacillated between fear of his own son and fear of the Spaniard.[67] Over Christmas 1623–4, Buckingham turned threateningly on Lord Keeper Williams, his client who was now earnestly supporting the match, and dismissed that policy as 'both dangerous to your countrie and prejudicial to the cause of religion'.[68] Throughout January, Buckingham tried to cajole the Privy Council into breaking with Spain. At the end of the month, Chamberlain wrote that, led by Arundel, Williams, Lord Treasurer Cranfield, Sir George Calvert, and Sir Richard Weston remained in favour of the match. Only Carlisle and Conway voted to end it. The Earl of Pembroke, despite his earlier support of Buckingham's motion for a parliament, and despite his distaste for the Spaniard, took the view that if the king had engaged himself and the Spanish did not violate the agreement then he could not with honour retreat from it.[69] Pembroke's concern with honour and engagement was typical of the behaviour of the early Stuart nobility. Buckingham was still in the minority, but in December the junta had voted to call parliament.[70] Council faction and

[64] *H.M.C. Mar and Kellie Suppl.* 183–4.

[65] *C.S.P. Venet. 1623–5,* 169–170.

[66] *Cabala,* 160.

[67] Locke to Carleton, 26 Dec. 1623, *C.S.P. Dom. 1623–5,* 134; *C.S.P. Venet. 1623–5,* 178.

[68] J. Packer to J. Williams, 21 Jan. 1623/4, *Cabala,* 86.

[69] *C.S.P. Dom. 1623–5,* 156.

[70] Salvetti Correspondence 5 Jan. 1624, Brit. Lib. MS. Add. 27962, vol. III, fo. 88, cited in D. H. Willson, 'Summoning and Dissolving Parliament 1603–25', *Am. Hist. Rev.* xlv (1940), 299 n. 66.

personal rivalries were now to be played out on the floor of both Houses.

In December, Arundel had opposed the summoning of parliament,[71] but when it was called he used his influence at the hustings. His secretary, Humphrey Haggett, obtained a place at Chichester, second to Lord Percy, son of Arundel's friend, the Earl of Northumberland. Sir John Borough, who collected antiquities for the Earl and who was made herald through his patronage, took the first place at Horsham.[72] But Buckingham not only exercised some official as well as private patronage, he also organized a clear programme to direct the Lower House. The Earl of Kellie observed in March, 'Monye of theis Parlament men that did disturb the last Parlament ar now als mutche for my Lord of Bukkinghame as thaye warr then against him.'[73] Against that organization Arundel could only promote delaying tactics: he suggested that precedents of former treaties be fully investigated before any decision was made; he sat on the committee to investigate allegations made against Buckingham by the Spanish ambassadors, who tried thereby to discredit the Duke.[74] Such tactics were not futile: Bristol was *en route* for home promising a full report of all the negotiations in Spain, and rumours were already rife of the scandalous behaviour of Buckingham there. However, on 12 March both Houses advised the king to terminate marriage negotiations, and proceeded to promise a supply.[75] In vain Arundel and Cranfield, Earl of Middlesex, argued that parliament's offer of support was too general to be a basis for a war: the prince snubbed them.[76]

But though he could do little in the Lords, Arundel planned, perhaps, to work through his clients in the Commons. In the Lower House, one voice stood out from the clamour against the match. On 19 March, amidst a debate on supply for the war, Sir George Chaworth argued that the treaties for the marriage and Palatinate were already at an end but that the old peace with Spain remained and prohibited any

[71] Willson, art. cit. 299.
[72] Ruigh, op. cit. 101–2.
[73] *H.M.C. Mar and Kellie Suppl.* 193.
[74] *L.J.* iii. 236, 238.
[75] *L.J.* iii. 259.
[76] *C.S.P. Dom. 1623–5*, 191.

assistance to the Low Countries. Chaworth maintained that
the kingdom was in no danger and hinted that war was in
the interest of a faction not of the realm: 'yf a war ensue
upon our petition wch you now wage were I to chuse, I had
rather be in ye office of Admirall of Engd than K of Engd.'
The country was too poor to finance a major campaign and
was in greater need of good laws and reform of grievances.[77]
The speech evidently caused a stir, and Pym observed that
'if there had beene bad humors enough in the Howse it might
have done some hurt.'[78] But Thomas Wentworth, Recorder
of Oxford, quickly rose to dismiss the speech as a 'diversion'
and Chaworth found no support.[79] By the end of the month
he was dismissed the House after they had 'pricked a hole in
his election'.[80] Chaworth's speech may have owed something
to his indignation at not obtaining the viscountcy which was
promised to him by Buckingham after his employment as an
ambassador to Brussels in 1621. Chaworth attributed Buckingham's hostility towards him to his continued support for the
Spanish marriage after the Duke had abandoned it.[81] In 1624
he sat for Arundel borough in Sussex. It is clear that the
election had been irregular, the mayor having returned
Chaworth over one Richard Milles by reopening the poll late
in the afternoon when many electors had gone home. The
mayor would not have risked this course without connivance
from above—from the Lord Lieutenant of Sussex, the Earl of
Arundel. Not only was Arundel Chaworth's patron for the
place, it appears that Chaworth's cousin travelled to Italy
with Lady Arundel, so there may have been closer connections
between them.[82] But despite the irregularities of the election,
the case against Chaworth was not clear cut. Even at the first
count four voters (all supporters of Milles) had arrived after

---

[77] *C.J.* i. 742; *C.S.P. Dom. 1623–5.* 197; *The Loseley Manuscripts*, ed. A. J. Kempe
(1836), 479–80; Northants Record Office Finch Hatton MS. 50 (Parliamentary diary
of John Pym), fo. 34. (I am grateful to Conrad Russell for lending me a microfilm
of this manuscript); Ruigh, op. cit. 224–5.

[78] Northants R.O. MS. 50, fo. 34.

[79] Ibid., fos. 34ᵛ–35; *C.J.* i. 742–3.

[80] P.R.O. S.P. 14/161/30. I owe this reference to Ruigh, op. cit. 224 n. 129.

[81] *Loseley Manuscripts*, 470–6.

[82] Ibid. 472.

voices had been heard but before a formal poll was taken.[83] Chaworth himself maintained that the polling continued with the consent of all and complained that he never received a formal hearing.[84] The situation might have suggested a completely new election, but Buckingham was suspicious enough to see that no new writs were issued and Milles took his seat.[85]

During the Easter recess, Buckingham attacked Chaworth, who laid his defence, and a copy of his speech, before the king. He claimed that James thanked him for it and swore 'that had [he] beene in ye House of Parlament he wold have spoken just my words'. When Buckingham upbraided him for his speech, James broke out in impatience against the Duke, 'By ye wounds, you are in ye wrong! for he spake my soule...'[86] There seems no reason to doubt Chaworth's account in that his speech was a precise statement of royal policy. If the Duke had triumphed in parliament, he had not as yet won the royal closet. His position was no stronger than it had been in the spring of 1623.

After Easter, Buckingham returned to parliament determined now to use it in order to break his opponents. His client, Sir Robert Pye, brought into the Commons charges against Lord Treasurer Middlesex who had continued a supporter of the match. When the case came to the Lords, of the principal officers of the household, only the Earl Marshal was not included on the committee to investigate the charges.[87] Yet encouraged, perhaps, by James I's half-hearted defence of Middlesex on 7 April, Arundel and Williams asked the House to excuse the Treasurer's passionate accusations against unnamed enemies and prompted him to name his persecutors.[88] John Holles, Lord Haughton, joined them in an effort to save

[83] For accounts of the election see Pym's diary, fo. 40; Brit. Lib. MS. Add. 36856, fos. 108ᵛ–109.

[84] 'And though I had 16 witnesses to cleare and justefie my election, yet ye Committee entred to ye hearing ye cause, but just as sunne sett and being then darkeish (before Easter) they made it such a [i.e. dark] worke, and in one quarter of an houre, without so much as hearinge one witnes for me, or more than one witness against me, they sentenced my election voyde.' *Loseley Manuscripts*, 482.

[85] See ibid. 482.

[86] Ibid. 480–3.

[87] *L.J.* iii. 301.

[88] Brit. Lib. MS. Add. 40088, fo. 25.

Middlesex, but he was inevitably found guilty and sentenced.[89]
Buckingham's next attacks struck Arundel directly. At the end
of April and in early May, Pye and Sir Robert Phelips raised
questions about the heralds and the jurisdiction of the Earl
Marshal's court. Sir Edward Coke's report that there could be
no commission for the Constable's office threatened the very
existence of Arundel's court.[90] If he failed to cajole the Privy
Council, Buckingham showed that he had gained a monopoly
of influence in parliament.

But his methods were both dangerous and caused offence.
On 5 April, Pembroke, no friend to the policy of a Spanish
marriage, yet urged moderation and caution in order to
avoid firing a religious war.[91] And he refused to support
Buckingham's plan to have Bristol, who returned in May,
committed to the Tower in order to silence him.[92] Buckingham
rightly feared that James had not been won over to the war
and that the return of Bristol to court would be a threat to
his very position.[93] Certainly James warned the prince and
Buckingham against using parliamentary impeachment to
crush their rivals and endeavoured to reconcile them with
Bristol.[94] Arundel, powerless to prevent what had happend
to Middlesex, determined to prevent its repetition against
Bristol and, perhaps, himself. On 28 May, he reported that
the subcommittee for privileges had decided to allow counsel
to the accused in parliamentary judicial prodeedings.[95] Three
years before, he had denied Yelverton even a hearing. But
times had changed: he could no longer look upon the Duke
as a friend, and even those who had voted to end the
match reacted against the obvious persecution of Cranfield
and Bristol. The decision to grant counsel to the accused had

[89] Hacket, *Scrinia Reserata*, i. 189–90.

[90] *C.J.* i. 786, 701; Pym Diary, fo. 81ᵛ; P. H. Hardacre, 'The Earl Marshal, the Heralds and the House of Commons 1604–41', *Int. Rev. Soc. Hist.* 2 (1975), 106–25. On 8 May complaints were also delivered against Bishop Harsnett of Norwich, a close friend of the Earl of Arundel, concerning his Arminian practices and alleged sympathy towards Catholics. *L.J.* iii. 362; Pym, fo. 89ᵛ; Arundel Castle Letters 1617–1632, fo. 225; Brit. Lib. MS. Add. 15970, fo. 15.

[91] Brit. Lib. MS. Add. 40088, fo. 13ᵛ.

[92] S. R. Gardiner, *Camden Misc.* vi, p. v.

[93] Ibid. v; speech of James I, 7 May reported in Pym, fo. 89.

[94] Gardiner, op. cit. vii; Clarendon, *History of the Rebellion*, i. 28.

[95] *L.J.* iii. 418.

been taken hurriedly and Arundel admitted the need for more consideration. But the main point was clear: 'God defend that an Innocent should be condemned.' The following day, parliament was dissolved.

Clarendon's belief that James I was openly displeased with Buckingham is confirmed by the Earl of Kellie who reported that the king rebuked the prince and Duke for courting too much popularity.[96] It seems that as the representative of justice and propriety (probably too of royal policy) Arundel rose in the king's estimation during the summer of 1624. On 5 June, James stayed at Arundel House and went stag-hunting while Buckingham lay ill at Newhall.[97] A week later, James made a second visit and it was rumoured that the Spanish ambassadors and Bristol met the king there in secret.[98] Both the prince and Buckingham were worried that Bristol's friends would gain him an audience.[99] Certainly Buckingham's position was insecure: in June, Bristol sent in answers to the questions posed about his embassy and was later to claim that James was satisfied by them.[100] In August, Sir Robert Phelips advised his patron Buckingham to win over Bristol, for the Spanish match was already broken and persecution of Bristol could only lead to trouble.[101] Lord Keeper Williams endorsed this advice and counselled him to behave more modestly to the king so as to avoid offence.[102] In October, Pembroke, who rejected advances made by Buckingham, was reported as one of a group opposing a war against Spain unless France could be secured as a reliable ally.[103] It was to separate Pembroke from his enemies, and to prevent the return of the Spanish faction to power that Buckingham hurried the negotiations for a French marriage. Arundel, Calvert, and Williams were dropped from the commission for negotiations in July and by December even Pembroke and Hamilton had been excluded, 'and as I am informed the great Lords of the

---

[96] *History of the Rebellion*, i. 29; *H.M.C. Mar and Kellie Suppl.* 201, 203.
[97] *C.S.P. Dom. 1623–5*, 267, 5 June, 1624.
[98] *C.S.P. Venet. 1623–5*, 343, 14 June 1624.
[99] Ruigh, op. cit. 361.
[100] S. R. Gardiner, op cit. xi–xii.
[101] *Cabala*, 264–6.
[102] *Scrinia Reserata*, 150.
[103] *C.S.P. Venet. 1623–5*, 453.

Consell . . . are not weill pleased, whoe was the Lords Stewart, Marshall and Chamberlaine . . . .'[104] In order to prevent Arundel and Pembroke becoming dukes, Buckingham resigned his Irish titles.[105] He had reason to fear the great lords.

Perhaps the death of James I in March 1625 saved Buckingham from the fate of Somerset. Rumours about the medicines he had administered to the king on his death-bed and the scandal of a possible poisoning of James can only have gained currency from a belief that Buckingham benefited by his death. Certainly Buckingham's survival as favourite into the next reign caused some surprise and added to the animosity towards him.[106] At first the situation was confused: Council factions jostled for the ear of the new king, and Buckingham postponed taking the proxies for the marriage to France for fear of losing his place. His fears were justified. At the first meeting of the Privy Council Arundel requested 'that the king should let his Council share the things which he wishes to announce'—a request which was a condemnation of Buckingham's behaviour since 1624 or earlier. Arundel's other proposal, to limit the sale of honours, not only reflected his contempt for the low-born who were raised to noble status, it overtly aimed at Buckingham's patronage and potentially at his influence in the House of Lords. Buckingham replied cleverly that there could be no limit to a king's ability to reward deserving subjects, and Arundel met with little support in a Council from which Middlesex, Bristol, Calvert, and the Earl of Suffolk were excluded for the first time. 'No one said any more and the Earl [of Arundel] was somewhat dashed.'[107] Buckingham had now secured the control of an emasculated Privy Council and the norms of Stuart government were brushed aside. As a body for the full discussion of business and as adviser to the crown, the Privy Council ceased to function until after Buckingham's death.[108]

The new reign, however, dictated the assembling of another parliament. Buckingham cannot have been happy at the prospect, for he was now identified with the policy of a

[104] *H.M.C. Mar and Kellie Suppl.* 206, 216.
[105] *C.S.P. Venet. 1623–5,* 511.
[106] *The Origins of the English Civil War,* ed. C. S. R. Russell (1971), 16.
[107] 18 Apr. 1625, *C.S.P. Venet. 1625–6,* 12; 25 Apr. ibid. 21.
[108] See above, introduction section V.

French marriage, which was only a little less odious than the Spanish match, and the war against Spain, intimated in 1624, had not materialized. There were bound to be questions raised, and there were enemies to take advantage of them. In 1624, Buckingham went to parliament because he could not get his way in Council. Now, having removed his enemies from the Council, he had to defend himself against them in parliament.

The parliament of 1625 sat for three weeks in a plague-infested Westminster before a final disastrous session in Oxford early in August 1625. The Commons' committee for foreign affairs began careful examination of the abortive Mansfeldt expedition and of the activities of the Council of War.[109] Dangerous precedents circulated in August concerning the punishment of corrupt ministers, and the session was abruptly dissolved. Buckingham was convinced that those who opposed him in the Commons—Sir Thomas Wentworth, Sir Dudley Digges, and his quondam client Sir Robert Phelips—were supported and encouraged by his enemies in the Lords. Three days after the dissolution, Kellie reported a rumour that Arundel, Williams, Pembroke, and Archbishop Abbot were to be questioned concerning their activities.[110] Sir Arthur Ingram confirmed it, warning his friend Wentworth that Buckingham suspected these lords and others of the Lower House 'that were depending upon them, among which you are not altogether free'. He assured Wentworth that Arundel was a 'good friend'.[111]

Buckingham's suspicions seem to have been well founded. Williams had advised the king not to reassemble the parliament at Oxford because some were out to attack the Duke.[112] The French ambassador reported that Arundel and Pembroke, 'personnes puissantes dans le Parlement', were aware that Buckingham would be called to account. Thomas Lorkin told his patron Buckingham that Arundel and Pembroke were conspiring against him.[113] There are close and interesting ties

---

[109] Brit. Lib. MS. Harl. 6645.

[110] *H.M.C. Mar and Kellie Suppl.* 282, 15 Aug. 1625.

[111] *The Earl of Strafforde's Letters and Despatches*, ed. W. Knowler (2 vols., 1739), i. 28. Wentworth had shown great concern about the treatment of Bristol, ibid. 21.

[112] *Scrinia Reserata*, i. 14.

[113] Brit. Lib. MS. Add. 30651 (French transcripts), fos. 12ᵛ–13; *Cabala*, 301.

between those Buckingham suspected in Lords and Commons. The precedents for punishment of corrupt ministers were collected by Sir Robert Cotton who had been closely connected with Arundel since 1616 and who, in 1625, sat for the Howards' seat at Thetford, Norfolk, where Arundel was Lord Lieutenant.[114] A copy of the speech containing those precedents has been found among Sir Robert Phelips's manuscripts at Taunton.[115] Though the speech was not delivered, the Commons echoed its spirit in condemning advice given by one man only and endorsed Arundel's plea to the king to consult with his full Privy Council.[116]

In the Lords, as well as his brother-in-law Pembroke, Arundel had a friend in Holles, now Earl of Clare, a client of Arundel's friend the Earl of Northumberland, and personal friend of Lord Keeper Williams.[117] In 1624 Clare had been conspicuous for his attempt to defend Middlesex. In 1625 he failed to attend the second session of parliament at Oxford because his house was under suspicion of the plague. But he assured Arundel of his intention to have attended him there and asked him to prevent a friend from being pricked sheriff and so incapacitated from standing for parliament.[118] In November Clare wrote to Wentworth expressing his hope that Phelips and Sir Edward Coke would not be pricked sheriff and his satisfaction that the 1625 session, though brief, might 'make great ones even more cautious in wrestling with that high court.'[119] For all their different reasons, the enemies of Buckingham were gathering.

The king's desperate need for supply meant that another parliament was imminent, and Buckingham set about protecting himself. Wentworth, Coke, and Phelips were pricked sheriff, and evidently Arundel, who as Earl Marshal helped to

---

[114] *Cottoni Posthuma*, ed. James Howell (1651), 273–81. K. M. Sharpe, 'The Intellectual and Political Activities of Sir Robert Cotton c. 1590–1631' (Oxford Univ. D. Phil. thesis 1975), 216–19.

[115] Somerset Record Office Phelips MSS. DD/Ph 216/19. I owe this reference to Conrad Russell.

[116] *C.S.P. Venet. 1625–6*, 146.

[117] *Memorials of the Holles Family 1493–1656*, ed. G. Holles (Camden Soc., 1937), Ch. 12.

[118] Earl of Clare to Arundel, 23 Oct. 1625, Arundel Castle Letters 1617–1632, fo. 277.

[119] Earl of Clare to Wentworth, *Strafforde Letters*, i. 31.

choose the sheriffs, was unwilling or unable to prevent it.[120] But if he had clipped the leadership of the Commons, Buckingham still had to reckon with the Lords—with Arundel and Pembroke. Before Parliament met on 6 February, Buckingham was presented with an opportunity to discredit Arundel. After nearly a year's delay, Charles was to be crowned early in February. The coronation was an important public function for all the nobles of the realm, an occasion on which to display their prominence at court and to show the new king that they merited his favour. Arundel, as Earl Marshal and one of the greatest nobles of the realm, prepared a grand reception for Charles in the garden of Sir Robert Cotton whose house in Westminster, next to parliament, backed on to the Thames. On the coronation day, however, the royal barges floated past the crowd at Cotton House and the king disembarked with some discomfort downriver. D'Ewes, a friend of Arundel and Cotton, observed that Buckingham had manœuvred to embarrass publicly both Arundel and Cotton on the eve of the new parliament. He thus demonstrated the price of opposition and his inviolable influence upon the king. Significantly, Buckingham had had himself made Constable for the coronation day.[122]

But clever manœuvres alone could not end his troubles with parliament. Indeed, they may have served to sharpen the distaste felt for him. The Lower House, now led by his former client Sir John Eliot, determined to call Buckingham to account. The Earl of Bristol, under confinement since May 1624, had become exasperated by his failure to obtain a hearing and resolved to bring his case to the Lords. The man behind all was Pembroke who, as Sir James Bagg warned Buckingham, had won Eliot to his circle, and had attempted to assist Bristol in the spring of 1625.[123] In the Upper House former supporters of the Duke, such as the Earl of Suffolk, shifted allegiance from him, and many seemed

---

[120] Brit. Lib. MS. Add. 6297, fo. 283.

[121] *The Autobiography and Correspondence of Simonds D'Ewes*, ed. J. O. Halliwell (2 vols., 1895), i. 291.

[122] D'Ewes to Sir Martin Stuteville, 4 Feb. 1625/6, Brit. Lib. MS Harl. 383, fo. 24.

[123] S. R. Gardiner, op. cit. xv–xxxi; *C.S.P. Dom. 1625–49*, 112, Sir James Bagg to Buckingham, Mar. 1626.

anxious to check his monopoly of patronage and influence.[124] On 25 February, Lord Mandeville reported from the committee of privileges a motion that no peer should hold more than two proxies.[125] This was a direct threat to Buckingham who held thirteen proxies in this session, many from newly ennobled Lords, and who depended on control of the Upper House lest charges be presented against him in the Commons. Amongst those who supported the motion were Arundel, Clare, and Arundel's friend the Bishop of Norwich, Samuel Harsnett. But the new ruling concerning proxies could not operate until the next session; it may have been intended as a warning to Buckingham not to use the House of Lords as the playground for his private vendettas. In 1626, Buckingham's most dangerous opponents were Pembroke, who held probably five, but whom the Duke still hoped to win over, and Arundel, who also held five proxies, and whom he looked upon as an inveterate enemy.[126]

Suddenly Buckingham was presented with a chance to remove him. In February, Arundel's son, Lord Maltravers, secretly married without royal consent the Duke of Lennox's daughter whom Charles had intended to match with Argyle's son. Arundel was imprisoned supposedly for this affront to the king, but more truthfully, as was observed, in order to remove him from parliament and so deprive the opposition to Buckingham of six votes and a leader.[127] Arundel, trusting still in Charles I, could not believe that he would remain long under royal displeasure, for the marriage had been desired by Lennox and by 'good Kinge James himselfe'.[128] An anonymous correspondent tried to discover for the Earl the cause of the King's displeasure. He had courted Buckingham to no avail—'I might as well concluded the busyness as I began it'—but thought yet that a judicious explanation

---

[124] The Earl of Suffolk transferred his proxy from his elder to his younger son who was an enemy of the Duke, *The Court and Times of Charles I*, ed. R. F. Williams (2 vols., 1848), i. 106.

[125] *Notes of the Debates in the House of Lords 1624–1626*, ed. S. R. Gardiner (Camden Soc., 1879), 113–14.

[126] For proxies see *L.J.* iii. 491; Ruigh, op. cit. 377 n. 76.

[127] *H.M.C. Skrine MSS.* 54; V. F. Snow 'The Arundel Case', *Historian*, xxvi (1964), 323–50. It is interesting to note that Buckingham had copies of letters between Arundel and his son Lord Maltravers on this question. Brit. Lib. MS. Harl. 1581, fo. 390.

[128] Tierney, *History of Arundel*, ii. 454; cf. *Court and Times of Charles I*, i. 90–1.

would settle everything: 'Let the Parlamt free those that stand in need of their helpe,' he advised, 'for God's sake make not yor case so desperat but ride it out with patience.'[129]

But Arundel's patience must have been taxed as the weeks passed without his release. Whether he wished to make his case desperate or not, his imprisonment raised in the Lords fundamental questions of parliamentary privilege and of the violated rights of those who had given their proxies to the Earl Marshal. The Lords' committee for privileges, after searching the precedents, discovered that no peer had ever been committed without trial while parliament was sitting. It was an issue that transcended the personal quarrel.[130]

On 30 March, Clare argued that proxies given to an absent lord should return to the peers who had given them that they might be conferred anew.[131] The question was raised again on 3 April.[132] The growing anxiety in the House about this question cannot be divorced from the show-down impending between Buckingham and Bristol, who in response to charges of treason against him had sent to the Lords similar charges (drawn up with Williams's assistance) against the Duke.[133] In the last resort, the outcome of that show-down would depend upon votes in the Lords.[134] On 19 April Bristol's petition was read in the House and the Lords made their first formal demand for the release of Arundel.[135] The House of Commons watched the proceedings in the upper chamber closely. Philip Mainwaring, a friend of Sir Thomas Wentworth, assured Arundel that he would soon be free: Bristol had presented his case and 'our house hathe some things now on foote in Parliament wch at the least makes a noyse.'[136] Buckingham showed relatively little anxiety about

---

[129] Arundel Castle Letters 1617–1623, fo. 284.

[130] H. Elsyng, *The Ancient Method and Manner of Holding Parliaments in England* (1660), 151–2.

[131] *Lords Debates 1624 and 1626*, 135.

[132] Ibid. 139.

[133] For the charges, see *H.M.C. 13th Report*, App. 7, p. 11; T. Ball, *Life of The Renowned Doctor Preston* (1885), 116–17.

[134] Bristol drew up for his own instruction a list of proxies held in the Lords, Ruigh, op. cit. 377 n. 77.

[135] *Lords Debates 1624 and 1626*, 144; *L.J.* iii. 504.

[136] Arundel Castle Letters 1617–1623, fo. 285; Arundel had recommended Mainwaring for a seat at Steyning in 1624. Ruigh, op. cit. 10.

the investigations in the Commons, but he was worried about the Lords and proposed the creation of twenty new peers to boost his following there.[137] Bristol launched his full attack on 2 May[138] and the case against Bristol and counter-case against Buckingham were now to proceed. The Lords continued to demand the release of Arundel and the king repeatedly gave evasive answers, hoping perhaps to force a vote on both cases while the Earl Marshal was absent and his proxies were neutralized.[139] The Earl of Clare, who led the committee to inquire into the charges against Bristol, awaited Arundel's return, while the House of Commons demanded the commitment of the Duke (and hence the loss of his votes) pending the investigations. Sir John Skeffington, M.P. for Newcastle under Lyme, told his patron, the Earl of Huntingdon, that the Lords 'want only the company of such a Lord whose example and courage would give animation and boldness to some such as dare not wel looke out of theyr cold neutralities'.[140] Lady Cornwallis regretted Arundel's absence, 'in regard of the want of so able a man at this tyme in the upper house', but feared he would not be suffered to return.[141] The Lords, however, proved adamant. On 2 June the House voted to conduct no business until Arundel returned.[142] Buckingham made inquiries about the proxies held by the Earl Marshal[143] but concluded that there was no alternative to Arundel's release. Arundel returned to his place on 8 June. Pembroke immediately moved 'That the Duke of Buckingham his answere now be receaved.'[144] Bristol petitioned that his case be hastened and on the 13th he delivered the names of his witnesses. Two days later parliament was dissolved.[145]

Albeit reluctantly, Arundel had become a martyr to the

[137] *C.S.P. Venet. 1625–6*, 390.

[138] *L.J.* iii. 576.

[139] *L.J.* iii. 591, 646, 652; *H.M.C. Skrine MSS.* 63, 65, 66.

[140] Bodl. MS. Carte 77, fo. 104.

[141] *The Private Correspondence of Jane Lady Cornwallis 1613–1644*, ed. Lord Braybrootle (1842), 146.

[142] *L.J.* iii. 653.

[143] Edmund Bolton to Buckingham, 29 May, 1626, *C.S.P. Dom. 1625–49*, 129.

[144] *Lords Debates 1624 and 1626*, 214.

[145] Ibid. 224–6; I have benefited greatly from conversations with Norman Ball and Conrad Russell on the Parliament of 1626. The above account is basically endorsed by J. Flemion, 'The dissolution of Parliament in 1626: a revaluation', *E.H.R.* (1972), 784–90. but Flemion pays little attention to Bristol's case.

cause of parliamentary privilege and head of the opposition to Buckingham. When he was expelled from court after parliament, his 'followers in consequence of this persecution have their ranks now swollen by a great part of the people in general....'[146] It was an unnatural alliance. No nobleman more despised the political activities of the lower orders than the aristocratic, reserved Arundel who had recommended the closing of all unruly taverns near Westminster.[147] No one was less suited to be a champion of the diverse discontented—the ambitious courtiers, the frustrated place-seekers, and the war-hawks. It was not a common policy that bound them but a common dislike for Buckingham and his rash bearing.

For eighteen months, Arundel remained debarred the court, months during which no parliament was called and the tangles of foreign policy demanded the subordination of domestic disagreements. As Lord Lieutenant of Norfolk and Sussex, Arundel was called upon to raise the county musters, and as Earl Marshal he was responsible for the discipline of billeted troops. Just as members of the Commons returned from parliament after heated debates to carry out their offices in the localities, so Arundel, ostracized from court, enacted Council orders.[148] There were still signs of tensions: Buckingham supported the petition of the herald Henry St. George against Arundel, who had evicted him from Derby House, and St. George requested that the Earl Marshal 'may not be allowed to prejudice him out of spleen to the Duke'.[149] But without co-operation government would have collapsed completely in 1627, and Arundel suppressed personal animosities for the sake of order and stability.

Indeed, an accommodation with the Duke could not be ruled out. In December 1626 it was rumoured that Buckingham sought a reconciliation with Bristol and Arundel as a means of re-ingratiating himself.[150] He had also arranged a pacification with Pembroke in August, and Calvert returned

[146] *C.S.P. Venet. 1625–6*, 512, 21 Aug. 1626.

[147] Brit. Lib. MS. Add. 40087, fos. 89, 96ᵛ.

[148] *H.M.C. Skrine MSS.* 76; *H.M.C. Cowper* i. 320; *C.S.P. Dom. 1627–8*, 461; *A.P.C. 1627*, 250. Arundel was not listed as one of the recalcitrant peers who refused the loan, *Diary of Walter Yonge*, 98.

[149] *C.S.P. Dom. 1627–8*, 230–1.

[150] *Court and Times of Charles I*, i. 175.

to court by the end of the year.[151] Clearly these moves were an insurance for the next parliament, and may help to explain its being called. Early in 1628, Arundel's client, Sir Robert Cotton, offered to the Privy Council a blueprint for a harmonious parliament. Having remedied the abuses of the forced loan and arbitrary arrests, Buckingham was to request a parliament in which he would champion the cause of reform and so avert distrust in his administration. In 1628 Cotton sat for Arundel's borough of Castle Rising in Norfolk, and it is most probable that he wrote *The Danger Wherein The Kingdom Now Standeth and the Remedy* in consultation with his patron.[152] Both wished for the restoration of traditional and effective conciliar government rather than the pursuit of private quarrels. The proposal met with favourable reception in Council and it seems that its outlines were followed. In early April it was thought that Arundel and Bristol would commence impeachment proceedings against Buckingham in the Lords; but by the 20th one John Hope reported an agreement whereby, in return for concessions to the liberty of the subject, Buckingham was not to be named as a cause of the nation's grievances. Buckingham had affected a reconciliation with Arundel, Bristol, and Williams, having led them 'to believe he is theyr frend and layed all the blame of theire discord on mistakeings and they are so foolish to believe it . . . .'[153]

Arundel certainly had no reason to place an unqualified trust in an agreement with Buckingham. On 6 May 1628 he reported from the committee of privileges recommendations that the liberties of peers and their goods be guaranteed during the session of parliament[154]—a precautionary measure against Buckingham's possible treachery. Yet throughout the debates on the Petition of Right, Arundel, as Miss Relf has shown, attempted to promote a moderate course in order to restore harmony.[155] While Buckingham abhorred all conces-

[151] C. Russell, 'Parliamentary History 1604–1629 in Perspective', *History*, 61 (1976), 18–19; S. L. Adams, 'Protestant Cause', 399–400.

[152] R. Cotton, *The Danger Wherein the Kingdom Now Standeth and the Remedy* (1628) and in *Cottoni Posthuma*, 309–20. The copy in Brit. Lib. MS. Lansdowne 254, fos. 258–69 is dated 27 Jan. 1627/8.

[153] *C.S.P. Dom. 1628–9*, 60; P.R.O. S.P. 16/101/43; cf. *Court and Times of Charles I*, i. 309.

[154] *L.J.* iii. 782.

[155] F. H. Relf, *The Petition of Right* (Minneapolis, 1917).

sions and while Lord Saye and the Earl of Warwick advo-
cated total support for the Commons' petition, Arundel and
Bristol led a centre group composed of Williams, Bishop
Harsnett, the Earl of Clare, and most of the old aristocrats.
They proposed acceptance of the substance of the Petition, but
modification of the language, 'with due regard to leave entire
that sovereign power wherewith your Majesty is trusted'.[156] It
was a position typical of Arundel's behaviour over a decade.
Only when impasse threatened the failure of the Petition did
Arundel's group join those who accepted it unrevised and then
insist upon Charles giving his answer in due legal form.

Throughout the 1628 session of parliament, Arundel worked
in close contact with his friends in the Lords and Commons.
His associates in the Lower House helped to assist the smooth
and rapid passage of his private bill (probably drawn up by
Selden) for the annexation of the hereditary lands to the title
of Earl of Arundel.[157] After the adjournment in June, Selden,
Arundel's legal adviser who had played an important part in
the debate on the Petition of Right, joined Cotton at Arundel
House. There they all studied the engraved stones and marbles
which Arundel had shipped from the East.[158] Sir John Eliot,
formerly a client of Buckingham and Pembroke, entered into
correspondence and friendship with Selden and Cotton and
rested his hope for future good government in the Earl
Marshal. The co-operation of these and others in 1628 was
founded on discontent with Buckingham's administration: it
masked differences of attitude to religion, foreign affairs, and
questions of government. The assassination of Buckingham in
August 1628 therefore undermined the foundations of that
alliance and opened the way to new connections and the re-
establishing of old associations. In late July Arundel had been
admitted to kiss the king's hand, but not until October was he
readmitted to the Council table.[159] Lord Percy believed cor-

[156] *Court and Times of Charles I*, i, 346–7, 349; *L.J.* iii. 801; V. F. Snow, *Essex the
Rebel: The Life of Robert Devereux, 3rd Earl of Essex 1591–1646* (Lincoln, Nebr., 1970),
170.

[157] *H.M.C. 13th Report*, App. vii (Lonsdale MSS.), 42, 11 June 1628; *L.J.* iii. 837–8;
C.J. i. 911, *H.M.C. Cowper* i. 351; Tierney, *History of Arundel*, i. 132.

[158] J. Selden, *Marmora Arundelliana* (1628); Hervey, op. cit. 279–83.

[159] *Court and Times of Charles I*, i. 381; *H.M.C. Skrine MSS.* 169. Salvetti commented
in October: 'Now that he [Arundel] is replaced he will take a distinguished part in
the government of the State.'

rectly that with Buckingham off the stage the Lord Treasurer Weston would hold the greatest power and that he would bring in Buckingham's old enemies, Arundel, Bristol, and Sir Francis Cottington.[160] Arundel returned to his Whitehall lodgings and to prominence at court.[161] Clare expected that with Weston and Arundel at the Council table all would change 'for both thear habilities be such as they need nether fear nor envy able men . . .'[162] Weston himself believed that, with the Duke off the stage, 'our Affairs may be settled in the Ancient way.'[163] He commented not on policies, but on modes of government.

The 1629 session of parliament ended in violence in the Commons after noisy debate over religion and grievances. But this time the Commons were alone. In the Lords, Arundel, echoing an old petition to Charles, moved the king in the Earl of Oxford's cause 'to preserve ancient Honor especially when it is accompanied with virtue'. He proposed the establishment of a learned academy to educate the young nobles, the natural advisers of the crown, for service in government.[164] It was again a plea for the old forms. Arundel emerged as a leading figure on the Privy Council, and in his friend the Earl Marshal, Bishop Harsnett rested his hope for the revival of that 'vital spirit' which preserved 'the gallant ancient composition of our glorious state [which] is much declined . . . .'[165]

II

In 1621 Arundel had led Buckingham's supporters in the Lords; from 1624, he emerged as the leader of his critics in the Lords and in the Council, and was looked to as a leader by the Commons. Why did Arundel break from Buckingham? Why did the enemies of the Duke look to Arundel as a leader? We must examine Arundel's circle.

Those who associated in opposition to Buckingham were often bound by ties of kinship. Arundel was Pembroke's

[160] *C.S.P. Dom. 1625–49*, 291–3.

[161] *Court and Times of Charles I*, i. 419. In December the king and queen paid the Earl the honour of a visit to Arundel House, ibid. 451.

[162] *The Wentworth Papers 1597–1628*, ed. J. P. Cooper (Camden Soc., 1973), 308, Clare to Wentworth, 15 Nov. 1628.

[163] *Strafforde Letters* i. 47, Weston to Calvert, 8 Sept. 1628.

[164] *L.J.* iv. 34, 39.

[165] *C.S.P. Dom. 1629–31*, 167.

brother-in-law; his wife's brother-in-law, the Earl of Kent, supported him in the Lords. John Selden was steward to the Earl of Kent as well as legal adviser to Arundel. Sir Robert Cotton's son 'married Arundel's niece, while Clare's daughter married Sir Thomas Wentworth, Arundel's 'good friend'. Such connections were important, but disagreements and political alliances could cut across the ties of blood. In 1614 Arundel had observed 'that suspicions of jealousies are nowe between parties grown to that heights to dissolve ... bondes of kindred.'[166] He remained estranged from members of his own family for most of James I's reign.

More recent historiography would trace the disagreements between Buckingham and Arundel and the emergence of Arundel's circle from attitudes to foreign policy. But Buckingham had no consistent policy: he wavered between the Spanish match and a war, while Arundel, though he has been described as one committed to peace, supported a proposal to intervene in the Palatinate and might have entertained, as he was to do in the 1630s, a war against Spain with French assistance.[167] The argument from attitudes to foreign affairs makes it difficult to explain the behaviour of Pembroke, who failed to support Buckingham though he was hostile to Spain. Religious divisions prove no more helpful. Buckingham advanced both puritan and Arminian divines until the last years of James's reign. Despite his probable private Catholicism, Arundel had openly taken Anglican communion in 1616. In 1617, Sir Dudley Carleton thought him to be the protector of the anti-Arminian group at court, yet in 1624 he supported the Arminian bishop Montagu.[168] The herald Edward Walker aptly remarked that 'in religion he was no bigot'. If Arundel was committed to the Spanish party and the Catholic faith, it becomes impossible to understand how he attracted as his followers men like Selden, Williams, Cotton, and Wentworth.

[166] Arundel to Sir Thomas Edmondes, 23 Feb. 1614, Brit. Lib. MS. Stowe 175, fo. 244.

[167] Ruigh, op. cit. 33; *C.S.P. Dom. 1625–49*, 336, Arundel to Vane, 10 Aug. 1629; Hervey, op. cit. 396.

[168] Carleton to Vere, Oct. 1617, Arundel Castle Letters 1586–1617, fo. 222; H. Bouchier to Ussher, *The Works of James Ussher*, ed. C. R. Elrington and J. M. Todd (17 Vols., Dublin, 1847–64), xv. 194; *The Correspondence of John Cosin*, ed. G. Ornsby (Surtees Soc. lii., 1869), 85, 91.

What is clear from a study of Arundel's associates is that many shared intellectual interests: in history and antiquities, in art and architecture. Arundel projected a history of his own family and planned a study of Roman Britain.[169] His library contained the major antiquarian works of his century and the great Italian histories of Machiavelli and Guicciardini.[170] A love of the past doubtless facilitated his friendship with Cotton, Selden, with Henry Spelman, his Norfolk neighbour, with John Williams and Samuel Harsnett who collected historical works for their own libraries and leisure.[171]

We need not document the artistic interests of the nobleman who is famous for his collections and for his patronage of Inigo Jones, Rubens, and Mytens. But it is less well known that the Earl of Northumberland, Arundel's friend, built up a classic collection of works on architecture and that the Earl of Clare studied the subject from books borrowed from that collection.[172] Sir Robert Cotton sat with his patron on the commission for buildings in London. Arundel's friends Cotton and Selden shared his interest in collecting antiquities and Pembroke was a friendly rival for the best pieces.[173] It may be that Buckingham developed his own interests in art and antiquities during his years of close association with Pembroke and Arundel, but he developed 'nothing of the older man's refinement or antiquarian sense'.[174]

These intellectual pursuits should not be ignored by the historian of faction and politics. Cultural attainment was of the essence of nobility in the seventeenth century. Competition for works of art was sharpened by more than aesthetic zeal. It is interesting that after 1625, when their political alliance had broken, Arundel refused to co-operate with Buckingham in collecting rarities from the East: he worked alone, to Buckingham's disadvantage, through his agent William

---

[169] Hervey, op. cit., App. ii; Brit. Lib. MS. Harl. 4840; G. Carracoli, *The Antiquities of Arundel* (1776), 213.

[170] *Bibliotheca Norfolciana* (1681); Brit. Lib. MS. Sloane 862 is a manuscript list of Arundel's library.

[171] *Cabala*, 105; G. Goodwin, *A Catalogue of the Harsnett Library at Colchester* (1886).

[172] *H.M.C. Portland*, ix. 152; *Memorials of Holles*, 112.

[173] Arundel Castle Letters 1617–32, fo. 251; *H.M.C. Downshire*, iii. 189–90; *C.S.P. Dom. 1611–18*, 356; Tierney, *History of Arundel*, ii. 435.

[174] M. Whinney and O. Millar, *English Art 1625–1714* (Oxford, 1957), 2.

Petty.[175] In 1626, writing to Buckingham at the time of his greatest crisis, Edmund Bolton understood the importance of these noble pursuits:

> By your favour I would say there is scarcely any greater cause of your loss of favour with the gentry and better bred sort, who usually delight in books, than that of late your Lordship hath not seemed to value the generously and soberly well-learned famous for free studies and liberal cyclopaedie....[176]

In short, interests in aspects of history, of art and architecture, of learning in general, reflected, and perhaps even inculcated, attitudes and values. In a letter to Arundel from Constantinople, his agent Sir Thomas Roe reported that there the arts were thought to debilitate martial spirits. 'But they are absurdly mistaken,' he argued, confirming Arundel's own beliefs, 'for civility and knowledge do confirme and not effeminate good and true spirits.'[177] When Arundel's librarian Franciscus Junius wrote on the paintings and artists of the ancient world, he outlined more clearly the links between aesthetic pursuits and social and political values. The arts, he argued, inclined men to peace, consecrated the memory of the great, and showed virtue as the pattern of the glorious life. For artists to work, they needed 'that stable tranquillitie of an unshaken peace', enjoyed during the greatest days of classical empires and praised by the humanist students of antiquity.[178]

We cannot divorce the political values of Arundel's circle from their interests in the world of antiquity. Arundel's own library and collections were a monument to classical scholarship and to an Italian intellectual tradition of classical scholarship. Arundel sent his sons to Padua so that there they would imbibe a classical heritage. In Harsnett's house another son was guided through classical texts, for Harsnett's library was a fine repository of humanist learning.[179] The Earl of Clare read widely in classical texts and projected a commentary on Bacon's essay 'of Empire'. Sir Thomas Wentworth read

---

[175] *The Negotiations of Sir Thomas Roe* (1760), 386, 434, 444–6, 495.

[176] 29 May 1626, *C.S.P. Dom. 1625–49*, 129.

[177] W. N. Sainsbury, *Original Unpublished Papers Illustrative of the Life of Sir Peter Paul Rubens* (1859), 283.

[178] F. Junius, *De Pictura Veterum* (Amsterdam, 1637).

[179] *C.S.P. Venet. 1619–21*, 34, 81; Arundel Castle Letters 1617–1632, fo. 267; *Briefwisseling Van Hugo Grotius*, Vol. ii. ed. P. C. Molhuysen (The Hague, 1936), 240.

and annotated Polybius in his rural leisure; Sir Robert Cotton's historical writing revealed increasingly the influence of classical and Italian models.[180] Perhaps they sought in the histories of classical Greece and Rome a remedy for the instabilities of the 1620s. And if Arundel (and Harsnett) avidly collected Holbein's portraits, it may be because they depicted a period of humanist learning in England, the great age of the aristocracy at the court of Henry VIII, when the Howard family was supreme.

Certainly Arundel came to symbolize for many the old values of order and sobriety in public life. The French ambassador was told that in negotiating with Arundel and Pembroke, 'il faut aller avec mesure...', while 'even such as were no parties in contention with my Lord of Buckingham blame him that he was very rash in managing business... keeping no Motion of order or Measure...'[181] By his ostentatious behaviour, his insults to the nobility, his homosexual involvement with King James and his vulgar familiarity with the prince, by his indecorous behaviour in Spain, Buckingham offended many who sympathized with his policies.[182] Arundel, by contrast, was a nobleman for whom the forms and methods were at least as important as the ends, a great master of order and ceremony, as his biographer depicted him. The elaborate ceremonial of the Marshal's court was not for him mere display, but the correct expression of the dignity and authority of the office. When he went on embassy to Holland in 1632, Arundel drew up elaborate rules to ensure the correct behaviour of his attendants there.[183] Such a concern for order and sobriety helps to explain his friendship with Harsnett who wanted the return to the old stability in local government,[184] and with Wentworth, the exponent of 'Thorough' and 'antiquas vias' in the 1630s. Buckingham had offended against this ideal of order by his meteoric rise to supremacy and by his irresponsible actions. Sir Dudley Digges (who became Arundel's client) and

[180] *D.N.B.* Holles; Bodl. MS. Firth B2, fo. 104ᵛ; Sharpe, 'Sir Robert Cotton', *passim.*

[181] Brit. Lib. MS. Add. 30651, fo. 53ᵛ; *Scrinia Reserata*, i. 183.

[182] Lord Percy wrote in September 1628 that Buckingham's sordid death befitted a life 'which was granted by all men to be dishonourable and odius', *C.S.P. Dom. 1625–49*, 291–3.

[183] Tierney, *History of Arundel*, 457.

[184] Ibid. 437; Arundel Castle Letters 1617–32, fo. 225.

the Earl of Clare compared him to a comet which unsettled the order of the heavens and eclipsed less flashy luminaries.[185]

In the terrestrial sphere, Buckingham had upset the social and political order by sale of honours and by blocking the king from his aristocratic councillors—'the great usurper', Lord Percy called him.[186] Arundel came to personify the interests of the old aristocracy and the values of honour and nobility. He refused to accept any duchy other than that of Norfolk to which he had a hereditary claim[187] and was anxious to preserve the honour of all noble families. Arundel supported the claim of Robert de Vere to the earldom of Oxford against the pretence of Buckingham's candidate Willoughby, and then petitioned the king to grant de Vere the estates necessary to support so ancient and so honourable a title.[188] In the Lords, Arundel was the champion of the privileges due to peers, such as the right to answer on honour not oath; in his Earl Marshal's court he made rigorous inquiries into claims to titles.[189] This concern for maintaining the old nobility caused friction between Arundel and Buckingham in 1620 when they agreed on major questions of policy.[190] In 1623 Arundel ruled that no man was to be made a baronet who could not prove gentle descent. In 1625, as we have seen, he petitioned Charles to stop the sale of titles.[191] He was not alone: the Earl of Northumberland was offended by Buckingham's ostentatious coach with its six horses; even the Earl of Clare, who bought his title, condemned the sale of honours.[192]

The members of the House of Commons were no less concerned with the maintenance of the aristocracy. Sir Dudley Digges advised the king 'above all to look into the several abilities of his noblemen and be served by ablest men for parts and breeding'.[193] In 1628, in support of Arundel's bill for the annexation of hereditary lands to his title, 'Sir Edward Coke wished every nobleman would do so that there might be

[185] *Autobiography of Simonds D'Ewes*, ii. 183; *Memorials of Holles*, 103
[186] *C.S.P. Dom. 1625–49*, 291.
[187] *H.M.C. Hatfield*, xv. 190; *Letters of Chamberlain*, i. 412.
[188] Bodl. MS. Ashmole 857; *L.J.* iv. 31.
[189] *L.J.* iii. 41.
[190] *Letters of Chamberlain*, ii. 286.
[191] *C.S.P. Dom. 1623–5*, 95; Bodl. MS. Ashmole 846, fo. 37.
[192] C. H. Firth, *The House of Lords During the Civil War* (1910), 14.
[193] *C.S.P. Dom. 1625–6*, 243.

convenient maintenance for the supporting the earl-doms....'[194] The charge of selling titles was included in judicial proceedings against Buckingham in 1626. Evidently the Commons preferred the decorum of the old aristocracy to the vulgar pretensions of the upstart. And in Arundel they believed that nobility of birth met truly noble behaviour and inclination. Ben Jonson, whose works during the 1620s show great interest in the theme of honour and nobility, thought Arundel the man 'to shewe and to open clear vertue the way'.[195] Franciscus Junius called his patron, 'the very pattern of true Nobility'.[196] All writers who dedicated books to Arundel stressed his nobility, his real worth, and solid virtues in contrast to the superficialities of the age.[197]

A concern with order and propriety, with honour and nobility—*gravitas* the Romans called it—alienated Arundel from a court dominated by Buckingham. His plain attire, scorned by Clarendon, separated him from the tawdry gaudiness of the new nobility; his formal behaviour distanced him from two kings who lived with their favourites in intimate familiarity. These values made Arundel appear, like Clarendon's Pembroke, to be of the court but never corrupted by it. They earned him the respect of those essentially conservative parliamentary gentry who loved the king but were contemptuous of Buckingham. Such values, the currency of political exchange in the 1620s, bound to Arundel a group of men in Lords and Commons.

Edward Hyde had no part in that world. He came to court in the 1630s when Arundel was at the height of his influence and when the Earl Marshal's court, which he hated, was most active. He came to a court dominated now by the former enemies of Buckingham, shortly after he had married into the Villiers family and had undertaken a tract to vindicate the memory of the favourite. He saw only Arundel's arrogance, his ambition, and his reserve, where others living in the world of Buckingham had venerated the Earl's decorum and nobility.

[194] *H.M.C. 13th Report*, App. vii (Lonsdale), 42.

[195] Ben Jonson, *Works*, ed. C. H. Herford and P. and E. M. Simpson, (11 Vols., Oxford, 1925–52), vii. 585.

[196] F. Junius, *The Painting of the Ancients* (English edn., 1678), Dedication to Countess of Arundel.

[197] e.g. *The Mirrour of Majestie* (1618); G. Markham, *The Booke of Honour* (1625).

Historians have singled out the 1620s as the decade of issues and conflict. The political activities of Arundel and his circle during these years suggest rather the importance of personalities and personal connections—not connections based on constitutional principles or ideological commitments nor connections founded on the mere pursuit of office, but connections strengthened by traditional beliefs about correct behaviour and modes of action, about methods not policies. The Arundel circle is a case study in the values and politics of Renaissance England.

VIII. The Divided Leadership of the House of Commons in 1629

Christopher Thompson

THE DECADE that began in 1620 was one of terrible conflict. It was a period of conflict in Europe that witnessed the almost continuous advance of Catholic armies and that threatened to end in the extinction of the cause of continental Protestantism. As those armies advanced and that danger became more acute, the anxieties of Protestant Englishmen grew correspondingly more pronounced. For they had seen not only the return of English forces from the continent in defeat and disgrace but also the even more alarming growth of irresponsible royal power in church and state at home. Naturally, they resisted. And the result of their resistance was the series of increasingly bitter parliaments that came to a disastrous climax in 1629.

The story of the parliamentary session of 1629 is well known, at least, in outline.[1] It is the story of the breakdown and failure of the last voluntary attempt made by King Charles to secure the co-operation of the assembled political nation. This was due, it has often been said, to the violence of his opponents in the House of Commons who abandoned the moderation and restraint they had shown in the previous session. The release of their pent-up anger led to an exaggerated attack on the king's ecclesiastical policy and to their refusal to come to terms on the issue of Tonnage and Poundage. In its frustration and despair, the House lost its sense of judgement and its members rushed incontinently from one uncompleted subject to the next. There was thus no clear pattern to their debates and no obvious advantage gained from their complaints. When the breakdown inevitably came, the provocation they had given Charles

---

[1] S. R. Gardiner, *The History of England from the Accession of James I to the Outbreak of the Civil War* (10 vols., 1899), vii, chs. 1 and 2. Harold Hulme, *The Life of Sir John Eliot 1592 to 1632* (1957), ch. 13.

justified his action in bringing the session to a close. Having found his parliaments to be unmanageable in practice, the king repudiated them for the present in theory.[2] He therefore dismissed his critics to their homes and resolved to do without them if he could.

This deft combination of the general argument that the breakdown was the result of the growing political tensions of the decade with an account of the force with which the House of Commons expressed its opinions seems straightforward enough. No doubt the general argument is sound, but it does not follow that the particular propositions by which it is illustrated are altogether convincing. The latter require subscription, in any case, to two surprising contentions—namely, that the Commons as a whole had lost its sense of political judgement and that the House's entire proceedings consequently reflected no more than inchoate anger. It is this view, or rather the assumptions that lie at its heart, that I propose to challenge in this essay. I shall attempt to refute it by examining the circumstances in which parliament met, by demonstrating that the debates in the Commons do, in fact, fall into an intelligible pattern and by showing that a close analysis of the proceedings casts a revealing light on the objectives of the House's leaders. Finally, I shall try to show that the famous events in the Commons on 2 March may be explained as much in terms of the victory of one group amongst these leaders over another as it is by the conflict between the House and the king.

It is possible, of course, to trace the origins of the quarrel between Charles and his subjects back to the war policy adopted with such apparent enthusiasm in 1624. It had then been assumed that Elizabeth's triumphs could be repeated in a shorter time and at less expense. But these illusions were soon exposed when the war involved hostilities with France as well as with Spain and parliamentary supply proved totally inadequate. Discontent about the continental strategy pursued and over the domestic role of the Duke of Buckingham compelled King Charles to turn to his prerogative powers to sustain the war policy from 1626 onwards. The subsequent imposition

[2] In his proclamation on 27 March 1629; J. P. Kenyon, *The Stuart Constitution* (Cambridge, 1966), 61.

of the forced loan, and the arbitrary imprisonment, martial law, and billeting that it brought in its train, aroused fears that the liberties of the subject were gravely threatened. This clearly inspired the decision of the leaders of the House of Commons to seek the redress of these grievances when parliament met again in March 1628.[3] But the procedure eventually adopted in formulating the Petition of Right was the result of internal divisions and of external pressures. For it was not only the consent of relatively moderate or of relatively radical members that had to be won but also that of a divided House of Lords and a hostile king. When, indeed, it seemed that no satisfactory reply from the king to the Petition would be forthcoming,[4] a much wider assault was launched by members of the Commons. In the closing weeks of the session, Charles again heard that the Duke of Buckingham was the source of all their grievances,[5] was again informed that Laud and Neile were the promoters of innovation in religion,[6] and was again warned that the collection of Tonnage and Poundage was contrary not only to the fundamental liberties of the kingdom but also to the Petition of Right to which he had belatedly given a second, acceptable, reply.[7] The combustible materials of political dissent were thus gathered together in June 1628 and all that prevented their ignition then was the king's decision to prorogue Parliament until October.

To contemporaries, the breach between Charles and his people seemed wider than ever. The king, indeed, made matters worse by proroguing parliament with a claim to continue collecting Tonnage and Poundage as a right[8] and by his subsequent promotion of the peccant Arminian divines.[9] Domestic affairs continued to be shaped by the exigencies of

---

[3] In a pre-session meeting at Sir Robert Cotton's house. On the background in 1628, see F. H. Relf, *The Petition of Right* (Minneapolis, 1917).

[4] For the king's first answer, see S. R. Gardiner, *England under the Duke of Buckingham and Charles I* (2 vols., 1875), ii. 277. Cf. Huntingdon Record Office dd M 36 Bundle 4, pp. 90–2, 115–18.

[5] Huntingdon Rec. O. dd M 36 Bundle 4, pp. 141–2.

[6] Ibid., p. 134.

[7] *H.M.C., 13th Report, App. VII*, 57; Gardiner, *England under the Duke of Buckingham*, ii. 291. Cf. J. P. Cooper, 'The Fall of the Stuart Monarchy', in The New Cambridge Modern History, vol. iv. 557.

[8] *H.M.C. 13th Report, App. VII*, 58; Brit. Lib. Harl. MS. 390, fo. 421r.

[9] Kenyon, op. cit. 149.

foreign policy, and preparations for the relief of La Rochelle were pushed ahead without interruption even when Buckingham was murdered in August. The failure, however, of the expedition to save the port made it likely that parliament—which was prorogued for a second time in October—would have to be faced again in January if the war was to go on. The king's position was incidentally eased by the decision of the Barons of the Exchequer in November that goods seized for refusal to pay the disputed duties of Tonnage and Poundage could not be recovered from his possession by means of a writ of replevin; the question of the right to the goods was one, they stressed, to be settled by the king and his subjects in parliament.[10] A deliberate attempt was certainly made to quieten religious passions. A declaration was therefore drawn up forbidding disputes about the interpretation of the Thirty-nine Articles and reserving judgement (with royal assent) on such abstruse questions to the clergy in Convocation.[11] To prevent renewed inquiries and further punishment in parliament, Richard Montague, the most prominent Arminian controversialist, was persuaded to repudiate the tenets of Arminius,[12] and he and three others were granted special pardons for past offences.[13] As a final gesture of conciliation, Montague's book, *Appello Caesarem*, was called in.[14]

Charles had done what he thought reasonable to secure an amenable parliament. He might certainly hope that, on this occasion, the House of Lords would offer less assistance to the Commons in thwarting his plans. Opposition to him there had been more moderate in tone than that in the Lower House in 1628, and Buckingham's death had permitted a series of personal reconciliations that depleted the ranks of his potential critics amongst the peers.[15] Other, more fortuitous, advantages

[10] Gardiner, *History of England*, vii. 5–6.

[11] Ibid. vii. 21–3.

[12] Brit. Lib. Harl. MS. 390, fo.463^r; *C.S.P. Dom. 1628–9*, 346. *H.M.C. Cowper, Appendix*, i. 373.

[13] Gardiner, *History of England*, vii. 23–4.

[14] Ibid. 23.

[15] e.g. with the Earls of Arundel and Bristol and the Archbishop of Canterbury. In fact, the House of Lords proved to be relatively quiescent in 1629. Since the proceedings in the two Houses were not connected as they had been in 1628 and did not impinge upon the calculations of the Commons' leaders to any significant degree, I have made very little reference to events in the House of Lords in the text below.

had been gained too. The elevation of Sir Thomas Wentworth to the peerage silenced one ot the more conciliatory leaders of 1628, just as the absence, through ill-health, of Sir Edward Coke deprived the Commons of a more radical spokesman. And this time, at least, there was no sign that the leaders of the Lower House had agreed beforehand on the course to be taken. But political problems are not solved by the exercise of tactical acumen or by the accumulation of such advantages as these. The actions of the king and his advisers were, in any case, open to grave suspicion. Ignorance about the technical nature of the Exchequer decision was widespread and it was commonly held that the right of the subject to his goods had been judicially infringed. Leaving the question to be settled in parliament meant that the king's claim to levy these duties without statutory authority was in effect maintained. If this went un-challenged, the need for parliamentary grant at all would soon be over. No less profound fears were held concerning religion. Doctrinal peace could scarcely be attained when the very same divines who had been condemned in parliament for their opinions were promoted to the highest offices in the church and their adversaries silenced by the king's declaration. However quiescent the House of Lords proved to be, to have expected the Commons' leaders who remained—common lawyers like Littleton, Noy, and Selden, country gentlemen like Eliot and Phelips, and subtle tacticians like Pym and Rich—to pass over these matters without comment would have been too sanguine. When parliament reassembled at West-minster on 20 January 1629, serious misgivings about Charles's policies and intentions thus persisted.

In fact, the king's most resolute critics in the Lower House were eager to exploit the opportunity they had been given. Once proceedings began on the 21st, it was soon discovered by a committee appointed at John Selden's suggestion that the king had commanded the entry of his controversial speech at the close of the preceding session into the Commons' Journal:[16] a request for delay in considering the question from John Pym

[16] Selden's request is to be found in the first sentence of Lowther's report. *H.M.C. 13th Report, App. VII*, 59. See *C.J.* i. 920 for the appointment of the committee and its immediate actions. Selden's report is given in *The Commons Debates for 1629*, ed. W. Notestein and F. H. Relf (Minnesota, 1921), 4. Lowther's report omits the speeches that followed from Pym and Eliot.

prompted Sir John Eliot to demand that a select committee be instructed to inquire into a matter that concerned the honour of the House and to investigate this and other violations of the liberties of the kingdom.[17] A proposal for a committee with similar general responsibilities was made by Selden himself when he opened the subsequent debate on the violations of the Petition of Right since their last meeting.[18] It was apparent, however, that the House was unsympathetic to the idea. For the first subject was postponed as Pym had suggested until a report could be made by an enlarged committee on the following Tuesday.[19] The second was far more controversial because it involved the establishment of a standing committee to inquire into the violations of the liberties of the subject and for these violations to be reported as grievances to the House. But such a body, it was pointed out by Sir John Coke, the Secretary of State who bore the heavy burden of speaking for the king, would usurp the function of the Committee of the Whole House for Grievances and render an accommodation with Charles more difficult. It evoked explicit comparison with the Spanish Inquisition and was vigorously resisted by a number of members. Eventually, a compromise was reached when it was ordered, on Sir Nathaniel Rich's motion,[20] that the House as a committee of the whole would consider how the liberties of the subject had been infringed contrary to the Petition of Right on Tuesday 27 January.[21] The more radical proposal was thus circumvented. Eliot and Selden had found the views of Pym and Rich preferred in turn. The House was evidently not yet ready to take such steps against the king.

A similar degree of reluctance to confront Charles was again shown on the 22nd. Proceedings began with a complaint from a merchant member, John Rolle, about the seizure of his goods for refusal to pay the duties demanded by the Customs officers, despite his offer to provide security for what was due in law

[17] *Commons Debates 1629*, 4–5. The first three sentences of Eliot's speech on page 5 constitute his reply to Pym. The remainder was given in the subsequent debate, as a comparison with Lowther's report shows. *H.M.C. 13th Report, App. VII*, 59.

[18] *Commons Debates 1629*, 5; *H.M.C. 13th Report, App. VII*, 59.

[19] *C.J.* i. 920.

[20] *H.M.C. 13th Report, App. VII*, 60. Rich deftly avoided offending either party by suggesting that it required a proper committee to undertake this work—i.e. a committee of the whole House but not the Committee for Grievances.

[21] *C.J.* i. 920. Cf. *H.M.C. 13th Report, App. VII*, 60; *Commons Debates 1629*, 4.

or granted by parliament. Neither of the replevins he had since sought had secured the restoration of his property.[22] Two vital questions were thus directly raised, the question of his liability to pay Tonnage and Poundage without statutory grant and that of his privilege as an M.P. which he had unsuccessfully pleaded.[23] The House's reaction was one of anger, but it was again divided on what should be done. According to Phelips and Coryton, a select committee should be appointed to examine Rolle's allegation.[24] But this idea was anathema to Eliot and Selden: it was improper, they claimed, to refer the question of the privilege of a member to a committee and they both asked that his information should be accepted as it was. They were quite content to refer the matter of the rights of the subject thereby raised to the Committee of the Whole House on the 27th.[25] Men who violated the liberties of parliament, Littleton, and later Eliot, insisted, should be summoned to answer for their conduct.[26] Once again, the radicals were frustrated. The examination of Rolle's information was entrusted, as Phelips had suggested, to a select committee of twenty, who were to meet at two o'clock in the afternoon. To assist this committee in its inquiries and to answer for their contempt to the House in Rolle's Case, six of the Customs officers were summoned to attend.[27] This was a small success for Eliot to set against his larger failures.

Unfortunately, precisely what was said or done in the afternoon is not known. It is, however, certain that Charles wished to prevent further discussion on the subject. On Friday 23 January, he employed Sir John Coke to ask the Commons to suspend further debate on the Customs officers' seizure of merchants' goods until after he had spoken to both Houses at Whitehall on Saturday afternoon.[28] With the initiative in his hands for the moment, the king then made it plain that his purpose was conciliatory, explaining that his speech at the end of the previous session had been intended to show the necessity,

[22] *H.M.C. 13th Report, App. VII*, 60; *Commons Debates 1629*, 7.
[23] See Littleton's speech, *H.M.C. 13th Report, App. VII*, 61.
[24] Ibid. 61. Cf. *Commons Debates 1629*, 8–9.
[25] *H.M.C. 13th Report, App. VII*, 61; *Commons Debates 1629*, 8.
[26] *Commons Debates 1629*, 8.
[27] *C.J.* i. 921.
[28] *C.J.* i. 921; *H.M.C. 13th Report. App. VII*, 61; *Commons Debates 1629*, 10.

not the right, by which he took Tonnage and Poundage. If a bill was passed in the form in which his ancestors had received it—that is, from the beginning of his reign—his past actions would thereby be included and his future proceedings authorized. This reassuring statement specifically rejected any claim to collect the duties on the basis of his hereditary prerogative and was thus welcome to the Lower House.[29] In an attempt to exploit this reaction, Sir John Coke urged the Commons on Monday 26 January to respond to the king's speech by reading the bill for Tonnage and Poundage which he then presented and which he supported with an account of the foreign dangers threatening the kingdom.[30] But Eliot was not persuaded by these strategic arguments and observed that, if the king had allowed time for its passage, the bill could have been passed in the last session. This measure, he continued, gave power to levy impositions at will: other matters, he insisted, should first be considered to facilitate its passage.[31] Selden, too, was against reading it now: it was contrary to the liberties of the House, he asserted, for a bill of subsidy to be introduced by the king, and against their custom to begin with a measure of this kind.[32] And Phelips was anxious that the work of the select committee should be completed before it was discussed.[33] So, despite some support from Harley and Digges for the bill, it was not read:[34] a political impasse had been reached.

The House's preoccupation with civil grievances had thus far been clear. But there had been no general inclination to precipitate a direct confrontation with the king. Eliot and Selden, who appeared to be working together, had, on the whole, been contained. Charles, however, was no less frustrated. For, despite his placatory gestures and his conciliatory speech, he had proved unable to secure even the first reading of the bill to grant him Tonnage and Poundage. Those who opposed the

---

[29] *H.M.C. 13th Report, App. VII*, 63–4; *Commons Debates 1629*, 10–11; Brit. Lib. Egerton MS. 2645, fo. 3ʳ.

[30] *H.M.C. 13th Report, App. VII*, 62. It is likely that Sir Humphrey May, the Chancellor of the Duchy of Lancaster, was originally intended to present it. *H.M.C. 12th Report, App. I*, 381.

[31] *H.M.C. 13th Report, App. VII*, 62; *Commons Debates 1629*, 108.

[32] Loc. cit.

[33] *Commons Debates 1629*, 109.

[34] *H.M.C. 13th Report, App. VII*, 62–3. *Commons Debates 1629*, 108–9. This suggests that the bill was not in its usual form.

proffered bill clearly wished to press on with their previous lines of attack. In fact, an altogether different assault was now begun and the attention of the House claimed by Pym's stepbrother, Francis Rous, for rights of a higher nature than those concerning their goods, liberties, and lives. In a speech of great force and passion, he pleaded for deep and serious consideration to be given to the dangers threatening religion. It was now being consumed by the popish assault upon the laws and statutes of the realm and by the infectious increase in Arminianism. The old heresy had bred a new heterodoxy that confronted them with the peril of the imposition of Roman tyranny in the church and of Spanish monarchy in the state. By separating the prince from his people or by discovering other, non-parliamentary, sources of income, their enemies could undermine true religion and introduce their own erroneous opinions. Were not the Arminians, indeed, the very same men who sought to accomplish these ends by attacking the goods and liberties of the commonwealth? The past showed how the decay in religion had brought in its train the decline in the honour and strength of the nation. But if they held fast to their faith by a vow and covenant, then their goods would be restored to them and the kingdom flourish again.[35] Rous's powerful appeal evoked a sympathetic response, and the speakers who followed emphasized the dangers that threatened from the growing numbers of papists and Arminians and from the power of those about the king who protected them.[36] Phelips now agreed with this diagnosis of their ills and it was at his suggestion that the Commons decided to petition the king for a general fast.[37] The entire subject of religion, it was resolved, should be discussed in the Committee of the Whole House that afternoon.[38] But when a request was then made to see what the remonstrance delivered to the king in June had contained on these topics,[39] it was revealed that the document had been conveyed by royal command into the hands of the Lord Privy Seal: the committee therefore decided to go no

---

[35] *Commons Debates 1629*, 12–14.

[36] Ibid. 14–16, 109–10. Cf. *H.M.C. 13th Report, App. VII*, 63. The emphasis on this point is worth noting.

[37] *Commons Debates 1629*, 16; *H.M.C. 13th Report, App. VII*, 63; *C.J.* i. 922.

[38] *C.J.* i. 922.

[39] *Commons Debates 1629*, 111. Cf. ibid. 246–7.

further until the House had been informed.[40]

Charles's reaction to this development was predictable. He had expected the bill for Tonnage and Poundage to have precedence, and that was still his expectation as he informed the Commons through Sir John Coke on the 27th.[41] But priority was again demanded for religion by Sir Walter Earle[42] and detailed proposals to ensure its preservation produced for discussion by John Pym. Popery was an old affliction and to combat it Pym sought inquiries into the neglect of the recusancy laws, into the favour shown to papists, and into the introduction of superstitious Catholic ceremonies. But the new disease of Arminianism was the more dangerous and subtle threat. To deal with it, he wished to open a way for the profession of the truth and to call upon the positive witnesses for their faith.[43] Doubts about the legality of preaching against Arminianism, which had arisen from the king's proclamation, should be cleared up. Men whose teaching had been contrary to the truth had been promoted since the last session. How, he asked, had they been preferred and what pardons had they obtained for their false doctrines? What, indeed, had they preached before the king on these contentious matters since they were enjoined to silence by that proclamation? And which books in favour of their doctrines had been published and which against them suppressed? It was the manifest duty of parliament in general and of individual Christians in particular to employ all possible means to eradicate these evils. Parliament should certainly know the established and fundamental truths of religion and it alone could deal with this mischief. Neither the Convocation of Canterbury nor that of York, each of which was a provincial synod, still less High Commission, which derived its authority from statute, could pre-empt parliament's judgement in such matters: that was, he said, 'the judgment of the King and of the three estates of the whole realm'.[44] The moment was evidently

[40] Ibid. 111. [41] Ibid. 18, 111.

[42] Ibid. 18–19; *H.M.C. 13th Report, App. VII*, 64. Note the contrast with his priorities in 1628.

[43] It is in this speech that the combination of statutory and non-statutory authorities was first advanced in this session. *Commons Debates 1629*, 20; *H.M.C. 13th Report, App. VII*, 64. There had been attempts to put the Lambeth Articles and those of Ireland on the statute book in 1626 and 1628.

[44] *Commons Debates 1629*, 20–1. Cf. ibid. 17 for Rich's use of a similar phrase on the 27th.

well chosen since the House adopted this programme of inquiries in its entirety.[45] Nothing had been heard of the report into the entry in their Journal or of the investigation they had undertaken to conduct into the violations of the rights of the subject contrary to the Petition of Right envisaged as their business six days before.

Once it had accepted Pym's guidance, the House was even more unwilling to respond to Charles's promptings on Tonnage and Poundage and immune—with the notable exception of Eliot[46]—to the immediate temptations offered by the petitions they received on the subject from Richard Chambers and from the Levant Company.[47] The king's demand that precedence be given to his bill was again made known to the Commons by Sir John Coke on the 28th and it was clearly stated that he expected no new remonstrance on religion.[48] But the assertion that gratitude rather than criticism was due commanded no agreement, and the draft heads of the House's reply to the two royal messages they had received made plain their determination to proceed first with religion.[49] The suspicion was indeed expressed that those who advised Charles to press for the bill to be read cared neither for religion nor for the king's service.[50] They had no intention, the draft declared, of discussing new points in religion but merely of suppressing novel opinions as former parliaments had done.[51] On both issues, therefore, the House rebuffed the king.

The assessment that Pym had made on the 27th of the relative dangers arising from popery and from Arminianism was adopted by Sir Benjamin Rudyerd when debate on the subject was resumed in the Committee of the Whole House for Religion on the 29th. His complaint about popery was of the failure to

[45] *C.J.* i. 922–3. Cf. *Commons Debates 1629*, 111–12.

[46] *Commons Debates 1629*, 112.

[47] Chambers's petition came in at the opening of business and was referred to the select committee dealing with Rolle's allegations. The Levant Company's petition came in at the end of proceedings and was referred to the Committee of the Whole House dealing with invasions of the liberty of the subject contrary to the Petition of Right. *C.J.* i. 923; *Commons Debates 1629*, 112, 115.

[48] *Commons Debates 1629*, 22, 112–13; *H.M.C. 13th Report, App. VII*, 65.

[49] *Commons Debates 1629*, 113–14; *C.J.* i. 923.

[50] *Commons Debates 1629*, 114.

[51] Loc. cit.

execute the laws against recusancy; but Arminianism, he observed, had lately crept into high places in the kingdom. As an antidote, he therefore proposed that the Commons should consider the articles of their faith—the 1552 Articles, the catechism in the Book of Common Prayer, and the Articles of Lambeth—and refine them so that they might proceed against those who dissented from them.[52] This argument was elaborated by Sir Robert Harley, who added to Rudyerd's list of formularies the Thirty-nine Articles of 1562, the Articles of Ireland, and the conclusions of the Synod of Dort. As positive remedies, he suggested that they make a public profession of their faith and that they seek a conference with the Lords to gain their support for a remonstrance to the king for the punishment of the Arminian divines and for the suppression of their writings.[53] The two men were evidently attempting to provide a list of the 'witnesses for our religion in the affirmative' of which Pym had spoken two days earlier.[54] The authorities they cited together carried a heavy weight of Calvinist teaching on predestination and would thus provide an effective answer to the Arminian doctrine of grace. Eliot, too, had a contribution to make in a long and important speech. In it, he specifically expressed his wish to carry out the House's intentions and to direct their labours to an end. For that reason, he was unwilling to enter into a discussion of the opinions of particular divines. He refused to believe that they were now ignorant of the truth in religion; they neither could nor would alter the faith they had so long professed. But he was afraid of the advisers about the king and of the declaration recently made in his name. Their faith rested upon the Thirty-nine Articles but, if any dispute about their interpretation arose, the power to decide lay with the bishops and clergy in Convocation. For all he knew, they might introduce popery and Arminianism by this means. How could such power be left to these men? How could they leave it to men like Montague? To avoid confusion in their proceedings, he therefore asked that the House presently consider the foundations of their religion and set down a rule on which all might rest. Having established the grounds on which they

[52] Ibid. 116.
[53] Loc. cit. Cf. *H.M.C. 13th Report, App. VII*, 66.
[54] *H.M.C. 13th Report, App. VII*, 64.

differed from the Arminians, they might then proceed against those who offended against that rule.[55] Now, despite the length of his speech, it is highly improbable that Eliot was attempting to persuade the House to define the doctrine of the nation, still less that he was proposing to turn the Commons alone into the supreme religious authority in the kingdom.[56] They already knew what true doctrine was, but it had to be defended against men who were willing to overturn it. So, he was requesting a definite statement on which to rest their case against the Arminians, who could be punished for their offences against this rule. The first response he elicited came from Sherland who proposed that they rely upon the Thirty-nine Articles as understood until seven or eight years before.[57] A second was made in a speech by Sir Nathaniel Rich in which he suggested that they should acknowledge as true the Thirty-nine Articles of 1562, confirmed by Parliament in 1571, as understood by the public acts of the Church of England and by the general and current exposition of its writers, and that they should reject the interpretations of Arminians, Jesuits, and all others.[58] The only other recorded comment was Selden's terse (but significant) observation that, since the 1562 Articles had not been confirmed in parliament until 1571, the reformation of their religion had not been complete until then.[59] But it was Rich's formulation that was none the less adopted by the committee and later by the House.[60]

The Commons had certainly moved some way towards an agreed position. And there appears to have been very little of that overt internal obstruction that had greeted the earlier proposals of Eliot and Selden. More skilful political hands seemed to be at work. But who were the men guiding the House and on what grounds were they acting? The surviving records

[55] *Commons Debates 1629*, 24–8, 117; *H.M.C. 13th Report, App. VII*, 66.

[56] Gardiner, *History of England*, vii. 40–1; H. Hulme, op. cit. 282–3. Eliot's confusion about the respective roles of parliament and Convocation can be inferred from Sir Robert Cotton's letter to him: *The Letter Book of Sir John Eliot*, ed. A. B. Grosart, (2 vols., 1882), ii. 35–8.

[57] *Commons Debates 1629*, 117.

[58] *H.M.C. 13th Report, App. VII*, 66.

[59] *Commons Debates 1629*, 117. This obviously raised the entire question of the relationship between the statutory and non-statutory authorities cited for this purpose since the 27th but no one else is recorded as having spoken after Selden.

[60] *H.M.C. 13th Report, App. VII*, 66–7; *C.J.* i. 924; *Commons Debates 1629*, 117–18.

do not offer certain answers to these questions but they do provide a number of clues. One such clue is to be found in the delay sought by Pym and Rich in turn to the discussion of the matters successively raised by Eliot and Selden on the 21st. Neither, it is evident, was anxious for inquiries into civil grievances to be too vigorously pursued then. It is possible, moreover, to suspect that Pym may have prompted the intervention of Francis Rous, his stepbrother, on the 26th, but no proof of this has yet been adduced. What can definitely be stated, however, is that Pym placed the discussion of religion first amongst his political priorities on the 27th and that it was he who laid down the lines of inquiry the House decided to adopt. It is also possible, perhaps even probable, that the Commons' prospective defence of its new priorities was suggested by Rich on the 28th.[61] It is certain that it was Rich who proposed the formula agreed on the 29th. The initiative may have been taken by others—by Rous on the 26th, by Earle on the 27th, and by Rudyerd on the 29th—but practical direction was coming from Pym and Rich. The suspicion that they were working together—in the way that Eliot and Selden appeared to have been doing in the earlier debates—may thus be legitimately entertained.

In fact, the House was now treading on most difficult ground. The arguments put forward by M.P.s on the definition of their faith had hitherto relied upon a combination of statutory and non-statutory authorities to delimit the orthodox position of the Church of England. If an effective weapon was to be found to use against Arminian teachings on grace, the latter had to be cited. But the resolution passed on the 29th had neither defined what the public acts of the church were nor stated how the church itself was constituted. These were the problems that faced Rich on Saturday the 31st, when he addressed the Committee of the Whole House for Religion once again. His

---

[61] Rich is known to have proposed the heads of an answer to the King: *Commons Debates 1629*, 113. The addition suggested by Kirton is not to be found in either version of the draft heads accepted by the House: ibid. 114; *C.J.* i. 923. Since no one else made any proposal concerning its contents, Rich perhaps may be thought to be its author. This would explain why Nicholas left a blank space in his notes; if the House accepted Rich's scheme, there would have been no point in taking the resolutions down twice. For the final text of the House's reply, see *Commons Debates 1629*, 29–30; for its compilers, *C.J.* i. 925.

purpose, he declared, was to discover who the Arminians were, and he therefore set out what he considered to be the public acts of the church. He defined them as the catechisms made and confirmed by Act of Parliament, the Thirty-nine Articles of 1571, the Common Prayer Book, the Articles of Lambeth and Ireland, the conclusions of the Synod of Dort, the readings of the public professors in the universities, and all the works of divines printed by authority.[62] Once again, a mixture of statutory and non-statutory authorities had been cited. The latter, however, were immediately rejected by Selden, who denied public authority to formularies without parliamentary sanction.[63] He was supported by Littleton and Hoskins, both of whom declined to accept Convocation as an independent authority constituting the church; the king and state alone, said Hoskins, could decide on a public act of the church.[64] The division thus revealed threatened to render nugatory the attempt to establish a fully Calvinist interpretation of the doctrines of the Church of England. But the dispute was not settled then: it was postponed for further discussion on Tuesday 3 February.[65] When the debate reopened, a compromise was suggested by Eliot. Having remarked that they had previously disagreed over the way in which the Lambeth Articles might be used, he proposed to rely on the declaration they had made on 29 January and proceed to charge the Arminians; they could then use the Lambeth Articles—which all agreed to be true— against them if they defended themselves.[66] Rous certainly approved. But Coryton was still unwilling to accept the Articles of Lambeth as public and binding acts of the church because of the danger that would ensue if another assembly of bishops decided against those articles on any point.[67] It was easier, as many members proclaimed, to move on to inquire into how Laud and Montague had been promoted and to discover how the special pardons had been granted.[68] The attempt to define the established and fundamental truths of religion—first made

---

[62] *Commons Debates 1629*, 119; *H.M.C. 13th Report, App. VII*, 68.
[63] *Commons Debates 1629*, 119–20; *H.M.C. 13th Report, App. VII*, 68.
[64] *Commons Debates 1629*, 120.   [65] Ibid.; *C.J.* i. 925.
[66] *Commons Debates 1629*, 33–4, 121; *H.M.C. 13th Report, App. VII*, 69.
[67] *Commons Debates 1629*, 122.
[68] Ibid. 34–5, 122.

by Pym and last defended by Rich in this session—had to be laid aside.

Of course, it was only a part of the programme suggested by Pym that had fallen through. Its abandonment promised to heal the differences between members and to make it easier to attack individual Arminians. It was now possible to ask whether Montague had been legally confirmed as Bishop of Chichester[69] and to inquire into the way in which the pardons for Cosens, Manwaring, Montague, and Sibthorpe had been obtained. Men like these, who had made the commonwealth sick, Rous argued on the 4th, should be cut off as rotten members; and both Kirton and Phelips wished to know who had induced the king to grant them pardons.[70] This was a line of inquiry that brought an almost immediate political dividend when Phelips reported that Attorney-General Heath had had instructions from the king in the previous summer, but had only acted on them after a discussion with the Earl of Dorset as a result of which he had received the necessary warrant from Viscount Dorchester and that his rough draft had been revised by Neile, the Arminian Bishop of Winchester.[71] Two days later, on the 6th, further evidence of the parts played by Dorchester and Neile was brought to light,[72] evidence confirmed in the latter's case on the 11th.[73] But at no time did the House proceed from the conduct of these inquiries to the formulation of charges.[74]

The most promising line of attack grew directly out of this investigation. For the Commons were informed by Sir Eubule Thelwall on the 4th of remarks alleged to have been made by Cosens in which he denied that the king had any more to do with religion than the man who rubbed his horse's heels.[75] Superficially, this seemed to constitute a clear denial of the royal supremacy in religion, and yet Cosens had received his pardon shortly thereafter. When Phelips reported the inquiries the Attorney-General had conducted into these allegations on

[69] Ibid. 36, 53–5, 123, 134–5; *H.M.C. 13th Report, App. VII*, 67, 69–70.
[70] *Commons Debates 1629*, 37–8.
[71] Ibid. 39–40, 125.
[72] Ibid. 45, 131, 175.
[73] Ibid. 59, 139, 192.
[74] But note Rich's plea on 6 February and Eliot's on the 7th. Ibid. 43, 50, 52.
[75] Ibid. 36–7.

6 February,[76] Heath's decision to abandon the investigation because he could not find corroborative evidence was vigorously censured. Eliot was particularly incensed; the charge, he said, was high treason, resting upon deposition, and could not properly be abandoned by Heath on such slender grounds as a certificate to him from the Dean and others at Durham. Those who had testified against Cosens should be summoned and Heath himself interrogated about his conduct; if guilty, he—and others—should not be spared.[77] But questioning Heath, Sir Henry Mildmay pointed out, should not be contemplated until they were satisfied of Cosens's guilt.[78] Eliot demurred: Heath had failed in his duty and would, he hoped, reveal those who had commanded him not to proceed when he was examined.[79] Once again, members were divided on what should be done. But eventually it was ordered that the witnesses should be sent for and that Heath should be heard on the following Monday if he so wished.[80] The Attorney-General had, however, learnt by now of the dangers involved in being too frank and declined the invitation: he merely sent a letter to the Speaker explaining his conduct.[81] Nothing further was said or done. The irony was that, as Bishop Neile had predicted,[82] the whole affair eventually came to nothing.

The failure of the Commons to press home either inquiry should not be exaggerated. A great many other matters—the printed versions of the Thirty-nine Articles and the practice of censorship by Laud's chaplains, for example[83]—required the House's attention. It is none the less true that the pursuit of these disparate matters meant that members were no longer following a well-directed course of action. It was for the purpose of drawing these lines of attack together that the House accepted a suggestion by Sir Nathaniel Rich on 11 February for the appointment of a subcommittee to collate what had already been stated about the dangers to religion, to identify the causes and to suggest the necessary remedies.[84] But it is

---

[76] Ibid. 43–5, 130, 174–5.   [77] Ibid. 45–6, 131, 175–6.
[78] Ibid. 176.   [79] Ibid. 176.   [80] Ibid. 46, 131, 176–7.
[81] Ibid. 133, 181 Cf. *C.S.P. Dom. 1628–9*, 466, 469, 470.
[82] *Commons Debates 1629*, 46, 176.
[83] Ibid. 40–1, 126–7, 138–9, 191–2; *C.J.* i. 926.
[84] *Commons Debates 1629*, 60, 194.

doubtful whether this was the way in which members like Sir William Bulstrode, who found the Court and City infested with papists,[85] or Sir Richard Grosvenor, who suspected that they were protected by ministers of state,[86] wished to express their anxieties. Even when clear evidence seemed to be available to convict Sir John Coke and others of dereliction of duty in the release of some detained Jesuits,[87] it dissolved in members' hands. It proved impossible to attribute responsibility to the judges, who were accused of refusing to allow vital evidence to be put in at the priest's trial,[88] or to anyone else.[89] Like the previous inquiries, this one came to a halt and nothing more was said after the 17th. By then, the revived question of Tonnage and Poundage was claiming the full attention of the House. Without decisive leadership on religion, the House had proceeded from one topic to another for a fortnight and had secured nothing.

The eclipse of Tonnage and Poundage by religion had placed control of the House, however briefly, in the hands of Pym and Rich. In the debates that followed on the definition of the orthodox interpretation of the doctrines of the Church of England, Eliot and Selden had been divided and had argued on rather different lines. That attempt at definition had, of course, failed and both men contributed to the subsequent investigations. Evidence certainly exists to show that Eliot's interest in the first subject persisted. On 28 January, the presentation of Richard Chambers's petition gave him an opportunity to attack the judges, the Privy Council, the Customs farmers and the Attorney-General for conspiring to trample on the liberty of the subject, and he proposed further legal action by Chambers to discover which ministers would refuse to do their duties in the matter.[90] It is possible that he was thus attempting to rekindle the House's interest in this grievance. He certainly exploited Charles's explanation of his earlier messages on 3 February to demand the expulsion from the Commons of Sir John Coke who had delivered them.[91] But on neither occasion did the House respond to his appeal. It is

[84] *Commons Debates 1629*, 60, 194.   [85] Ibid. 64, 144–5.
[86] Ibid. 65–9.   [87] Ibid. 70–1, 145–6, 205–6.
[88] Ibid. 79–80, 82–3.   [89] Ibid. 78.   [90] Ibid. 112.
    Ibid. 32–3, 121.

surprising, therefore, to note that the initiative for reconsidering the subject came from those who had earlier sought precedence for religion. On Friday 6 February, Sir Nathaniel Rich argued that members should now act to content those who had sent them there by sending Montague's business to the Lords and by proceeding to that of the king and commonwealth.[92] He was followed on the 7th by Kirton, Earle, and Waller, all of whom had previously argued for priority to be given to religion and who now wanted Tonnage and Poundage considered.[93] Earle's remark that their discussions on religion had hitherto gone on with leaden feet and had been spun out with business of less importance is testimony to the shift in his position since 27 January.[94] So, at the suggestion of Benjamin Valentine, it was agreed that the question would be debated on the 12th.[95]

In fact, the select committee appointed on 22 January to inquire into Rolle's allegations had continued to function. Its work had, however, been hampered by the prevarications and contradictory answers of Sir William Acton, one of the Sheriffs of London who had appeared before it as a witness. Since the committee could make no progress with him, Eliot reported to the House on the 9th, they had decided that he should answer to the Commons as a whole for his conduct.[96] The subsequent debate showed speakers to be divided on whether or not to summon him as a delinquent. Some, like Eliot, Long, and Vaughan, clearly thought that he should be summoned;[97] others, like Goodwin, Waller, Moulson, Coke, and May, preferred to send him back to the committee to answer their questions again. On this occasion, Eliot and his supporters had their way.[98] When Acton appeared at the Bar on the 10th, he was sent to the Tower, despite pleas on his behalf.[99]

To men who were already alarmed at the infringement of their privileges, the news members received on the 10th that John Rolle had been served with a subpoena to appear in the

[92] Ibid. 43.
[93] Ibid. 177. Note the qualifications in Waller's speech.
[94] Ibid. 177. Cf. ibid. 18–19.
[95] Ibid. 177; *C.J.* i. 927.
[96] *Commons Debates 1629*, 52–3, 133–4.
[97] Ibid. 182.
[98] Ibid. 53; *C.J.* i. 928.
[99] *Commons Debates 1629*, 56–7, 136–7, 187–9. He was released upon his submission

Star Chamber was an intolerable affront.[100] Phelips spoke angrily of the unprecedented insolence of the messenger who had delivered it,[101] and Eliot asserted that the happiness of the kingdom was dependent upon the preservation of members' liberties which were contracted in the House.[102] The violation of their privileges came, he believed, from those who wished to divert them from their inquiries on religion, and responsibility lay not with the Attorney-General but with those over him who had acted without the king's knowledge.[103] Sir Humphrey May, the Chancellor of the Duchy of Lancaster, agreed that it proceeded from some error or mistake and asserted that neither the king nor the Privy Council had known of it.[104] But Selden could not accept this explanation: he was sure it sprang not from error but from their negligence in defence of their privileges.[105] So Rolle was granted his privilege and the messenger was summoned to answer for his contempt.[106] Another select committee began work, reporting the next day on its findings, when they were referred for debate with the main issue on the 12th.[107]

The implications of that issue and of the choices open to the House were grave. The goods of merchants had been detained by the Customs farmers for failure to pay Tonnage and Poundage, although it had not been granted by parliament, and yet the farmers had defended themselves in the Exchequer on the imprecise grounds of staying the goods for duties due to the king.[108] One member had already grasped the distinction between the grounds on which the Star Chamber action had been brought[109] and the king's repudiation of a right to the duties in his speech to both Houses on 23 January. Was the House now to make a grant of Tonnage and Poundage to the king, thereby approving the Exchequer proceedings, or was it

---

on the 12th. Ibid. 195.

[100] Ibid. 55, 186.

[101] Ibid. 186. The 'True Relation' combines speeches by Eliot and Selden. Ibid. 55.

[102] Ibid. 186.

[103] Ibid. 135–6, 186.

[104] Ibid. 55–6, 136, 187.

[105] Ibid. 56, 136, 187.

[106] *C.J.* i. 929.

[107] *Commons Debates 1629*, 56, 136, 190; *C.J.* i. 928–9.

[108] *Commons Debates 1629*, 140–1, 195–6.

[109] Kirton on 11 February. Ibid. 137–8.

first to seek a restitution of the merchants' goods? There was always the danger that, if these goods were left in the king's possession, the Commons' failure to act now might be cited against the right of the subject in the future.[110] But how could they proceed against the Customs farmers when their detention of the goods was supported by the Exchequer order? One way out of the House's difficulties was suggested by Eliot and Selden on the 12th: they were quite clear that no grant could be made until the goods were returned. But if the Barons of the Exchequer were informed, they argued, that the merchants' goods were detained for Tonnage and Poundage—which could only be granted by parliament—the receipt of this information would cause their decrees to be withdrawn, the replevins to succeed, and the merchants to recover their goods.[111] This involved the danger, as Wandesford shrewdly pointed out, that failure to convince the judges would leave the merchants without their goods and the House no nearer its ends.[112] Sir Humphrey May informed members that they would, in fact, find the Exchequer proceedings legal. The alternative that Noy suggested was to declare the Exchequer and Star Chamber evidence void in their bill and thus to secure the rights of the subject.[113] Other speakers were, however, convinced that the proposal made by Eliot and Selden would remove all obstacles, and it was therefore adopted.[114] Unfortunately, Eliot was wrong and May right. The reply of the Barons on the 14th stated that suing for a replevin was not the proper course for recovering those goods from the king's possession and that it was for this reason that they had inhibited the actions: the owners were free to take such course as the law allowed.[115] Selden's reaction was to question whether the court had acted according to its own practices and, at his suggestion, a select committee was appointed to inquire into the matter.[116] There was, as May had warned, no simple way to solve this problem.

The situation was complicated still further by a second petition from Richard Chambers on the 17th. In it, he com-

---

[110] See, e.g., Noy's speech, ibid. 199.   [111] Ibid. 141–2, 143, 196–7, 199.
[112] Ibid. 197. Cf. ibid. 61.   [113] Ibid. 61–2, 142–3, 197, 199.
[114] e.g. Glanvile and Littleton, ibid. 143. Cf. ibid. 144, 201.   [115] Ibid. 73–4.
[116] Ibid. 147, 207; *C.J.* i. 930.

plained of the seizure of goods he had imported since his last supplication to the House for refusing to pay duties due in King James's time: he was unable to gain possession of them because of a warrant from the Privy Council dated 15 February to stay all goods until the customs were paid.[117] The issues that now confronted the Commons, Phelips and Eliot agreed, could not be considered at once but should be deferred for debate on Thursday the 19th. Eliot took the view that it was the Customs farmers who were at fault in this and that, having offended against parliamentary privilege, they should then attend to be punished.[118] It was certainly alarming, Selden pointed out, that there was no way in which the merchants might legally obtain their goods: if their property could thus be taken away, no man's goods were safe.[119] And, at his suggestion, the House agreed to refer the problem of securing the restitution of Chambers's property to the select committee investigating the reply of the Barons of the Exchequer.[120]

It was obvious that the crucial issues could no longer be avoided. The interrogation of Dawes and Carmarthen, two of the Customs officers, at the Bar on the 19th confirmed that they had known that Rolle was an M.P. when they took his goods, although they denied being aware that parliamentary privilege extended to them. They also admitted that they had taken them for duties due in King James's time under a commission issued in 1627 but refused, under instruction from the king, to state that the duties meant were for Tonnage and Poundage.[121] Eliot once more took the initiative in the House, asking whether they were guilty of breach of privilege or not and, if they were, what punishment they should receive.[122] But he was resolutely resisted by Wandesford, who cited the king's interest in the question as the reason for his reluctance to consider the Customs officers as delinquents at that time: as an alternative, he proposed a remonstrance to Charles for the purpose of recovering the merchants' goods before they passed any bill.[123] Pym, too,

---

[117] *Commons Debates 1629*, 217. The warrant was dated 15 February.
[118] Ibid. 217.
[119] Ibid. 217–18.
[120] Ibid. 218; *C.J.* i. 931.
[121] *Commons Debates 1629*, 84, 155–6, 221–2; *H.M.C. 13th Report. App. VII*, 72.
[122] *Commons Debates 1629*, 85, 222.
[123] Ibid. 156, 222.

was anxious not to discuss this now: the liberties of the Commons were inferior to those of the kingdom and their main purpose was to establish the subject in possession and to remove the various records that told against them. It was better, he insisted, to do this first and then to proceed to vindicate their privileges.[124] Selden, however, could not accept these counsels of caution and argued that the Customs officers—who had commission only to levy and not to seize—should be put to the question for their delinquency.[125] Rich rose to oppose Selden. He could not, he said, discern the grounds on which the House would insist that a breach of privilege had occurred: they had never before punished an officer for breach of privilege when he had acted at the king's command and they still had to decide whether privilege for goods held against the crown. Further inquiries were clearly necessary and he suggested that a committee be appointed to do this job.[126] But Eliot could not be persuaded that the privileges of the House were inferior to any liberty in the kingdom and rejected such cautious advice as that given by Pym.[127] He went on, moreover, to spurn Sir Humphrey May's plea not to appear to put the king's commands in question and to disregard his claim that remedy might be found for the breach of the liberty of the subject in the work of the select committee investigating the Exchequer decision.[128] The House had a clear choice between relatively conciliatory and relatively radical courses of action. It chose to be radical and to consider the violation of its privileges by Dawes and Carmarthen on the 20th.[129] Eliot and Selden had triumphed at the expense of Wandesford, Pym, and Rich.

The radical leaders had been clearly warned of the dangers of the course they were now following. But the vindication of the privileges of the House was essential, in their view, if there was to be any point in the Commons continuing to sit.[130] The Lower House's position would, moreover, be much stronger if, as Eliot alleged on the 19th, the king's command to Dawes and Carmarthen had been merely a pretext for their action: to question a direct royal command would be 'high treason in us all'.[131]

---

[124] Ibid. 156–7, 222–3.   [125] Ibid. 157.
[126] Ibid. 85, 157, 223.   [127] Ibid. 223.
[128] Ibid. 157–8, 224.   [129] Ibid. 158, 224.
[130] See the remarks by Eliot and Selden, ibid. 85.   [131] Ibid. 204. Cf. ibid. 158.

The whole issue therefore turned on determining in whose interests the goods had been taken in Rolle's case. There could be no dispute—as the interrogation of Sir John Wolstenholme and the reading of the Customers' commission together showed on the 20th[132]—that they had been taken for Tonnage and Poundage. That commission, Selden again observed, gave power only to levy and not to seize. But there still remained one vital point raised by Wolstenholme to be disposed of before they could proceed. If, as Wolstenholme claimed, there was a clause in the Customers' lease or commission under which the king was bound to bear any loss on the farm, could they not be said to have acted in Charles's interests rather than in their own? The possibility that they could be regarded as the king's officers in this rather than as farmers alone was one that Noy and Pym were eager to explore.[133] Inconclusive inquiries were made at once, but nothing was produced to show that the farmers were accountable to the king.[134] The argument between Eliot and Selden on the one hand and Noy and Pym on the other had been converted into a minute examination of the subordinate clauses in the relevant documents.

In fact, this one remaining obstacle to the punishment of the Customs farmers proved to be most insubstantial. When the royal sign manual protecting them against loss was read on Saturday 21 February, it was found to be as deficient as the commission and lease had been as grounds for seizure.[135] And since the king had no right to these duties, the grant was in itself void and the parties concerned could be proceeded against as trespassers.[136] No effective argument was interposed by the king's servants, May, Coke, and Sheldon. May's claim that parliamentary privilege was invalid in cases concerning the king's revenue was ignored, and Coke's assertion that the king's possession of the goods led to a presumption of a right to them in Rolle's Case, together with its corollary that he was entitled to retain them as a component part of parliament himself, was entirely overlooked. The House found Solicitor-General Sheldon's argument that, if the lease was void, so, too, was the interest of the Customers and that the goods must therefore

---

[132] Ibid. 86, 225.   [133] Ibid. 159–60, 227.
[134] Ibid. 160 for Noy's inconclusive report.   [135] Ibid. 86, 163, 226.
[136] See Glanvile's speech, ibid. 164, 230.

have been taken for the king no more convincing.[137] On the grounds of precedent, the members were convinced by Littleton and others that Rolle had been and was entitled to the benefit of parliamentary privilege.[138] The Commons could go even further now. For if, as Noy argued, there was no evidence of a royal command to seize the goods at all, then the king need no longer be regarded as involved and the House could safely proceed to the punishment of the Customs farmers.[139] Rich was delighted by this observation and Coke and May were forced to give way for lack of evidence to support their contention that power to seize had been granted. Even they agreed that the House might proceed to the question.[140] It seemed as though Eliot and Selden and their supporters had come within sight of a momentous political victory.

The agreement, however, within the House on the issues of privilege in general and on privilege in Rolle's case in particular[141] had done nothing to heal the deeper divisions between the Commons' leaders. It was one thing to decide these questions in theory, quite another to determine what should next be done in practice. How was Rolle to regain possession of his goods? And how were the Customers to be punished? Phelips, who opened the debate in committee on the 23rd, clearly indicated his preference for settling the question of delinquency and therefore of punishment first as the most effective means of securing restitution.[142] But he was opposed by Sir William Constable, who, with the support of Rous, Rich, and Rudyerd,[143] wished to take the more conciliatory line of obtaining restitution first.[144] There was no reason, Rudyerd argued, to suppose that the distinction they had drawn between the king and his officers could be extended to encompass the punishment of the latter, even if members were allowed time: having come so far in the matter of religion, they might now be frustrated if they took this action.[145] May hastened to add his voice to this chorus of moderation.[146] But Eliot and others—Valentine, Glanville, Jones, and Holles—

---

[137] Ibid. 89–90, 163–4, 230. [138] Ibid. 88–9, 91, 164–5, 232.
[139] Ibid. 91. [140] Ibid. 91–2, 165–6, 232–3.
[141] Ibid. 166. [142] Ibid. 234.
[143] Ibid. 167, 234–5. [144] Loc. cit.
[145] Ibid. 167. [146] Ibid. 93, 167, 235.

would have none of it: justice had to be done and judgement given.[147] The old divisions between the leaders were again apparent. But the House was no longer allowed to suppose that the king and the Customs officers could be separated: responsibility for the seizure of goods was openly avowed by Charles in a message delivered by Sir John Coke.[148] In view of this admission, what could the House do? They might, like Eliot, attribute it to the fears of those about the king that their own faults and sins were to be exposed[149] or, like Selden, ask if a royal command could protect men already judged to be delinquent.[150] The privilege of the House, perhaps even the fate of the kingdom, was in the balance. Such grave issues required the most careful consideration.[151] Proceedings were therefore adjourned until Wednesday the 25th,[152] when the House was again adjourned, this time by royal command, until Monday 2 March.[153]

Very little is known of the events that followed between 25 February and 2 March. It is, however, certain that an attempt was made by the king and his advisers to come to terms with those most determined to punish the Customers and that this attempt failed.[154] The result of this failure became apparent when the House reassembled and the Speaker, Sir John Finch, announced a further adjournment at the king's command until the 10th.[155] The House's reaction was openly hostile, and Eliot stood only to hear Finch state once again that the king had given an absolute command that there should be no speeches or other proceedings and that, if anyone tried to speak, he should at once leave the chair and wait upon him. None the less, there was a loud shout to have Eliot speak, and when Finch tried to leave he was forced back into the chair by Holles and Valentine.[156] Once the House had settled again, Eliot stated that an order for adjournment had been given only once before—in the previous week—and that it was the fundamental liberty of the House to adjourn itself. The Commons' proceedings had been misrepresented to the king, possibly on

---

[147] Ibid. 167–9, 235–6.   [148] Ibid. 167–8, 236–7.
[149] Ibid. 169.   [150] Ibid. 169, 238.
[151] See the speeches by Price and Phelips, ibid. 169, 238.   [152] *C.J.* i. 932.
[153] Ibid. 932.   [154] *C.S.P. Venet. 1628–9*, 579–80.
[155] *Commons Debates 1629*, 252.   [156] Ibid. 252–3.

the grounds that they had encroached on his sovereign power. But nothing they had done was contrary to Charles's justice and he was confident the king would perform what they were about to ask of him. He therefore offered to their consideration a short declaration of the House's intentions.[157] This paper he threw down on to the floor of the House, where it was picked up by Sir William Fleetwood and carried to the Clerk.[158] Finch rose once again to tell members of their practice not to listen to speeches after receiving the king's message to adjourn and of his own resolution to ignore the cries to have the paper read.[159] Kirton was certain that the king had been misinformed and demanded to know by what warrant the Speaker had delivered the message. But when Earle alleged that it was customary in such cases for the Speaker to bring the king's letter with him as a warrant, Finch took the opportunity to refute the claim in some detail. Coryton, however, sternly condemned the Speaker for his failure to obey the House and urged him to put the question of reading Eliot's paper to the members. If he did not do so, Bellasis warned, they would choose another in his place.[160] Member after member urged Finch to allow it to be read or put to the question.[161] Eliot now went further, threatening that, if the Speaker refused to submit to the will of the House, he could be called to the Bar as a delinquent: the command of the House, he cajoled him, would satisfy the king.[162] Finch, however, was prepared to face the threat and ignored the appeals of Earle and Giles, begging the House to allow him to go to the king.[163] Once again, Eliot threatened Finch with the displeasure of the House and demanded the return of his paper so that he might read it to the Commons. But Finch was adamant and told Strode that he dared not put it to the vote.[164] The attempt to coerce the Speaker had failed.

It was obvious that the order to adjourn had been anticipated by Eliot and his allies. But they could not have foreseen that Finch would be so obstinate in his refusal to allow the declaration Eliot had prepared to be read. Eliot therefore came

---

[157] Ibid. 253.   [158] Ibid. 240, 254.
[159] Ibid. 254.   [160] Ibid. 254–5. Cf. *C.S.P. Dom. 1628–9*, 479.
[161] *Commons Debates 1629*, 256–7.   [162] Ibid.
[163] Ibid. 241, 257–8.   [164] Ibid. 258.

down from his seat and proceeded to vindicate his loyalty to the king. The miserable condition of the kingdom made him, he said, sympathetic to the person of the king and to the subject. They knew how Arminianism was undermining them in religion and how popery was creeping in. The Jesuits were favoured and protected by men with power to inhibit the enforcement of the law and it was their fear of punishment that had brought the House to this impasse. Eliot named the Bishop of Winchester and his followers as being amongst their number and went on to accuse the Lord Treasurer, Viscount Portland, of being the person in whom all these evils were contracted. It was from Portland, as head of the papists in England, that all danger in religion came. And he described him as building in both politics and religion upon the foundations laid by his former master, the Duke of Buckingham. In politics, in the great affair of Tonnage and Poundage, the men who had acted had been his instruments and it was in his interest rather than the king's that it had been taken. Portland intended to ruin the trade of the kingdom. He was thus the man responsible for misrepresenting their proceedings to the king. It was to show their affection to the country and their desire to preserve the safety of the king and realm that he proffered the protestations in his paper. They should declare all that they were suffering from to be the result of new counsels in the government and protest against the persons, great and small, who were innovators in religion, who introduced new customs duties, and who advised or counselled the king to collect Tonnage and Poundage without parliamentary sanction. All such men were capital enemies of the king and kingdom and those who willingly paid the duties were their accessories. When he next sat there, as he was sure he would, Eliot declared his intention of falling upon the person of that great man.[165] The two strands of parliamentary complaint were drawn together by Eliot in this great attack upon Portland and his associates and instruments in the king's inner circle of advisers.

In the charged atmosphere of the House, this assault fell upon receptive ears. The king needed their help, said Coryton, but

---

[165] Ibid. 259-61.

the men named by Eliot kept it from him. It had indeed been their intention to grant Tonnage and Poundage when they came—and any further supply the king might need. But the laws had been broken under pretence of the king's command, an offence previously considered treasonable. Parliament could not allow such a defence to be advanced. He therefore asked that Charles might be advised to consult with his grave counsel and omit those against whom they had complained.[166] But Portland's son was not prepared to allow his father's fidelity or religion to be thus questioned, and Sir Henry Vane expressed his confidence that the Lord Treasurer would be cleared when any charges came to be debated.[167] Eliot, however, was not prepared to vote anything against Portland yet: he was afraid that their difficulties sprang from him, but he intended to prove it before voting it to be so. He asked the Speaker and others to convey the House's wishes to the king during the adjournment.[168] Other members agreed that no one should yet be named.[169] Selden, too, concurred but reminded the House of the predicament the Speaker's refusal to read Eliot's paper had placed them in. The Clerk, he thought, should be commanded to read it.[170] Eliot, however, confessed that he had burnt his declaration.[171] Holles was most critical of this action and proposed to leave no merchant free to pay Tonnage and Poundage.[172] By then, however, one voice, that of Digges, had been raised in favour of adjourning and another, that of Wandesford, against Holles's proposal.[173] With Maxwell, the king's messenger, at the locked door, time was short. It was just possible to hear Holles's summary of Eliot's paper and for the House to decide to adjourn.[174] The political impasse had been brought to an end.

Charles now had no alternative but to act if his authority was to be preserved. The House of Commons had passed beyond the vindication of parliamentary privilege to an unprecedented defiance of a direct royal command. It had compounded its offence by condemning innovations in religion and the collection and payment of Tonnage and Poundage with

---

[166] Ibid. 261–2.   [167] Ibid. 262–3.   [168] Ibid. 263.
[169] Ibid. 243, 263–4.   [170] Ibid. 264–5.   [171] Ibid. 265.
[172] Ibid. 265–6.   [173] Ibid. 172, 265.   [174] Ibid. 172, 267.

unparalleled vehemence.[175] The king therefore took the only course he considered open to him. On the 4th, Eliot, Selden, and seven other M.P.s involved in the demonstration on the 2nd were arrested by order of the Privy Council and, on the 10th, parliament was dissolved.[176] He would call no more, Charles proclaimed a little over two weeks later, until his actions and intentions were more clearly understood.[177] It was his acknowledgement of the breakdown that had occurred.

It is possible, of course, to say that the condemnation of royal policies was alone responsible for the outcome. But such views had been expressed before and had led to no such final breakdown. The problem of explaining what happened therefore remains. It is one to which no easy solution can be advanced. It is, however, clear from an analysis of the debates that the House of Commons was divided in its political priorities and on the remedies it was prepared to sanction. When the session began, it was apparent that members were reluctant to be rushed into a confrontation with the king over civil grievances of the kind being sought by Eliot and Selden and that they preferred to give precedence to the subject of religion introduced by Rous on 26 January. The Commons were persuaded to adopt the programme of inquiries suggested by Pym on the 27th. But the attempt he then made to define the limits of doctrinal orthodoxy had to be abandoned when it became clear that non-statutory authorities were unacceptable to the common lawyers, led by Selden, in the House. Thereafter, the attack on religion concentrated on detailed, though ultimately unproductive, inquiries into the actions of individuals until it was eclipsed by the question of Tonnage and Poundage after the 17th. The strong lead given by Eliot and Selden in the first of these periods was successfully resisted, while that of Pym and Rich foundered on these legal objections: no one could subsequently have been said to have played a dominant role in the debates on religion. It is also clear that the initiative for reconsidering the question of Tonnage and

[175] Ibid. 267.

[176] Kenyon, *Stuart Constitution*, 31; I. H. C. Fraser, 'The Agitation in the Commons. 2 March 1629, and the Interrogation of the Leaders of the Anti-Court Group,' *B.I.H.R.* 30 (1957), 86–95.

[177] Kenyon, op. cit. 85–6.

Poundage came from those who had earlier demanded precedence for religion. The temperature of the House was still relatively low when it discussed Sheriff Acton's conduct on 9 and 10 February and, although it decided to punish him, the members were not inclined to be vindictive. But the failure of the attempt sponsored by Eliot and Selden to convince the Barons of the Exchequer that they had been inadequately informed and the discovery of the Privy Council order on the 17th placed the Commons in an acute political dilemma. The attempt by Eliot and Selden to blame the Customs officers for this obstruction and to induce the House to consider the violation of Rolle's privileges as a member was openly resisted by Wandesford, Pym, and Rich on the 19th. When it seemed that a way had been found to punish them without involving the king on the 21st, Eliot and Selden were on the point of triumph. But the leaders of the House were again divided on the question whether the punishment of the delinquents or the restitution of Rolle's goods should have precedence on the 23rd when the king's message blew away the fragile distinction on which Eliot and Selden had rested their proposed course of action. No compromise between them and the king was possible and the disaster of 2 March ensued. The pattern of debates and of the divisions amongst the Commons' leaders in those debates is thus clear.

The connection between this pattern and the position within the House of Eliot and Selden seems straightforward enough. Initially frustrated in their desire to prosecute the investigation of civil grievances, they were later successful in persuading members, alarmed by the revelation of obstruction after obstruction in the matter of Tonnage and Poundage, to insist upon the punishment of the Customs officers as delinquents. It is possible, indeed, to argue that neither of them was much interested in the discussion of religion. The difficulty, however, with this argument is that it obscures the rather different grounds on which they argued in the debates on religion between 29 January and 3 February and that it renders supererogatory all their subsequent speeches on the subject. There can be no doubt that Eliot was concerned to promote the investigation of civil grievances when the session opened, and that that was still his view in the second week is confirmed by his reaction to the introduction of the bill to grant the king Tonnage and Poundage on 26 January. It could certainly be argued that his attack on the judges, the Privy Council, the Customs farmers, and the Attorney-General on the 28th constituted an attempt to reclaim the House's attention from religion.[178] So far, so good. But Eliot's speech on the 29th was notable for its profession of sympathy with the House's objectives in religion and for its exculpation of the king from blame: that rested on the king's advisers.[179] His willingness, moreover, to employ the Lambeth Articles for the purpose of striking at the Arminians definitely separated him from Selden.[180] It is difficult to see how this proposal or his subsequent speeches betray any lack of interest in religion. On 6 February, he launched an attack on Attorney-General Heath for his failure to investigate charges against Cosens thoroughly and expressed the hope that his examination would reveal those who had commanded him not to proceed.[181] The revelation of Neile's role in procuring the Arminian divines' pardons caused Eliot to denounce him as 'the great cause of our religious misery' and to suggest that a charge be drawn up against him for transmission to the House of Lords.[182] Eliot even dared to suggest on the 10th that the Star Chamber subpoena on Rolle sprang from those who wished to divert them from religion.[183] Fear of those who protected the Jesuits detained at Clerkenwell from the operation of the law was again expressed by him on the 14th.[184] 'There is', he said three days later, 'some Malus genius some ill angell that walks between us and the King and State, for we see the Kings care and the Councell Boardes, to have the law put in execucion against Recusants.'[185] All these points are to be found in the first half of his declaration on 2 March, in which he denounced those in authority who countenanced the introduction of Arminianism and of popery and named the Bishop of Winchester and his allies as their coadjutors. He was speaking of the subversion of the laws of the realm by men who held power about the king. This had been his argument in the debates on religion from first to last. But it is not—it is vital to

[178] *Commons Debates 1629*, 112.
[179] Ibid. 24–8. Cf. ibid. 32.
[180] Ibid. 33–4, 121.   [181] Ibid. 175 6.   [182] Ibid. 50, 180.
[183] Ibid. 186.   [184] Ibid. 77, 149.   [185] Ibid. 155.

note—a theme confined to his remarks on religion alone. It can be seen in his violent outburst on 28 January, with its proposal that Chambers should institute a second action for the recovery of his goods so that the House might 'see what Ministers will refuse to doe their duty therein',[186] and in the reasons he gave for pressing for the expulsion of Sir John Coke from the House on 3 February.[187] A week later, on the 10th, he expressed his wish to punish not only Sheriff Acton but also all those officers who had acted in any way against Rolle: responsibility for the subpoena did not rest with the Attorney but came 'from a higher hand . . . without the Kings knowledge'.[188] On the 17th, he denounced the Customs officers for the interposition of the Privy Council order. Fears of a dissolution he dismissed on the 23rd by cursing those who sought to hinder their proceedings.[189] When that fear became a real threat, Eliot was certain that it sprang from the 'fear of great men'[190] about Charles of being exposed. The climax came in the speech setting out his declaration on 2 March: the threads of his argument were drawn together in a bitter denunciation of royal advisers in church and state, culminating in his attack on the Lord Treasurer.[191] Eliot's analysis of the dangers facing the kingdom in civil and religious matters consisted of a recognition of the pernicious role played in England's affairs by the inner circle of the king's advisers. He had therefore been conducting nothing less than an assault upon those advisers and their agents throughout the session. This amounted to an attempt to separate the king from his 'political court' and to destroy its influence.

The problem, however, of explaining the conduct of Eliot and Selden can only be considered partly solved, since the importance of the means by which they sought to accomplish their objectives and indeed the relationship between them have not yet been clarified. The support they lent one another in the early stages of the session seems clear, and yet they were divided in their attitudes towards the attempt to define the limits of doctrinal orthodoxy in religion. Selden refused to accept the non-statutory authorities that Eliot was willing to employ.[192]

---

[186] Ibid. 112.   [187] Ibid. 32–3, 121.   [188] Ibid. 136.
[189] Ibid. 236.   [190] Ibid. 169.   [191] Ibid. 259–61.
[192] Ibid. 119–20. Dr. N. R. N. Tyacke has pointed out to me that Selden may have had other reasons for rejecting these authorities.

Once this disagreement was over, Selden, too, was able to play an important role in the debates on religion. He was deeply involved in investigating the pardons granted to Montague and the other Arminian divines and, like Eliot, acknowledged his fears about the protection given by 'great persons' to the Jesuits at Clerkenwell.[193] Both men were absolutely determined to protect the privileges of the House: 'every Court in Westminster', Selden remarked on 10 February, 'has the power to protect suitors in it.'[194] Two days later, he expressed the opinion that the obstructions the Commons faced in the matter of Tonnage and Poundage were due to the actions of the king's ministers rather than to Charles himself.[195] If those about the king misrepresented the House's actions, he said on the 19th, let the curse be on them.[196] And he urged the Commons on the 23rd to proceed to the punishment of the Customs officers as delinquents, despite the king's message accepting full responsibility, like any other court in Westminster.[197] It is hardly surprising that he should have encouraged Speaker Finch to read Eliot's declaration on 2 March[198] and that he too should subsequently have been arrested. He and Eliot had diagnosed the same disease and prescribed the same remedy. The one difference they had had was, however, of vital importance. For whereas Eliot had viewed the House as the supreme council of the realm,[199] even in matters of religion, Selden had conceived of it as the highest court, especially in matters touching the liberties and property of the subject. Eliot was therefore prepared to face the dangers inherent in the course advocated on religion by Pym and Rich: Selden and the other common lawyers, who saw the House as bound only by its previous actions, could not contemplate the introduction of extra-parliamentary authorities as binding upon the Commons. It was on that point that Pym and Rich were frustrated early in February. Thereafter, their conceptions of the role of the House proved compatible. The absence of certain words in the instructions to and bargains with the Customs farmers enabled them to argue that no royal authority had been given for the seizure

---

[193] Ibid. 131, 175.   [194] Ibid. 136.
[195] Ibid. 143.   [196] Ibid. 85.
[197] Ibid. 169, 238.   [198] Ibid. 171.
[199] Brit. Lib. Add. MS. 27878, fo. 343ᵛ.

of goods for refusal to pay duties demanded and thus to proceed to the punishment of those officers who had violated John Rolle's privileges as an M.P. It was therefore upon the twin claims of obedience to the law by the king's ministers and of the absolute right of the subject to his goods that the two men had been able to mount their attack upon the 'political court'. It was because that attack threatened to deprive the king of his power to command and to protect his servants that Charles was forced to intervene. Protecting the 'political court' was essential to the preservation of the king's ordinary prerogative.[200]

Eliot and Selden had been able to go so far because they had won control of the House in the latter stages of the session. The course of action they had first proposed had been blocked by the reluctance of the House to precipitate an immediate confrontation with the king on civil grievances. But the strategy subsequently suggested by Pym on religion had partially broken down early in February, and the House confined itself to the investigation of the activities of individual Arminians and their protectors. To all intents and purposes, this united members. It is, however, noticeable that no further major speech was made by Pym or Rich in the debates on religion[201] and that a much more prominent part was taken in these inquiries by Eliot, Phelips, and Selden. The subsequent actions of Pym and Rich seem rather more puzzling. Rich certainly gave notice of the change in his priorities on 6 February and was followed in this by other speakers on the 7th. But the revival of Tonnage and Poundage placed the initiative in Eliot's hands as chairman and thus reporter of the select committee dealing with Rolle's case. The difficulty, moreover, of explaining their behaviour grows when their silence on the 12th, when faced with a choice between Eliot's proposal for a message to the Barons of the Exchequer and that of Noy to proceed by bill, is considered. Eliot's stratagem failed. Once the Privy Council was known to have intervened, the House had to choose between seeking a compromise and attempting to secure an outright victory. It is important to note that Pym and Rich

---

[200] See Francis Oakley, 'Jacobean Political Theology: The Absolute and Ordinary Powers of the King', *Journal of the History of Ideas*, xxix (1968), 323–46.

[201] Note, however, Rich's proposal on 11 February.

were outspoken in their opposition to Eliot's proposal to find
a way out by punishing the Customs officers as delinquents.
Pym thought the liberties of the kingdom to be of greater
importance than those of the House and wished to secure the
rights of the subject by passing the bill to grant the king Tonnage and Poundage. They might then proceed to vindicate
their privileges when the king had been sweetened.[202] Rich was
uncertain whether privilege held against the king in this case:
if his doubt was well founded, Eliot would have no grounds
upon which he could advocate proceedings against the Customs
officers.[203] Pym scouted the possibility on the 20th that these
officers had indeed acted in the king's interest as they
claimed.[204] Rich's conduct in welcoming the separation of the
king and Customers by Noy on the 21st and yet preferring to
secure the restoration of Rolle's goods rather than punish the
officers as delinquents on the 23rd is still more quixotic.[205] How
can this apparent inconsistency be explained?

This is, indeed, a difficult problem but a solution may perhaps be advanced. For both men began by attempting to secure
the delay of the discussion of major civil grievances and by
guiding the House in its early debates on religion. The breakdown, however, of the attempt to define the limits of doctrinal
orthodoxy was a setback for Pym, who had first made such an
endeavour on 27 January, and for Rich, who had been responsible for elaborating the House's position since then. If this was
his principal purpose, then Rich's new priorities on the 6th
become more comprehensible. There appeared to be ample
time available for all the House's purposes. Unfortunately,
however, while Eliot and Selden were consolidating their
positions in the Commons, the initiative was lost. There was,
after all, no good reason to oppose the course suggested by
Eliot and Selden on the 12th: if it worked, if the Barons of the
Exchequer withdrew their order, the House's difficulties would
be greatly reduced. But, of course, it did not. Neither Pym nor
Rich was prepared to countenance the direct assault upon the
king's servants that Eliot had in mind on the 19th because
concessions to the king on Tonnage and Poundage seemed more

[202] *Commons Debates 1629*, 156–7.
[203] Ibid. 85, 157, 223.   [204] Ibid. 160, 227.
[205] Ibid. 91, 166, 232, 235.

likely to produce effective results than aggressive action. Pym's remarks on the 20th would, if substantiated, have compelled the House to seek a compromise since the danger involved in attacking the king would be too great. In fact, it was possible for the king and his servants to be separated—hence Rich's relief at and welcome for Noy's remarks on the 21st—but it was still wiser to leave those servants alone as far as possible, as he argued on the 23rd. It seems clear that neither Pym nor Rich was willing to place the House in a position of direct confrontation with the king because of the likely consequences of such defiance. Other members shared these fears.[206] But when they resisted Eliot and Selden, they were unable to carry the House with them. Circumstances and their position within the House had changed. If delaying the passage of the bill for Tonnage and Poundage had originally been intended to allow discussion of (and presumably remedies for) religious grievances,[207] the failure of the attempt to define the limits of orthodox belief meant that particular inquiries would, even if successful, supply no general remedy against Arminianism. The struggle between a political strategy that placed vaccination against this disease first and the elimination of its carriers second and one that identified the carriers as the disease itself had been won and lost very early on in the session. But because they overlapped to a certain extent, the House had been able to proceed on an apparently united course for some time. And it was in that period that Eliot and Selden had consolidated their hold on the House. The later struggle had been won by Eliot and Selden because circumstances within the House had changed, and with them the fears that dominated members' apprehensions: each succeeding revelation of royal or conciliar obstruction strengthened their position. It had been lost by Pym and Rich because the ground beneath them had moved and the course they proposed at the end seemed too conciliatory. The two strategies had overlapped on religion and this had enabled Eliot and Selden to recover from their early reverses. But this should do nothing to obscure the fundamental differences in political judgement that divided these leaders during the session.

It is, of course, rather simpler to analyse the position of Eliot

---

[206] e.g. Rudyerd and Glanvile, ibid. 235, 238.
[207] Ibid. 114.

and Selden if only because they are more frequently recorded as having spoken. Eliot set out the kernel of his position when reciting his draft declaration on 2 March. Nothing of a similar kind is known to survive for Pym and Rich. What does, however, survive is the draft of a declaration to the king on religion prepared by the subcommittee appointed at Rich's instigation on 11 February. This document's place in the session has never been altogether clear. It catalogues the fears that had existed and grown since the House last met, fears that sprang from the 'unfaithfulness and carelessness' not of the king but of his ministers.[208] Protestants abroad were dangerously threatened and those in the neighbouring kingdoms were at risk. In England, popery had grown extraordinarily and was openly— sometimes even insolently—practised; worse still, there had been a subtle and pernicious growth in Arminianism which, if left unchecked, would consume their religion by dividing Englishmen at home and separating them from the Reformed churches abroad. These developments were due to the suspension or negligent execution of the laws against recusancy, the defence of popish doctrine by Arminian divines and the introduction of many new and offensive ceremonies. Orthodox teaching, contained in the Articles of religion and approved in 1571 in Parliament, had been restrained and suppressed. On the sense in which these articles were to be understood, the subcommittee were quite specific: they were, they wrote, to be interpreted by the Book of Common Prayer established in parliament, the Book of Homilies, and the Catechism. To this list they added Bishop Jewel's works, the public determination of divines in the universities and the published decisions of the divinity professors, the articles of Lambeth and Ireland, the conclusions of the British divines at the Synod of Dort, the uniform agreement of the writers published by authority, and, lastly, the recantations of those who had taught to the contrary. Unsound opinions, they complained, were published while those refuting them were not. The persons, indeed, who countenanced these erroneous opinions had been favoured and preferred and it was their power about the king that was

---

[208] Ibid. 95–101. The quotation is on p. 96. Cf. Kenyon, *Stuart Constitution* 149. These were not 'resolutions' but rather the remonstrance envisaged on 28 January. See *Commons Debates 1629*, 95, 114.

responsible for these evils. Having listed their fears and apprehensions, they suggested the necessary remedies, including the appointment of sound bishops with the advice of the Privy Council and the provision of competent means for the support of a godly and able minister in every parish by parliamentary action.[209] On balance, there was little enough in this statement to cause dissension amongst members. It is certainly unfortunate that nothing is at present known about those who composed it. It does none the less reveal two important points about its authors—namely, that they included the non-statutory authorities on the definition of doctrine that Selden and others had earlier declined to accept as binding, and that they still anticipated having time to pass legislation on the support of the ministers of the church. It is legitimate, therefore, to ask whether the subcommittee was not the means by which it was intended to reverse the breakdown that had occurred on 3 February. If this conjecture is sound—and it must be stressed that it is a conjecture—then an attempt was being made to rescue this portion of the strategy first advocated by Pym and elaborated by Rich. But whatever the truth about this, the draft declaration does constitute a statement of the House's original concerns on religion. It may also serve as an epitaph to their failure.

The reasons for the political breakdown should now be clearer. No king of England could have contemplated the punishment of his servants for obedience to his commands with equanimity whatever pretext was found. And no king could have surrendered to the abridgement of his prerogative so stridently demanded in the name of the inviolable privileges of parliament. Between this absolute demand and the absolute discretion of the crown, no compromise could be found. To protect his servants, high and low, and to preserve the policies in church and state for which he was ultimately responsible, the king was obliged to accept the challenge thrown down by the Lower House. If his government could not be conducted with them, he would rule without them. The fact that Charles was willing to go so far meant that the assault launched by Eliot and Selden was bound to fail in the short term. The narrow grounds on which it rested had implications that other

[209] *Commons Debates 1629,* 95–101.

M.P.s preferred to repudiate. 'Princes should in pollicye haue some time & way left to euade', Sir Thomas Barrington wrote, 'when point of honor is in competition; if theay acknowledg theire acts past, illegall, and theire Ministers confess it, & pleade ignorance, I know not why it were not better to take reasonable satisfaction for ye rest, and declare our right to posterytye by a law, & ye errors past, then by laboring to punish more to lett fall ye end of or desyres in yt and all.'[210] There could be no more eloquent condemnation of Eliot's strategy than that. But even the more subtle intentions of his rivals had a flaw. For although Pym and Rich and, indeed, the other leaders who were prepared to come to terms with the king on Tonnage and Poundage might have been able to reach an agreement there, it is unlikely that they could have persuaded Charles to make any substantial concessions on religion. The cosmetic measures taken just before the session represented the limits to which Charles was ready to go. Just as the king mistakenly thought that such adjustments might win parliamentary approval as a means to further supply, so the members of the House of Commons thought that the old process of complaint and bargaining might extract further concessions. As events proved, they were all wrong.

It is natural to think of the dissolution of Parliament in 1629 as a watershed in Charles I's reign. All that was achieved then was a recognition that the king had abandoned the process of seeking political consent by the customary means. The consequences—peace abroad and personal government at home— were profound. The dominance of the Arminian faction in the church was inevitably confirmed and there was a further extension of prerogative rule in the state. One decade of conflict came to an end: another began.

---

[210] Brit. Lib. Egerton MS. 2645, fo. 13ʳ. Sir Simonds D'Ewes blamed the subtle practices of parliament's enemies and of some M.P.s who were in no way favourably disposed towards religion. *The Autobiography of Sir Simonds D'Ewes*, ed. J. O. Halliwell (2 vols., 1845), i. 404–7. He wrongly named Noy amongst the latter group.

Index